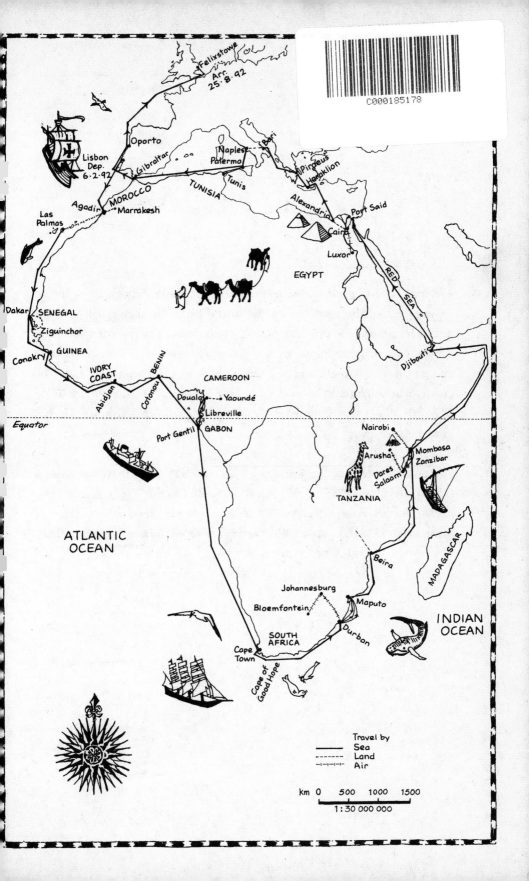

Felixstowe
Arr.
25·8·92

Oporto

Lisbon
Dep.
6·2·92

Naples
Palermo
Bari
Piraeus
Gibraltar
Heraklion
Tunis
TUNISIA
Agadir   MOROCCO
Alexandria
Port Said
Marrakesh
Cairo
Las
Palmas
Luxor
EGYPT
RED SEA

Dakar
SENEGAL
Ziguinchor
GUINEA
Conakry
Djibouti
IVORY
COAST
BENIN
CAMEROON
Abidjan
Cotonou
Douala   Yaoundé
Libreville
Equator
Port Gentil   GABON
Nairobi
Mombasa
Arusha   Zanzibar
Dares
Salaam
TANZANIA
ATLANTIC
OCEAN
Beira
MADAGASCAR
Johannesburg
Bloemfontein
Maputo
INDIAN
OCEAN
SOUTH
AFRICA
Durban
Cape
Town
Cape of Good Hope

Travel by
———— Sea
------- Land
-¹-¹-¹- Air

km 0   500   1000   1500
1 : 30 000 000

C000185178

*A*bout the *A*uthor

*P*eter *M*arshall grew up by the sea in Bognor Regis, Sussex. At eighteen, he went round the world as a cadet in the P&O. He then taught English in Dakar, Senegal, before returning to continue his studies in England. He subsequently taught philosophy and literature in several British universities and in the late seventies helped set up a rural community. In 1986, he crossed the Atlantic in a small yacht. He is now a full-time writer living in North Wales where he regularly sails a dinghy in the Irish Sea. He has visited Africa many times.

His publications include: *Journey through Tanzania* (1984), *William Godwin* (1984), *Into Cuba* (1985), *Cuba Libre: Breaking the Chains?* (1987), *William Blake* (1988), *Journey through Maldives* (1992), *Demanding the Impossible: A History of Anarchism* (1992) and *Nature's Web: An Exploration of Ecological thinking* (1992). His voyage around Africa features in a major TV series.

Around Africa

*f*rom the
*P*illars of *H*ercules
to the
*S*trait of *G*ibraltar

Peter Marshall

SIMON & SCHUSTER

LONDON · SYDNEY · NEW YORK · TOKYO · SINGAPORE · TORONTO

First published in Great Britain by Simon & Schuster Ltd, 1994
A Paramount Communications Company

Simon & Schuster Ltd
West Garden Place
Kendal Street
London W2 2AQ

Simon & Schuster of Australia Pty Ltd
Sydney

A CIP catalogue record for this book is
available from the British Library

ISBN 0-671-71066-4

Typeset in Perpetua 12/15 pt by
Hewer Text Composition Services, Edinburgh
Printed and bound in Great Britain by
Butler & Tanner Ltd, Frome and London

For my mother Vera

To James Byam Shaw,
From one lover of boats
to another,...
      Best wishes,
            Peter Marshall

'You will never enjoy the world aright till the sea itself floweth in your veins, till you are clothed with the heavens, and crowned with the stars.'

Thomas Traherne

Acknowledgements

One of the most enduring impressions of my voyage has been the generosity of the countless people who helped me around Africa. Many are mentioned in the book, but I would particularly like to thank the following who made my crazy adventure possible: John Alton of The Strand Cruise Centre (London), João A. P. Galamas of Pinto Basto Navegaçáo (Lisbon), the Portuguese Sail Training Association (Aporvela), Jaime Medina Tacoronte of Olsen & Co. (Las Palmas), Capt. Henryk Netzel of *Pol Europa*, Capt. Pierre J. Noël of *Delphine Delmas.*, Capt. Fritz Witts of *Tilly*, Mr Tsanis of Delmas Shipping Agency (Douala), Anil V. Patel, representative of WEC Lines (Dar es Salaam), Capt. Simon Dyer and Capt. Mohamed A. Hatimy of Beacon Shipping Lines (Mombasa), Captain Georgios Kastis of *WEC Rotterdam*, Captain Till Hülsbergen of *Ulf Ritscher*. The companies Laurenço & Neves, Polish Ocean Lines, Delmas, and Southern Steamships all kindly offered me free passage on their ships.

I would also like to thank the following people who guided me on my way, often through troubled waters: Hugo Gil Ferreira, David, Maggie and Simon Burke, Peter and Christina Cracknell, Mamadou Seyliou, Outi Kaarina Badji, Valerie Treitlein, Regina Ofeiba Quist Arcton, Jean-Philippe Chauzy, Eugène and Michael Fanguinoveny, Ebony Wesley, Roger Milla, Steven Shapiro, Chaim and Jeni Rabinowitz, Martin and Barbara Versfeld, Alvin Kushner, David Schlapobersky, Felicity Potter, Mongane Wally Serote, Judith Mokhetle, John and Nanou Guthrie, Nancy Barnes, Admasu

Haile, Dipan Shah, Duncan Willetts, Mohamed Amin, Juma Shomari, Issa Mlongoti, Amant Macha, Gerald Msuya, Ressa Izina, Silvester Dilli, Jan van Liere, Chanel Croker, Sami Hassan and Tanya Matthews.

My friends back home, Richard Feesey, Jeremy Gane, Graham Hancock, David Lea and John Schlapobersky, all inspired me in different ways to complete my task. I much appreciated the interest of the pupils of Croesor School who followed my voyage and sent me letters of encouragement. I appreciated the support of the members of the Porthmadog and Trawsfynydd Sailing Club, especially Andy Holmes of *Fadeaway*.

My editors Carol O'Brien and Sian Parkhouse of Simon & Schuster deserve my special thanks for their excellent advice and warm inspiration. John Schlapobersky kindly read part of the text. Thanks also to Emily Gwynne-Jones for producing the map.

I am indebted to the HTV crew David England, Elayne Muth and David Williams for their unforgettable company and great assistance, and to the shore-based staff Emyr Daniel, Dilys Morris-Jones, Giles Randall and Menna Richards for helping to realize the TV series.

Jean-Victor Nkolo of Radio Netherlands International gave me some wonderful contacts and kept in close communication.

Finally, my deepest thanks to my family, Jenny, Emily and Dylan, who undertook their own voyage and came out of it the stronger and wiser. The concern of my brother Michael and mother Vera proved invaluable. Without all their unfailing support, I would never have been able to make it.

Croesor, 28 March 1994

Contents

Contents

Chapter One

Drawing *the* Circle

'No can do. If you'd tried twenty five years ago then perhaps I could help you, but today the shipping world is no longer what it used to be. It can't be done.'

I was talking on the phone to a clerk from the Union-Castle Travel Company about a voyage around Africa I wanted to undertake. I imagined the shipping clerk sitting in a dingy office, with heavy wooden panels, somewhere in the City of London.

'Nothing doing with British companies,' he went on. 'The British Merchant Navy is greatly reduced. Try the Poles or the Germans. They might come up with something.'

I put the telephone down disappointed but determined. I was not going to be put off at the first hurdle. I was sure it could be done. I was sure that I could manage to find a passage on working ships to circumnavigate Africa. But where to start?

After several more calls, I was at last directed to The Strand Cruise Centre at Charing Cross Station, London.

'Yes, we do specialize in cargo-carrying passenger ships,' said the efficient voice of John Alton, the Cruise and Ocean Voyages Manager. 'Why not come in and see us?'

His office was situated in a corner of the underground concourse of Charing Cross Tube Station. I could not imagine a place further from the sea and sky, but on the wall of the inner office I saw a

1

reassuring painting of a fine ocean-going ship. At last I seemed to be getting somewhere.

I told him about my plan.

'I'd like to leave in the New Year. Any chance of getting me a ship at least from Lisbon down the West Coast of Africa?'

'Why Lisbon? It'll be much more difficult from there than from a North European port.'

'Well, it's more or less five centuries since the first European, Vasco da Gama, found a passage around South Africa into the Indian Ocean. I want to follow in his wake – in as many different boats as possible – and look at the contacts between Africa and Europe ever since. I want to see what makes Africa tick.'

'It sounds fascinating but first we've got to get you a boat.'

That's the spirit, I thought, first things first: Boats, Visas, Vaccinations, Equipment . . .

'I'll let you know as soon as I come up with something, but I can't promise.'

As I was about to leave the office, a document called *The ABC of Shipping* caught my eye. It listed all the passenger-carrying cargo ships in the world, with a small section on Africa. Although John Alton was unable to come up with a ship which fitted my itinerary, without knowing it he helped me no end. His readiness to take my voyage seriously was a great inspiration and his copy of *The ABC Shipping Passenger Guide* was to prove my Bible.

But why on earth was I planning to go round Africa by boat? To my knowledge, no writer had attempted to circumnavigate the continent in one go. It was a grand design which immediately excited my imagination. It seemed one of the last great journeys left on earth. To try to draw a circle around Africa had a perfect symmetry which I found deeply appealing. It also combined my love of Africa with my love of the sea.

I was born and grew up in Bognor Regis in Sussex, a hundred yards from the beach, and my earliest memories are of the sea crashing over the railings and swirling across the promenade on a winter's day. By the time I was ten, my brother and I had acquired an old clinker boat and we spent nearly every day of our holidays out in the Channel. We were later to sail across the Atlantic together in a small yacht.

After leaving boarding school in the Sussex Downs, I joined the Peninsular and Oriental Steam Navigation Company (P&O) as a purser cadet and sailed around the world on a great passenger liner, taking the wealthy on cruises and the young to and from the Antipodes. It sealed my love of travel but I found the work repetitive and unfulfilling. I was already writing poetry and short stories and wanted to go on to university. But first I went to Dakar in Senegal, West Africa to teach English for a year. It proved one of the happiest of my life and left me with a lifelong fascination for Africa.

In Senegal, I got to know my future partner, Jenny. She came from Martinique in the French West Indies. We later had two children and through my family I became indirectly linked to Africa. Jenny's forebears might well come from West Africa and mine came from the West Country. By some quirk of history, a great great grandfather of my children might well have travelled as a sailor on a ship from Bristol down the West Coast of Africa to take another great great grandfather as a slave across the Atlantic to the sugar plantations of the New World. What had once been separated by empire and capital has become united in our family by love and affection.

It was partly for these reasons that I wanted to come to terms with Africa, to consider what Africa means for the West and the West for Africa after 500 years of contact. The early Portuguese discoverers were in search of slaves, ivory, gold and the legendary Christian king Prester John. I too was also on a quest, but in search of understanding. I wanted to go beyond the romantic myths which see Africa as a savage paradise or the Garden of Eden turned into Hell. I wanted to go beyond the headlines of famine, disease and war, and to experience the everyday life of the African people. I wanted to see what light shines in the heart of the continent, to sing of Africa and its golden joys.

Having decided to go, come what may, my first task was to get some visas. I knew from experience that it could be very awkward arriving in an African country without the appropriate visa; either one is turned back or obliged to pay a hefty sum to the corrupt officials. But while getting visas for Africa before leaving is good practice, it is easier said than done.

When I telephoned the Cameroon embassy in London, a girl in the visa section asked me how I intended to enter the country. When I said by boat she said curtly: 'We've never heard of anyone entering the country by boat', and put the phone down. I quickly redialled and explained that I was intending to sail around Africa by boat.

'We've never heard of anyone coming into Cameroon by boat. Come in and see my boss.'

'What's his name?'

'I can't give you that. Ring back later.'

I did but still to no avail. Only by the intervention of a Cameroonian friend was I able to get a visa. It helps to have friends in Africa – and in African territory in London.

It was even worse at the Nigerian Embassy. I was bounced like a ball about four times between the information section and the visa section located in different buildings in London. I was invited to London for an interview and on my arrival they said they had never heard of me. They had lost all my papers. Only after four weeks of continual harassment – I was determined not to give up – I had an interview with the visa attaché. He told me to return the next day, when he finally stamped my passport with a flourish. An imposing man in flowing robes, he handed over my passport and said with a beaming smile: 'I wish you a pleasant stay in my country!' Outside the Nigerian High Commission in Fleet Street, I looked at my passport: he had only given me a one-week tourist visa. Was palm oil the missing ingredient in my application papers?

I decided there and then that I could not face getting any more visas. I headed for a place called the Visa Shop which promised to ease the pain for a handsome fee. It was worth it. They managed to get me visas for Guinée, Mozambique, Algeria and Angola. I would have to take my chance with the others. In comparison with the rest of Black Africa, the South African embassy was all sweetness and light. The staff were over the moon at the time. United Nations' sanctions had just been lifted: the South African cricket team were cleared to visit Pakistan and the next Miss World Competition was to be held in South Africa. But I noticed the reality of the apartheid system in the notes to my visa application: so-called 'nationals' from the black homelands needed a valid passport and a visa if they were 'visiting' South Africa for more than fourteen days.

4

I was most impressed by the Consulate of the Democratic Republic of Madagascar. They sent me a useful information pack on their country and even a map to find their consulate in London. The notes were disarmingly frank: Madagascar is very poor and has 'one of the worse public transport systems in the world'. Hotels can be very basic (not suitable for 'the squeamish'). On the other hand, I was reassured to learn that the Malagasy people are very gentle and friendly, and 'touchingly honest'.

After explaining my intention of sailing in the wake of Vasco da Gama, I had some lofty replies: the second secretary of the Embassy of the Islamic Republic of Mauritania declared in French from Brussels: 'I am convinced that you will enjoy in our country a welcome and assistance to the measure of the fascinating enterprise that you envisage.' The First Secretary of the Embassy of the Kingdom of Morocco in London wished me nothing less than 'total success'. I hoped he was right.

After visas, my next concern was health. I had already travelled widely in Africa and knew the risks involved, especially in a continent which had the lowest life expectancy in the world. Along the tropical coasts, the main worry would be malaria, especially cerebral malaria which could kill you in a few days. The West African coast had earned its reputation as the 'White Man's Grave'. Then there was the AIDS epidemic sweeping across the continent, especially in Central Africa where one in four people were probably infected. Over ten million people in Africa could be HIV positive.

To make sure that I would not be infected by all these and other horrific diseases, I went to the School of Tropical Medicine at Middlesex Hospital in London and got a health travel kit, a mosquito net and a water-purifying system. There are of course many unpleasant microbes waiting to ambush the unwary traveller: yellow fever, cholera, typhoid, tetanus, polio, diphtheria, meningitis, hepatitis (Types A and B), rabies. I got jabbed for all these before leaving and became the not-so-proud owner of an yellow International Vaccination Card to prove that I was not the carrier of some loathsome plague. Or rather I was, since I had been vaccinated, but I hoped it would not break out.

But there are many illnesses for which there is no vaccination, such as bilharzia, caused by blood flukes passed on by snails, or sleeping sickness, transmitted by the tsetse fly. To avoid vomiting, diarrhoea, dysentery and giardiasis, I was advised to have no unpeeled fruit, eat no uncooked vegetables, drink no unboiled water.

Reading about all the potential diseases and illnesses was deeply depressing. If I had continued, I would no doubt have become a chronic hypochrondiac – a particularly nasty condition. I therefore decided to take the basic precautions and to forget about the rest. My principle was that I would stimulate my defences and increase my resistance by feeling strong and positive. I wanted to show that if I travelled well and with care, I would return home healthier than when I first set out.

Apart from invisible germs which could attack my body, there were much more obvious dangers to consider. I was certainly leaving at a time when Africa was in turmoil. The headlines said it loud and clear: 'Africa at the Edge', 'Long haul through years of despair', 'Waiting for the Wave of Death'. Civil war was raging in many countries, notably Somalia, Sudan, Angola and Mozambique. As a result of the cold war, the continent was awash with arms. There was widespread ecological devastation, largely man-made: expanding deserts, cyclical drought in savannah regions and dwindling tropical rainforests. Harsh governments and dictatorships ruled over the troubled land. The gap between rulers and ruled, rich and poor was forever widening. Cities, which hardly deserved the name, were breaking down. Food production declined while populations were soaring. Unique human cultures as well as animal species and habitats were disappearing fast. There seemed no end to the downward spiral.

African countries, south of the Sahara, suffered the greatest human deprivation in the world. Westerners had grown used to seeing in the media bellies of children swollen with malnutrition, and women holding 'stick' babies to their withered breasts. The statistics disguised the harsh reality: Africa had the lowest life expectancy, the highest infant mortality rates and the lowest literacy rates. Its average per capita income fell by a quarter in the 1980s. Two thirds of all Africans are denied access to clean water for cooking and drinking. Over four million children die each year from malnutrition, while another thirty million are underweight. Most citizens have become worse off in real terms since independence, and every year they are getting poorer.

Given the risks, it was not surprising that I had some difficulty in getting insurance. When I first contacted an agent and explained what I was doing, he replied: 'You'll have to go to Lloyd's of London and deposit a gold bar at their door!' In the end, I was able to get a policy which covered medical expenses for up to a million pounds; if I broke a leg, I could be airlifted out – provided, of course, there was an airfield nearby. I consoled myself with the thought that Vasco da Gama was not insured and he made it all right; then I remembered that he lost over a third of his crew.

Chapter Two

To Die a Little

THE night before I left, I went out for a walk for the last time with my dog Cai, a stray sheep dog who had moved into our house in the Welsh mountains overlooking the Irish Sea. It was a dark, cold night in early February, with a black mass of clouds blocking out the stars. I trudged along a track through the stunted oak copse, scattering a few sheep which had sought shelter for the night below some ancient stone walls. I came out into the clearing overlooking the sea which we called the 'Crab Apple Field' because of the bushy tree there which was full of white blossom in the spring.

The tree bore no fruit in this season and stretched its gaunt branches up to the darkening sky. I felt my head spinning and my heart racing at the thought of leaving my family whom I pictured going about their familiar tasks in the warm interior of our brightly lit cottage. To steady myself, I put my arms around the gnarled, moss-covered crab apple tree.

I returned to the house half an hour later, the cold of the winter's night biting into my body.

My thirteen-year-old daughter was worried about a cross-country race on the coming Friday which everyone expected her to win. I would be out of the country then.

'I'll look after Black Jack, you know.'

I knew she would. I had seen the black silhouette of the horse in the lower field below the copse, motionless after his evening's feed.

'And I'll put the spuds in the garden on Easter Monday, as we normally do!' said my ten-year-old son, Dylan.

'When the earth is warm, I'll dig in the cherry tree you brought us, to replace the dead laburnum,' Jenny said.

Jenny was suffering from a semi-dislocated jaw and was not sleeping well. She had a lot to worry about too. In deepest winter in the Welsh mountains, the half-mile track to our remote cottage was a sea of mud, blocked by cattle. Everyday she would have to get the children to school and travel by car to the college where she taught French. I could not have been leaving at a worse time. It seemed like I was going to have adventures in the sun while she would be struggling in the rain.

'I admire what you're doing,' she said, 'but aren't you running away? What about me? I've got to stay and pay the bills while you're enjoying yourself on the high seas. You'd rather face the obstacles of getting around Africa than stay here and mend a burst pipe!'

She had a point. Why was I going? Why, when sitting by a roaring fire in the midst of my family did I listen to that siren voice which said: 'Give up the comfort of your home and take a voyage across the sea!' I had run away to sea as a boy – was I running away again in middle age?

To make matters worse, my mother in Devon was not very well, unable to eat properly. She had lost a lot of weight recently, and I was not sure that she would still be alive on my return. She wished me well, blissfully unaware of the dangers ahead.

My daughter was involved in her own teenage problems at school, but she tried to make light of the whole thing, sending me notes addressed 'Captain Vasco de Peter Scot Columbus' or simply 'Adventurer Dad'. I hoped I could live up to her expectations. Other letters came addressed: 'To my super-Galactic, extra-spesiall DAD. Dr Scott Marshall, Peter Vasco da Gama. Have courage my good fellow companion! Adress: Somewhere in Africa, the World, the Universe.'

Saying goodbye to Dylan was especially difficult. On New Year's Eve the year before, he had burst into tears at the thought that we might be apart the following year. I had deliberately postponed my voyage several months so that we could be together for New Year and his birthday in

January. When it came to saying goodbye, I had difficulty in holding back the tears.

'It's all right, dad,' he said. 'I'll be with mum. I'm not going to be without both parents, am I?'

I nodded my head, unable to reply. 'Only if Jenny stays well', I thought.

'We really work together, don't we dad? Sometimes, you ask me to do things and I've done them already . . . You must go to Africa, now, after all the preparations.'

Many a time, I had gone over my proposed voyage with Dylan on his illuminated globe, tracing the outline of Africa with our fingers. He knew all the coastal countries and the major towns by heart, and would fall asleep at night with the brightly coloured continent of Africa glowing in the dark corner of his room.

We had estimated that it would mean travelling at least 15,000 miles to circumnavigate Africa. How long it would take was a piece of string: off the top of my head, I said between six and eight months. I knew that I would have to pass through four of the world's greatest seas – the Atlantic and the Indian Oceans, the Red Sea and the Mediterranean. I would cross the Tropic of Capricorn, the Equator and the Tropic of Cancer twice. I would pass through many of the world's most fascinating and varied ecosystems, from deserts to equatorial rainforests, temperate highlands to savannah. On my way, I would see a kaleidoscope of places, peoples and cultures – as colourful and bright as Dylan's illuminated globe itself.

The physical preparations for my voyage had gone smoothly. I had a big enough advance from my publishers to pay for my travelling expenses. When I had mentioned the idea to the television company HTV there was immediate interest and a deal was soon struck for a six-part series. A film crew would meet me at half-a-dozen agreed places around Africa and I would film with a video camera in between. It all seemed to come spontaneously together, a fine example of work without effort, action without striving. The physical pieces of the jigsaw had all fallen into place as if they had a life of their own. But though the physical preparations had gone so well, I realized when the time came to depart, that my feelings were in turmoil.

Not sure that I would ever return, and keen to set my affairs in order, I wrote a will for the first time the night before my departure. Surveying the sum of my worldy goods, I realized that at forty–five I owned no house, no property, no shares, no capital. I was less well off than when I entered the world since all my bank accounts were in the red. All I had to show for all my years' work were several degrees and half-a-dozen books to my name. These were of little use to my nearest and dearest who might be strapped for cash in the future.

The only thing I could offer to my children was an old sailing dinghy, a roomful of books and memories of a father who had tried to bring them up to question authority and think for themselves. I gave my partner Jenny the unenviable task of trying to edit a collection of poems and the manuscript of an autobiographical novel which I should have burnt.

'It is my will,' I concluded, 'that my brother arranges for my body to be cremated and my ashes scattered in Tremadog Bay as the tide begins to ebb. *I love you all.*'

I underlined the last sentence with three lines in a choking burst of love, love for my family, love for the earth, love for life.

After writing my will, I began to pack my luggage. I was determined to try to travel as light as possible. I stuffed in a backpack my health kit, mosquito net, yellow light-weight waterproofs, deflated life jacket, one pair of stout deck shoes, two pairs of trousers and shirts, underwear and socks. In the way of documents I took a large map of Africa, *The ABC Shipping Passenger Guide*, *Africa on a Shoestring*, an address book, notebooks, pens, travellers' cheques (in dollars and pounds), vaccination card and my passport with its precious visas. A friend sent me copies of Lao-tzu's *Tao te ching* and of Walt Whitman's *Leaves of Grass*. I also had another bag with a Sony Hi-8 video camera, a Canon stills camera and a tripod. My only luxury was a fine Panama hat bought in Jermyn Street, Piccadilly, London. Of course I found I had too much and had to abandon a large pile of books, medicines and sweets.

I put on my wrist a blue-and-red 'friendship band' Emily had given me, and around my neck a silver St Christopher's medallion chosen by Dylan.

Although not usually superstitious, I felt they would somehow protect me from evil forces. I also put in my pocket two small stones they had chosen from the house field, so that I could throw them into the sea when passing the Equator for the first time.

I got up early the next morning, 6 February 1992. I said goodbye to Emily and Dylan as quickly as possible before they went to school. I was too sad to linger; to leave is always to die a little. I wrote on the slate slab above the stove where we normally leave messages: 'I go – to return – All my love, Peter.'

I don't know how long it was before my message was rubbed off.

The fields and woods were white with frost that early February morning but the yellow sun brought a hint of spring in the air, after a week of icy nights. The snowdrops were already out, and the tight buds of the daffodils were showing above the frozen ground. I would not see them come out this year.

At Llandudno Junction, I met the HTV film crew who were to see me in Portugal and we drove to Manchester Airport: the producer and director David Williams, who was suffering from mysterious headaches but whose wry sense of humour helped in difficult situations; David England, a young cameraman in his twenties, a vegetarian who had a Zen-like stillness when filming; and Elayne Muth, the sound recordist in her thirties who had a great passion for organic gardening and independent travel.

As Wales merged into England, the towns grew uglier and roads dirtier. I thought I would not greatly miss the grey conformity of Britain at the end of the twentieth century – its people squabbling amongst themselves, scrambling for goods to consume, kidding themselves they were still a great power while in reality a poor cousin of Europe. Once upon a time huge swathes of Africa had been pink but that had faded and now Thatcher's Britain was a murky blue, the artificial blue of blue rinse, not the wondrous blue of the sea or the sky.

The Press covered my departure with phrases like 'North Wales adventurer' or 'globe-trotting author' off to 'darkest Africa' on an 'epic voyage'. The phrases did not somehow fit. My mind was still on what I was leaving rather than where I was going. I had travelled abroad many times for different travel books, but I never imagined that it would have been so difficult to leave this time.

When the plane took off and veered west towards the setting sun, I saw England for the last time clamped in winter, with its sprawling cities, villages, and patchwork of ploughed fields and neat woodlands. Louis Armstrong was singing over the loudspeaker the sentimental tune: 'Skies are blue, the clouds are white . . . a bright blessed day . . . And I think to myself, what a wonderful world!'

During the flight, David said: 'You know, Peter, every journey is an exercise in self-destruction.'

I also read in Lao-tzu.

> Without stirring abroad
> One can know the whole world;
> Without looking out of the window
> One can see the way to heaven.
> The further one goes,
> The less one knows.

If they were right, I was setting off on a voyage which would destroy me in some way and leave me more ignorant than before. But then it dawned on me that there was a positive side to it. Perhaps I would destroy part of my old self, my restless ego, which would be no bad thing. And maybe in the process I would discard some of the useless knowledge I had acquired over the years and get down to essentials. Perhaps the voyage I had just begun was a test, a challenge I had to go through, a necessary stage in the cycle of experience. My quest was a spiritual as well as a physical one, the discovery of my self as well as of a continent.

13

Chapter Three

On the Waterfront

*M*y first night in Lisbon was spent in a small hotel called the Albergaria da Senhora do Monte on a steep hill reached by a cobbled road. When I opened the shutters on my little balcony next morning, I had a wonderful view over the old Alfama quarter of the city to the Castle of St George opposite which dominated the river Tagus. Seagulls and pigeons flew below me and landed on the rooftops and chimneys of the buildings in the steep valley between the castle and the hill on which the hotel stood.

I remembered visiting Lisbon as a boy with my uncle during Salazar's fascist dictatorship when it had seemed like a quiet backwater compared to London. But now, anxious to 'catch up' with the rest of Europe and wallowing in its presidency of the European Economic Community, it was expanding fast. The narrow cobbled streets and alleys designed for horse and carts were packed with cars and the rush-hour jams lasted all day. I soon found the best way to travel was on the trams which clattered up and down the hills; they had been imported from London in the fifties when the metropolis had given them up.

My first concern was to find a boat to take me down to Africa. During an earlier visit to Lisbon I had by chance come across a shipping agent while wandering around the Cais do Sodré area down by the waterfront. It was called Pinto Basto Navegaçáo, founded in 1771. I was introduced to the agency manager, João Galamas. His modern office was in the cellar of an old wharehouse.

He was large man, with a round face, thick glasses and thinning hair. He had a fine command of English, peppered with quaint, old-fashioned phrases. As a believer in free trade and strong leadership, he was a great admirer of Margaret Thatcher. Despite our political differences, I could not help warming to him.

He was immediately excited by the idea of the voyage. As he chatted on, I glanced out of the window. The wind was blowing hard and I could see people fighting with their umbrellas in the pouring rain.

'You realize, of course,' he said, catching my eye, 'that you are sailing from Lisbon in the worse season: in February, we usually have a month of south-westerly gales. Sometimes ships with deep draught have to lay off the port for several days in this weather. But we're happy about the rain. We've had a drought for two months in Lisbon; we need this rain very much.'

'It's very important that I get a boat. You will do your best, won't you – as soon as possible?'

'You can rest assured that I will do my level best, Dr Marshall. But why do you want to go to Africa and upset the poor blacks? Let them lie on the beach, kicking the coconuts as they fall. You should stay here in Portugal.'

On my arrival, the country was celebrating its part in the Age of Exploration, presenting itself to the outside world as the 'Land of the Discoverers'. It had always been a rocky outcrop at the south-west edge of Europe jutting out into the Atlantic Ocean. The poorness of its soil and its closeness to the sea made it look outwards, and for one extraordinary period in its history in the fifteenth century, it became the cradle of Europe's age of discovery and the centre of world trade.

The man chiefly responsible was Prince Henry 'The Navigator'. As a young man, he had taken part in the battle of Ceuta in 1415 (opposite the rock of Gibraltar) which checked once and for all Arab expansion into Europe. From his base in Lagos in the Algarve, he sent expedition after expedition down the west coast of Africa in search of gold, ivory and slaves. In his struggle against the Moors, he also hoped to link up with the legendary Christian king Prester John – probably inspired by rumours

15

of the Christians in Ethiopia – who was thought to live somewhere in Africa. By the time of Henry's death, the Portuguese had reached Sierra Leone. Bartolomeu Diaz then rounded the Cape of Good Hope in 1588, and the first person to round southern Africa and find a passage to India was Vasco da Gama ten years later.

The initial contacts between Africa and Europe were bloody and based on conquest; they set the tone for what followed. The Portuguese had no interest in the indigenous peoples and cultures, but were entirely preoccupied with what they could get from them. They were ostensibly concerned with spreading Christianity and Civilization but in practice their principal aim was plunder. And that could only be achieved by force: the gun went hand in hand with the cross.

As part of its official celebrations, the government had formed a National Commission to commemorate the Portuguese Discoveries. It was housed on the bank of the river Tagus. As I was looking through some documents there, I was approached by a well-dressed man who asked me what I was doing. When I explained my intention of sailing in the wake of Vasco da Gama around Africa, he said:

'Ah ha, I am a descendent of Vasco da Gama! I can tell you something that perhaps you do not know. Christopher Columbus was a secret agent for the Portuguese king, King John II.'

I did not have any more time to explore this intriguing hypothesis, as I had an important meeting to keep. Before I left, he said:

'You must discuss all this with our king.'

'Your king? I thought Portugal was a republic . . .'

'I mean the Duque de Bragança. He is the heir to the Portuguese throne. You can find his telephone number in the directory. He lives in Cintra. Try the Colares wine there, it's very good.'

That was novel; should I look his name up under 'Pretenders' in the Portuguese equivalent of the Yellow Pages?

'Who are you going to see now?' he insisted on knowing.

'Brigadier General Pezarat-Correia. Do you know him?'

'Do I know him! That man is a dangerous leftist! You must be very careful with him . . .'

My contact with the Brigadier General was Hugo Gil Ferriera, a Professor

16

of Physiology at the Gulbenkian Institute of Science in Lisbon. He had worked with my brother Michael at the Cavenish Institute at Cambridge University and they had written a book on the Portuguese Revolution together. His friend, the Brigadier General, was a formal, dapper man. Like many young middle-ranking officers fighting in Portugal's colonial wars in Mozambique and Angola, he had come to the conclusion that not only was the cause of the enemy just but the war itself could not be won. He played a key role in the revolution in 1974 and in the decolonization of Africa. As military governor of the whole of the southern region of Portugal, he had tried to implement a major land reform and create a socialist democracy out of the ruins of the Salazar dictatorship.

'What made a man like you, a professional officer in the army, become a revolutionary?' I asked him over lunch.

'When I was in my twenties serving in Goa, I became friendly with a young conscripted officer. Over a drink in the evening on my verandah after sunset, we would discuss politics and history. He convinced me that Portugal would have to give up the colonies since to hold on to them was unjust. Our conversations also turned me into a socialist: I am socialist because I believe in social justice.'

'Why do you think there is so much trouble in Portugal's former colonies?'

'It's partly a question of development. It's a myth to say that the Portuguese were in Africa to spread civilization. They at first occupied only the coast and formed different alliances with tribal chiefs for slaves. When they settled, they never bothered about educating the Africans.'

'But why haven't the revolutionary governments in Angola and Mozambique been able to bring peace after winning independence?'

'The situation was made worse by the cold war. But there is an even more important factor at work.'

'What's that?'

'The nation state. The state is different from the nation. Europeans went wrong by cutting Africa up and imposing states on different local nations. It meant that the states that the African independence movements inherited were completely artificial. There will have to be a lot of redrawing of boundaries in Africa before things settle down.'

17

Before leaving for his country house, the Brigadier General gave me some good contacts in Angola and Mozambique, and in case I ever made it to landlocked Guinea-Bissau, the address of Dr Vasco Cabral, the brother of the famous revolutionary leader Amilcar Cabral.

While waiting for Mr Galamas of the Pinto Basto Shipping Agency to find me a boat, I decided to travel down to Sagres in the most south-westerly tip of Portugal where Henry the Navigator was said to have set up the first navigation school in the sixteenth century. I soon found out that the idea of the school was a myth but the setting was stunning.

Sagres was situated on a rocky promontory, a wild and barren headland, covered in heather, wild daisies and scattered sisal. At the other end of a bay, Cape St Vincent stretched a rugged finger into the sea, with a lighthouse on its tip where an old convent used to be. Several hundred feet below the sheer cliffs, the Atlantic rollers crashed on the jagged limestone rocks, sending surf and spray high into the whistling air. Lone fishermen were perched like seabirds on the tiny ledges, throwing their lines into the swirling waters below. The sailors who set off with the early Portuguese explorers probably came from the same sturdy stock. I was standing at Europe's Land's End, but in Henry the Navigator's time it was the edge of the known world.

At dusk, I went for a walk along the cliffs. In the hazy distance, I could just make out a little trawler smashing through the waves off Cape St Vincent, bobbing up and down like a tiny cork in the swell of the vast Atlantic. It was a sobering thought to think that I could be in a similar boat heading south in a few days. Looking out to sea, I said to myself: 'I am the hard rock. I am the yielding water. I am the pounding of the waves. I am the whistling wind. I am the the seagulls flying. I am the sun setting and rising . . .'

On my return from Sagres to Lisbon, I contacted the Portuguese Sail Training Association – Aporvela – which had recently built two replicas of the caravels used by the early Portuguese explorers. I was invited to join the *Boa Esperança* (Good Hope). Captain João Lucio welcomed me on board, a short man with a big presence dressed in a navy-blue pullover and bright red woollen hat.

Once we were underway, the light wind gently filling the sails decorated with red crosses, he told me that the first great obstacle was to round Cape Bojador off the Moroccan coast: 'They thought that it marked the beginning of a Sea of Darkness, where the seas boiled, the pitch in their boats would melt, and they would turn black for ever. It was a great psychological barrier; once they managed to round the cape and return, there was no holding them back.'

Although top-heavy, the thirty-three metre caravel was still a seaworthy ship, with the ability to sail at about seven or eight knots. Its two masts carried a main lateen sail and mizzen sail. As with the ancient Arab dhows, the correct set of its triangular lateen sails was very important. If too close hauled, there could be considerable leeway. Sailing straight downwind also caused rolling. But the crew seemed to have the knack of it all right, and even though the winds were light, it was exhilarating to be sailing out into the Atlantic Ocean in a caravel just like the early explorers five centuries before me.

Sailing towards the open sea and the setting sun, we passed under the great suspension bridge which spans the Tagus. We sailed by the imposing monument to the early discoverers, built like the bow of a ship, with Henry the Navigator in the prow and his team of scientists, cartographers and mathematicians behind him. In the distance was the Jerónimos Monastery built in the first years of the sixteenth century on the spot where Prince Henry had ordered a small chapel for the Order of Christ. It was the most obvious sign of the wealth and power which the early colonies brought Portugal. The last famous monument to pass before making for the open sea was the ornate white Belém Tower on the waterfront, built at the same time, the first and last landmark in the capital for the early explorers.

I was unable to sail south towards Africa in the *Boa Esperança* because the weather forecasts were for gales and she had to get ready to sail across the Atlantic to commemorate Columbus's epic voyage five hundred years before. I still had to find another boat to get me down the west African coast. At one point, it seemed that my friend Mr Galamas of Pinto Basto Navegaçáo might get me on board a ship on a geographical expedition, but it fell through. He was as philosophical as ever; with a broad sweep of his large hands, he informed me: 'The best laid-up plans of mice and men can suddenly come to nothing!'

I had no choice but to kick my heels in Lisbon. David Williams had gone home the day after our arrival because of his terrible headaches, and David England and Elayne went back to Britain a week later. I was on my own for the first time. I found the solitude difficult at first. Jenny was still ill at home and was not sure whether she could cope. I especially missed the children and worried if they were going to be all right.

I would wake up at night in my hotel room for no apparent reason and my stomach would drop like a stone off the edge of a cliff. During the day, I often experienced a kind of free-floating anxiety, with hot waves flowing up the back of my head making me feel light and dizzy. I wondered if it might be the effect of the malaria tablets I had been taking or the cocktail of vaccinations coursing in my veins.

Waiting for my boat to come in, I spent a week strolling around Lisbon. Every morning, mist from the the river rolled up the hills of the city, but by midday the winter sun broke through in the pale blue sky. I would go down by tram to Black Horse Square – a neo-classical square built after the great earthquake of 1755 which devastated the city. From there I would stroll along the waterfront by the swirling, brown waters of the Tagus. It was the haunt of young lovers who walked hand in hand, of old men who sat on benches with gnarled hands and brown wrinkled faces, of unemployed Africans trying to keep their body temperature and spirits up.

The river was criss-crossed by ferries, heavily laden with passengers going to and from work, their blunt bows creating an impressive wake. Large cargo ships slowly swung at anchor with the tide. Seagulls soared in the wintry sky. Occasionally a ship was escorted by tugs under the great suspension bridge which straddled the river towards the wide estuary and the open sea.

My life in recent years had become a ceaseless round of activity, and I enjoyed the opportunity to stroll and sit, stand and stare. I would try to do just that during my voyage: take it nice and easy, not straining, not forcing, open to new encounters and adventures. I would let fate take its course, allowing chance to unfurl within the tight circle of necessity.

Mr Galamas of Pinto Basto Navegaçáo did not let me down. He came up with something much more interesting than a cargo ship: a fishing trawler.

It was owned by a company called Laurenço and Neves and her name was *Susana*. She was bound for the Moroccan fishing banks. I received a fax in my hotel one morning with the message: 'For your guidance owners aforementioned trawler do welcome Dr P. Marshall on board and will assist to the best possible.'

Mr Galamas took me down to the docks in his car on the morning before the trawler was leaving to introduce me to the owners and the skipper. There was tight security in the fishing port: 'There's a lot of smuggling of drugs going on from north Africa,' he informed me as the police double-checked our papers.

'You'll find the fishermen very nice people. They come mostly from the north. They look rough; they are not educated, but they are very good people. At sea it's so quiet; they help each other like in a small village. I used to go fishing with them when I was a boy. They're good people.'

The last words of Mr Galamas were: 'If you want my help, contact me anywhere in the world.'

That afternoon, I went to the Jerónimos Monastery where Vasco da Gama's tomb was and lit a candle. It was not only to the memory of the early Portuguese discoverers, although I admired their courage, but to all those who had suffered during the scramble for Africa. It was also for my family in the hope that they would stay well during my absence.

Sitting on a bench of the waterfront for the last time, I wrote a poem:

> I sing a song of Africa and myself,
> A song of sorrow and joy
> Of hardship and hope.
>
> Africa, slumbering across the Equator,
> Your head in the warm waters of the Mediterranean,
> Your feet in the cold currents of the Antartic,
> Life teems across your broad limbs.
>
> Africa, under the sheltering sky,
> Trouble began when we emerged from your side,
> Cutting down your forests, killing your animals,
> Inflaming your skin with war.

Africa, the severed head of the world,
I shall tread carefully around your shores,
Respecting your moods and manners,
Seeking the light in the heart of your soul.

I sing a song of Africa and myself,
A song of sorrow and joy
Of hardship and hope.

In the evening, I went to my favourite little restaurant in a cobbled alley near my hotel and ordered a bottle of cool vinho verde with my dinner. David Williams, feeling a little better, rang me back at the hotel and said: 'Remember that the way to heaven is the way.'

I also spoke to Jenny on the phone. She said she was still in pain with her jaw, was sleeping badly, but was coping for the time being. She insisted that I was not to return.

After tossing and turning for a long time that night, I eventually fell asleep and dreamt that I was shipwrecked on an unknown shore. Thick jungle came down to the beach. Strewn around on the sand under the blinding sun were the blackened bodies of dead lions and elephants in different stages of decomposition. I could not tell the cause of their deaths but I knew that some catastrophe had occurred in the heart of Africa and that I was the last man alive. I woke up soaked in sweat at five o'clock in the morning – the hour of the wolf. I lit a candle at the side of my bed and lay awake until dawn.

When I threw open the doors of my balcony, I was not in good shape but I found the Alfama district below bathed in winter sunshine. The mist which had welcomed me every day had gone. On the terraced slopes of the Castle of St George opposite, the leaves of the orange trees were deep green and the almond trees were covered with delicate white blossom. It was a Sunday morning, and the narrow streets were quiet and empty. A dog barked in a backyard and the distant melody of a flute floated from an open window. Pigeons courted on rooftops, the males bobbing their heads and making fans of their tail feathers.

Then just opposite my balcony a beautiful white seagull with red legs landed on a chimney pot. It looked me straight in the eye and then flew off in a long and effortless glide across the house tops to the orange grove below the castle on the other side of the valley.

It felt like a sign. The thought came into my head: 'Yes, I shall travel like that seagull, alone, independent, but intensely alive and at one with the elements. It comes and goes and leaves nothing behind. That seagull will be my guide.'

Chapter Four

Jumping Ship

WHEN I saw the trawler moored in the fishing port, my heart sank. It was the rustiest there and much smaller than I had expected, like the old trawlers which used to push out into the Channel from Brixham in Devon where my mother lived. Although owned by a Portuguese company with her homeport in Lisbon, the *Susana* was registered in Tangiers, a ploy which I later learned enabled her to fish in Moroccan waters.

I was welcomed on board by the skipper Lucio Vigia, a short taciturn man with gnarled hands. He had left school at twelve and spent eight years off Newfoundland fishing for cod in the freezing waters of the north Atlantic. He had learned his navigation the hard way from another seaman during those lonely years away from home.

I was given the top bunk in a tiny cabin which I shared with the second engineer, Carlos, a large kindly man in his thirties with black drooping moustaches and hair all over his body. He came like most of the crew from the northern coast of Portugal. All the men in his family had gone to sea; his grandfather, uncles, brothers and cousins.

'There is no other work, and this is the best thing we are good at,' he told me.

The galley and the mess were only a few yards down the corridor from my cabin. I smelt them as soon as I went below. On one wall was a garish picture of Christ and of the Virgin Mary, '*Nossa Senhora do Bon Viagem*'.

Everyone gave me a warm welcome and a hard handshake, including a couple of Moroccans who were members of the crew. I was handed a tin mug half full of rough brandy; they all wished me '*Bon viagem*' by clinking the mugs together high in the air with a flourish. I had to get by with my Spanish since no one spoke English.

The weather forecast was not good – gales coming in across the Atlantic. It was sunny with a light breeze, but the barometer pointed to change, and rain and strong winds were expected. The skipper was eager to get away, as they had already been delayed several days by a dock strike. The crew had returned from leave, and he did not want to hang around any longer in port.

'We leave tomorrow at 0400 hours!' he announced.

In the late afternoon, the trawler shifted its moorings to the refrigeration depot in the fishing port to take on fifty tons of ice, and then crossed over to the other side of the Tagus to fill up with oil. The men went about their tasks quietly, their minds already on the voyage ahead, trying to repress thoughts of their families and girlfriends. They would be away for four weeks, with only a couple of days in Agadir on the way out and back. Back in the fishing port in the early evening, a lorry arrived with the final stores; I joined the human chain and helped stow them on board.

I turned in early that night, but it took me a long time to fall asleep. After the months of preparation, followed by two weeks of kicking my heels in Lisbon, I was at last underway. I would be leaving Europe tomorrow for Africa . . .

Someone was gently shaking my shoulder. It was Carlos. I looked at my watch; it was three thirty on Wednesday, 20 February 1992.

'We're leaving, Pedro,' he said. I could hear the engines thumping.

I quickly got dressed and went up on to the bridge, barely big enough for three men at a time. The skipper was issuing orders to his crew who were casting off the mooring ropes. I noticed that the wind had picked up during my sleep. '*Vamos con Dios*,' said the skipper as the quartermaster steered the ship out of the fishing port into the choppy waters of the river Tagus. We passed by the monu-ment to Henry the Navigator by the Jerónimos Monastery where I had lit a candle, and then passed the Belém Tower. As we swung out of the estuary to face the Atlantic rollers I suddenly felt very vulnerable. I imagined the ship to be a little cork tossed about in a vast expanse of sea.

By breakfast time we were heading due south, but we could not see the coast because of poor visibility. The sea and sky were grey, and the wind was blowing at gale force. As the plucky trawler pushed through the surging white horses, it began to pitch and roll heavily. Seagulls screeched and dived in our wake. The waves must have been running fifteen foot high, but so far I felt fine. It was bitterly cold; I was told that it had been snowing in northern Portugal overnight.

By tea time, we were fifteen miles off Cape St Vincent and Sagres, but the coast was still veiled in low cloud. The skipper regularly checked the radar; we were passing by the Pillars of Hercules, the two promontories at the eastern end of the Strait of Gibraltar, one of the busiest shipping lanes in the world. I was leaving Europe behind once and for all; there was no turning back.

Carlos asked me out of the blue: 'Are you thinking of your family?' I was and so was he. He went on to complain about the seaman's life: 'We are always away from home; we spend a month at sea and only a week on leave. The children grow up without you seeing them. All my family is at sea. We have to go to sea to work for the wife and the kids and to pay for the house. All there is is the sea, the sea, always the sea.'

The trouble began when I took up Carlos's invitation to visit the engine room. It was immaculate, with fresh green paint, and seemed much cleaner than the galley. My mistake was to stay too long. The trawler was pitching horrendously, and with a sudden lurch a great wave of nausea rolled over me. I staggered for the gangway and made straight for the deck and fresh air and wide horizons. I just made it in time. Almost falling over the railings, I was sick and sick and sick until I could retch no more. It marked the beginning of two days of severe seasickness, sickness which slowly merged with homesickness. I took to my bunk. I managed with a great effort to unscrew my porthole, and found that I could just squeeze my head through it in order to retch. I had reached bile and beyond. I fell asleep in the early hours only to wake with a splitting headache, nausea and depression. 'Why the hell am I here?' was my first thought as I held on to my pitching bunk.

Unfortunately my cabin was just down from the galley and mess room, and the smell of rancid olive oil used for cooking was terrible. For the crew, the meals were the high points of the day; eating and drinking were their principal pleasures and only moments of rest. They each had their own large pitcher of wine and bottle of strong spirits with which they washed down their huge plates of food. They always seemed to be shouting at each other, as if they were angry, but I soon realized it was just their way of talking over the sound of the engine. Most of the fishermen were in their thirties but there were a few older ones who hardly said a word.

Determined not to feel sorry for myself, I staggered up to the deck as soon as the first light of dawn appeared on the grey horizon. To my surprise, the waves seemed smaller and the ship appeared to be rolling less. The cold fresh air did me good although any thought of the galley or the engine room below immediately sent me to the side.

'*Bon dia*,' said the skipper Lucio, smiling. Experienced seamen always find seasickness amusing in others. 'Today we see the sun and tomorrow we arrive in Agadir.'

I had been assured in Lisbon that there would be no trouble at all in picking up a fishing boat from Agadir to Las Palmas: 'They go across there everyday.' When I broached the subject with the skipper of the trawler, he was less sanguine: 'There's a war on down there between the government and Polisario guerrillas who want an independent state in the Western Sahara. When we go fishing, two Moroccan soldiers come on board to escort us. You won't be able to pass through the war zone.'

'But your owners and the agent in Lisbon said that you would be able to find me a boat to Las Palmas,' I reminded him.

'*No es fácil*. There are only Korean boats going to the Canaries and they will not take you.' I hadn't intended to travel on one; Carlos had told me that Korean trawlers are filthy, full of cockroaches and rats. Portuguese trawlers refuse to moor alongside them for fear of the rats running across the mooring lines.

'Look,' said the skipper, showing me a document, 'you are officially an *observador* on this boat and you must return with us to to Lisbon. If you leave the boat in Agadir, you are officially jumping ship. That's illegal. You will not be able to land.'

'But I was told that you would be able to help me find a boat to Las Palmas!' I insisted.

'I'm sorry but I can't change the law. You must stay with us and go fishing for three weeks and then return to Lisbon.'

This bit of news was the last straw. I had hardly slept for two days and had felt continually seasick and homesick. I would have to get off the boat one way or another, even if it meant jumping ship. A prison cell would be preferable, as long as it was in Africa.

The next day dawned beautifully. The sea had calmed down and the red sun rose above the light brown cliffs of the Moroccan coast. I could soon make out the hills behind Agadir and slowly the hotels along the beach and the masts of the fishing port came into view. When we entered the port, it was a mass of rusty trawlers, piled high with nets and swarming with Arab fishermen. We eventually moored alongside a Moroccan trawler, four abreast from the quayside. The place stank of fish and rotting vegetables, and I was careful not to fall into the oily water. A warm wind blew fine dust from the desert.

Carlos came to say goodbye and warned: 'Pedro, Marrocos is a dangerous place. You must not talk in Marrocos' – he drew his fingers across his mouth – 'there is no freedom of speech. It is all religion and no culture. There is plenty misery, plenty beggars, more thieves than flies. Be careful in Africa!'

I asked him the name of the local shipping agent:

'His name is Moustapha. Moustapha is a very big man. He shaves his head and beard. He has many *bambinos* in Agadir. Money, he always want money. There is much corruption in Marrocos; also much *miseria*. Be careful in Africa, Pedro!'

Soon after we had moored alongside, I saw a huge man clambering over the adjoining trawlers, accompanied by a young Arab boy. He was dressed in long robes and a thick colourful pullover. His head was entirely shaved. He must have been over six foot three. He was Moustapha. Just as he was about to jump into the *Susana*, the bearded Moroccan fisherman Mohamed came up to me and said with a broad grin: '*Attention à Moustapha; il est pédé!*' It seemed that I now had legal, military and sexual obstacles to overcome.

After he had seen the skipper and collected a great box of goodies from the cook, I explained my case to Moustapha. He shook his great shining head and said '*C'est très difficile! très difficile!*' He then took my hand in a great soft paw and said '*Viens avec moi!*'

I left my things on board and clambered over the trawlers moored alongside us to the quay where Moustapha had left his battered white Peugeot. He drove, very erratically, through the port, bouncing over potholes and nearly running down several people. By the time we arrived at the main offices in the fishing port, he was sweating profusely and gave off a sickly smell of cheap perfume. On the way, he explained to me that it was the King's coronation day and all next week there would be celebrations. That also meant empty offices.

As we entered the Police headquarters, Moustapha spotted a man in a suit slipping away. He managed to usher him back into the office. He was the *chef de la police*. His office was empty except for a desk and few chairs, with a badly hung portrait of the king of Morocco on the grimy walls. After listening carefully to my case, he replied:

'*Monsieur*, you are not allowed to enter the port by fishing boat and you have no proper papers. You will have to return to Lisbon.'

'But I must get a boat to Las Palmas.'

'I am sorry, *monsieur*, but you do not have the right papers. Anyway it's impossible to take a boat from here to Las Palmas, it's a war zone.'

'But I must visit Morocco. It is a very beautiful country and I am a writer.'

'Ah, *vous êtes écrivain*.' He seemed immediately interested. I've blown it now, I thought.

'A writer? I am a great lover of literature! You have a fine profession, *monsieur*,' and he beamed in appreciation. This was to be one of the few times in my travels that being a writer would go down well with the authorities. Whatever Carlos might say, the Moroccans were very civilized.

The *chef de la police* flicked through my passport, glancing at all the visas I had managed to get for countries along the west coast of Africa. He then looked up and fixed me with his clear brown eyes.

'*D'accord*, I will let you enter this time. But it is not correct.' He stamped my passport with flourish, shook my hand and said: 'Welcome to Morocco!'

*   *   *

Moustapha agreed to take me back to the *Susana* to collect my things. But when I clambered back across the moored trawlers, nearly losing my camera in the process, I found the white Peugeot was gone. Moustapha was nowhere to be seen.

Mohamed then turned up out of the blue. 'Why has Moustapha cleared off?' I asked him.

'Customs. He doesn't want any trouble with customs!'

It then hit me. I was not yet in. I still had immigration and customs to clear. More hassle, and, if Carlos was to believed, money. I then had a brainwave. I had seen some tourists arrive in a taxi to visit the port. An ancient taxi was just passing me at that moment; I hailed it down. I insisted on putting my luggage in its oily boot.

'*Centre ville, s'il vous plaît,*' I declared and off we went, dodging the dockers, fishermen and their wares scattered all over the quayside. At the port gates, my heart began to thump; our taxi was waved down by a policeman with a rifle.

'What's in your bag there?'

'A camera, that's all. I'm a tourist visiting the fishing port.'

'A tourist?' he asked, uncertain what to do. He looked carefully on the back seat. Allah be praised that the driver had put my luggage in the boot.

'*D'accord,*' he said at long last, and waved me on. I was saved. At last I was in Morocco.

On the other side of the gate stood Mohammed, beaming all over. He seemed to come and go like a genie.

'So you made it. *Inshallah.* Now you can give me a lift into town.'

Chapter Five

False Guides

I HAD arrived in Agadir at the back end of the season, and only a few elderly Europeans ventured out along the promenade, huddled against the off-shore winds which bent the palm trees. The sky was overcast and rain threatened.

I asked to be dropped off at a travel agent in town. It was just about to close for the weekend as I staggered through the door with all my gear.

A smart young Moroccan, clearly impatient to be off, informed me that there were no boats west to Las Palmas or north to Casablanca – '*absolument pas!*' My worst fears were confirmed. Was there a plane then to Las Palmas?

'Yes, on Wednesdays, but it is fully booked. It's a small plane and it's always fully booked.'

'And to Casablanca?' He telephoned the only airline, Air Maroc, and replied:

'They are all fully booked for weeks to come.' It seemed that I was well and truly stuck. Relax, go with the flow, I told myself, but it was difficult. If this is what was going to happen during my voyage around Africa I might as well go home. I still had not recovered from the trawler and my brush with the Moroccan authorities. Despair welled up like a spring of crude oil.

At that moment, the French *patronne* of the agency came in, a chubby middle-aged woman with staring eyes. She had the confidence of a *pied-noir* who had spent years dealing with the natives. I explained my predicament

31

to her. She said she would do her best over the weekend but she did not hold out great hopes. In the meantime, she booked me in a four-star hotel by the beach at a special rate.

The Atlas Hotel was just what I needed. My room was airy, quiet, clean, with a balcony overlooking the sea. On the wall was a splendid engraving of a Berber on a rearing horse, both full of fiery haughtiness. I showered off the salt, sweat, fish and diesel fumes of the trawler. After a bottle of mineral water, a sandwich, and pot of piping-hot Moroccan mint tea, I felt like a new man.

At dinner that night, I realized that I was virtually alone in the ten-storey hotel. There were five huge Germans with beer bellies round a table in the centre of the dining room. On the periphery at separate tables sat two single Frenchwomen of a certain age; the handsome waiters paid them special attention, to their obvious delight. There was also a middle-aged Frenchman with a beautiful Arab boy.

After dinner, I got chatting with the manager of the hotel who joined me for coffee in the huge empty lounge.

'It's the Gulf War. As soon as the Gulf War started, the tourists stopped coming. The English were against all the Arabs. The king also fell out with the French after President Mitterrand's wife offered support for the Polisario. I can remember when this room was full of laughter; now there are more staff than clients. I keep them on in the hope that things will improve. We live in difficult times.'

The next morning, I went to explore Agadir a little. Much of its old architecture had been destroyed in the famous earthquake of 1960, and the new buildings in the Arab quarters were drab and functional. Along the seafront there were large hotels catering for European tourists; it could have been on the Costa Brava in Spain. Its saving grace was its wide curving bay.

With the sun, the citizens of Agadir came out on to the beach. Schoolboys were playing football in the sand, and a wide circle of girls with long robes and headscarves threw balls to each other. They collapsed in giggles when I tried to film them, and told me to clear off. Quite right too. There was even a lone camel with a European lady in a straw hat being led along the seashore. On the promenade, the open air cafés were filling up with Moroccan couples. It all seemed very sedate and calm.

My dinner in the dreary hotel was enlivened that night by the presence of an English couple, David and Maggie Burke, and their son Sim who were travelling by car down through Morocco. They were recovering from a spell in Tanzania where they had been teachers at the international school in Dar es Salaam and caught giardiasis. It was a pleasure to talk to this family in a familiar tongue after being in a world of half-understood Portuguese for so long. We agreed that we should visit Marrakesh together the following day. We booked – by computer in a smart office – tickets in a state-run coach which was to leave at four o'clock in the morning.

When I told my plan to the maid with the gold teeth who cleaned my room she said: 'There are many rogues in Marrakesh. You must be very careful!'

The last thing that the hotel receptionist warned as we left for our coach in the dark next morning was '*Attention aux faux guides!*'

We set off on a cold morning after a night of heavy rain. After a hour or so the dawn began to break, grey and bleak. On the road we passed only an occasional overloaded lorry and a few lean peasants. As we travelled through the Atlas mountains I could see neat villages of mud buildings nestling along the valleys. The first tender white buds of the olive trees were opening. We then crossed a barren rocky plain. The recent heavy rains had left large puddles here and there. By nine o'clock we reached the walled fields and a few factories on the outskirts of Marrakesh. We got off at the coach terminus and, dodging the cars and horse-drawn carts, made for the souks of Marrakesh.

While we were looking at a map at a street corner, a man in a blue anorak pulled up on his bike and said: 'You want a guide. Me good guide. Here see my papers.'

He showed me a crumpled identity card which declared that he was an assistant accounting clerk.

'We not worry about money. You pay me after what you think,' he insisted. We agreed to take him on. I noticed that he had dark circles around his eyes and had a nervous disposition. He could not stand still.

The souks he took us to see were extraordinary. It was like entering a medieval city, crawling with all manner of people. Some of the alleys were covered, others open to the sky. Because of the recent rains it was necessary to jump across the puddles which formed amongst the filthy mud. It smelt of rotting vegetables, with the occasional waft of incense. After a while a kind of pattern emerged in the labyrinth, with different quarters devoted to different trades: blacksmiths, jewellers, carpetmakers, woodcarvers, leatherworkers, butchers, spice merchants and so on. Beggars and sellers accosted us from all directions.

Our guide, who seemed to become more agitated as the morning wore on, made a big show of chasing away the hustlers. Things started to turn sour after we refused to buy some goods in a tiny weaving workshop he showed us.

Whenever a policeman appeared, he detached himself from our group and dropped back far behind. He then told me that if I continued to film in the souks, I would have my camera smashed. As if to make his point, he shouted something in Arabic to some young men who then came at me menacingly. One guy drew a knife, shouting '*Tu me fais chier, schisse*, fuck off!'

'You're scared! You're scared!' screamed our guide dancing around, his sunken eyes rolling. It then dawned on me that the man was high as a kite.

We continued down an alley, but he deliberately trod on our shoes and ankles, trying to provoke a fight. With a hostile crowd gathering around us, I tried to calm things down and said:

'Take us to the main square, and we will pay you off.'

He took us around a couple of blocks along the narrow streets and soon we came to a deserted spot where two alleys crossed. High walls were on either side.

'Here is main square. Now you pay me.' When we gave him some notes, he spat on the ground. With his face twisted in rage, he shouted: 'Fuck Off! Bullshit! Bloody Tourists!'

We had, as they say in the trade, been had. Our guide was indeed false. He had abandoned us not in the main square but in the centre of the labyrinth of the souks, in a dangerous quarter, with no obvious way out. The Arabic names on the alleys meant nothing. There was only one thing to be done: to travel due west according to the sun until we hit the 'civilized' quarter built by the French with its classical grid pattern of wide roads and squares.

By now it was midday and hot and humid. The fetid pools along the endless alleyways stank. The lack of fresh air made us all feel faint. Eventually, we managed to find a Moroccan who spoke French and directed us out of the labyrinth. We came out suddenly into the great square of Djemas el Fna and, *inshallah*, the wide open sky.

The heat, din and hassle were still oppressive. It was with great relief that I saw the entrance to a Club Méditerranée hotel. Going into its cool interior, with its Oriental carpets and cushions, was like entering an oasis of peace.

Determined to see as much of Marrakesh as possible, I set off again into the heat of the town in the afternoon. I made for the Palais de la Bahia, a palace with secluded gardens and shady courtyards. But when I tried to enter its main building, armed guards blocked my way. The palace had been occupied by the court followers of the king who would be soon passing through as part of the round of celebrations in the country for his coronation day.

Modern Morocco might be in a mess – in economic decline, at war with its southern neighbour, torn between European and African ways, suffering the rising tide of Islamic fundamentalism – but its past rulers, however tyrannical, certainly knew how to live graciously in beautiful surroundings. The underground irrigation channels built by Yussef Ibn Tashfin in the eleventh century in Marrakesh still refresh the city's gardens.

I returned to the main square Djemas el Fna in the late afternoon to witness one of the great daily pageants in Africa. I was constantly hassled by beggars, old and young, and by men who wanted to be my guide and who would not take 'no' as an answer. Pimps also accosted me; it was possible to have sex with a woman who lifted her long dress against a wall for a few dirham. Dope was freely available.

The square was lit by fires, and swarming with people. It was like a Brueghel painting come to life; we had entered a medieval peasant world of naked passion. Snake charmers, palmists, story tellers, craftsmen, jugglers, acrobats, street sellers, charlatans, hustlers and madmen all jostled for attention. Pickpockets, drugdealers and prostitutes kept to the shade to ply their trade. On the outside of the pageant stood kiosks selling food and drink, lit up by kerosene lamps in the darkening night.

Men passing by with monkeys on their shoulders would suddenly throw them into your hair, demanding money before they released you from their clutches. Dancers suddenly ran up to you and started performing. However much money you gave, it was never enough: ingratiating demands would be followed by insults and abuse. One of the main centres of attraction was a band of acrobats, with boys and girls in dirty red clothes doing incredible contortions with their stunted bodies. Assistants hustled the admiring circle for contributions.

What attracted the noisiest crowd were two men dressed as women who gyrated their thighs and swung their false breasts in the most suggestive way. One came to dance up against me; the only way to disengage myself was to throw a note, not in appreciation, but in desperation. The rhythm was definitely African; the melodies Arabic.

After the exhausting events of the day, I looked forward with pleasure to the long coach drive back to Agadir. When we got on the modern coach, the only seats available were at the back where several young men in sharp clothes giggled. Women in purdah with their children and old men were already long ensconced with their luggage and shopping.

When the coach left Marrakesh, it was already dark. I settled down to sleep. I was then awakened by an American video which was shown on two screens so that none could turn a blind eye. Since the state-run coach was full of devout Muslim women and their children, I assumed that the film would be family entertainment. I could not have been further off the mark. Called 'Angel of Vengeance', it was a story about a gang of Vietnamese veterans holed up in a desert stronghold who capture and rape a woman writer. She is then released in the sierra and proceeds to kill her rapists one by one in the most vicious way. If this wasn't bad enough, it soon became apparent during the show that the young men next to me at the back of the coach were lovers. Their passionate petting during the film soon gave way to mutual masturbation, trousers down.

It was a delight to get out of the coach at last in Agadir, to see the star-studded sky, to feel the cool sea breeze on my face, and to hear the crashing of the surf.

When I returned to my hotel, the receptionist at the Atlas Hotel passed me a fax from Mr Galamas, the shipping agent in Lisbon: 'VERY MUCH SURPRISED WITH YR NEWS, OWNERS SUZANA GUARANTEED PLENTY TRAFFIC FM AGADIR/LAS PALMAS'. The next morning, there was another fax waiting for me in my pigeon-hole: 'MUCH REGRET SITUATION FOUND AT AGADIR, STILL CANNOT UNDERSTAND WHY OWS SUZANA STATED PLENTY VSLS THAT END'. He asked me to accept his sincere apologies, and said that he had already spoken to the agents in Las Palmas who would do their 'very best' to assist me.

I decided to put more pressure on my travel agency to see if I could get out of Agadir and Morocco. I had had enough. It was all very well to go with the flow, if you felt it was flowing in the right direction. Since there were no boats travelling across to the Canaries because of the war, I had no choice but to see if a plane could take me the hundred miles or so to Las Palmas.

As soon as I entered the office, the *patronne* declared: '*Vous avez la chance, monsieur*'. She had telephoned a friend in another agency who had come back to say that she had found a ticket to Las Palmas that had been reserved for two weeks but had not been taken up. The plane would be leaving tomorrow.

'You'll enjoy Las Palmas,' she added. 'It's carnival time there!'

My exit from Morocco was very different from my arrival. I caught a taxi with a Berber driver. He was a descendent of the people who had controlled the trans-Saharan gold and ivory trade and had exchanged goods with the Phoenician who had settled along the coast a thousand years before the arrival of the Portuguese.

After a long straight highway, we arrived at the huge new empty airport outside Agadir. So far, so good. When I checked in, the customs officials made me unpack every single item of my rucksack and camera bag. I soon had the contents strewn all over their table. They were clearly after drugs and arms. They were highly suspicious of my medical kit and checked each little item. They took so long that it seemed that I was going to miss my flight to Las Palmas, probably the only flight I would ever be able to get. At the last moment, as they were unscrewing a bottle of mosquito repellent, they suddenly said: '*Allez, monsieur, allez!*'

I stuffed my worldly belongings in as best and fast as I could and ran for the aeroplane. I was the last person to board, but was welcomed by a beaming steward who kissed his fingers and outstretched his hands at the top of the gangway.

I settled down next to an attractive Moroccan woman in her thirties, with long dark wavy hair and beautiful brown eyes. She turned out to be a teacher travelling to the Canaries for the carnival.

'You must go. After Rio, the carnival is the best in the world. *Tout le monde est en fête.*'

'You can't say that about Morocco.'

'Yes, I'm afraid you're right. If everyone were allowed out of the country, only four people would remain. There's so much poverty and wealth side by side. The government has banned the political opposition; they let people steal and kill each other so that they can have an excuse to remain in power.'

'Is it difficult being a woman in an Islamic country like Morocco?'

'It used not to be too bad, but the fundamentalists are making it very difficult for us. They want all of us to stay at home and wear purdah. They don't even want a teacher like me to go out; my neighbours now are always criticizing me for living my own life. I'm a Muslim myself, but what the fundamentalists teach is not true Islam.'

The flight across the narrow strip of sea between the Moroccan coast lasted only half an hour. Before we landed the beaming steward handed me a slip of paper. On it he had written: 'It is an illusion to think that more comfort means happiness. Happiness comes from the capacity to feel deeply, to think freely, to enjoy simply, and to be needed.' He wished me the very best in all that life can bring, adding: 'When you need salt, sugar won't do.' I could not have had better advice.

Chapter Six

Carnival Time

I HAD no trouble with immigration and customs in Las Palmas, Gran Canaria. By a quirk of colonial history, this barren windswept rock off the African coast was a part of Spain and therefore part of the European Economic Community. I joined the flocks of tourists in the airport who were escaping from the cold northern winters.

Waiting at the bus stop outside the airport, I met a tall blond Englishman, with round gold-framed glasses, who was dressed in jeans and a pullover. Since the bus would not be coming for some time, we decided to go and have a pot of tea in a nearby café.

His name was Peter Cracknell and he was a painter. Since his girl-friend was an air hostess in a charter company flying regularly between Stockholm and Banjul in the Gambia via Las Palmas, they had decided to spend half the year in Sweden and half in the Canary islands. He liked the relaxed pace of life in the Canaries and in his sunny and airy flat by the sea he painted his watercolours, with their lakes, seashores, birds and flowers, in tranquil contentment.

When he invited me to stay in his flat, I immediately accepted. It was on the fourth floor of an apartment block overlooking the long sweep of Canteras beach in Las Palmas with rugged hills rising at each end. At low tide, a reef emerged from the sea opposite. We soon settled down to a regular routine. While he got on with his painting, I would go and visit the shipping agents down by the docks. In the late afternoon we would go for a jog along the deserted beach, play beach tennis, and swim. We then headed home to make ourselves a light meal with a bottle of wine under the stars on his balcony. In the mornings, I would be woken up by the sound of children playing and the cooing of doves.

I soon discovered that there was some fine colonial Spanish architecture in Las Palmas, especially in the old town with its cobbled streets, little squares and grand houses. The main square down by the docks in the new town was also a fine place with its gardens and bustling cafés. But much of the town was turned over to selling: a free port, it provided every consumer good that money could buy. The shops stayed open late into the night, enticing passing sailor and tourist alike.

I was struck by the stockiness of the islanders who had replaced the original blue-eyed cave dwellers. They were short, dark and swarthy, many with pock-marked faces. The older women seemed to age quickly, many dressed in the black of widows, but the young ones had long hair, curvaceous bodies and incredibly short and tight mini-skirts. Their boys in crew-cuts would hurtle around the narrow streets on their mopeds, making as much noise as possible. In the season, they eyed the foreign girls who bared their breasts on the beach to the sun.

Although it was carnival time, my first priority was to find a ship to take me down to Dakar, Senegal. The initial response was not good. I first went to the shipping, Perez & Co., agent recommended by Mr Galamas in Lisbon but it only knew of a ship with a Russian crew owned by Mac Lines which was leaving three weeks later to Banjul. 'Try Menendez & Pelay,' the director suggested. 'They're agents for Polish Ocean Lines.' After tracing them down two hours later, I still had no joy. I seemed to have come to a dead end.

The next day I went down to the harbour master to see if I could find a tramp ship going down the west coast of Africa. Tramps follow no fixed itinerary, but travel to ports where they can pick up cargo at short notice. Again the response was unhelpful: 'There's no saying when they come and go; they're in one day and out the next. At the moment, there aren't any in the port.'

I had sailed across the Atlantic from the Canary Islands with my brother and two friends in his yacht six years earlier; perhaps I could hitch a lift as a crew member on one going down to the Cap Verde islands. I went down to the yachting marina but again drew a blank. It was too late in the season; there had been quite a few French yachts sailing down to Dakar from November to January but the trade winds had now swung round.

Once again, I had ground to a halt, sitting on the dock of the bay, miles away from home, waiting for a ship to roll in. But at least it was Friday afternoon: the carnival would be reaching its climax at the weekend, so I decided to go with the flow.

When Franco decided to rebel against the Spanish Republic in the thirties, he launched his military campaign from the Canary islands before going to Spanish Morocco. He repaid their hospitality by banning the carnival. I could see why. Carnivals are by their nature subversive, great outbursts of popular energy and creativity. Music and dance have always threatened dictatorships. Since the fall of Franco, the Canaries like the rest of Spain have made the best of the new freedoms.

The carnival had become a great annual festival and big business, comparable to Rio de Janeiro's in size and energy. Every night the coloured lights went on along the promenade near the docks and music blasted out. In the main square on a huge open-air stage, groups played until the early hours. The most popular music was the rumba, with its African rhythms and Latin American melodies. Disguised young and not so young people danced wildly; clowns leapt around; men on stilts swept by. Behind their disguises, everyone lived out his or her fantasy to the hilt. After a while, I gradually realized that there were a great number of men dressed as women in the most outrageous and provocative costumes.

Peter put me right: 'Didn't you know? Las Palmas has become the tranvestite capital of Europe during carnival time!'

Until the early hours of the morning, the bars were full of tranvestites and tough young Canarians who flirted with them good-humouredly. But the carnival had its down side. Seeing lonely tranvestites returning home to their cheap hotels, soaked by the rain, mascara running, their carefully designed dresses ripped and dragging in the dirt, was not a happy sight.

Next morning in the main square all was quiet; the streets were swept, the pigeons picking up titbits left by the revellers, and the warm sun soon dried the washed pavements. The newsagents and flower sellers opened up their kiosks and old men gathered in a corner of the gardens for coffee and chess.

The day after the final night of the carnival I woke up with a headache and with a sinking feeling that I was marooned on this island. There was only one way to exorcise the mood – visit more shipping agents. By chance, I entered the office of Olsen & Co in a busy street down by the docks and was introduced to the director Mr Jaime Medina Tacoronte, a fastidious man in well-ironed shirt and tie. He said that there was indeed a ship – the MV *Pol Europa* – sailing to Dakar at the end of the week, and then on to Conakry, Freetown, Lagos, Abidjan, Tema and Douala – 'the dark side of Africa'. It was a new ship owned by Polish Ocean Lines but chartered by CMB – Compagnie Maritime Belge – based in Antwerp, Belgium. Although he thought it a waste of time, he said he would fax the company's head office to see if it would let me join the ship.

When I went to see Mr Medina the next day, he was all smiles:

'Ah, señor Peter Marshall. Good welcome at Olsen's! I have good news for you!' Over coffee, he recounted how he had spent three months twenty years ago with a family in Swanage in Dorset to learn English; he then lived in Bayswater in London for two years importing tomatoes from the Canaries. He liked all things English, recalling how as a boy his friends would call the British sailors 'Johnnies' without knowing why. The words cake, play, bacon and beefsteak had all gone into the local dialect. He also claimed that the British community had made a considerable impact on the island: tomato and banana plantations, the golf course, the Hotel Metropole, the Anglican Church and the British Club.

On his wall was a photograph of the SS *Queen Elizabeth* visiting the port. In the old days, British ships were the main ones that called, but not any more: it was now the turn of the Germans, Poles, French, and Russians. Our conversation was suddenly interrupted by a gruff Russian voice on the ship-to-shore radio which asked whether they wanted to sell any frozen fish and 'fish flour' (presumably meal). Not today, thank you.

As we said goodbye, Mr Medina said: 'I hope you have a good trip around Africa. Tata and toodle-oo!'

I continued my routine with Peter, except that one day we climbed the mountain at the end of bay which gave us a magnificent view across Las Palmas. At the top of the mountain, a couple of old men and some boys were trying to catch pigeons with lines. Goats, introduced by the Spanish centuries ago, had devastated the local flora and fauna and had reduced the wooded island to a bare rock.

We also visited in the old town the ornate Spanish cathedral and the house where Columbus had stayed on his voyage across the Atlantic five hundred years ago. Bartholomeu Dias and Vasco da Gama also put in here during their voyages south in search of a passage to the Indies in the opposite direction. There would have been no carnival for them until they got home.

During my stay with Peter, his girlfriend Christina joined us for a few days after returning from Banjul. 'It's funny how the Scandinavians are drawn to Africa,' she observed. 'Many Swedish women marry Gambians, but when they go and live in Sweden the marriages usually break up. There's a lot of prejudice still, and the African men do not settle down in Swedish society; they miss the sun and ease of their own country. They usually drift back.'

Despite the certainty of a ship, I was delayed for a further two days in Las Palmas by a strike by pilots opposed to privatizing the service run by the Port Authority. At midday, the African sun was warm, but cold winds blew across the islands, and the night before I left a thunderstorm broke out. It seemed to clear the air in my mind as well as in the sky.

My first sight of the MV *Pol Europa* was at night. I was waiting on the dock of Las Palmas with Peter when this huge ship, her rear accommodation ablaze with lights and her forward deck piled high with rectangular containers, towered out of the darkness. As soon as she had moored alongside the dock with the help of tugs, the overhead gantries swung into action to lift the containers out of the ship. Trucks with enormous wheels roared forward to collect them and stacked them like so many boxes of matches.

I said goodbye to Peter with some sadness; he had proved a good friend at a difficult moment in my voyage. It was great however to have found a ship and to be on the move again. I had no regrets when I saw the mountains of Las Palmas disappear over the horizon next morning as we sailed down towards black Africa.

The ship was brand new – on its second voyage in its short life. The bunk in my comfortable cabin had not yet been slept in and I was the first to shave in the small bathroom attached. I had a square porthole on the port side of the ship.

The ship had been made in Germany. Although owned by Polish Ocean Lines. Compagnie Maritime Belge had chartered it and its Polish crew; they drummed up the business and told the captain where to go. It was a good deal for both of them. Ever since Conrad's time, the landlocked Polish had a fine maritime tradition and were reliable sailors; they were also now about half the price of their Western counterparts.

In the mess room, I was placed at a small table with a dour and taciturn German engineer from the shipyard which built the *Pol Europa*; he was there to fulfil the terms of the guarantee and to check the ship's performance. None of the Poles spoke German, so the language of communication was English as it is throughout the merchant navies of the world.

For much of the voyage, there was about a force four wind blowing and the sea was choppy, but the large container ship ploughed through the waves with ease. After my recent experience, I did not envy the trawlers we passed which were crashing through the white horses and twisting and turning like corkscrews.

I had the free run of the ship so, after taking a walk around the decks under the containers to the quiet forecastle, I would go each day up to the bridge. One morning I fell into conversation with the second mate Jarek Kondraciuk and asked him why he had gone to sea in the first place?

'The romance of the sea. But I soon learned different. Now the romantic days of shipping are over. With containers, we are in and out of port in hours rather than days. It is like a bus service; we have no time to go ashore and to get to know a country and meet people. We don't even use the sextant any more to plot our position: the satellite navigation tells us exactly where we are. It's becoming completely mechanized.'

As we spoke the cadet who was in the starboard wing of the bridge started shouting and pointed down to the sea. I rushed out to see what all the commotion was about. It was a whale, a huge one! It surfaced right next to the ship, blew a spout of water, dived with a flip of its wide tail and then resurfaced 200 metres behind in our wake. We were travelling at about thirteen knots an hour; it could not, or did not want to, keep up with us. It was the first whale I had ever seen at sea.

The first mate's name was Wladyslaw Szymanski. He reminded me somehow of Captain Aheb: he was tall with a beard which he carefully trimmed around the neck and cheeks. As a boy, he had been seduced by the 'dream of Communism' with its vision of abundance and leisure, but had recently played a leading role in the Solidarity movement within the Polish Ocean Lines. Although it had managed to get rid of the corrupt Communist Party in Poland, he was not happy with the result:

'I am very ashamed now', he confided in me, 'that we have not realized our goals. My Solidarity work hasn't helped me either. I know I'm a second-class citizen in the company because of it and I may not get promotion to become a captain.'

'What made you lose your faith in Communism?'

'Communism has ruined the African people and Eastern Europe. They were told that communism was inevitable, so no one made an effort. With no race or competition, you become lazy. It is natural for people to become inert, to do nothing, unless pushed to. That is the trouble with Africa.'

I soon found that virtually every sailor I met, whether Asian or European, had a low opinion of Africa and Africans. This is partly due to the inefficiency of the ports and the dockers, but also due to the corruption of the authorities and the widespread presence of thieves, pirates and muggers. Ports anywhere in the world are dangerous places, but especially so in Africa where few countries are stable and well organized.

Captain Henryk Netzel of *Pol Europa* particularly complained of the corruption of the port authorities. On each voyage down the West African coast, he had to take 10,000 cigarettes and a hundred bottles of whisky to give as 'presents' to the immigration, health and customs officials who swarm on board as soon as the gangway is lowered.

The captain was a serious man who kept a tightly disciplined ship. His eyes were mere slits; they were puffed up and had dark rings around them which suggested that he hardly slept. With a new ship, the pride of Polish

Ocean Lines, in difficult waters, he felt his responsibility. Yet behind his serious veneer, he had a good sense of humour.

The dangers for sailors along the African coasts were not just imaginary. The captain told me how on a previous voyage they had been unable to enter Freetown in Sierra Leone because of congestion in the port. Knowing it to be a dangerous place, he decided to stand off forty miles out to sea. He placed a lookout fore and aft, and the chief officer was on watch on the bridge. He went to his cabin, confident that they would not be disturbed. But in the early hours, unbeknown to him, pirates came out in fast speed boats. They boarded the ship silently, and seized the nightwatchmen. The first thing that the chief mate knew about it was a knife at his throat. The pirates proceeded to go through the cargo and then slipped away as stealthily as they had come. When the alarm was at last raised, the officers found that they had only stolen a few drums of chemicals. It was another time for celebration.

Chapter Seven

Keep Calm

THE night before we arrived in Dakar the captain of the *Pol Europa* warned me: 'When you go ashore, you'd better take $10 to $15 to give to anyone who stops you. Africans can get angry and dangerous. Many sailors get into fights with them. Take care. Africa is very dangerous just now.'

He seemed to be talking about a different Dakar and a different Africa to the ones I had known a quarter century earlier when I had been a teacher of English in Senegal. It was in Dakar that I really got to know Jenny; it was like coming home and revisiting my youth.

After spending her early childhood in Fontainebleau outside Paris, Jenny had grown up in Dakar from the age of eleven. Her father, Joseph Zobel, a writer from Martinique, had been a friend of the Senegalese President Léopold Senghor when they had been students in Paris together.

Senghor, a poet, had helped develop the cultural movement known as *négritude* which took pride in black consciousness. It had a considerable vogue, and was a precursor of the 'Black is Beautiful' and 'Black Power' movement in the United States. Yet for all his celebration of African civilization, Senghor married a Frenchwoman, bought a château in France, and became the first African to become a member of the French Academy. His socialism did not prevent French military bases in Senegal or the importation of French strawberries and mineral water for his élite, educated in France.

The legacy of French colonialism in Africa was much stronger than that of Britain's Africa. Senghor's successor, President Abdou Diouf, was said to travel on a French passport. Where the British were primarily interested in making money, the French wanted to administer and spread their civilization. Their rule was authoritarian and centralized, and they invested little power in appointed chiefs. Their success was reflected by their close economic, military and cultural links with their former colonies.

Jenny's father had come back to Africa hoping to rediscover his roots, but had been sorely disappointed. Like so many West Indian's and black Americans of his generations who returned to Africa, he was forced to realize that not only the terrible voyage of the slaves across the Atlantic had severed roots for ever, but that their descendents had irredeemably become part of Western 'civilization' with its values of efficiency, punctuality and comfort. Joseph did not like people arriving late, civil servants who put their hands in the till, or an administration which did not clean the sewers and maintain the roads.

My coming to Senegal was much more arbitrary. After spending two years in the P & O, I had decided to try to get myself an education. But first I wanted to spend a year teaching in Africa. Through Jenny, whom I had met briefly on holiday in my home town in England, I got a job as a English teacher at the age of nineteen at the Collège St Michel. It was in the centre of town and run by French Canadian brothers. I enjoyed every bit of my stay. Senegal had recently won its independence, Dakar was still being run efficiently, and there seemed hope in the air. I was not only in love but had the pleasure of discovering a new culture and continent completely different from my own.

Returning twenty-five years later was a big disappointment. The port of Dakar was filthy, the dockside covered in oil and rotting garbage and dust. No one seemed to bother with cleaning. Fortunately the captain's gifts did their usual work and I did not have too much trouble with the authorities. My passport was stamped '*Navigateur en Transit*'. I declined the caviar that one of the officials tried to sell me.

I took a taxi to a hotel outside of town on a beach opposite the little island of N'Gor, a favourite weekend haunt of Europeans in the old days. The taxi was falling part.

'What's life like these days in Dakar?' I asked the middle-aged driver. 'Difficult', came the reply. 'Senegal is an underdeveloped country and there's lots of unemployment.'

The streets were dirty and overcrowded; the buildings were drab and in need of paint. Waste lots were strewn with blue plastic bags carried by the wind with the slogan 'I love Africa'. By contrast, on the road to the airport and the coast there were many new luxurious villas behind high walls. The women were as beautiful and elegant as ever. Hot, tired and irritable, I arrived at the hotel only to be stung by the taximan.

The spectacular view from the balcony of my room soon put me in a better mood. Fine gardens led down to the beach. Buzzards soared on the thermals below and above the balcony. Beyond the grounds of the hotel, brightly coloured narrow boats called *pirogues* were ferrying people from the neighbouring fishing village across to the island half a mile away. Atlantic rollers crashed along the rocky coast and the far side of the island, but within the inner lagoon there were only a few ripples and a slight swell. The casuarina and palm trees swayed in the light wind.

There was a reddish haze in the grey sky and visibility was poor. It was the back end of the Harmattan, which blew every year from December to February, and covered all with sand. The sands of the Sahel were inexorably reaching Dakar, covering up fertile soil on the way, forcing people to move to the city. The Sahara had originally been flourishing savannah, but overgrazing by domesticated animals had created a desert thousands of years ago. Now it was the largest desert in the world, occupying over a quarter of Africa. There was nothing to check its gradual expansion; even trees in its path which might help were being cut down for firewood. The sands of the desert would eventually reach the sands of the beach.

The hotel N'Gor had special memories for me. I had spent New Year's Night here with Jenny and a group of friends when I was nineteen. We had danced until dawn and then gone across to the island for breakfast. I still remembered the tight mini dress she wore and her lithe body. The power of place seems stronger than the passage of time.

The hotel had been managed by a luxury French chain, and recently sold to a local owner. In the bathroom of my vast two-tiered room on the eighth floor, there was a picture of a black child drinking water from a tap, with the slogan in French: 'Don't waste water. Waste not, want not.' Another sign offered the good advice: 'In case of fire, keep calm', but did not tell one how to escape.

Things already had become to slip. When I asked for a coffee in the poolside bar, the barman pulled down the handle of the defunct coffee machine and smiled disarmingly: 'It's broken a little. *Tu veux un Nescafé?*' I got a big tin of instant coffee and a big pot of hot water to help myself. He went back to surveying the topless wives of the French business men, tapping his big fingers on the bar counter to the rhythm of James Brown. Out of a population of two million, there were still about 20,000 French still living in the country.

When the receptionist looked at my credit card later in the evening, with its shining bright colours, she exclaimed wistfully: 'How pretty it is!' Adjusting her loose *bou-bou* which had fallen off her well-shaped shoulder, she could not help sighing: 'What a fine life it is here for the white settlers!' From a financial point of view at least, she was right. After me a South African business man began complaining about the room service.

In the evening, I had dinner on my own by candle light under the moonlit coconut trees down by the beach. The crashing of the Atlantic surf mingled with the rustling of the palms; the perfume of frangipani filled the air. I felt at home for the first time in Africa, listening to the singing of a wandering kora player. He weaved his way among the roaring braziers of charcoal, carefully avoiding a pregnant cat warming itself on the nearby flagstones.

I chose the Senegalese national dish *tsheb bou djen* – rice with fish and hot sauce and a mixture of vegetables. It had once been made for me by the family of a pupil. We had sat cross-legged on the sand in their shack by the sea and helped ourselves with our hands from a central dish. His mother had pushed the choicest pieces towards me. Whenever possible, it was a Senegalese tradition to cook more food than necessary, in case there might be an unexpected guest. If he or she did not turn up, the food would be given to the inevitable beggars. With daily alms-giving being a duty of every devout Muslim, it was considered a normal part of everyday life. In a society without a welfare network beyond the extended family, it was a lifeline to many in the city.

The next day, 6 March, was the first monthly anniversary of my departure. I heard on Network Africa of the BBC that an Englishwoman had been stabbed to death by a spear in Masai Mara National Park in Kenya; that there was a national emergency in Zimbabwe because of the drought; and that Nelson Mandela of the African National Congress and President de Klerk of the National Party in South Africa were beginning yet another round of talks. Another day in Africa. But the real Africa slumbered on in the villages, where children woke to the smell of wood fires cooking maize meal porridge, the rattle of gunfire, or the screeching of birds in the forest.

It was also the first day of Ramadan, a month when all good Muslims fast between sunrise and sunset. Strictly speaking, they should abstain from food and drink, and not even swallow their saliva. The result is a great increase in spitting in public places, which makes travelling in an overcrowded bus a not very pleasant experience. In West Africa, Ramadan becomes the universal excuse for feeling tired and going slow. It is virtually impossible to get anything done during this period, and offices and factories grind almost to a halt. After dusk, when people can eat and drink their fill, the drums come out in the shanty towns and villages.

Through a Cameroonian friend, I arranged to meet a young man called Mamadou Seyllou who offered to be my guide during my stay. I met him outside the ornate Chamber of Commerce – one of the few old colonial buildings left – in the Place de l'Independance. He was a stylish young man who worked as a clerk in a ministry and aspired to be a professional photographer. He seemed diffident but there was another side to him. When I came out of one of the central banks bordering the Place de l'Independance, I saw him suddenly leap on to a much bigger man, bring him to the ground and start punching and kicking him in mad frenzy. He had to be held off by the crowd, while the man was led away by a bank guard.

'He's a pickpocket.' Seyllou panted, wiping a bleeding lip. 'They make me ashamed of my country. I saw him trying to take the money from a young European leaving the bank. I could have killed him.'

This display of rough justice shocked and bewildered me.

'Don't you think you should leave it up to the police?'

'Why should I? They're never around when they're needed. Here if someone sees a thief escaping, everybody has a go at him. I've seen a crowd beat one to death. There's no other way; thieves are everywhere now, and often armed.'

My first port of call was my old school which was a few minutes from the Place de l'Independance. It was still called Collège St Michel and it had not changed except that it was in more need of repair and paint. As usual some students were playing basketball in the yard, but since it was the weekend there were no classes. My old headmaster had gone to live in Ziguinchor in Casamance in the south of the country, but a young brother let me look around.

Seeing my old classroom, I remembered the day when my best pupil caused uproar in my all-boy class by passing round a French pornographic magazine. I gave him some sort of punishment but my heart was not in it; I had been accused myself of a similar misdemeanour in my primary school. I also seemed to hear the faintest echo of the Joan Baez songs an American Peace Corps teacher used to sing with her guitar to the delight of her pupils next door. She was so kind and beautiful anything she did would have been wonderful to the pupils.

When I visited the Collège Sacré Coeur where I used to sleep on the outskirts, I was knocked over. It had been on the edge of a desert, with great knobbly baobabs raising their trunks like upturned roots to the sun. Now it was amongst the concrete of a fashionable and wealthy quarter. In the central courtyard, the tiny plants I had once watered were now towering coconut trees. The sight of them brought tears to my eyes and a sudden awareness of the inexorability of time. The philosophy teacher had hung from the balcony outside my old room: 'One does not wash one's face with a single finger.'

In the late afternoon, we went down to the Soumbédioune beach to see the fishermen come in with their catch in their *pirogues*. We parked next to an artisanal village, and were immediately accosted by boys and a leper pulling himself along on a board with wheels. To get to the beach, we had to cross over a narrow wooden bridge over an open sewer. The stench was so strong that it felt like acid fumes biting into my nostrils. And the worst of it was that emaciated children with pot bellies and scabrous skin were playing in its black liquids as they flowed into the sea.

Despite the presence of this sewer, the beach beyond filled up every evening with crowds coming down to buy the day's fresh catch. Women butchered the big fish on the beach while the smaller ones were spread out in groups on the sand. Because of the Russian, Japanese and Korean trawlers fishing off the coast, the catches of the inshore fishermen were getting smaller as the population and poverty of Dakar grew. The fish were still four times cheaper here than in town. Despite the smell, the market was a colourful scene in the late afternoon, with *pirogue* after *pirogue* landing on the sandy beach, and the elegant women in their flowing colourful robes buying their evening meal.

All day my stomach had been feeling bad and when I got back to the hotel, I suddenly vomited in a hot wave of nausea. The thought of the open sewer did not help. I vomited all the first night, until I could only retch yellow bile. I had such runs that all that was left was rice water. Coupled with the nausea was a slight fever and severe stomach cramps. I was pretty certain it was the fish in Senegal's national dish which had laid me so low. It had no doubt been defrosted several times in the hotel's kitchens during the inevitable electricity cuts.

I looked up my symptoms in my traveller's guide and my manual from the School of Tropical Medicine of London University. I decided that at best it was a bout of food poisoning, but at worse it could be dysentry, giardiasis, or even cholera. In the days that followed, confined to my bed in an alien room, I felt completely desolate. 'Death-warmed-up' seemed the aptest description. Depression, I read, is often a symptom of giardiasis, which can takes months and even years to clear up. Keep calm, I told myself.

I assumed that it was food poisoning. I tried to starve the bugs, eating nothing but drinking plenty of bottled water with salts to avoid dehydration. I had none of the pellets of opium which my guide book suggested chewing.

I was lucky. My regime of mineral water and salts worked and on the third day I rose again from my bed. It took at least a week before my appetite came back, and much longer before I felt relatively normal again.

Chapter Eight

A Black Thing

ORIGINALLY built as the administrative centre of French West Africa, Dakar might be a great city, but it was hopelessly overblown for the small, impoverished country of Senegal which relied on the monoculture of peanuts. To escape the city, I decided to take a ship down to Casamance in the south of Senegal, a fertile region below the Gambia. Casamance had been Portuguese for a couple of centuries, and still felt different from the French-dominated northern Senegal. There was even a small but vigorous independence movement there.

While I was recovering from my spell of food poisoning the TV crew arrived. That evening we boarded the new German-built ferry boat in Dakar. Our white Peugeot was stowed in its hold alongside sacks of onions from Holland and a group of tethered goats which shat in front of the gangway leading to the upper decks. The ship rapidly filled up, with people crammed everwhere: in the restaurant, lounges, corridors and on the decks. Some devout Muslim peasants prayed in the corridors, angering the city slickers who kicked them out of the way.

The passage was calm and pleasant. When we started to steam up the wide Casamance river groups of dolphins joined us, leaping and playing in the greenish water. On anchoring off the town of Karabane nestling in palm trees at the mouth of the river, *pirogues* rushed at us like so many coloured sharks; when they reached our sides, they transferred passengers, food, empty drums, dried fish, live chickens and babies. It was a miracle that none fell in the water or the swaying *pirogues* did not overturn. For all the apparent chaos, the transaction was quickly done, and we were soon on our way towards Ziguinchor. Mangrove swamps came down into the water and beyond the river's banks the flat land stretched out for miles with its scattered bushes and trees. Only a few pelicans and cormorants and kingfishers interrupted their flight as we went by.

As I went out of the bridge on to the deck to look more closely through my binoculars at the bird life of the river, a sudden gust of wind blew off my Panama hat. I could do nothing except watch it floating upside down alongside the ship and then swirl away in our wake. I half expected a crocodile to grab it and pull it down to the depths. It was the one great luxury that I had brought on the trip; it was also a necessity under the tropical sun. I hoped that it would end up, a little worse for wear, on the head of village chief along the river bank.

The captain saw my dismay and laughed:

'Don't worry. If your hat is blown off into the water it will bring you good luck for a year.'

When we came to moor at Ziguinchor, it seemed as if half the town had come out to meet us. Boys were swimming in the river by an ancient wreck of a ferry. Sellers held up beautiful round baskets of oranges and mangoes. Friends and families were waiting to welcome the passengers. Ziguinchor stretched below us full of trees and flowering bushes and wide avenues.

What looked exciting from the bridge proved hellish on foot. As we tried to walk off the ship, we were taken up in a scrum which moved with its own momentum. I had no choice but to go with the flow. As soon as we stumbled out of the mainstream, sweating young men in Bob Marley shirts with Rasta hats descended on us offering their dubious services. 'Come with me! Come this way! I show you town.' They tried to grab my luggage. On one sweaty and grimy shirt I read: 'Africa – Land of Opportunity'. Another quoted the American Marcus Garvey, leader of the thirties Back-to-Africa movement: 'Let us guide our own destiny.' I agreed, and tried to throw them off.

As we reached the car, our would-be guides tried to get in with us, one muscular man even trying to sit on the lap of Elayne, the TV sound recordist. Seyllou, as calm as ever but concerned about his carefully ironed jeans, observed '*Voici la brousse, quoi!*' Here's the bush, what!'

The last time I had come to Casamance, with Jenny and her parents, we had travelled overland and stayed in a friend's village. All the inhabitants turned out to give us a great feast with copious servings of palm wine; we fell asleep in a well-swept hut to the sounds of the drums and dancing in the early hours. This time we stayed in an expensive hotel recommended by Seyllou's local contact with a swimming pool and thatched chalets. The great redeeming feature was the beautiful gardens, a botanist's dream full of local trees and flowers, well-tended and carefully marked. I fell asleep trying not to listen to the buzzing mosquitoes around my head.

The next day I visited my old headmaster Frère Emmanuel, a short man in his seventies who had gone to live in Ziguinchor after being unable to settle in Canada on his retirement. He lamented the present state of public education in Senegal. There had been a strike for months by teachers and students for books and many schools had closed down. The government was not even paying the teachers. But his main news was the visit of the Pope to Ziguinchor during the previous week.

'I was one of those who had the honour of shaking his hand. From the airport in Dakar to the city centre, the streets were lined for twelve kilometres with people, Muslims as well as Christians. Senegal, you know, is a very tolerant country; we have a Muslim President who has a Catholic wife. When he came to Ziguinchor for a day, the Pope was going to visit our school, but he got held up on the way and it was cancelled. You can imagine how disappointed the pupils were after all the preparations!'

After a beer we visited the school grounds outside where girls and boys were playing basketball. In Senegal, Frère Emmanuel had become famous not for his piety but for his school's basketball teams which would regularly win the national championships. His was the human face of missionaries in Africa: tolerant, knowledgeable of local culture, keen to help develop the country, and not imposing his own religion. Indeed, in a country with only ten per cent Christians and eighty per cent Muslims (the rest were animist), he realized that persuasion and not force is always best: 'We pray to the same God,' he observed, 'except they go on pilgrimage to Mecca and we go to Rome'.

We brushed Africa's animist traditions the following day. Seyllou contacted through his friends a famous *griot* called Bacary Diédhiou who had represented Senegal at a drumming festival at the Smithsonian Institute in Washington. 'A *griot*,' Seyllou explained, 'used to sing the praises of the king and be his messenger to his people. Now they uphold the traditions of the clan.'

We called on Bacary in the morning on the outskirts of Ziguinchor. His wife was sweeping the yard in front of their thatched hut when we arrived; children played nearby, and chickens scratched in the dust. He came out of the dark interior of his hut to welcome us, a squat, powerful man with massive biceps and a toothless grin. Friends and neighbours immediately gathered round on our arrival.

Seyllou remarked: 'Have you noticed the women? The women in Casamance are short and famous for their *grosses fesses*, their big bums!'

The *griot* went through an elaborate ritual with the drums before playing them, which involved spitting in the dust. In small leather pouches tied to his upper arms, he had *gris gris*, lucky charms to ward off evil spirits, which sometimes included the owner's umbilical chord. The drum skins were then heated by his assistants over a special fire made from burning grass. He explained that certain drums are considered sacred, and if a woman touches them she will become barren or have a very difficult life. Another ploy of patriarchy, I thought.

One of his assistants in a Rastafarian wool hat had a T-shirt with a map of Africa and the unanswerable slogan: 'You won't understand: it's a black thing'. Following in the footsteps of Alex Haley of *Roots* fame many black Americans had visited the region in search of the African Arcadia only to be ripped off by wily natives. They corrupted them in turn with their greenbacks and fancy gear.

The sun was growing hot and many in the neighbourhood were fasting. People looked dull and they walked slowly. But when the drums were brought out a crowd of women and children quickly formed. As the *griot* began to play, the tired faces suddenly began to smile, and bodies started to move with the rhythm. Pieces of wood were distributed through the crowd, so that they could knock them together to accompany the drums. Then a woman threw herself in the ring and started to dance, opening and closing her dress provocatively. The rhythm increased to a crescendo when she threw back her head laughing and gave a final kick in the dust with her foot before retiring to the throng. Another young girl took her place and so it went on. The *griot* was soon sweating profusely, his massive biceps relaxing and taking the strain. The spirit of the ancestors stirred deep inside him; he loosened his numb fingers to let their message pass through his vibrating body into the drums.

It was an amazing experience. The whole neighbourhood had been transformed. The men might play the drums for the women, but the women excelled in the dancing. The two together made Africa pulsate.

I would like to have stayed in the village, and taken my place on the bench with the men under the towering tree, but as a wanderer I had to move on. I was condemned by my Promethean quest not to take root. We decided to return back to Dakar overland, and drove over the long bridge spanning the river Casamance and headed north towards the Gambia.

We were the only car on the road, except for the occasional trundling juggernaut overloaded with peanuts which we tried to overtake in a cloud of red dust. The main road linking southern with northern Senegal was full of potholes which made driving a nightmare. On many occasions, we had to leave the road altogether and drive alongside on a bumpy track created by the lorries. Children in some of the infrequent villages were ostentatiously filling in the pot-holes, hoping to be thrown a few coins for their enterprise from passing vehicles. Little could be expected from the ministry of transport in Dakar in this forsaken region. The *independantistes* had a point.

After four hours of back-breaking jolts, we eventually arrived at the village of Senoba, a run-down frontier post of the Gambia. We had to cross this thin strip of land along the river Gambia, grabbed by the British in the scramble for Africa. We had decided to take the higher route since the lower one would have led us through Banjul, the capital, with all its road blocks, corrupt policemen and inevitable delays.

Senegal and the Gambia had officially joined up to form a federation called Senegambia some years before but the shot-gun wedding between Francophones and Anglophones was going nowhere fast. The Gambian government still refused an open corridor of about six miles for Senegalese citizens to reach the two parts of their country, and the Senegalese government did not want to prop up a regime which was even poorer than itself. The Senegalese had offered to pay for a bridge over the river; the Gambians, eager to maximize on local trade, declined. The result was considerable hostility at the grass roots.

Police and customs at the borders determined to make life as difficult as possible for those who were foolhardy enough to try to cross them. One set of police in French uniform would shout '*Salauds d'anglais!*' to another set of policemen dressed as bobbies who would reply 'bloody, Frogs!'; both came from the same tribe and spoke the same language. Such is the legacy of colonialism in these parts.

Once over the frontier, the Gambia seemed even more run down, and rubbish and litter gathered in any corner where the wind blew them. Even the street sellers were lethargic. Men sat on benches outside the poorly built, corrugated houses watching the odd vehicle go by. A rusty sign at an angle, courtesy of Pepsi Cola, announced 'Welcome to the Gambia'.

At the big sign which declared 'Stop-Police', we stopped. David England went into the post and a hostile constable asked to see his international licence. David did not have an international licence, only his British one. 'This is very serious, Mr England,' said the constable. 'Very serious. You do not have the right papers. You must stay in our country until the next court hearing.'

'What?' said David, going deathly white. He could envisage himself, as I did, rotting in some mosquito-infested jail waiting for a court hearing that would never come.

'What have I done wrong?'

'It's a serious offence to travel without an international licence. You must wait here until your friends send us your international licence.'

If the post was as efficient as the customs, that could be for ever.

I realized that there was only one thing that would quickly solve this little problem: MONEY. Yet you never knew whether offering money would get you into more trouble: the cry could go up: TRYING TO CORRUPT A POLICE OFFICER. Pondering on this matter, Seyllou came to the rescue. He gave a long speech in Ouolof which sounded very eloquent and convincing although I did not understand a word.

'So you are not tourists?' asked a sergeant who had been leaning back in a seat throughout the proceedings.

'No,' replied David, 'we're a British film crew.'

'And you have someone ill with you.'

'Yes, very ill. We must get him to a hospital quick.' This time it was for the police to envisage the rubbing down they might have with their bosses if the arrest of a Mr England of British television became a major diplomatic event. That surname was particularly worrying. And what would they do with the sick man?

'Well,' the sergeant said after a long pause, savouring his authority 'you can go this time. But I give you a last warning. This is very serious.'

And with that he returned the licence and waved us on. He need not have warned us; we wouldn't be coming back for some time.

'Phew, we're saved!'

'Not quite,' said the cautious Seyllou. 'There are many more police and customs posts to pass.'

There were nine to be precise. Fortunately, most waved us on, too tired to be bothered. At the last one before the ferry to cross the river Casamance, we were told by a policeman that we would have to get a ticket at an office several kilometres back along the road. There had been no clear sign on the road indicating the ticket office; presumably every stranger had to return on their tracks to get their ticket.

The man who pointed out our error greeted us with 'Good afternoon, for Great Britain' and offered to accompany us back to the ticket office. He piled in, young, spotty-faced, sweaty and willing.

His English was idiomatic, Gambian style: 'Far away we go. You go straight, bend by left. Go, okay, you turn here. No board indicating.' You can say that again.

As an upholder of the law, he warned us: 'You must lock, even if in car. Too many thieves and bandits.' Even if we're in the car? 'You can mistake your vigilance!' As we thanked him, he said: 'Don't mention. You nice man. Nice to meet.'

We then took our place in the queue which had grown even larger in our absence. All along the road, people sat on benches in front of leaning shacks. Flies covered everything, including the people, who were too tired in the heat to shoo them away. In the middle of nowhere, there was a sign which declared 'City Centre Enterprises'. The difference in exchange rates meant that goods in the Gambia were much cheaper than in Senegal, so the vendors did a steady trade, especially in clothes.

I got out to stretch my legs but the heat was so great that it was impossible to stay under the midday sun long without feeling like a damp rag. We had the air conditioning on full blast, so our solid Peugeot fortunately did not boil over in the sun while we waited in the queue. It felt like being in an aquarium, with young children pushing their faces up against the windows, trying to sell boiled eggs and peanuts or get some sweets and pens from us. We were the rich *toubabs*, holding Africa at bay with modern technology.

After an hour or so we were at the top of the queue, but when the ferry arrived, the man in charge of loading let only one car on and waved on four tankers and a bus who had come after us.

'Don't worry,' said Seyllou. 'I'll fix it.' He went up to the supervisor, talked for some time and then passed on some notes. He came back beaming: 'Relax. It's all right now . . .'

It had taken two and a half hours to cross the six-mile stretch of the Gambia. As soon as we passed the Senegalese frontier on the other side of the river, Seyllou gave a great sigh of relief: 'My country at last!' He did not have a very high view of Gambians: 'Gambian man stupid. It is a small country, with only one million population. They only need a little imagination, and they could take all the tourism in West Africa.' Well, maybe.

Once we were back again in Senegal, the road improved, although there were still pot-holes to negotiate, smoke-belching, overloaded juggernauts to try to overtake, and goats and cattle and children to avoid. All these came together, along with hundreds of car-defiant pedestrians, in the regional capital of Kaolack, a busy crossroads on the river Saloum.

On the other side of the town, we stopped at a small roadside village. From a distance it appeared a model of rural tranquillity, the thatched roofs of its round mud huts surrounded by a few baobabs. Close up, things were very different. Entering a compound with Seyllou, we came across a mother with her baby on her back and an older woman preparing the evening meal on an open fire: a handful of rice and a little peanut sauce. The pot-bellied children sat listlessly. Scrawny chickens scratched in the carefully brushed sand.

One man who seemed to have some authority – no doubt because of his emaciated horse which he wanted photographed – explained that because of the encroaching Sahel desert the villagers were desperate. Sand was covering the fertile soil and the wells were dry. The women had to walk ten kilometres every day for water and carry twenty litres back on their heads. With this, they had to make do for drinking, cooking, and washing. And then there were the animals to water.

'I don't like to stop at these villages,' admitted Seyllou, 'because the people do not have an adequate life. The government does nothing for them. This is no life. We come on this earth to learn and work, not to die in the dust.'

Chapter Nine

Chez Madame Dakar

O N my return to Dakar, I discovered thanks to to my *Abc of Shipping* that Delmas, the pride of the French Merchant Marine, had ships regularly calling at francophone countries in West Africa as far south as the Congo and Zaïre. They did not usually take passengers. With faxes and phone calls to Paris and much pressure on the local shipping agent, I eventually managed to find a passage on the new container ship *Delphine Delmas*, one of four sister ships doing the West Africa run. She was not sailing until 23 March; it would involve a wait of ten days in Dakar.

I saw the film crew off at the airport. If I could make it, our next rendezvous would be Douala, Cameroon. I moved out of the grand hotel where I had once passed a New Year's night but which was now sullied by recent memories of food poisoning. Seyllou had introduced me to a Finnish lady called Outi Kaarina Badji who had a fine villa with a beautiful garden in a leafy suburb a little further up the coast. 'She's so well known that in town they call her Madame Dakar,' he said. Her home proved a haven of peace. I loved waking up under my mosquito net in the morning to the sound of the birds singing in the garden below and of the distant surf crashing on the rocky shore.

Outi Badji had been married to a Senegalese business man; they had four children before he had died of stomach cancer. Three of them were now working in Finland, but she had decided to remain in Senegal as long as her youngest daughter was at school. I asked her whether it had been difficult bringing up children with parents from such different backgrounds?

'I decided early on to put our two countries and cultures in balance. Though my older children live in Finland now, they feel Senegalese because they grew up here. They're not completely accepted by Finnish society because they're "African", and not by Senegalese society because they're *toubabs* "Europeans". I tell them they have to realize that they are what they are – *métis*, of mixed race – and that they should feel good with that fact.'

Having been the wife of a Senegalese, she had unique insight into the lot of women in Africa. She told me that they do most of the work: 'They bring up their children on their own and ensure that the community survives. They are the ones who work in the fields, collect the water, and prepare the food. The men make the decisions but the women do seventy per cent of all the work in Africa.'

'Do they mind?'

'The African mentality is different from the European. The main concern of women in Africa is food and shelter for their families. If they get that, what need do they have for a new way of life?'

'So they're happy with their lot.'

'They want to retain the equilibrium and harmony in their society, including female circumcision which has no religious meaning. Even educated women in Dakar accept their submissive role as part of the African consciousness. Ideas of equality are considered part of Western corruption and decadence.'

'And marriage?'

'Most Senegalese are Muslim and can have several wives. But it doesn't stop prostitution; about a quarter of young women in Dakar are now probably prostitutes. The figures are unbelievable. It's a sign of the times.'

Whether the women liked it or not, things were changing fast in Senegal, especially in the capital. I read a slogan on a wall during a bus trip into town which declared: 'To become civilized is not to abandon your past but to adapt it.' But the unemployed young in Dakar were losing their ancient traditions and gaining nothing new except survival skills in a concrete jungle. The capital had become 'Hustlerville'. I remembered it as a friendly and relaxed place, but now the tension in the streets was electric. There were simply too many young men with too little to do.

The hassle was a direct result of the country's economic decline and political stagnation. A taxi driver explained the problem to me: 'Every person in Dakar who works has about fifteen mouths to feed. Relatives from the bush come to Dakar because of the drought and you cannot refuse them. That's the African way, that's the African family. The trouble with us Africans is that we don't plan for the future. If we get money, we buy a big car or give it to our women who then waste it on jewellery or clothes. I've known Senegalese women spend all their money on gold necklaces while their children go hungry. We live for today, for the present. Money soon goes, and then we're poor again.'

Outi Badji blamed the élite for the economic crisis: 'In Senegal now, ten per cent of the population own eighty per cent of the wealth. It's meant to be a socialist state. Those in power have grabbed funds for themselves and put them in foreign banks. The rich control the government who will not tax themselves. They have not invested in agriculture and industry but in property. The result is that you have all these expensive villas to rent around Dakar but no production. Even the banks will not invest in agricultural projects because of the drought. The majority of the population is now under thirty, but they have no education, no work and all around is conspicuous consumption. It's a recipe for disaster.'

Outi Badji's analysis seemed spot on to me, but I wanted to find out the official government line. Through Seyllou I managed to meet the Minister for African Economic Integration. When I first heard his name – Jean-Paul Jazz – I thought he must be a philosopher and musician in one, but I was disappointed to find out that it was spelt 'Diaz'. He was from Casamance and had some Portuguese ancestry. I traced him down to an office in a high-rise building called the Former Building of the Ministry of Urbanisation and Population. Dressed immaculately in a French suit like most wealthy Senegalese, he called me '*tu*' in the African way.

He talked dutifully for some time about the need for the economic integration of West Africa, conveniently overlooking that Senegal was nearly at war with its northern neighbour Mauritania over the river which formed a common border, that the federation it had formed with its central neighbour the Gambia was in shreds, and that tension was rising with its southern neighbour Guinea-Bissau over oil. If there were any conflicts in the region, he insisted that it was the cause of colonization:

'The micro-states left by the colonialists are the problem. Since they have only a few million inhabitants, it means that only a few thousand people in each country are capable of buying goods on the market. The result is that it's impossible to make industries work. In Senegal, in the last two years, a company has closed every twenty-four hours. The economies of West Africa are in a desperate state.'

The only solution, in his view, was regional and international co-operation. He was for free trade, including economic contacts with South Africa: 'I believe whites have a place in Africa. Gabon wants to Africanize its administration, but Africans are not trained to do the job. In the Ivory Coast, attacks against the whites have meant that the community is reduced by half, from about 40,000 to 20,000, which will have a severe effect on the economy. As far as I am concerned, whites should have a place in Africa. I see the future as *métis*, racially mixed.'

But would the wave of Islamic fundamentalism sweeping through north Africa upset the government's new-found zeal for *laissez-faire*? I went to Dakar University, where I met Professor Sérigne Khadima Mbacké, Director of the Department of Islamic Civilization, at the Cheikh Anta Diop Institute at the University of Dakar. He was a gentle man in a *bou-bou*, a long flowing robe embroidered around the neck. Although he came from a leading *marabout* family, he said he was 'intellectually free'. A *marabout*, he explained, was a defender of Islam; in Arabic, it meant a 'soldier who defends the frontier'.

'There are four main Muslim brotherhoods in Senegal who wield considerable power,' he told me, 'but at the moment they are mainly concerned with educating the Muslim masses.'

'What makes Islam so popular in Africa?'

'It's popular in Africa because of the similarity between Islam and traditional African religion. It is very simple and easy to understand. Above all, it has a suppleness and an ability to adapt which makes it open to foreign cultures.'

As we chatted, I could see the sun beginning to set over the sea, and remembered that the professor had not eaten or drunk since dawn. I asked him what Ramadan meant to him.

'For me fasting in Ramadan is above all a means of spiritual regeneration, a period during which one tries to repair internally, on a spiritual level, all that which is not quite right, and to regain what one has lost during the rest of the year. It is a relatively strict period. I pray, I meditate. When I abstain from eating and drinking I am obliged to think about why I accept to support hunger and thirst. It is very purifying, very spiritual.'

Politics and religion might have been on every one's mind in Senegal during my stay, but what most people wanted to hear was music. Like everywhere in Africa, music was a central part of life. In recent years, Senegalese music had become internationally famous. Thanks to Seyllou, I managed to trace down Ismael Lo, the 'Bob Dylan of Africa', in his modest villa in a suburb of Dakar. He was a tall, slim, handsome man with an infectious smile and a warm manner. It was Friday, and he had just returned from the mosque in his embroidered blue *bou-bou*. We sat in a garden under a palm tree, the sun playing through its leaves on to the sand. I asked him who had been his most important influences:

'The American rhythm & blues singers Otis Reading and James Brown played a big influence on me when I was young, but my main inspiration has come from traditional African music. Music is universal, but it is through the rhythm that music has its own identity.'

I asked him what he tried to express in his music.

'It is my dream that we should all become happy and peaceful in the world. We are not in life for suffering, but here to enjoy life.'

As the afternoon flowed away, he invited me to come with him for a jam session. He got into a silver car with darkened windows with his fellow musicians and was whisked along tracks of sand to a half-built house on the outskirts of town. The rehearsal room was on the ground floor. The other musicians were already beginning to play. When my eyes eventually got used to the dark, I was surprised to see a thin, sallow-faced European at the keyboard.

His name was Kevin Willoughby, and he came from England. He had once been an oboist in the Irish Guards Band but had left to study music in Africa. For four years he had been living entirely with Senegalese people, eating their food, learning their music, shivering from their malaria. He earned enough playing in a night club to keep body and soul together. He had no wish to return to Europe:

'Perhaps I will one day, but not for the time being, I want to deepen my understanding of Senegalese music. Anyway, the people know how to live here. They have so little compared to us in Europe, yet they know how to enjoy themselves.'

I loved staying chez Madame Dakar while waiting for my boat. I appreciated the orderly rhythm of her house. The cook Kalifa, who had been made redundant from a grand hotel, would join us while we ate. The two maids with old-fashioned French names, Marie and Françoise, were kept on though not needed; they would spend the day brushing the yard, tending the garden, doing the washing, and sleeping in the shade on the verandah.

During the day I would often walk along the rocky coast, past the little shops at the corners of the grand villas which sold baguettes of fresh bread and packets of cigarettes. The men on the bench nearby greeted me with *Salaam malekum*- 'Peace be with you'. Squatters had erected small huts from paper and plastic, trying to grow a few vegetables and flowers in the sandy waste ground. Women with babies tied to their backs pounded maize. It had the atmosphere of a village and there was no hassle from the strollers along the rocky seashore.

Outi had adopted a son, a distant nephew from Casamance, called Fally. After dinner he would invite me into the garden to have tea. It was usually very dark, and our faces were only lit by the small charcoal burner on which the kettle was boiled. Kalifa the cook would turn up and a few friends from the neighbourhood would drop in. After a while they took no notice of me. Kalifa would usually make the tea, which involved putting strong tea leaves, mint and sugar in a pot with a long spout and then pouring the contents back and forth into a small glass about forty times until it was well-blended and frothy. It was the custom to have three brews from the same leaves, a process which took up a couple of hours. I loved those evenings, sitting around the fire in the warm African air, watching the clouds pass by the moon, not understanding a word of the conversation, but feeling part of the friendly circle.

One morning we got up early and I went with Fally to visit Gorée, an island about three and half kilometres off the the port of Dakar. We took a ferry crammed with French tourists and islanders returning home laden with essential goods. About 1,200 people live permanently on the island, including a few foreigners.

The Portuguese had first landed there in 1444, and on 6 March 1502 Vasco da Gama heard mass in the chapel on his second voyage around Africa. At different times, it had been occupied by the Dutch, the British and the French. It was now a haven of peace with fine eighteenth-century colonial buildings, quiet squares and narrow alleyways shaded by palms and bursting with bougainvillaea. There were no cars to disturb the serenity. Children splashed and laughed on the sheltered beach by the little harbour.

It had not always been like this. At one end of the island, there was a large moated fort and on the only hill there were strong fortifications abandoned by the departing French. More ominously, the island had been the most important slave entrepôt of West Africa until the British abolished the trade in 1807.

Three million slaves had passed through Gorée during the height of the trade, part of the 200 million who were taken from West Africa to the New World. The slaves travelled in atrocious conditions, packed side by side like matches in a box; about a third died during the passage. On arrival they were then sold on the open market, the value of women measured by the size of their breasts; the men, by their weight and muscle; and the children, by the quality of their teeth.

The curator of the Old Slave House told me how the rebellious slaves had been submerged up to their necks in sea water in windowless cells, and how the sick had been thrown to the sharks below, their mangled bodies washed up on the rocks to be picked by the crows. The place evoked painful feelings. My ancestors from the West country could well have manned the boats from Bristol which took slaves from Gorée across the Atlantic, some of whom could have been Jenny's ancestors. Recently many black Americans had come on a pilgrimage to the island and to the hinterland beyond, including Alex Haley who had traced his roots to a village in the Gambia. In the visitors' book to the Slave House I came across an entry dated 9 August 1990 by another pilgrim, Angela Davis, the black American radical philosopher: 'To return home; to relive the profound suffering of my ancestors; to know that humanity's worst crimes were committed on this site. It must never happen again'. The worst moment was to stand at the door which led to the open sea along a dark passageway – the door of no return – and to imagine what the shackled slaves must have felt as they turned their back on Africa for the last time.

Strolling up to the old fortifications at the top of the hill on Gorée, Fally introduced me to some of his friends who had cleared out the old bunkers and had moved in with their families. They were members of the Baye Fall sect, an extreme Muslim sect who dressed colourfully with dreadlocks, lived by begging and swore complete obedience to their spiritual leader or *marabout*.

We went into one small bunker and met the wife and baby of Fally's friend who were lying asleep on a mat on the hard floor. Lianas were working their way through the cracked concrete: nature was gradually reclaiming its own. On the top of the hill, his friend had erected a post with 'peace on earth' written in English, Arabic, Japanese and French. He gave a short speech to me in English, his handsome black face illuminated by the noonday sun:

'This post commemorates peace on earth. It calls on the light within all of us to shine. We are all one race of humanity. Right on!'

Fally was impressed, and not knowing what to do with his life, thought of joining the Baye Fall on Gorée.

The time eventually came for me to join my ship and I rang home to hear how things were. I had found it increasingly difficult to speak to my family on the telephone and preferred to write. A short call on a bad line evoked so many painful feelings, especially when talking to the children. Dylan would always answer in a deliberately cheerful voice: 'I'm fine. Everything is okay at home. We're getting on fine. But I don't like walking home from school along the river alone.'

When I rang her from Dakar, Jenny decided to be frank:

'All your friends say I'm all right. I want to tell the truth. I'm not all right. I can hardly get through each day. I've still a got painful jaw. I can't

71

sleep properly at night. The neighbours say they can't understand how you can leave me like this.'

'But you've said that you were coping all right up till now.'

'It's been raining here for a week and I've had to bring the food down the muddy track through the cattle in a wheelbarrow. I can't go on living like this.'

All this was devastating. I had tried to appear cheerful on the phone, saying how well my voyage was going, not to worry anyone at home. But I had had my own dark night of the soul and had coped with illness, loneliness, sleeplessness and anxiety. I was always on the move, not knowing what was waiting for me around the next corner or in the next port – if I could get a boat there. The most difficult thing of all was worrying about those I had left behind.

'If you want me to come home, I will.'

'No, not at the moment. Let's see how things go for the time being.'

'Well, spring is not far away and you have the children to help you.'

'Yes. They're very good. Good luck Peter.'

'Good luck.'

We both needed it.

Before I left Dakar, I visited the British Embassy in the former European quarter on the highest point of the city by the sea. I spoke to the vice consul about my next port of call, Conakry in Guinea. His advice was not encouraging:

'I don't advise you to descend the gangway. There's a lot of rising tension in Conakry at the moment with the approaching elections. If you take out a camera, you're likely to end up behind four grey walls.'

Well, at least I'd been warned.

The last person I said goodbye to in Senegal was Seyllou. He shook me firmly with his left hand: 'In Africa, the left hand is the hand of the heart. We use it when saying goodbye to a friend.'

I could not have been more honoured or left with a better memory of my stay in Senegal.

Chapter Ten

Calm Days

A t last the day came when I was to embark on the *Delphine Delmas*. She was a new container ship, about 180 metres long, built in Yugoslavia and registered in Dunkirk. The ship was crawling with dockers. I met the first mate, a short round Corsican with thinning hair and a midday shadow. As he was overseeing the unloading of the containers, he passed me on to a steward who showed me to my cabin.

It was a spare cadet's cabin with a bathroom, bunk and writing desk, with a picture of a northern French landscape under snow. It was situated two decks below the bridge and had a rectangular porthole. By my door in the passageway a picture was hung of a crescent moon embracing stars with the words: *Impasse de Matins Calmes*. My cabin steward was a gentle Senegalese man in his fifties called Demba Bakary. Since only French nationals were employed on the ship, he had a French passport.

The last time I had been in a cadet's cabin was over a quarter of a century ago, when I was eighteen and travelling around the world on the SS *Oronsay*, a large white passenger ship of the P & O. My life had come full circle. My brown wavy hair was now thin on top and grey at the temples, my blue eyes had crow's feet but I still felt it was the same me. I was not merely a continuous succession of selves, but an evolving self. I had now realized – more or less – my burning childhood ambition to be a writer, and felt clearer about what I did not want to do. But I was still searching for certainty about the nature of truth, the possibility of justice, the existence of God, and the afterlife. I felt like a gardener in my long years of studying philosophy, clearing the undergrowth to reveal a few fine trees of questions waiting to be answered. It had occurred to me during this long labour that perhaps the search itself was the meaning, but I still was not sure.

We left Dakar the next morning at six o'clock on 23 March. It was 470 nautical miles to our first port of call, Conakry, Guinea, and we were due to arrive in two and a half days. I saw the pale sun rise over Dakar for the last time and by seven thirty, the island of Gorée had disappeared over the grey horizon. The sea was calm but the ship vibrated everywhere. I had to stow my things away carefully and slip pieces of paper in to stop the cupboards and drawers rattling in my cabin. I had forgotten during my fortnight in Senegal how everything constantly moves at sea. The *Delphine Delmas* turned south and settled down to about thirteen knots an hour.

I was invited by telephone for an aperitif before lunch in the captain's cabin. The chief engineer – Jean-Pierre Palfray – introduced himself. He was a large man with a tentative smile under a short grey moustache. He was from Le Havre and proud of being Norman. The captain, a slim, trim man was called Pierre Noël – which to the shoreside staff he sometimes shortened to Père Noël (Father Christmas). He was a Breton, born in Rennes, grown up in St Malo, and proud of being a Celt.

Over our Pastis, we discussed the results of the French regional elections which were coming through that day on the ship's radio. It soon transpired that I was in a hotbed of right-wing French nationalism. The captain, chief engineer and first mate all supported Le Pen, the rabid anti-Semitic leader of the Front National. The captain said: 'The only thing they've got against him is that he said that the Holocaust did not happen. I don't see what all the fuss is about.'

I ate with the senior officers behind a partition in the dining room dominated by an enlarged eighteenth-century print of La Rochelle harbour. For lunch and dinner there were five-course meals and a choice of wine, the best that France could produce. Coffee was taken in the officers' mess in an adjoining room.

The meals were leisurely affairs – the best on my voyage – and the conversation flowed with the wine. The Breton captain had a horror of the

Saxons du Nord and saw the Germans as the greatest threat to European peace. He disliked their crass materialism: 'One doesn't want to end up measuring life by the length of one's Mercedes'. Sometimes he would jokingly rail against *l'Albion perfide*; on other occasions, he would declare that France and England were one country divided by a river. As for Africans, amongst whom he had traded for half of his life, he commented ironically: 'Africans don't steal but merely take from the whites who are so generous and have given them so much. The trouble is they simply can't wait until they are given their presents, so they take them'.

The redeeming feature about the captain was his literary interests – he was writing a novel – and his sense of humour. He pretended to consult an imaginary dog, a philosopher: 'He is very wise, and I am sure he has hands although he does not show them'. He reminded him of the saying attributed to Socrates: 'There are three types of being – the living, the dead, and those who go to sea'.

When I asked the captain one day whether the sea was good along the West African coast, he replied: 'The sea is always good. It is humans who are the problem'.

'What does the sea mean to you?'

'After all these years, I still do not understand the sea.'

I knew what he meant. Ever since I was a boy, the sea had a strange fascination for me yet I did not know why. Perhaps because it is a symbol of life, constantly changing yet always the same. At the same time, I associated it with easeful death. Watching the sea pass by the ship for hours during my voyage down the west coast of Africa, I would often feel the urge to slip overboard and become part of it for ever, to be dissolved in its vast being like a drop of wine in water.

I often found during my voyage that officers would confide in me in a way that they would not with their fellows. I was supernumerary on board and did not have a clearly defined role. I was not exactly a passenger, because I was working; but neither was I a member of the crew, because I would be leaving soon. My anomalous position meant that the officers, and especially the captains, welcomed the opportunity to speak freely and unburden themselves. By their power and responsibility, captains are generally lonely men, giants amongst dwarfs on board ship, but dwarfed somewhat in civilian life on shore. Having lived so long in a tight community where they have absolute authority at sea, they are often at a loss in the flow of civilian life on land.

After breakfast, I usually went for a walk up forward. To reach the bow, I had to pass under the groaning containers along a narrow passageway on either side of the ship. Little piles of sugar on the metal deck, scattered amongst the red dust from the Sahel, revealed the nature of the cargo unloaded in Dakar. There were a couple of trucks destined for Conakry. A large wooden crate had written on its side: 'Soeur Benoit, Procure des Missions, Cotonou, Benin'. I wondered what she was like, sister Benoit, toiling for Christ on the Equator far away from home, fighting a losing battle against paganism and Islam.

The bow was the quietest part of the ship and the place I most liked to be. The mooring ropes, as thick as a man's arm, were coiled neatly and the chains of the anchors secured. The great capstains and well-greased winches waited until they took the strain again. The enormous derricks which had been working through the night were silent. Salt and dust covered everything. All you could hear was the swishing sound of the bows cutting through the water and the gentle hum of the engine aft. No one was to be seen. It was almost as if I were on a ghost ship gliding through the seas. The sun grew hotter and quickly evaporated the morning dew.

I often found that however agitated, homesick or anxious I might feel, a sense of peace descended on me in the bow. It almost had a religious atmosphere, like being in a simple church or temple. All around the pure sea and the sky expanded into infinity. I felt completely safe and at one with all things. Leaning over the rails in the bow, I could see a hundred feet below the great bulbous hull gliding like a torpedo through the sea. It would rise with the swell like a great whale, throwing off the tumbling water from its sides, only to dive down again into the dark green waters.

A large frigate bird soared overhead; I recalled his cousin the seagull in Lisbon who tried to show me how to be independent and at ease. Six weeks into my voyage, I was slowly getting there, but not without lapses. Melancholy would sometimes descend on me for no apparent reason, especially in the late afternoon, like a sea mist; I put it down to my lack of clear orientation and dependence on chance. I never quite knew what would happen next.

Having been travelling up and down the Western African coast for more than a quarter of a century, the captain had a low opinion of its ports. He warned at our first meeting: 'You must be careful in the ports. You must not go out at night, or you'll soon have a knife at your throat. If you don't have any money, they'll take all your clothes and leave you naked at the roadside. If you take a photograph, you must speak to them and explain that you're taking it for your family. They think that when you photograph them, you take their spirit away, their soul'.

Although the nationality of all the officers was French, the second mate came from St Louis on the river Senegal in the northern part of the country. His name was Gorgui Sy. Apart from the captain, he was the most interesting man to talk to on board. Although only thirty-eight years old, he had been taught in school with French textbooks that his ancestors were white and came from Gaul. He believed it at the time. Even recent events had been censored by the French:

'You know after the Second World War, there was a massacre of a group of returning Malian, Senegalese and Niger soldiers in the military camp outside Dakar, but it's been hushed up. It's still not in the history books'.

Sy bore no malice for this cultural imperialism and joked amiably with the rest of the crew, however racist their sentiments and right-wing their politics. He had married a Frenchwoman and his home was in France.

He too warned me that it was dangerous to walk alone in West African ports. It seemed that all the sailors, white or black, were obsessed with danger; the seafaring community, superstitious at the best of times, turned rumour into blood-curdling reality. In their feverish imaginations, the West African Coast not only lived up to its old name 'The White Man's Grave' but had become the 'Black Man's Grave' as well.

'Ça bouge,' Sy said. 'Things are moving in West Africa. There's rising tension everywhere because of the economic crisis. It's part of a long process. Europe took primary materials but introduced some development. The new rulers are not interested in their countries; only in their pockets. They don't invest funds to industrialize or diversify the country's economy but put it in foreign banks. Since independence, the same men are still in power.'

'At least the wave of democracy passing through Africa at the moment should make a difference.'

'I fear it could make matters worse.'

'How's that?'

'Africa has never known parliamentary democracy. Africans have always been subjugated; they're used to obeying a chief. With multi parties, there will be confusion and fights. Africans want power and money and a new dictatorship will inevitably emerge.'

'Is there any hope for the future, then?'

'Not much. Africa is getting poorer and poorer. When it has taken all our products, Europe will drop Africa. It is already turning to the the Far East and towards Eastern Europe. I'm afraid Africa will soon be left to fend for itself.'

After two days at sea, we anchored off Conakry, Guinea, waiting for clearance to enter the port. Nearby there was a beautiful island with rich foliage and a palm-fringed beach. It looked like a classic desert island hideaway.

'It's called Kassa island,' the captain said. 'It's part of an old volcanic crater. It's recently become the centre of an international scandal. A local company, involving the Norwegian consul, got a contract to dump waste there and to make building bricks from it. It was not long before the islanders came out in sores. There was an enquiry; it came to light that they had been dumping half-burnt hospital waste; some of it was even said to be radioactive. Soon afterwards the government took action and turned back a ship from the United States with a cargo of waste.'

Worse things had been going on in Guinea. It had been the first French colony to opt for independence in 1958. Sekou Touré, the future president, told De Gaulle: 'Guinea prefers poverty in freedom to riches and slavery'. In the outcome, it got poverty and slavery. Touré spoke the language of African nationalism and socialist equality, but he became a warlord whose repression sent a third of the country into prison or exile.

The Soviet Union had provided arms, eager to find an ally in West

Africa at the height of the cold war. They did nothing to develop the nation.

'You know what they did?' the chief engineer recounted with delight, 'They sent them snow ploughs instead of tractors, snow ploughs with heaters. Can you imagine it, in this climate! They stood rusting on the dock for years.'

Chapter Eleven

Angels *in* Red *and* White

I WAS woken up the first day in Conakry by a telephone call from the captain. 'Please come to my cabin. There is someone here to meet you.'

I climbed the two decks to his cabin below the bridge and found a middle-aged, well-dressed woman and a young man about twenty. She introduced herself as Mrs Valerie Treitlein, the honorary British consul in Conakry; her son Tilo was out during his college holidays. She had been contacted by the consul in Dakar and told of my arrival aboard the *Delphine Delmas*. She offered to show me around Conakry; I accepted.

She had come with her Guinean chauffeur in a Range Rover. With the Union Jack flying from its wing, we had no trouble sailing through the dock gates.

Conakry was built on a long narrow peninsular, part of a sixty-five-kilometre wide coastal plain which had large areas of mangrove swamps infested with mosquitoes. After a quarter of century of President Touré's 'Marxism in African clothes', the infrastructure of the country had virtually collapsed. Roads were not mended. Clean water pipes had burst. Schools were closed down since they might by accident encourage the young to think for themselves. French was abandoned as the language of instruction. The literacy rate was reduced to about thirty per cent.

Since Sekou Touré's death in 1984, the new President Lansana Conté, who came to power in a military coup, had rejoined the French franc

80

zone and military umbrella. Wandering through the streets of Conakry, I detected only a slight improvement. The streets were busy, chock-a-block with cars, and some attempt had been made to fill in the worst pot-holes and clear up some of the garbage. But under its beautiful spreading trees, the city of 800,000 souls still looked dirty and shabby.

We had coffee at the Hotel de l'Independance at the posh (formerly European) end of town. From its roof, I saw the palatial villas and gardens Touré had built for the delegates of a summit of the Organization of African Unity attended by the Presidents of Africa; a whole district had been flattened to house them. They were now occupied by international organizations and embassies. I could see that French businessmen, with their dapper suits, briefcases, and expense accounts had moved back into town. There were also some balding Russians in baggy suits in the hotel.

The British consul insisted on showing me the Niger market, the main one in town. It was a rabbit-run of alleys. Large women, with massive buttocks and biceps, sat behind wooden stalls selling every fruit, vegetable and consumer good imaginable. Old canvas and sacking above kept the sun off their heads; below filthy water trickled in small channels between their feet. The choice of goods was excellent.

Deep in the market by the fruit section, Valerie Treitlein introduced me to the wife of the US ambassador, a thin, pale, beakish woman with blue-rinsed hair. You could not miss her amongst the solid black ladies of the market. She had in tow several young boys in red shirts with the word '*Ange Securité*' printed on them. 'They're "angels of the market",' she explained beaming. 'They would probably have become delinquents, but I've organized them into a group to help shoppers for a small fee. It's modelled on the voluntary "Angels" who provide security for passengers on the New York metro.'

As we left the covered Niger market, I saw a few more angels in red shirts lounging outside waiting for trade. It seemed a good arrangement for the European shoppers to be followed by porters rather than pickpockets but I wondered how long this institution, plucked from the bowels of New York, would last on the steamy coast of West Africa. As long as the money lasted, probably.

'You know,' Valerie Treitlein, 'it was a real police state during Sekou

Touré's time; his soldiers did what they liked and took what they liked. They could beat you up and imprison you and you couldn't do anything about it.'

'Was there anything good about those times?'

'One thing which the people appreciated was the ration cards. They were issued to everybody, including the expatriates, for all the basic foodstuffs – sugar, rice, oil, tomatoes, even tins of sardines. No one starved. Now life is much harder without them and the prices are constantly rising in the market.'

'What happened to all those who went into exile?'

'They're coming back but often they find it difficult to settle down as they have developed a different way of life abroad. There are also refugees pouring over the borders escaping the conflicts in Liberia and Sierra Leone. The Liberians are particularly dangerous; they are heavily armed and have nothing to do.'

We continued our tour of the city, down towards the old port which was full of wooden ships and dug-outs. Many had been abandoned, and their ribs stuck out of the sand like skeletons. As I made to film the scene, angry fists were raised, fortunately on the other side of a river channel. Once back in the Range Rover, I continued to take some tracking shots with my video camera of the streets through the open window. As we slowed down at a crossroads, I noticed in my lens that a crowd of young men got off their benches at the side of the road and came angrily towards the car. I quickly put the camera at my feet.

By this time the Range Rover had stopped. In a bound, the youths were upon us. I was sitting in the front seat and a large black fist came through the open window which I just manage to avoid. The sweating driver quickly pressed the automatic button to close the windows and tried to speed away; he fumbled with the gears. The situation was becoming very nasty. The youths began to rock the car and some had stones in their hands.

The driver was just about to pull away when two armed policemen on a motorcycle waved us down. The pillion rider had a Kalashnikov slung over his shoulder; not a man to argue with.

'Photography is forbidden. You all come to the police station!'

While I was imagining the worst, Mrs Valerie Treitlein, honorary British consul in Conakry, rose to the occasion. She got out of the Range Rover and squarely faced the the police sergeant and the other officer.

'Can't you see the Union Jack flying from my car and the number plates,' she said haughtily in French 'I'm a member of the diplomatic corps.'

'I'm sorry *madame*, but that man there was filming and it's forbidden. You must all come with me to the police station.'

'I will not. Photography is no longer forbidden. If you try to arrest me you will be in trouble.'

'They want money,' she said over her shoulder to me in English, 'but I'm not giving it to them.'

'I'm afraid I must arrest you all,' insisted the policeman, although his tone was beginning to falter.

'Ring the Chief of Protocol first. He will tell you that you cannot do this. He is a personal friend and you will be in deep trouble if you carry on like this. You should not aggravate visitors; they can get a wrong idea of Guinea.' She looked very stern.

After this onslaught, the policeman suddenly wilted. He smiled, embarrassed: '*Madame*, you must realize that you should not take photographs. We came here to save you from those delinquents. You were in a very dangerous situation. We don't want people to see how bad our country is; our country has nothing. We are only trying to do our best.'

'All right. I thank you, *monsieur*. I will not take the matter any further. I will look out for you in the future.'

All smiles. We quickly got into our Range Rover and sped away. The police on their motorbikes who a few minutes ago were about to arrest us were now our escort through the busy streets.

After an expensive pizza in a small restaurant run by a Frenchwoman – one of the few opening up – we headed out of town into the interior towards the fishing village of Boulbinet. The potholed road soon gave way to sections of sand. Cubans apparently had helped lay the road but they chose the wrong kind of stones, and it was now breaking up. The wrecks of cars at the side of the road were stark reminders of the regular accidents.

Passing through the shanty villages on the outskirts of Conakry, we overtook great groaning lorries belching black smoke with completely bald tyres. One lorry was going at a walking pace, accompanied by four boys at each wheel carrying a large stone. Valerie Treitlein explained:

'They're old Russian trucks. They can't get any spare parts for them, especially brake pads. The only way they can stop them is for those car boys to throw large stones in front of the wheels.'

A large limousine went by followed by a jeep full of soldiers. 'That's the President going to his village for the weekend. He's got one of the best herds of cattle in the country. Chinese advisers came to help irrigate the land for vegetables and rice, but then they left; within two years it came to nothing.'

After the little port of Dixi, where trees which had once defended the northern coast ended up, the land gradually became more undulating. Scattered homesteads emerged from the the mango trees alongside the road. Bare-breasted women went about their tasks; here, as elsewhere in West Africa, they did most of the farming. Boulbinet was a scattered village by a creek with mangroves growing down its muddy banks. Not far off were two mountains peaks, one called 'The Smoking Dog' because of its shape and the constant cloud around its summit. While we were having drinks in the restaurant a platoon of soldiers with a white officer suddenly emerged out of the bush: the French were back, training the Presidential Guard.

It was not only the French who were back in a big way. Valerie Treitlein introduced me to Michael Wilson, the resident representative of the World Bank. His luxurious office was at the top of a large new building overlooking a bay on the edge of town. Michael Wilson originally came from the Midlands in England, but he had acquired a soft American burr. He proudly boasted that the World Bank had invested $550 million dollars in the defunct economy of Guinea and was now advising the government on how to cut down the bloated civil service. Since Sekou Touré had virtually eliminated the intelligentsia, there was, as he put it, a shortage of 'human resources'.

What interested the World Bank and the Russian, French and American guests holed up in the Hotel de l'Independance was not the human but the 'natural resources' in the country. Guinea not only had the world's largest deposit of bauxite but huge reserves of iron ore. In addition, there was uranium, gold and diamonds in them there hills.

I asked the director of the World Bank in Guinea what he was doing to regulate the mining.

'There are strict controls,' he insisted, 'and taxes and royalties are imposed by the government. The conditions of operation are carefully thought out, and when mines run out the companies must landscape the area.'

And what was the World Bank doing to protect the environment?

'A great deal. An accord has just been signed between the United States, the World Bank and the Guinean government to ban logging throughout the country. The Guinean tropical forests are some of the best in the world, but they have been sadly depleted. The strip mining for bauxite has destroyed large areas, while Guineans regularly burn down primary forest to plant pluvial rice and coffee, and to create pasture for their cattle. When the soil loses its fertility, they move on. The result is severe erosion.'

As he was talking, I noticed Valerie Treitlein shot him a quizzical look. As we emerged into the steamy heat of Conakry, she said, 'My husband has a different story to tell about logging!'

Mr Treitlein was an old African hand. German by nationality, he had spent a quarter of a century in Liberia and Guinea, and claimed to know the forests better than any other man in West Africa. He was the first European to set up a mine under Sekou Touré in 1980. Until recently, he had crossed the Sahara every year from Algiers to Conakry with a convoy of lorries. When I met him at their spacious home by the sea outside Conakry, he was still recovering from an attack of amoebic dysentery which had almost killed him.

After dinner, he told me over a piping hot cup of lemon grass tea:

'The government and the World Bank can announce one thing, but what happens on the ground is very different. Only last week I was approached to see whether I wanted to join in a massive logging operation which is actually going on at the moment in the north west of the country. The logging company has shifted its equipment from Liberia because of the civil war there. You can be sure they will pull down massive forests before anyone catches up with them – and you can be sure that they will do nothing to replace them.'

'Can anything be done about it?'

'Logging has become an ecological disaster. Even if the international companies obey the rules and only take out trees of a certain size in order to allow the forest to regenerate, it doesn't save the forest. By putting in roads in remote areas, they allow access for Africans to follow who then cut down the trees for firewood or burn them to clear the ground for crops such as pluvial rice. Many rare species of trees have already gone. The rainforests, I'm afraid, are disappearing at an alarming rate.'

As we were talking a young French couple called. The man was gaunt and sun-tanned and wore fancy leather boots. His girlfriend was dressed in tight quarter-length slacks and blouse and displayed a lot of gawdy jewellery. They appeared very anxious, with dark rims around their shining eyes. I thought at first they were both high, but I quickly realized that they were suffering from a far more dangerous fever: diamonds. They had just signed an accord with a government minister allowing them to begin the first phase of exploration. They had come to buy some diesel.

After they had left, he said: 'I've seen it all before. Entrepreneurs like that come and go all the time. They've reached the first stage of being allowed to take up equipment to explore a diamond mine in the interior. But it's all a front. When they get up there they won't bother mining. They get their diamonds from the *clandestines* – well-organized Africans who sell the diamonds found by their people to the Europeans. They can buy a diamond for $4 million which is worth $10.5 million on the world market. And the man who finds it in the first place gets hardly anything.'

The next day I woke up on board the *Delphine Delmas* to find that a beautiful white cruise ship called the *Anastasis* had moored alongside during the night. I could not imagine what a cruise ship was doing in Conakry, of all places, and strolled over to investigate.

A black American sailor in immaculate tropical uniform with shorts greeted me on board at the top of the gangway, and directed me to the old Purser's Office. I was introduced to the director, Mrs Simonne Dyer, who explained that I was on a Christian Mercy ship spreading the Good News and offering free medical operations, especially to those suffering from cataracts and from facial deformities such as cleft-lips and cleft-palates. The majority on board were American, but there were thirty different nationalities and thirty Christian denominations represented.

I could not help thinking that this ostentatious show of Christian charity was no replacement for proper health care in Africa. As I visited the operating theatres, I thought of the radioactive hospital waste which had been dumped on Kassa island by other American ships. The Mercy Ship also reinforced the myth of the whites in Africa as the master race with all the technology and wealth and power. Moored in the docks, the great white ship illuminated by a thousand lights only underlined the darkness and disease of Conakry where there was no electricity or clean water.

The people I met on board were undeniably well-intentioned. I met an American surgeon called Gary Parker who was being sponsored by a congregation in Rhyl in North Wales. He was in the middle of operating on a girl with a disfigured face who had travelled with her mother from Burkina-Faso. When I talked to him, he had been operating for eight hours.

'Traditionally in Africa, a child born with a facial disfigurement like a cleft-lip would be considered possessed by evil spirits and buried alive. It is considered a crime against nature which could bring disaster to the community. Even now their parents feel obliged to leave their villages and go and live in the towns.'

In a region where one in fifty are thought to have been infected by AIDS, I asked him about the danger.

'A good point. Take this girl from Burkina-Faso whom I've been operating on. Well, her last test was HIV positive. As I was sowing her up, I could have pricked myself through my rubber gloves with a needle.'

What motivated him to carry on faced with such enormous odds in Africa?

'I consider that evil is everywhere in Africa as well as in our society. But there is hope for all if they believe in God. I want to bring hope to people by letting them know that there is a caring, loving God. What I can do is only a drop in the ocean of suffering, but every individual counts. You can't just believe in helping others; you have to get down and practise it.'

One fact I learnt during my visit to the Mercy Ship: eighty per cent of all human illnesses are due to the absence of clean water and basic sanitation;

in Africa two-thirds of the population do not have access to clean water. Operations can help, but the basis of human health in Africa as elsewhere lies in satisfying basic needs. And it does not require high technology and visiting angels in white coats to do that.

As I was about to leave the Mercy Ship the chaplain from Merthyr Tydfil warned me: 'Be careful in Abidjan. I had a watch stolen there and two members of the crew were stabbed walking across the bridge from the dock into town. The night before we left a European sailor was murdered'.

I looked at my wrist. My watch was still there but it said three thirty: my ship was due to sail! I ran as fast as I could along the dock and just climbed up the gangway as it was about to be lifted. I had arrived just as the moorings were being cast off. Sweat poured from my brow in the steaming heat, and my heart was pounding in my chest. I had made it back to my air-conditioned cabin, but the grotesquely disfigured face of the HIV-positive girl from Burkina-Faso continued to haunt me for a long time after.

Chapter Twelve

Number *one* Peasant

*T*HE captain said at lunch next day:
    'The containers were broken into in Conakry – twenty-five of them. We think the thieves must have had inside information from the shipping agent's office because the containers were well-chosen.'

I had noticed too that sacks of flour and sugar on the quayside had been broken open during the unloading, with the dockers scrambling to fill plastic bags with their contents. They had also fought over scrap wood from the hold.

'We also had some trouble with the Guinean watchmen. One of the crew caught them stealing a television and they had to be threatened with a knife before they got off. An outboard engine also has gone missing.'

But the captain was philosophical:

'It happens in every West Africa port. You have to understand that they're very poor and suffering from *le mythe des blancs* – the myth that the white man has everything and is loaded with priceless goods. If the dockers don't take some sugar, flour, wood or cigarettes back to their family in the evening, they would be ashamed and their relatives greatly disappointed. Conakry is bad but Lagos is worse.'

On the second day out from Conakry, I visited the engine room. Compared to the bridge which was quiet and cool, it was incredibly hot and noisy. Not only their position, but also their nature made the bridge and engine roome like heaven and hell on a ship. The average temperature was about 40° centigrade, but in the generator room it was nearly 55°. Stripped to the waist, and sweating profusely, men were working there in the dim light as the ship gently rolled and pitched. But despite the conditions, I was moved by the poetry of machinery, by the sight of well-oiled pistons, the faces of the instruments, the grand prospect of an enormous 6,000 kilowatt engine moving thousands of tons of steel smoothly through the ocean. Working my way down to the lowest point aft, I could see the massive propellor shaft turning – the end point for all the energy and ingenuity above. Beyond the solid plates of the hull, millimetres thick, I wondered what strange sea creatures might be swept by.

In the comparative quiet of the air-conditioned control room, the chief engineer Jean-Pierre Palfray explained:

'Everything has changed since I was an apprentice. We had to check everything manually in those days but now it's all done by computer. An alarm goes off if there are any anomalies, if the pressure or temperature changes in some part of the engine room.'

'What happens if the automatic system fails?'

'In that case, we still have the old equipment and manual command; if the bridge asks me to go astern or forward, I can pull the appropriate lever.'

It took us three and half days to travel 765 nautical miles between Conakry and Abidjan in the Ivory Coast. I was not too disappointed to sail past Freetown in Sierra Leone where renewed fighting had broken out. I was positively pleased not to call into Monrovia, the capital of Liberia, where a civil war was raging between war lords with tribal rivalries but no clear political line. Both countries had been dumps for freed slaves, but the slavery of the gun and ignorance had returned with a vengeance. Ironically, much of the world's shipping was sailing under a Liberian flag of convenience; the government which was meant to ensure that international safety standards simply no longer existed. In Liberia's case, colonialism could not be blamed for its troubles, since it was the only country apart from Ethiopia which had not undergone foreign rule.

By comparison to Conakry, sailing up the long Vridi canal which linked the sea to the lagoon of Abidjan, the capital of the Ivory Coast, was like visiting a great American city. The lagoon stretched as far as the eye could see and beyond – for 300 kilometres along the entire eastern half of the coast. The Harmattan wind had stopped blowing from the north, but it was still cloudy and very hot and humid.

Under the presidency of Félix Houphouët-Boigny, a former agricultural trade unionist, the Ivory Coast had flourished compared to its neighbours. The 'Number One Peasant', as he liked to call himself, had been in power ever since independence in 1960. He had deliberately kept good relations with France and encouraged expatriates to stay. He was a wily, pragmatic fox: at the height of the call for sanctions against South Africa, he continued to trade with the African pariah. By stressing agricultural diversity and development, rather than trying to compete with industrialized nations, his country had prospered, especially the élite. The President naturally became a large plantation owner himself, but most of the cash crops of coffee, cocoa, pineapples and palm oil were produced by small farmers.

Although the country was mainly Muslim, the Catholic President had built in his home village Yamoussoukro in the south a huge church from imported marble, an unvisited monument to his megalomania. He had designated the place the new capital but no one wanted to go and live there. The grand hotels were empty, the eight-lane highways deserted, and the broad avenues petered out in the bush. Crocodiles in a moat protected his palace.

On my arrival, it was clear that both the economic recession and the drive for multi-party democracy sweeping throughout West Africa were making their mark in the Ivory Coast. Attacks on whites were encouraging many to leave. A recent anti-government march had degenerated into the worst rioting seen in the capital. Hundreds of demonstrators had been arrested and the main opposition leaders jailed. They were protesting against the army who had gone unpunished after rampaging through the university campus, raping and beating students. In the meantime, the Number One Peasant was on his annual vacation in France.

I took a taxi and gave the address of a friend who lived on the plâteau, the former European district which overlooked the fashionable city centre. It was a Sunday and there were few people in the wide streets of this modern tropical metropolis. Near where my friend lived I saw the windows of a huge bank broken and burnt-out vehicles in front of the law courts. I was not allowed by security guards to photograph the cathedral, a vast modernist structure, because a service was in progress. Perhaps God might have been disturbed.

My contact in Abidjan was Regina Ofeiba Quist Arcton. With parents from Ghana, she was born in Oxford and educated in London and Paris. A former colleague of Jenny's in the BBC World Service, she had achieved a double first, and was the first woman and the first black correspondent in West Africa. Her flat on the eighth floor of a tall building had the best collection of West African statues, carvings, and furniture that I had ever seen in private hands.

Chatting in her flat overlooking the city, she observed:

'Things have never been so bad in the Ivory Coast. The economic recession is affecting the country badly. *Le Vieux* – the Old Man – seems to be losing touch. There is very high unemployment, especially amongst the young. The population of the Ivory Coast is twelve million, with four million immigrants, mainly from Burkina-Faso. No part of the town is now safe for a European walking alone after dark. An eighty-year old French priest, who has spent most of his life here, has just been gunned down in the streets.'

Regina introduced me to Jean-Philippe Chauzy, a producer in the French Service of the BBC. We set off to visit Abidjan. Our first port of call was the Hotel Ivoire, an enormous skyscraper with a huge turquoise palm-fringed swimming pool dotted with islands. It is the most famous hotel in West and Central Africa, with everything from a casino and a bowling alley to an ice-skating rink. From its summit garden, Abidjan seemed like a slice of Manhattan rising out of the Africa bush next to the sea. Its saving graces were the green areas between the buildings, many of which were vegetable plots and gardens.

The people who built it all were to be found in the three sprawling shanty towns outside the futuristic oasis of concrete and glass. Amongst their sprawling masses, the real Africa pulsated, where music, dance, and AIDS made their heady brew.

Regina took me to see a writer, the novelist and poet Véronique Tadjo.

She was married to the chief correspondent of Reuters in West Africa; their young baby, crawling in the coarse tropical grass amongst the fallen frangipani flowers of their beautiful garden, was completely white with blue eyes. Her mother was carrying another child.

Véronique was the product of two cultures; her father was Ivorian but her mother was French. Although she had studied at the Sorbonne, she told me that she felt more African than European. 'This is my country. I'm Ivorian first and foremost.' In her poetry and novels, she drew on African myths and legends. She dedicated a delightful book illustrated and written in English called *Lord of the Dance* to my children with the words 'May life bring you a blue sky and green hopes'. She had spent three years teaching in the land of the Senufo, a farming people in the north of the Ivory Coast, and was inspired by their drawings and sacred masks which represented different spirits hidden in nature. Did she find any tension between her two cultures?

'Not really. I like to take the best from both. I write in French because I can reach more people. But I am concerned about Afrocentrism, about not losing the authentic African experience.'

During my stay in Abidjan, I went with Jean-Philippe Chauzy and Mark Doyle, BBC correspondents, to visit Grand Bassam, a town situated forty kilometres to the east of Abidjan. We drove through the outskirts on an excellent road, the best I had ever seen in Africa. But the six-lane highway was like a race track, with death-defying drivers overtaking on the inside lanes, weaving crazily between the roaring traffic. I was only slightly reassured to learn that the Ivory Coast is the only country in Africa to make it illegal to drive without a safety-belt.

On the way to Grand Bassam, we passed a huge French military base near the airport: the ageing President's best guarantee of dying with his boots on. Nearby, to remind us we were still in Africa, a herd of humped-back cattle grazed at the roadside, brought hundreds of miles by nomadic Hualpalu tribesmen from the north to feed the insatiable inhabitants of Abidjan. We passed a bridge named after De Gaulle and a college after Voltaire. As we turned off the main road to Grand Bassam before a lagoon, I also noticed a large crowd at a volley-ball match. It was a factory works match, and in the seats of honour high on a dais were two Europeans, eloquent reminders of France's involvement in the country. French civil servants played a central role in every government ministry.

Grand Bassam was built on a narrow strip of land between a lagoon and the sea. It was the capital of the first French colonists who built the handsome and spacious two-storey buildings and laid out the open sandy roads. A yellow fever epidemic at the end of the nineteenth century resulted in the capital being shifted to Bingerville (where the French administrators no doubt continued their alcoholic habits).

It was sad to see what had happened to this once fashionable seaside town. The fine colonial buildings were collapsing. Lianas wrapped themselves around the balconies, the paintless shutters hung off their rusty hinges, the red tiles on the roof were slipping. Squatter families cooked over open fires in once magnificent drawing rooms. Goats wandered in and out. A pastel-coloured pulpit, with a statute of Jesus at its base, stood in the open air surrounded by shacks in the sand.

Expatriates from Abidjan were drawn to the place at the weekends for its nostalgia, tranquillity and scale, so different from the capital. We had lunch by the lagoon in a delightful local *maquis* called chez Gaston. Its French name was just a front for this authentic local bar–restaurant which grilled food in the open-air on charcoal braziers. Whole families were sitting on benches outside their houses in an adjoining side alley. Local specialities were on offer: *kedjenou*, chicken and vegetables with a mild pimento sauce to be eaten with *foutou*, boiled yams or plantains pounded into a paste, and *attiéké*, grated manioc. The owner's daughter, with her spider-like hair-do, flashing eyes, and great white teeth, served us with the local beer, Flag.

'The food here is probably better than in the Hotel Ivoire', Jean-Philippe observed. 'It's fresh and cooked over a fire. I've never been ill after eating in a *maquis*.'

On our way back to Regina's flat in Abidjan, we mingled in the crowd which was pouring out of the main football stadium. The Abidjan team had won and in the frenzied celebrations wild men dressed in their team's colours were blowing whistles and leaping in the air. In the crush, I had my glasses stolen, taken from the open window of our parked car.

Before leaving Abidjan, I rang home. It was a great relief to learn that Jenny was feeling much better: her jaw did not hurt so much and she was getting more sleep. The children were flourishing: Emily was becoming more and more self-reliant and Dylan was a great help. The daffodils were out in the fields surrounding the house, and birdsong filled the trees. Some lambs had been born already. Even the muddy track to the cottage was beginning to heal with fresh shoots of grass. I could imagine just what a cool, green delight it must be – light years away from the sweltering heat and extreme contrasts of the West African coast. I continued my voyage much more relaxed, knowing that life at home was renewing itself with the spring.

Chapter Thirteen

Crossing *the* Line

BEFORE leaving Abidjan, we took on forty African crewmen, swelling the total number on board to sixty-one. They were taken on board to help maintain the ship but more importantly to handle the great trunks of hardwood which would be loaded from floating rafts in our scheduled ports of call, Port Gentil and Libreville in Gabon, and Douala in Cameroon. At first I thought the French sailors called them 'crewmen', but in fact they were 'Kroumen', an ethnic group who lived along the West African coast. Since state borders cut arbitrarily across ethnic groups, there were four Liberians, and one Ghanaian amongst the Ivorian Kroumen.

There were special quarters for them in the forecastle and special rations. The chief steward told me that he had fruit and vegetables for them but all they wanted to eat was rice and meat, washed down by red wine. They ate and drank huge quantities, making the best of their month on board before disembarking in the Ivory Coast on the homeward voyage. They went about their work in good humour, mainly chipping paint and repainting. Under the bright equatorial sun, their glistening black bodies contrasted with the gleaming white of the ship.

While at sea between Abidjan and Cotonou, our next port of call in Benin, I spent a lot of time on the bridge. I got to know the first mate from Corsica better. He dreamed of the old days at sea when the officers wore uniform and were respected for it.

96

'You know, in my village in Corsica a captain is treated like a *seigneur*, a lord . . .', he boasted to me.

He also regretted the new system of '*polyvalence*', in which officers have to serve as engineers as well as navigators. The automation of the ship was turning sailors into mere technicians; it did not matter whether the computer consulted was on the bridge or in the engine room. Under the new system an officer could become a captain or a chief engineer depending on the wishes of the head office in Paris.

I found his love of authority and past grandeur a pain in the neck and much preferred chatting to the Senegalese second mate during his watch on the bridge. One afternoon, after checking the position of the ship on the satellite navigation, we talked about the validity of the old beliefs of Africa. He recounted how when a baby is born in Casamance, the elder of the village will still take a ring and hold it against a sacred tree and pronounce the names of the ancestors. If the ring does not fall to the ground, it means that the spirit of the dead has been reincarnated in the baby.

Putting down the dividers on the chart, he observed:

'*Tu sais*, I'm in perpetual contradiction. Brought up in Africa, I've seen things with my own eyes that I cannot explain. I've absorbed European civilization, but there are many things which cannot be explained by *l'esprit Cartesien*, by reason alone. The body is not separate from the spirit. If you have a little spot on your arm and you think it is a cancer, it will become one. In Fan hospital in Dakar I've seen a doctor bathe a madman in bull's blood to exorcize the evil spirit which possessed him. It worked; it's a question of mind over body.'

At this stage in my voyage, I too was prey to irrational feelings. In the morning, I often woke up centred and alert, but by mid afternoon a strange weariness and melancholy still descended on me. I recorded in my journal as we travelled along the coast of Ghana, formerly the Gold Coast:

'I feel the nothingness of life in the vastness of the ocean and sky. I feel the isolation of each person, the crushing weight of solitude, the indifference of any possible Creator. Without bearings, without familiar landscapes and faces, I feel lost and alone, aware that my death would make no real difference to those around me, except perhaps a sigh of regret and an unfortunate legal complication. Life would continue as before in the warm swamp of being.'

After two days at sea, we arrived at Cotonou on 31 March. It was the capital of Benin, formerly Dahomey, a strip of land sandwiched between Togo and Nigeria. From the seventeenth to the nineteenth century, it had been the centre of a great empire in West Africa; about 140 kilometres out of town, there were still some ruins of the great palace of Abomey. Many of its beautiful statues are locked in the vaults of museums in Paris and London.

Benin had also been a major slave centre; south Benin was formerly known as the Slave Coast. For more than a century, an average of 10,000 slaves a year were shipped from Cotonou across the Atlantic. With them went their beliefs – the gods and goddesses of the Yoruba and the voodoo of the Fon – to form a central part of Caribbean and Latin American culture, especially in Brazil, Cuba and Haiti.

Dahomey had gained its independence from France in 1960 during De Gaulle's unexpected withdrawal from West Africa. This small country of four million had the dubious honour of having had the largest number of coups, after Nigeria, in Africa. It was just recovering from a Marxist Revolution under Mathieu Kérékou, a former Catholic and French-trained paratrooper, who had changed the country's name, abolished Christmas and Easter, and presided over its rapid economic decline. One positive legacy of his era was that Cotonou proved the safest port I had visited so far during my voyage.

The captain, through the local Delmas shipping agent, arranged a minibus for me. The driver's name was Luc. As we drove through the busy, sandy streets of Cotonou with its low-rise buildings, the relics of a workers' state could still be seen. One square was called Place de Lenin, with a great statue of the old scoundrel, and another Place de Martí, named after the national hero of the Cuban Revolution. The country was about to have its first multi-party elections, contested by eleven parties. Luc had no doubts where he stood:

'The Revolution ended two years ago. It was very hard. The Cubans, they did nothing. Now they have gone, and the French military have returned, life is much better. You can do and say what you like. *On est très content.*'

Unlike in Guinea, I found that I could film whatever I liked, whether it was a group of schoolgirls joking under Lenin's neglected statue, or a bloody bull's head, its tongue sticking out, on a greasy trolley in the market.

'Is there enough to eat?' I asked Luc.

'Weyyyy! Enough to eat? There's too much to eat!'

At lunchtime, Luc took me to his house situated by a broad sandy avenue behind a tall breeze-block wall. Young children were playing in the sand with chickens. It was not clear amongst the several women present who were relatives and who were servants; they were probably both at the same time. Although a Catholic, Luc confessed that he had a wife in town and another in the country:

'It's the custom here. The two women get on well and my city wife comes with me when I go to my village. My country wife works my land there: women prepare the ground, the men sow, and women do the harvest.'

Although his fellow Catholics might say he was living in a state of mortal sin, he was undoubtedly standing in a long local tradition. King Glélé of Abomey had 800 wives, who took part in the royal hunts, and a thousand female slaves to attend them. Believing that women are more trustworthy than men, he had 6,000 Amazon bodyguards, although it must be said he also had 10,000 male soldiers to fall back on. One unpleasant habit he had was to pound his enemy's head in a mortar with a dismembered leg.

Next we went to visit his sister – Luc's, that is, not Glélé's – who was managing his shop selling football pools. It was a bit like a fetish temple. My driver was something of an entrepreneur in newly liberated and capitalist Benin. He was an agent of a company based in Nigeria which relied on the results of British football teams. Unfortunately no one had yet won in Luc's neighbourhood and sales were dropping off. In this French-speaking country, there was no way of checking the results.

'What is the secret?' asked Luc, taking me to one side. This was a difficult question since I had never played the pools and was not even clear how they worked. Now was the time for a touch of voodoo, if ever there was. Unfortunately I did not have any fetishes at hand. I decided to come clean.

'There's really no secret,' I replied. 'You simply have to guess how many goals the teams are going to get. It's like a lottery, although I suppose those who follow football in England have a reasonable idea.'

'Well can you tell me three teams which are likely to have draws?' Out of the top of my head, I said Newcastle United (where my brother lived), Portsmouth (my local team as a boy) and Manchester United (whom everybody knew).

'*Merci, monsieur Peter, merci beaucoup!*' he said in triumph, as if I had shared a profound secret.

I hoped he did not bet all his money on it. Even if he did win, it would not be beyond his Nigerian brothers over the border to make a little adjustment to the results . . .

After the hassles of Agadir, Dakar and Conakry, I found walking in Cotonou delightful, despite the sweltering heat. In the artisanal market, there were some magnificent brass and iron sculptures which recalled the grandeur of Dahomey's lost civilization. I bought an example of *appliqué* tapestry (the colourful symbols of different Fon kings sewn on black cloth) without any overpowering sales talk. I left the man-made fetishes, not knowing what voodoo spirit it might represent or what evil force it could evoke. Walking along a roadside afterwards, a young man pulled up on his motorbike politely offering a lift. I felt sure that the experience of socialism, however resented, had contributed to this honesty and public spirit.

Luc seemed to be right about the new order. There were no apparent shortages. Strolling through the vast sprawling market of the Grand Marché de Don Tokpa bordering the lagoon, there seemed everything available in quantity, from meat to flour to vegetables. It was not only the well-dressed who were buying. With news on my radio of growing drought and famine in southern Africa, this was a pleasure to see.

Before I left Cotonou, I wanted to make one more visit out of town. Paul, a matelot on the *Delphine Delmas*, urged me to go to Ganvié: 'It's one of the most interesting places in all West Africa. It's a town built entirely on stilts in a lake. I've got friends over there and I'd take you myself, but I can't get any leave today. Watch out for the women; they've got beautiful tattoos on their breasts!'

It took about half an hour by car travelling through fields of sugar cane and groves of mangoes to reach the shores of the green lake of Nokoué north of Cotonou. I then hired a dug-out *pirogue* with two young men to take me to see this fabled town. Women from the settlement were landing at the jetty and selling their fish and buying vegetables and fruit at the market on the lakeshore. Many had beautiful straw hats with broad rims. A refreshing breeze carried their canoes in under sail, some made from old sacking.

My guide introduced himself as Christophe Honfo; his friend concentrated on boatwork. As we made our way out into the lake, he pointed out some boats piled high with loosely woven bamboo nets:

'The people harvest fish here. They encircle an area of the lake with those nets and let the fish grow inside them until they are ready to catch. They also put branches in the lake and when the fish come to eat the rotting leaves they catch them in a net.'

'What made these people come and live in the lake in the first place?'

'It's a long story. Several hundred years ago the Tofinu people were fighting against their enemies the Fon in the north. Since they were a small people they soon began to lose. They knew that there was a taboo for the warriors of Abomey to go near water, so they decided to try to live in a swamp. The story goes that a bird led them to this shore. They built their houses on the lake and their enemies have left them alone ever since.'

The town was several kilometres from the shore. It first appeared as a large huddle of grey huts on stilts, but gliding through the waterways of the town was like visiting an African Venice. There were many different types of house made from bamboo and reeds, some much grander than others. The children swam and played in the water; presumably the waste from the 20,000 inhabitants was not enough to pollute seriously such a vast lake. The dead, my guide told me, were buried on the shore of the lake.

Some inhabitants appeared to resent my intrusion, and I did not blame them. I was not the first European to pry into their lives, and I would not be the last. One or two had been quick to exploit the interest and turned their houses into rest houses and bars. We landed at one such, run by two young girls who looked like twins. They immediately brought beer and began to flirt with one of my gondoliers. They had tattoos on their cheeks. One of them took me round the back of her house on stilts and showed me a dark room with a bed, implying that we should go and test it. I declined. Not only was she a teenager but the damp, mosquito-infested interior had no attraction. And of course there was the threat of AIDS. I never did have the opportunity to find out about Paul's more intimate tattoos.

I left the village at dusk, as the setting sun turned the water into a golden green. Ducks were flying in low over the reed beds. The breeze had picked up. The returning boats, loaded down with goods and their sails filling out, pitched merrily over the small waves sweeping across the darkening lake. A few kerosene lamps had lit up in the houses in the distance. I wondered how long it would be before visitors would finally corrupt these people who had adapted themselves so skilfully to their watery environment.

We left Conakry late at night on 1 April. At dinner, the captain announced that following the recent elections in France, the socialist prime minister had resigned and that the right would be taking over. There was general jubilation amongst the French officers, except for Sy who remained quiet. Then the captain made his *coup de grâce*: '*C'est un poisson d'avril*, an April Fool's joke!'

We were now heading in a direct line down through the Bight of Benin, past the great delta of the Niger, across the Gulf of Guinea and down towards Port Gentil in Gabon. I was disappointed to have to bypass Nigeria, despite the desperate tales about Lagos, since it contained a quarter of Africa's population and was a nation to be reckoned with. French ships tend to keep to French-speaking countries.

The *Delphine Delmas* was travelling at top speed in an effort to catch up lost time, and my cabin vibrated from top to bottom; it took me a long time to trace the worst of the rattles. My neighbour in the *Impasse de Matins Calmes* – the third officer – had the deadman's watch from midnight to four, and in the mornings I had to take extra care not to wake him up as he was a light sleeper.

Visibility was good, but it was cloudy, hot and humid in this equatorial zone. Sometimes dark clouds would gather and a few drops of warm rain would fall into the grey-green sea and on to our newly painted decks. Watching the bows of the ship cut through the boiling waters below, I appreciated the simple fact of being alive in such a remote spot in the Atlantic Ocean.

After two days at sea, on 3 April at 13.12 hours, we crossed the Equator, about eighty miles off the coast of Gabon. I watched the degrees of latitude on the satellite navigation click from north 005 degrees north to 000 to south 005. It was the ultimate in navigational aids, for at a flick of a switch any mariner could find out his exact latitude and longitude, something which was way beyond the imagination of the early Portuguese navigators who had to rely on a simple astrolabe and quadrant to get a reading of the sun or a star.

Not so long ago, sailors would have a great party if one of their number crossed the line for the first time. This had happened to me when I was eighteen in the Pacific Ocean, but now in the age of containers and tight schedules ships' crews were too busy to celebrate. It is all part of the creeping automation of life on sea and land. Sailors no longer feel the need to propitiate Poseidon, the god of the sea, like the ancient Greeks, or call up Neptune from the depths to judge in a mock court and pronounce sentence on a young tar who was foolish enough to leave his home and take to the wandering life of the sea.

I celebrated the crossing of the line for the first time on my voyage by throwing two small stones chosen by my children from our garden in Wales. According to the chart, the depth of the sea at this point was a thousand fathoms – 6,000 feet. I would like to have been small enough and aquatic enough to hitch a ride on one of the stones, as it gently swung to and fro down to the mysterious sea-floor which no human had ever seen.

We arrived in Port Gentil, Gabon, in the afternoon of 4 April. Port Gentil is a large island in the estuary of the river Ogooué just below the Equator. Sailing up the river Ogooué evoked for me the memory of Albert Schweitzer who established a leper colony and hospital at Lambaréné on its banks. After giving up a career as an organist and university lecturer, he had at the age of thirty trained as a doctor and decided to come to Africa in an attempt to serve humanity. Seeing a herd of hippos in the river triggered off a sudden revelation that 'reverence for life' should be the basis of all morality. He tried to make his hospital attractive by providing patients with familiar surroundings; they were fed by their families who camped nearby. Some visiting Europeans complained of the hygiene, but the formula worked.

Schweitzer himself was a complicated man. He shared the typical view of missionaries earlier this century that they were bringing Christianity and civilization to darkest Africa. 'I feel for them like a brother,' he wrote, 'but like an older brother. The Negro is a child in a primitive culture, and nothing can be done with children without authority.'

Port Gentil was not only a port for the timber floated down the river Ogooué from the forests of the interior; it had become a boom town thanks to the discovery of black gold – oil – on and off shore. The French presence was so strong that formalities on my arrival were unnecessary.

The expatriates lived nearby in luxurious compounds, their large houses, spacious gardens and expensive high-powered boats all carefully guarded behind barbed wire fences. Armed security guards stood at the gates. After recent riots, most women and children had left. For this reason, I was surprised to see a young blond girl of about five wandering alone at the roadside; perhaps she had momentarily escaped from her parent's comfortable zoo.

The gap between rich and poor on the island was staggering. In the town centre, there were bright lights, high-rise hotels and offices, a casino, nightclubs, supermarkets and shops bursting with goods. But just outside, kilometre after kilometre of run-down shacks bordered the road. Large areas were flooded by the rains. When dusk came the townships fell into darkness; there were no street lights but only kerosene lamps to light the dim interiors of the mosquito-infested shacks.

Tension was running high according to my driver, and he advised me not to photograph anywhere. He had a hunting knife at his side, to protect me, he said, from 'savages and wild men'. There had been a bloody riot in the previous year which had led to the burning down of the police headquarters and president's palace. The rioters emptied all the big stores. The French paras flew in to hold the airport while the expatriates were evacuated.

I drove past the charred ruins of the palace and saw many burnt-out trucks. The anniversary of the burning was approaching, and the people were impatient to rid themselves of the president who had singularly failed to share the immense wealth of this small country. The spectacle of the

Europeans in their compounds and local managers in their limousines was a daily insult.

President Albert-Bernard Bongo of Gabon was only five feet tall but he liked to play big. The loss of a palace in Port Gentil was no great deal: he had many more throughout the mainland. His country had probably undergone more dramatic change than any other country on the continent. The discovery of oil and minerals, especially manganese and uranium, made it the richest country in black Africa.

Bongo was the archetypal African leader who creamed off all the power and wealth of his people. Every seven years on his birthday, he had elections in which he ran unopposed. Apart from being the president, he served as minister of defence, information, telecommunications, planning, national guidance, and women's advancement. Because of his readiness to do business – both commercial and military business – with France, they propped up his one-party rule as long as the country remained reasonably stable. Uncertain of his own people, he employed Moroccan and French mercenaries as a presidential guard. Despite his love of pin-striped suits designed in Paris, he had converted to Islam and now called himself El Hadj Omar Bongo.

'You know,' the chief engineer recounted with delight, 'throughout the period of sanctions against South Africa, Bongo operated "Air Bidoche" (Meat Airline) between Libreville and Johannesburg. When the African heads of state came to call for sanctions, they would tuck into tender steaks flown in specially from the hated racist regime!'

The Gabonese were notorious amongst the French for being slow and work-shy. In the equatorial heat, these of course are virtues, since any great effort immediately brings beads of sweat to the brow. But there are also historical reasons. When the French and British ships first arrived on the coast they were after slaves and ivory. The coastal tribes quickly learned to do their dirty work, and raided settlements in the interior. These included tribes like the Fang who not only produced beautiful masks, but were fierce hunters and allegedly ate their enemies. The coastal slave traders grew rich and eventually got their own slaves to produce for them. The tradition continues: the well-off in the coastal towns still do not overly exert themselves; they employ cheap foreign labour.

We sailed from Port Gentil at 22.00 hours on 4 April and arrived in Libreville eight hours later. It had started as a settlement in the late nineteenth century when the French captured a slave ship and released its human cargo at the mouth of the river Komo. The slaves called their settlement Libreville (Freetown). It grew rapidly and became for a while the capital of the French Congo, before it was moved to Brazzaville. It was now the capital of Gabon.

I had telephoned a Gabonese acquaintance of mine called Eugène Fanguinoveny from Port Gentil and had left a message for him to meet me. His brother Michael came on board with the agent and port officials. He could not have been better placed: formerly the director of Port Gentil, he was now director of the staff-training programme in Libreville port.

Michael had a car waiting for me on the quayside to go and visit his family. A devout Christian (like many Gabonese), he was a thoughtful and modest man. He smoked but did not drink. His half-brother Eugène was very different: as the public relations manager of Air Gabon, he was an affable *bon viveur*. Their family home was in Lamberéné where they had grown up near Schweitzer's hospital. They could rememember as boys hearing the Grand Old Man playing his organ.

As we drove through the wide streets of Libreville, the spectacular bonanza which had hit Gabon was clear to see. It might have been a sleepy settlement at the turn of the century, with its back to an unexplored hinterland, but now it was a mini Miami. Stretching along the coast, it had a wide highway – the Boulevard de l'Independance – lined with fancy hotels and expensive shopping centres. The big French multi-nationals were all there. I stopped at the Novotel Rapotochombo hotel – the tallest one in town – to take it all in from its rooftop. It had a fine view of the coast, with the coconut palms leaning over the white beaches washed by the deep azure sea. We did not linger outside the high walls of the President's Palace, with its Greek columns, its marble throne imported from Italy, its two theatres, night club and its banquet hall for 3000 stooges.

The centre of Libreville had a empty feel and there were few people about. We stopped at the Hypermarché de M'Bolo which was bursting with as many goods – virtually all imported – as any supermarket in a European capital. Having got used to bustling local markets and small stores lined with basic necessities, it was a real culture shock to wander along its brain-killing aisles to thin musack in the heart of central Africa. It was good to rediscover the real Africa in the townships outside the sterile city centre.

I had arrived in the rainy season and it was incredibly muggy. Usually it rained in the late afternoon, and during the day it was unbearably hot under the hazy sun. It was a pleasure to catch the slight sea-breeze on the balcony chez Eugène. He lived with his wife, two maids and several children in a modest villa – certainly by presidential standards – in the suburbs of Libreville, overlooking a valley dotted with houses amongst lush vegetation.

He put on a magnificent lunch for me of stuffed crab, red snapper, and wild boar, served with manioc, plaintains and rice, followed by fresh pineapple. The whole was washed down by the best of French white and red wines, and of course, Champagne. Gabon, Eugène proudly announced, was one of the world's largest consumers of Champagne. It was difficult to tally with my vegetarianism, but I thought in this case to refuse to eat some of the food he had specially prepared for me would be unforgivably rude. Any abstract moral principle should be adapted to the demands of particular circumstances.

Eugène admitted that the economic bubble could easily burst. Recession had begun to bite in Gabon, as elsewhere on the west coast. During my visit there was growing tension between the Gabonese and their guest workers. Some politicians were calling for their repatriation and some of the young unemployed were becoming openly hostile. Gabon for the Gabonese was the cry. This was beginning to apply even to the 50,000 French expatriates.

Eugène was not impressed: 'Gabonisation overnight won't work. There are so many French here running things that if they pull out the country will ground to a halt. There should a gradual training programme for Africans to replace them.' In the meantime, let us enjoy our champagne!'

*   *   *

Before the *Delphine Delmas* left Libreville, the Kroumen took on more huge logs and chained them to the decks which had been cleared of containers. It was *okoumé*, a semi-hard wood from the equatorial rainforest which the Gabonese use for canoes and the French for plywood.

Beyond the coastal strip stretches dense equatorial rainforest, archetypal jungle, for thousands of miles down through Congo and Zaïre. Since such vegetation prevented the development of the kind of cities and kingdoms further north in Benin, this region was considered by Europeans who arrived a hundred years ago as the most primitive and savage part of Africa: the heart of the Dark Continent. Much was still inaccessible, with only 400 kilometres of road in the whole of Gabon.

It might not be so for long. The great trees were crashing down, with the noise of the chain saws terrifying the animals and birds in the surrounding rainforest. Despite the minerals and oil, timber was still Gabon's second major export. The logging companies were going deeper and deeper into the jungle. With the coastal forests exhausted, the new railway crossing the country – the four-billion-dollar *Transgabonais* to President Bongo's hometown of Franceville – had opened new virgin forest for exploitation. The outcome could be devastating not only for Gabon but for the world.

And we on the *Delphine Delmas* were all adding to the process, whether we liked it or not.

Chapter Fourteen

Man know Man

AFTER leaving Libreville, the *Delphine Delmas* continued to head north to Douala in Cameroon, the armpit of Africa. I was doubling back on my wake, once again in the northern hemisphere, but the extra 250 nautical miles amply made up for the hundred miles or so I had lost flying from Agadir to Las Palmas. I was arriving in the season of the light rains.

On Sunday 4 April, I wrote in my journal: 'It's two months now since I left home. I feel much better than at the beginning, with the friendly company and regular routine on board *Delphine Delmas*, interspersed with the excitement of the ports of call. Africa is slowly revealing itself and I am slowly relaxing into my voyage.'

That evening was a beautiful starry night. I went out on deck in the warm, humid air. The silvery sea slid along the ship's hull with a soft murmur, the seething bubbles of the wake slowly disappearing in the surrounding darkness. I could see Orion with his studded belt to the north, and the Southern Cross rising above the horizon. I felt the purity of the sea and the air and the cold indifference of the constellations above which guided us to our port.

The day before we arrived in Douala the radio officer received a report from our sister ship, the *Polande Delmas*:

Informed by the Consul Général of France. Renewed attacks directed against Europeans ashore. Attacks on moored ships each week by commandoes, twenty or thirty individuals, with hold-ups of the crew.

A little after setting sail at night, containers broken into on the terminal and canoes attempting to take them away.

One is sometimes relieved to be at sea again.

I was not, it seemed, arriving at a very good time.

Douala lies on the bank of a wide river. As we sailed slowly up its green waters, fishermen in their small dug-out canoes bounced in our wake. I soon made out the wharves of the port which were piled high with huge trunks of *azobé* timber waiting to be loaded on the *Delphine Delmas* by the Kroumen. To the north, its summit hidden in cloud, rose Mount Cameroon, the highest mountain in Central Africa. It was very sultry, despite the sea-breeze.

I was pleased to land in Cameroon for the country had strong associations with the early navigators. Hanno from Carthage, who founded colonies along the west coast of Africa in the sixth century, was probably referring to Mount Cameroon when he described in his *Periplus* an active volcano in the region as the 'Chariot of the Gods'. Hundreds of years later, when the Portuguese arrived in 1472, they were amazed at the number of giant shrimps along the coast and exclaimed '*Camaröes, Camaröes!*'. Henceforth, the country became known as Cameroon.

I experienced a certain quiet satisfaction to have proven wrong the girl in the Cameroonian Embassy in London who had insisted that 'no one comes to Cameroon by boat'.

We moored early in the morning. As I was packing my trunk and filming equipment before breakfast, I got a call from the captain: 'You have some friends waiting for you in the mess room.'

There were two men and a woman, all expensively dressed. I immediately recognized Jean-Victor Nkolo, a Cameroonian colleague of Jenny's at the BBC World Service. A large man in his mid thirties, he was a veteran reporter of civil wars in Africa as well as a great lover of music and sports. He introduced me first to the beautiful young lady – 'a princess from Douala' – and to his friend Ebony Wesley who carried a swagger stick like a brigadier. Powerfully built, at ease in the unusual surroundings of the ship, Wesley gave a winning smile. Above his stiff white shirt collar, his jugular vein pumped slowly.

Wesley had been trained in the Foreign Legion as well as in the US Rapid Deployment Force. As a company commander he had invaded Grenada with a force of 200 black Americans and fifty Cherokees. He now lived in Paris, where he was a neighbour and friend of Mitterand's son. He was a black-belt in judo, and Jean-Victor had chosen him to be our bodyguard.

With a visa in my passport and Jean-Victor and Wesley at my side, we had no trouble getting through the customs and immigration officials. We went to the old Hotel Akwa Palace in the town centre on Boulevard de la Liberté to hire a car to take us to Yaoundé, the capital of Cameroon about 250 kilometres away in the interior. Although Cameroon is one of the richest countries in Africa, and Douala has a population of almost a million, it has none of the high-rise buildings of Libreville or Abidjan. Many of its fine old colonial buildings had been left to decay. As we passed one set in an overgrown garden with tall mango trees, Wesley observed in an American drawl: 'That's been a police brothel for twenty-five years'. Cameroon had long been one of the more stable countries in Central Africa, despite long hostility between Muslim northerners and more Westernized southerners, and between the English-speaking minority in the south-west and the French-speaking majority. But things were coming to a head. Since independence, two presidents had failed to check the growing corruption and graft, and the people were becoming sick of the same self-serving barons. The country was slipping into civil war.

The road to Yaoundé which cut through the equatorial forest was new and fast. Outside Douala, the trees were being cut down and burnt for firewood and cleared to plant crops. As elsewhere in Africa, wherever a road penetrated, people soon followed.

Jean-Victor had just flown in from Holland to meet me, and was very happy to be home again after four years. The great trees of the rainforest, swirling with mists in the hills, replenished his soul.

'Not long ago, there used to be gorillas in this forest. The whole forest is criss-crossed by tracks linking up the scattered villages. In the old days, people would walk along them from Douala to Yaoundé. Outside the towns, life still hasn't changed very much.'

On the side of the road, I occasionally saw dead monkeys hanging upside down, their hands and feet tied to sticks. A huge headless snake dangled at the end of a pole. They were for sale to the passing drivers, as were the large glass containers of petrol smuggled in from Nigeria at about a third of the official price.

There was something eerie about the highway as we sped through the equatorial rainforest. Then I realized what it was. There was no traffic.

'It's because of the growing tension. People are too scared to travel. During a go-slow of workers some months ago, the security forces were handed out guns, but they didn't return them. Some of them have got into the hands of bandits, but some of the police themselves are freelancing as bandits. They want to create as much confusion in the country as possible. If we see a road block with two policemen, we wont stop!'

On the rest of the way to Yaoundé, Jean-Victor filled me in on the history of Cameroon:

'Unlike the British colonies, who ruled indirectly through the existing village chiefs, the French imposed direct rule. They chose leaders amongst the chiefs and sent them away to be educated. They wanted to form administrators to carry out their policies. When independence came, the trained élite just took over the government from the French and carried on the same policies.'

'But doesn't Cameroon have English and French-speakers?'

'Yes. At the time of independence, the Anglophones in the north chose to become part of Nigeria. Those in the south-west highlands at first formed a federation with the Francophones and then they joined together in a unitary state. It has never worked well. Today many Anglophones want to break away and form their own state.'

'I suppose this is partly due to the artificial boundaries imposed by the colonialists.'

'Yes. Cameroon is one of the most artificial countries in Africa. It has a population of twelve million and there are more than 240 ethnic groups with their different languages. The geography too is very diverse.'

'Does tribalism still play an important role?'

'Very much so. Many of the tribes are very hierarchical and the *chefs* still have a lot of power. Politics is still basically tribal; as they say in pidgin "man know man".'

'Isn't tribalism the scourge of African politics?'

'Well, it has a positive and negative side. The positive side is that all members of an ethnic group are expected to help each other; in a country without a welfare state or social security, that can mean the difference between life and death. Everybody feels that they belong to a family, a clan and a tribe. The negative side of course is nepotism and the rivalry between tribes which can lead to civil war. All African politics have to take tribalism into account.'

'And I suppose it's the basis of the corruption you see everywhere.'

'Corruption is certainly a part of everyday life. It's silly to try to get things done in a straight way, because you won't get anywhere. It's very complicated to explain. You can call it corruption or you can call it doing something for a friend. If I give a T-shirt to a receptionist and chat her up a bit, then she might knock ten per cent off my bill. If the manager is an old school friend, he will take fifty per cent off. It works like that.'

On the outskirts of Yaoundé, schoolchildren were walking dangerously close to the road. Pick-up trucks, overflowing with people, bumped along. The undulating, winding streets soon became crowded with people who walked slowly, conserving their energy. It was reassuring to be back amongst people after the menacing silence of the rainforest hiding bandits with automatic weapons. We dipped down into the business centre of Yaoundé, with its new Hilton and high-rise office blocks, and then climbed one of the many surrounding hills, green with lush vegetation. The traffic cops, in pith helmets, white uniforms and white spats, blew their whistles and waved their gloved hands with amazing grace.

We headed for the Mount Fébé Hotel. It was perched on a hill overlooking the city, with a vast golf course dotted with trees below it. At 1,000 metres above sea-level, it was wonderfully cool compared to Douala. Walking on to the balcony of my room, I saw yellow weaver birds singing in the flamboyant trees with their fernlike leaves and red flowers. The thud of tennis rackets came from the courts hidden by bushes, drowned for a moment by the cry of a young Cameroonian girl pushed by her French boy friend into the wide swimming pool.

Swallows swooped down low across the water, scattering the blue dragonflies.

In the distance on the right, I could make out some wooden shacks with tin roofs, set in small gardens of bananas, yams and maize, creeping up the steep hill. On the left on another hill was an impressive round building with a flat top.

'That's the president's palace,' Jean-Victor told me. 'Strictly forbidden. If you go anywhere near it, they shoot first and ask questions afterwards. A few years ago, when there was an attempted coup, the president took to his nuclear bunker there for a few days. If there's any trouble, we'll be all right here. Like the president's palace, this hotel is strategically placed and easy to defend.'

At £5 a sandwich, it was also one of the most expensive hotels in one of the most expensive countries in Africa.

By a strange coincidence, I had arrived at the time of the eighty-seventh Interparliamentary Conference which was being held in Yaoundé from 6 to 11 April. The main events took place in the Palais de Congrès built by the Chinese on a hill opposite my hotel. The government slogan for the conference was 'Cameroon: Land of Peace and Hospitality'. The host was President Paul Biya, the well-known democrat and advocate of human rights who jailed opponents (including Jean-Victor's father) without trial, did not allow fair elections, and encouraged *agents provocateurs* to provide an excuse for his iron rule.

The Interparliamentary Conference was a free beanfeast – or rather steak-and-wine feast. It was an opportunity for the MPs of the world to attend another talking shop in an exotic place, confident that none of the high-sounding resolutions would be implemented. There were 750 delegates scattered in hotels around Yaoundé.

The British delegation was led by the young Lord Lindsay, member of that deeply democratic assembly known as the House of Lords. But he was in good company; many of the other world parliamentarians were not elected either. He might have had a lot to say about tribalism and hereditary chiefs back home but instead he praised in his speech the Cameroonian government for its environmental record. In the mean time, the trees came crashing down in the forests and the logs piled up on the wharfs in Douala.

In the morning at the hotel, MPs from Denmark and Germany would jostle me at breakfast in their scramble for the free exotic fruit and imported cheeses. In the erratic lift on the way down, I had met a Thai MP and a Spanish MP, all dressed up to go golfing; unaware of my nationality, the Thai observed: 'This is one of the slowest elevators in the world – like an English gentleman'.

A couple of days after my arrival, the film crew turned up at the hotel full of the news of the British elections. David Williams, who had been covering them for HTV, was confident that this time the Labour Party would win. I heard the result standing on a huge volcanic rock overlooking the capital. Through the crackling shortwaves of the BBC World Service for Africa, I heard that the Tories had been returned by a short majority.

My friends, who had been following the minutiae of the elections at home, were deeply disappointed, but to me in Central Africa it all seemed utterly remote. Only a slight difference in emphasis over education, health and defence separated the main parties in Britain; in Africa, it was a question of dictatorship or a slight semblance of democracy. As I heard in the rest of the news bulletin, the former Portuguese colonies of Angola and Mozambique were tearing themselves apart, South Africa was about to explode, and the whole of Southern Africa was suffering from the severest drought in living memory. In the Horn, famine still stalked the land: Ethiopia was only just beginning to recover from a prolonged civil war and Somalia had completely collapsed.

Law and order were also breaking down in Yaoundé. When we went to visit the railway station, we were attacked by a mob of stone-throwing youths. I was sitting in the back of the Toyota four-wheel drive and one stone hit me through the open window. My natural instinct was flight, but Jean-Victor jumped out of the car and squared his broad shoulders in his perfectly cut white jacket and slowly walked along the side of the car. One severe glance at the youths made them hold back. I then remembered that he was a karate black-belt. Anyone could sense he was not a man to tangle with. In case there was trouble, Wesley had his eight-millimetre revolver out, half hidden in a white towel which he had taken from the hotel.

'Those porters and banana boys steal more than they carry,' Jean-Victor observed afterwards. 'Unfortunately, apart from harsh repression, the government has no policy for violent crime. There is no social work, no prevention, no education. And the repression only makes things worse.'

That evening we went to an open-air restaurant run by a family friend. Sitting around a table under a thatched awning, we suddenly heard about a hundred yards away behind some buildings the staccato firing of automatic weapons, a screech of brakes and then some terrible screams.

'It's started; it's started!', said Wesley excitedly. He disappeared in the night, revolver in his hand. Unlike him, I had never heard people shooting at each other and did not like the sound of it. Jean-Victor, who had been under fire in all the major wars in recent times in Africa, remained as cool as ever and continued to eat his chicken. He was not going to worry about this local incident. Everybody else in the restaurant, I noticed, carried on as if nothing had happened.

'But someone might have been killed or injured?' I said. I could still hear the shouting in the distance.

'We can't do anything about it. The people there will take care of it.' Wesley came back about half an hour later and gave us the low-down: 'Some bandits tried to raid a garage, but the owners were armed. As they tried to make their getaway, one of them was unable to get into the car. He tried to make it to the swamps but the crowd got him; they nearly killed him.'

On our way back to the hotel we came across a group of men who had stopped a car by a large roundabout and were dragging a girl out at gun-point. Jean-Victor overtook at speed.

'We can't do anything. They're armed with automatic weapons and we've only got a revolver. That girl will probably be raped. You see, Peter, what happens in a country where the police become bandits.'

'I don't think I'll sleep well tonight.'

'The best way to sleep is to close your eyes.'

The atmosphere in the hotel was becoming increasingly bizarre. In the bar on the ground floor, where beautiful Cameroonian music was played on

116

large xylophones called belafons, young prostitutes lounged every night eyeing up the punters. No doubt some were budding Mata Hari's; the security forces certainly knew who they were. On one occasion, a beautiful young girl in a short dress followed me into the toilet. She did not turn right into the ladies but left with me into the gents. As I came out of the cubicle, she ran the water for me and got some soap.

'Thank you,' I said.

'Can I come to your room tonight?' She tried to sound mischievous but ended up embarrassed. She was so young.

'It's all right. I've got a lot of work to do.'

'Can I come to your room for five minutes only?'

'I'm sorry but I'm with someone. Thank you all the same.' She barred my way out of the small toilet, then suddenly shrugged her shoulders and let me pass. 'If you change your mind, I'll be here!'

She returned to sit with two other equally beautiful young girls. When I met Jean-Victor in the bar the following evening, he seemed to recognize her and gave her a mouthful. She went red under her dark skin and looked very ashamed.

'She's a cousin of mine. I told her she should be studying and not hanging around here. But it's very difficult for her. She came to the city looking for a job and couldn't get one. This way she can earn money quickly and send some home to her family who'll think she's doing well.'

'Is she really a cousin?'

'Well, she comes from the same region as my family so she's a cousin.'

I could see a slight resemblance.

The hotel was crawling with security. There were armed guards at the gate of the hotel who checked all local visitors, and allowed through only those prostitutes who were prepared to pay them a big cut. In the lobby one morning, I counted twelve heavily armed soldiers in combat gear. Plain clothes agents strode about talking down their walkie-talkies.

Wesley slept at the end of our corridor with the filming equipment; at night, he kept his loaded revolver under his pillow. 'You can't trust anyone here,' he told me, taking off his dark glasses for a change. You know the room-boys – well, they're all secret agents.

Don't leave any notebooks on your desk, if you don't want them read.'

'I'll take your advice.'

'Good. If there's any trouble I'll shoot him down! You know I was the first man to fire a stinger rocket in Cameroon!'

While all this was going on, there was talk of an army coup. The country was strictly speaking without a government. After rubber-stamp elections in which the president was re-elected unopposed again he retained all the executive power. He had appointed a new prime minister, an Anglophone, no doubt to stem the separatist tide, but he had not yet formed a government. With the growing tension in the city, the ministerial hopefuls had come to the hotel and were encamped on the floor above me. In the grand confusion, I received one morning in my pigeonhole a fax intended for the new minister of finance in the room above mine. Jean-Victor talked to the minister of information on my behalf in order to get an interview with the president, only to find that he had become overnight the minister of communications. In the outcome, the interview never materialized. The president clearly had bigger fish to fry – and wanted to keep out of the fire. Maybe he was already hiding in his nuclear bunker. And there was also the little matter of Jean-Victor's father being in jail.

Not only was there no government during my stay but there seemed every prospect that the Cameroonian state would spilt asunder into its French-speaking and English-speaking regions. Cameroon was a classic illustration of the arbitrary nature of the borders of African states. After the First World War, German rule was replaced by the French in most of the territory and the British in the south-western highlands and the north. The latter area became part of Nigeria while the former merged in 1972 to form a single republic. But it had never been a happy marriage. This became clear when I visited a bi-lingual primary school in the centre of Yaoundé.

The headmaster, a large man in thick glasses, came from the English-speaking part of Cameroon. 'The children here are mainly from fathers who are English-speaking government officials and businessmen living in the capital,' he explained. 'They have no problem with bi-lingualism; they all speak English and French; in fact, most speak several other local languages.'

I visited a classroom full of girls in neat blue dresses and ironed white shirts who sat bolt upright at their desks. Standing in front of a large classroom of eager young faces took me straight back to my teaching days in Senegal. I explained where I came from and described how I was trying to sail around Africa by boat. Like every other African I met during my voyage, they beamed with interest. They seemed to love the idea that someone, especially an Englishman, should bother to try to go round their continent.

Chatting with the headmaster, it soon became clear that he was not happy about the present constitutional arrangements:

'The people in the south-west of Cameroon developed differently under the British from those under French rule. After independence, there used to be a federation between the two regions, but now there's one state. I would like to go back to a federation. We feel dominated by the French-speakers. The president has just chosen an English-speaking prime minister but it won't make any difference.'

Soon after this encounter, we decided to visit the English-speaking region around Mount Cameroon in the former British Cameroon. We travelled to Douala along the highway and then crossed the river Wouri. We sped past many small factories and workshops, with several containers gone missing from the port used as houses. Amongst the shacks which bordered the road, a few fine villas had sprung up behind high walls.

'Anything goes in Africa,' Wesley observed.

The road then climbed gently through plantations of palm oil and rubber trees which stretched in neat rows as far as the eye could see. The volcanic soils in this area were extremely fertile. From some boys at the side of the road, we bought some footballs made from strips of latex taken from the small cups catching the rubber sap. They soon deflated but it was a clever idea.

I gradually became aware that I was in a different country. At the crossroads in Tiko, the street vendors sold delicious sweet loaves of bread, not French baguettes. When we bought some for lunch, people spoke in 'pidgin', English mixed with words from the local language. The houses were different as well as the food. There were many small bungalows with tiled roofs built by the British in the forties. The business signs had their own special appeal: 'Beaufort – the Ultimate Thirst of Quench', 'Goodwill Medicine Store', 'Striker's Car Wash and Recreational Sport', 'Los Angeles Beauty Salon' and 'Bertha's Paradise Shopping Bazar'.

The only common denominators between the two parts of Cameroon seemed to be the economic crisis, the political stagnation, the popular frustration, the palm-wine specialists, and the '*mangemille*' – the thousand franc-eating policemen.

'We're close to the Nigerian border here,' Jean-Victor observed. 'Many Nigerians come down by *pirogues*, smuggling petrol, drugs, guns. Nigeria is a country of eighty million, with a quarter of Africa's population, but it's the worst example of capitalism. Nigerians will do anything for a fast buck.'

On the outskirts of Buea in the foothills of Mount Cameroon, I made out the severe lines of the old German governor's residence. The Germans before the First World War had chosen it as their capital because of the climate, and had started off the plantations of tea and coffee with forced labour. The British carried on the tradition. One of the last buildings of the town was an old post office, with a British red postbox outside. God only knows when the last collection was made; I posted a letter home out of pure nostalgia.

The weather was beautifully mild, with bright sun warming our backs. In the gardens and along the roadside roses and daisies had gone native and were flourishing. Although we were near the Equator apples and pears were growing well at this altitude.

Climbing in the foothills of Mount Cameroon, Hanno's 'Chariot of the Gods' reminded me of the highlands of Tanzania and Kenya. I loved the atmosphere; the air felt so clean and fresh, and the views were spectacular. Even the coarse grass underfoot and the scattered pine trees were reassuring. I decided there and then that I was designed to live in such a climate, not in the sultry steaminess of the equatorial coast. Unfortunately, the mountain summit was covered in cloud and without a map and compass we would have been foolish to try and climb it. For a tantalizing moment, the clouds lifted and the bright sun revealed a thick forest at its base, its alpine meadows growing over the old volcanic flows, and the jagged grey rock of its 13,352-foot high summit. I hoped one day I would return and climb the highest mountain in Central and West Africa.

Chapter Fifteen

The Heart of Africa

JEAN-VICTOR had not been back in Cameroon for four years, and festooned with presents, he took me to visit his family. Several strong young men opened the gates to his mother's house in Yaoundé and embraced him warmly; they were cousins up from the country looking after his mother while his father was in jail. She was delighted to see her son who hid himself away for years on end in the cold of northern Europe.

I was introduced to his sister, whom he had once described as 'Maître Felicité – skinny but tough and bright'. She was all of that, and a barrister and young mother to boot. Because she had complained at the Bar about the illegality of her father's imprisonment, she was no longer able to practise law. Such is the price of speaking out in such a regime. Felicité now changed nappies rather than briefs.

'Your family seems to have really run foul of the regime.'

'People say we're too arrogant. We don't beg for anything. We're too self-sufficient, too independent, and too educated for most people!'

The next day Jean-Victor's mother came to to see him in his room at the hotel at five-thirty in the morning. He had been out with Wesley to the early hours living it up in the night clubs. It is a tradition of their people that the mother sees her son very early in the morning before dawn if she has something important to discuss with him.

After much negotiation, Jean-Victor was also allowed to visit his father in prison for a couple of hours. He had been detained without trial for a couple of years, and there was no knowing when he would be let out. As a wealthy and influential man in the country, his conditions were not too bad, and he could get reading material and have visitors. But the uncertainty and confinement were depressing his spirits. Jean-Victor returned from the visit, visibly depressed.

'My father can't take much more of it. And I can't do anything about it. God knows I've tried. Only if there is a new regime will he be released.'

'With all the talk of multi-party democracy sweeping Africa, do you think Cameroon will ever be democratic?'

'It's democratic at the local level. Democracy exists in my village for instance: everyone participates in making decisions. But at the national level, that's something else.'

'Do you believe that people must be educated before they can be free.'

'That's what the colonialists said about Africans. You don't have to have formal education to be able to decide on how to run your affairs. We shall have to solve the problem of democracy in Cameroon as we have always done, in our way, in the African way, through debate and participation. I think by the end of century there will be democracy in my country.'

'I hope you're right.'

'I'll tell you what, I'll take you to see my village. You can discover the real Africa for yourself.'

We set off in a Toyota jeep and Mercedes Benz, piled up with presents and food. After leaving the Yaoundé–Douala highway, we bounced along a red dirt track. The heavy tropical showers had turned sections into mud baths, and on one bend the car slithered off into a ditch. Everyone got out, rolled up their trousers, and with Jean-Victor as the cheer leader, it was manhandled back on the road after a great deal of grunting and puffing. Everyone was splattered with red mud; Jean-Victor's expensive French shoes were no longer recognizable.

We passed neat homesteads by the roadside. The yards in front of the houses were planted with flowers, and nearby vegetable gardens flourished. In the rich equatorial soil, everything grew fast and well.

We eventually came to a bend by a small bridge. Tall trees of the forest grew up a hill on one side and down the other. We pulled off the road to a huddle of houses with corrugated roofs and mud walls. It was Jean-Victor's village, Mvila-Asi. About ten people lived there; most of the young had left to study or to find work in town. As we approached the yard in front of the house, Jean-Victor's grandmother and aunt got off a bench and let out a cry of delight. Arms outstretched, they came up and received a bearhug from their wayward boy. A couple of older men, less demonstrative, shook hands with us and bid us welcome.

'Where's your house?' I asked.

'They're all my houses. No one individual owns a house. Everyone shares things here. The village has been here for centuries.'

In the sparsely furnished meeting room, there was a faded photograph of Jean-Victor's grandfather. His relatives brought us coconut juice and delicious roasted peanuts. Wesley sat in a chair, his sun glasses on and his gun at his side. In a few minutes, he fell asleep.

Although the trees had been thinned out around the houses, the thick, luxuriant vegetation came right up to the backyards.

'When I was a boy of about ten, I went out of this door and saw a gorilla right there in the yard,' Jean-Victor recalled. 'They've gone much deeper in the forest now, but you still can see chimpanzees.'

'What do they grow here?'

'Yams, plaintains, sugar cane, vegetables. Let's go and look at some of the fields.'

We walked over the little bridge and then turned off the road up a muddy slippery path into the forest.

'You know before the First World War Cameroon was a German colony and my grandfather, who has only just died at the age of 102, remembered being beaten up by a German officer by that bridge. He would often go off into the bush to look for viper and cook it for himself. Usually, men never go into the kitchen. I always remember him smoking a pipe.'

We continued in single file up the path hacked out of the jungle. Insects buzzed, and the odd butterfly fluttered in the dappled light under the overarching canopy of huge trees. Invisible birds sang in the foliage. A flying snake leapt from one branch to another. Silence then settled for a few seconds like a newly launched boat. Jean-Victor's cousins continued to slash through the undergrowth with their machetes, clearing a path. I was deep in the heart of Africa.

'A machete is a man's best friend in the forest. They say you can tell how good a man is by how he uses his machete.'

After crossing a stream and walking up a slippery, narrow path, we came out into a small clearing. The ground had been tilled, and green shoots grew up here and there amongst the burnt stumps of trees. 'The men cut down the trees of the forest, but the women cultivate the land and plant the crops. They work very hard, from seven o'clock in the morning to mid-afternoon, without a break. They then have to go home and do the cooking and look after the house.'

There was a woman in the distance, bending over and putting her tools and firewood in a big wicker basket.

'Is that woman there a relative of yours?', I asked.

'Since she is working here on our land she must be. I say our land but we don't own the land, the land owns us.'

The fine looking woman came over, hugging Jean-Victor but avoiding eye-contact. Dark clouds were gathering overhead, and suddenly there was a flash of lightning and a clap of thunder.

'We'd better hurry. It'll rain soon.'

I asked Jean-Victor how old the woman was. He spoke to her in their lilting language; in the process she gave me a puzzled, sidelong look.

'Fifty-six. But she's surprised that you ask such a question.'

To make things worse, I then asked how many children she had had.

'Twelve deliveries. Nine children are still living.' It was difficult to believe; she looked so fit and strong.

As she gathered her things up and swung her heavy basket on to her back, thunder rumbled across the darkening sky. By the time we got back to the village, the heavens opened with a great crack of thunder overhead. We rushed onto the verandah of the meeting house, and splashed cool water gushing from the roof over our faces and arms.

After twenty minutes, the storm rolled on, the sun came out, and steam rose from the damp earth. Water gurgled in the countless gullies and streams hidden on the bottom of the forest floor.

'You know, Peter,' Jean-Victor said, 'I might leave here and travel the world but I'll always come back. This is where my ancestors are buried. This is where I belong.'

Before we left, he disappeared for a while. He came back carrying some guavas.

'I've taken them from around my grandfather's grave. I'll make a drink from them later.'

'Are you sad to leave?'

'Yes. My village is very important to me. The clan gives you spiritual as well as material support. Wherever you go they are always there waiting for you to come back. The real wilderness is in the city, not in the forest!'

As we drove back through the city centre, we heard gunfire and the screech of brakes; we were back in 'civilization'.

Not long afterwards Jean-Victor took me to see Roger Milla. At first, his name did not register. But then it dawned on me, he must be *the* Roger Milla, the star of the Cameroon football team and the 1990 World Cup in Italy, who used to dance in the corner whenever he scored a goal. He had not only led his team from nowhere to the quarter-final against England, but had suddenly brought enthusiasm and excitement back into a dull competition.

It turned out that Milla was Jean-Victor's brother-in-law. We turned up at his modest house in Yaoundé in front of which was parked his silver turbo-boosted Renault sports car.

We were let in by some of Milla's young assistants.

Africa's greatest football player was sitting in a white short-sleeved shirt and beige slacks in his lounge on a sofa. He was about to take his breakfast: a glass of grenadine, a glass of milk, and a strong coffee with French bread and jam – a habit he no doubt picked up while playing for clubs in France. He was now in his early forties but remarkably fit. His short-cropped hair was greying a little, and he had a front tooth missing.

We got talking in French about his projects.

'I'm working with young people and I've also become very concerned about the pygmies.'

'What's happening to them?'

'*Eh bien*,' said Milla between mouthfuls of fresh white bread, 'as the trees are being cut down, pygmies are being forced further and further into the forest. Those who make contact with the outside world often become lost. I'm trying to help them integrate into modern society, by organizing cultural and sporting activities. I've already brought two pygmy football teams to Yaoundé who were a great success. They make very good football players.'

'Any chance of meeting them?'

'As it happens, I'm going to visit a pygmy encampment in the forest in a couple of days; if you're interested, you can come along.'

When the time came to leave, Milla was not to be found. 'He's often like that,' Jean-Victor laughed. 'Once he was invited to play at a friendly match of the World's Masters in Antwerp. He missed the first half, but turned up for the second in a helicopter. As he was lowered on to the pitch, he was still doing up his football boots. Within two minutes, he scored a goal. The crowd went crazy. That's his style!'

As he was talking, I vaguely remembered a scandal about Milla which had hit the British tabloid papers. Jean-Victor explained: 'The British Football Association invited Cameroon to have a friendly match with England after the World Cup meeting early in 1991 at Wembley Stadium. They sold all the tickets with a photograph of Milla on them. When it came to the selection of the players, for some reason Milla was not included. The FA insisted that Milla play in the team and he was eventually persuaded to come over, but when the Cameroon football authorities and the FA still refused to pay him, he decided to return home. Milla has a maverick mind, which is not always to his own good.'

Milla wisely did not take his silver sports car with its low wheelbase. Instead we sat together in the back of a Renault driven by one of his associates. We first went to Edea where we bought some presents for the pygmies we were going to visit: salt, soap, rice, wine, cigarettes, and matches. I was not sure how appropriate these gifts might be, but that's what they wanted. Jean-Victor told me: 'Pygmies are very special people. They don't deal with money, only exchange gifts. In the old days, if you gave them a little salt, they would give you half an elephant.'

Walking through the streets with Milla, I realized what it was like to be a national hero. As soon as he got out of the car, a crowd immediately gathered around us. People came forward nervously wanting to shake the hand of Africa's most famous footballer. He returned the worship with good humour, shaking people's hands, observing to me in his deep guttural voice: 'That's Africa for you. You have to say hallo to all the family!'

We then travelled to Kribi on the coast. Beautiful white sand stretched along the isolated, palm-fringed beaches. The Germans had settled here at the beginning of the century, to be followed by the British, and finally the president who had a palace on a headland. We called on the regional police headquarters to get permission to go up country into the jungle to make contact with the pygmies.

After travelling another seventy kilometres inland, we eventually ended up several hours later in a village called Bipindi, where we presented ourselves to the police headquarters, a small house with a large pole in front flying the national flag. There was a Catholic Mission nearby so our white faces were not entirely shocking. At 37° centigrade, it was unbearably humid and hot. Jean-Victor informed me that it sometimes went up to 45°.

We were now deep in the equatorial forest. We drove down a narrow track, which was heavily rutted and often disappeared in flood water; when this happened everyone piled out to push the car out of the slippery mud. The tall trees and thick vegetation of the forest hemmed us in on both sides. The sun barely penetrated the luxuriant foliage above our heads. We then abandoned the car and walked on foot through the forest to come to a small encampment with several huts made from palm fronds. A group of women and children huddled together around a fire under a canopy. There were no men around. We had arrived.

When some of the women got up shyly to meet us, I was surprised to see that the pygmies were not as small as I had expected; perhaps a little under five feet tall. As we exchanged greetings, they huddled together to form one organic mass of humanity.

'Have you noticed how they look at us?' Milla said. Their eyes were gentle and sad and unfocussed. They did not look at us, but through us. It was an eerie experience.

'The men heard us arrive and have disappeared into the bush. We must wait until they come back.'

It turned out that they had been expecting us the day before and prepared a feast with music and dancing. While we waited, a little girl played on a finger harp a complicated rhythm and half-sang a most moving melody. She was ten years old, but looked six and had a swollen belly.

'Pygmies are some of the most subtle singers and musicians there are,' observed Jean-Victor. 'They are masters of polyphony'.

After about twenty minutes, the men started to reappear in twos or threes out of the forest. They carried machetes, catapults and bundles of leaves. Their faces were grave and wary at first, but then one or two suddenly broke into smiles. In the end, there must have been about thirty people in the encampment.

The distribution of the gifts began. Milla and I gave the rice, soap, wine, cigarettes, and salt to individuals who queued up but they then put them all back in one pile.

'You see, they don't take anything for themselves but share everything here,' said Jean-Victor. 'They have no concept of private property, of mine and yours. When they return to the camp after hunting and gathering, they share all that they bring.'

'Do they have any chiefs?'

'They value the wisdom of the elders and those who have special skills but they do not have chiefs like other tribes. It is something that outsiders find very frustrating; they always want a chief to deal with, but pygmies all decide on the things that matter to them together.'

In fact, pygmies are the world's greatest anarchists. They have no hierarchy or domination in their society, no leaders, law-makers or government. They have a deep-seated reluctance to lead or to be aggressive; if someone pushes himself forward, everyone else feels embarrassed. They have customs and rituals, as every people in the world, but no laws, judges, police, courts or prisons. If some members fall into dispute or harm others, then the whole group tries to restore the harmony and not wreak vengeance. In the end, the forest itself will deal with any serious disruption of the natural order. For them, the forest is God, and God is the forest.

The encampment we visited was one of the nearest to the road. The influences of the wider society were already apparent. The men had fine physiques, muscular and without an ounce of fat. Normally in the forest, living as hunter-gatherers off small animals, snakes, birds and wild plants, pygmies are fitter than surrounding farming people. But as the gifts we had brought showed, they were supplementing their traditional diet with white rice and malnutrition was creeping amongst their children, some of whom had swollen bellies. One man had a nasty goitre in his neck.

The pygmies took us deep into the forest, cutting a path with their machetes through the dense vegetation, in order to show us some of their traps. They walked carefully with bare feet. The forest floor was seething with life: ants, beetles, all kinds of insects. The traps were so well concealed that it would have been impossible to spot them without being shown. One consisted of a long pole set overhead by a stream; any snake or monkey would naturally want to use it, only to be caught in a noose at the far end. The men walked in single file through the forest, machetes in their hands, spears over their bare shoulders, chanting a tune which I shall always remember but cannot repeat.

Back at the camp, I noticed an old woman lying in a hut.

'She's from a neighbouring tribe,' explained Milla. 'They bring their sick people to the pygmies because they have great healing powers and understand the medicinal value of the herbs and plants of the forest. We can learn a great deal from the pygmies about medicine.'

'They also have a special way of giving birth', Jean-Victor added. 'It's never a problem. People come to them to learn how to do it.'

Pygmies, about a quarter of million of them, are spread right across central Africa. As hunter-gatherers, they represent the oldest kind of human society. Unfortunately none of the nation states in the region accepts that they have any legal rights to the forests which have always been their home. Governments claim ownership of the forests and are keen to turn the pygmies into farmers. In the process, they lose their way of life, identity and culture.

While we had been walking in the jungle to see the traps, Wesley had being doing some of his own business back at the encampment. Dressed again completely in white, he was sitting on a log with a couple of tiny children on his knee. In his free hand, he was holding the leg of a tiny bird which he was eating with extreme delicacy. Next to him was a young woman holding a bowl containing several other little birds together with bananas in a sauce. She wanted him to stay.

'These people are very intelligent people,' Milla told me, waving his hand around his head to chase away the insects. 'When they go to school, they are always at the top of the class. But they find it difficult to integrate – that's why I'm trying to help them. I know the case of two pygmies who went to university in Yaoundé and got some good jobs. Then one day, they just took of their ties and shoes and returned to the forest. No one heard of them again.'

The forest for the pygmies is their whole world. Inside it they are relaxed, alert and playful; outside, in the world of big people and buildings and cars, they are wary and retiring. Even in the settled villages, they move slowly and appear resigned.

The pygmies say: 'The forest is our home; when we leave the forest, or when the forest dies, we shall die.' They are potentially the guardians of the green lung of the earth. If the logging continues at the present rate in central Africa, they are a doomed people. With them will disappear great wisdom, not only of the forest creatures and plants, but of a whole way of life which is in profound harmony with the earth.

Chapter Sixteen

To Think *in* Front *of a* Lion

O<small>N</small> my arrival in Cameroon, I had no ship lined up for my onward
journey down towards South Africa. I rang from Yaoundé the Delmas
shipping agency in Douala; having travelled down with the *Delphine Delmas*,
I was in a position to call on the company's goodwill. I found in Africa,
where things are so unstable and uncertain, that people tend to help each
other more than in Europe, and pass you on from friend to friend. This
benevolent tribalism worked in European and African quarters. I spoke to
a Mr Tsanis who said:

'Ships from Europe don't go down much further than the Congo, because
of the war in Angola and because of sanctions in South Africa. I don't see
you being able to get there. Still, I'll keep a look out for you.'

He came back a few days later confirming that the only ship available
within the next few weeks was another Delmas ship to Pointe Noire in
the Congo. I looked the Congo up on my map and decided that if I
could not find a ship there to take me further south I would travel on
the famous railway which cut through the jungle from Pointe Noire to
Brazzaville. I would then try to catch a plane to Namibia, or failing that
to Cape Town.

With this plan in mind, I went to the Congolese Embassy down a
bumpy mud track in the suburbs of Yaoundé, where the receptionist
in a sparse room took my passport and returned it the next day with
a visa for a month. It was stamped with the slogan '*Unité – Travail –*

Progrès' which clearly expressed an aspiration rather than a fact. I also rang a contact in Brazzaville whom Jean-Victor had described to me as '*my very* good friend, the rich but lovely and nice Miss Motse Akanaty, fashion designer.' I telephoned her in Brazzaville, without any difficulty, but sadly this intriguing lady was out.

While I was at it, I also went with Jean-Victor to the headquarters of Cameroonian Frontier Police where, after a long family chat, his 'uncle' stamped my passport with a visa which was valid for several entries and exits. My guidebook suggested that it can be very difficult renewing a visa in Cameroon. Once again, in Africa it helps to have contacts.

After about ten days, it came time for Jean-Victor and the film crew to fly back to Europe. On the way back from the airport to my fortress-hotel in Yaoundé, Wesley stopped the car and borrowed $5 to buy a viper from a boy at the side of the road. It was about five foot long and as thick as a man's arm.

'Are they very dangerous?' I asked him.

'They can kill you. If a viper bites you, you must immediately put some white fur from a woman's vagina on to the bite and then treat it with herbs two days later.'

'What are you going to do with the viper?'

'It's for my colonel. He loves it for breakfast; it gives him strength.'

We then called in on Colonel Ze ('Lion') Akono, who had been responsbile for retaking Yaoundé during the attempted coup in 1984. The Lion was a huge man of eighteen stone. He sat, sweating profusely, on a sofa in his spacious house in a track suit, his legs apart and his belly loose. We were served soft drinks by a young woman who looked tired.

'I've just returned from the north where we're expecting trouble. I caught fever up there. If you like I could take you up to see the gorrillas.

'Are there many left?'

'A lot. The people up there hunt them and eat them.'

Wesley showed great deference to the colonel. After our meeting, he told me:

'Colonel Ze is looking after you in Cameroon. 'His men are looking after your security. He's a very powerful man in Cameroon. That's why I have to keep in with him.'

The daily stories continued of attacks on garage stations, shoot-outs in the streets, and rumours of a military coup. The British chargé d'affaires rang me at the hotel and told me not to travel at night. 'It's very dangerous. Only yesterday during the day one of our officers was stopped in broad daylight near the US embassy and had his car stolen.'

He also invited me to have lunch with the ambassador, who drove a Jaguar with the number plate 007, to meet another traveller, Ffyonna Campbell, who was passing through. She had been walking from South Africa for three months and intended to cross the whole of the continent on foot. She had a support team in two Land Rovers who followed her, but the chargé d'affaires told me that she had recently encountered great difficulties, 'especially as a woman'. Unfortunately, I was unable to go to the lunch and never met the intrepid traveller.

On Palm Sunday, 12 April, I wrote in my notebook a list of the day's tasks:

How to get a spoon at breakfast
How to tell the difference between a waiter and a secret agent
How to find a lift that works
How to keep cool
How to charm my way around Cameroon
How to see God in a policeman's face

Now that the provisional government, Jean-Victor and the film crew had all left, life calmed down at the Mount Fébé Hotel. I went for a walk in the wooded hill above it and came across a Benedictine monastery set in some beautiful grounds with a wonderful view of the hills surrounding Yaoundé. A young African monk unlocked a few rooms which had one of the finest collection of masks, sculptures and furniture in the country. I found it ironic that it had been left to Benedictine monks to preserve the artefacts of the ancient animist traditions.

On the way back to the hotel, I thought about the close connection between the spiritual and natural in the traditional African view of the world. The main goal of most traditional societies in Africa was to possess as much vital force as possible; all the myths, rituals, ceremonies and artistic endeavour are intended for this end. But this can have a positive and negative side. Colonel Ze and Wesley both had vital force, but they sometimes used it for violent ends. In a democratic and decentralized society, families and individuals all shared vital force, but in a strongly centralized kingdom like Dahomey it became personified in one individual who was considered a divine king.

Something of the calm of the monastery stayed with me when I returned to the hotel. I sat in the shade of a large mango tree near by and observed a yellow weaver bird making its nest, weaving bits of grass with frenetic haste into a ball. There was not only one bird, but dozens of them, all at their task, lightening the dark green leaves of the mango tree with flashes of bright yellow.

I suddenly realized how much I loved Africa. Not the Africa of imported luxury all around me, but the Africa of the mango tree and the weaver bird, of the pygmies and Jean-Victors, of the woman cultivating her field in the forest and the teacher in his school, of the young prostitute and the balafon player. Whatever the dire state of its politics, at the heart of Africa there is not darkness but light. The darkness lies in the European mind, not in the eyes of the children on the river banks or at the roadside.

When I finally left my place under the mango tree, I found a nest had fallen out of the tree. It was made of interwoven strands of dry coarse grass and smelt wonderfully of the sun-drenched earth. I placed it carefully in my pocket and carried it with me for the rest of my voyage.

On my return to the hotel, I found a message waiting for me from Delmas shipping agency. The diligent Mr Tsanis had found out that in three weeks time there was a ship called MV *Tilly* of Tropic Lines travelling down to South Africa, calling at Libreville (Gabon), Pointe Noire (Congo), Matadi (Zaïre), and then Cape Town and Durban. He contacted the German owner who agreed to take me provided that I paid $50 a day, signed a master's indemnity form against any possible insurance claims, and made a written declaration that I was not in any way connected with drug trafficking.

They were taking no chances. At this stage, I would have signed virtually anything. The *Tilly*, the agent assured me, was the only boat leaving from

Douala to Cape Town for months. I had been incredibly lucky to get a passage on board, even though it meant kicking my heels for a few weeks longer than I had intended in Cameroon.

Out of the blue while staying at the Mount Fébé hotel in Yaoundé, I got a message from England to say that my friend Jeremy Gane would fly in to see me. Jeremy was my oldest friend, and we had shared a house together as students. After travelling widely around Europe and north Africa, for the last decade he had been making a living as a clock maker and repairer.

I went down to Douala airport to meet him from the Nairobi plane. I searched the faces of the passengers passing from the baggage lounge. No Jeremy. Apart from a few European businessmen, they were all Africans, in smart suits and overloaded with baggage. I checked at the airline desk, but they had not heard of him. The next plane from Nairobi, they informed me, would be in a couple of days. Before leaving the airport, I decided to check with the police.

It was just as well. I immediately recognized my friend in an old-fashioned check shirt, with his rucksack thrown over his broad shoulders. He was leaning over a table trying to explain something in French to the police officer in a small office. In the corner stood a rifle.

'Jeremy, arrested already! You could have waited a little!'

'Pete, am I pleased to see you! They arrested me when I got off the plane because I arrived without a visa. They want 20,000 francs for the visa, but I've only got some Kenyan shillings and a few dollars.'

By Cameroonian standards, the sum was not great, and I went off to change some money. Once it was handed over, a girl stuck some stamps to that value in Jeremy's passport and we were free.

'*A votre service, messieurs!*' said the police officer saluting. Not all were corrupt.

We took a taxi to the Sawa hotel in Douala, and I caught up with the news. He handed over some mail and sweets from home; the chocolate, already melted in the heat, was delicious.

It was great to see him, but why, I asked, had he come out to Africa?

'I wanted to see you of course, but I also I wanted to break out of a rut. I was very close to becoming suburban man. I may be middle-aged but that doesn't mean my days of adventure are over. It's the same for everyone. They just have to decide to get off their butts.'

He had climbed Kilimanjaro in the wrong season, and despite the swirling cloud and reluctance of his guide, had made it to the top of Africa, over 19,000 feet above sea level.

'It was an incredible experience. I don't think I'll be the same again.' I had climbed Kilimanjaro ten years previously and knew what he meant.

The next day Wesley called at our hotel in a four-wheel-drive white Toyota. He was dressed again all in white – trousers, shirt, socks and shoes – carrying his black swagger stick and wearing his black sun-glasses. He was accompanied this time by two very beautiful women. Even his teeth seemed whiter than usual as he smiled. He was clearly in a good mood.

'I can take you to Yaoundé if you want. Jean-Victor asked me to keep an eye on you until you leave.'

We readily agreed and, thanks to Jean-Victor's friend behind the desk, paid our bills at half-rate, the tariff for residents. This time, we cruised at top speed, a hundred miles an hour, and made it to Yaoundé without stopping in a couple of hours. The same deserted highway. The same brooding rainforest. The same thoughts of gorillas in the mists. The same road blocks which we sped through without slowing down.

Before he left, Jeremy gave me a slip of paper with some lines written on it. He had been practising *aikido* and *T'ai-chi* for some years, and passed on some of its wisdom:

> If you can find the point of balance in the body,
> You can easily settle the details.
> If you can settle the details,
> You will stop rushing around.
> If you stop rushing around,
> Your mind will become calm.
> If your mind becomes calm,
> You can think in front of a tiger.
> If you can think in front of a tiger,
> You will surely succeed.

It seemed excellent advice, especially for a traveller in Africa who has to encounter unpredictable security forces, steet crazies, bureaucratic delay and occasional disorientation. I replaced the 'self' for 'body', thinking it more appropriate to centre one's whole being, and 'lion' for 'tiger' since there are no tigers in Africa. I also saw the lion as a symbol of danger within and without; a psychological fear as well as a man with a gun. Thereafter whenever I was confronted with a difficult situation, I reminded myself of the lines and relaxed. It really worked.

I said goodbye to Jeremy who was taking a flight back to Nairobi and then home after a few day's visit. It had been great to see my old friend, even if we had been restricted in our movements around town and the country. I think he was quite happy to leave the hotel; he did not like being picked up all the time.

After Jeremy left I returned to Douala and stayed at the Sawa hotel. It was virtually under a state of seige. Everyone advised me not to go out at night and even during the day. That did not prevent me from touring the city. Built on swamps, by a wide river, it was not particularly appealing. It had no grand architecture, and the fine old colonial buildings were being left to fall down. Yet despite the sultry heat, most Cameroonians prefer Douala to Yaoundé; as Jean-Victor put it, Yaoundé stands for 'food, politics, plain-clothes policemen and expensive girls, while there is something special about Douala, something more civilized'.

Wesley turned up one day at the hotel and took me to visit his parents in the suburbs. 'When I see my parents, it's hard for me,' he said as we pulled up outside the white villa. The house was comfortably furnished, with a cassette player and large Chinese clock. His parents were looking after his son while his young wife was in Paris studying for a doctorate in economics; when she had finished he hoped to make some money and then come back to Cameroon and start up a camp for training security forces.

Wesley's son was eighteen months old. The father was broad-shouldered and thick-necked but the son was half Charles Atlas and half Michelin man – or rather a black version of one of Michelangelo's cherubs.

'He's very strong, eh,' Wesley chuckled as he passed over to his mother some tins of powdered milk with extra vitamins he had brought from Paris.

When I approached the child, he started to cry out. 'Don't worry. He's frightened of whites. You know, when he was born, Colonel Ze got his soldiers to shoot a gorilla for me as a present. The custom is to take the bones of the gorilla and grind them down into a powder. You then mix it with the mother's milk for the baby. You also make a paste and rub it all over the baby's body. That way the baby becomes as strong as a gorilla!'

The last count I had heard was that there were about a thousand gorillas left in the mists of the whole of Africa.

'*L'Afrique est très mystique!*' Wesley observed as we left.

On 3 May, I was three months into my voyage and still on the Equator. I could see the ships steaming up and down the wide green river every morning from my balcony. I was assured by the Delmas agent Mr Tsanis that *Tilly* was expected from Abidjan in a couple of days' time.

I rang home. It was my daughter's fourteenth birthday, and it was a pleasure to hear that Jenny was better, the sun was shining, and they would be having a cake in the garden under the beech trees with friends. I promised them I would try to get them to come out and see me during my voyage if I ever made it to East Africa.

As for me, still sweating and waiting in the tropics, I did some yoga on my balcony as the sun rose, and then went down to the spacious garden of the hotel. A multi-coloured lizard bobbed its head up and down, looking at me askance with a round beady eye, and then ran away when I threw it some crumbs. Black butterflies flittered around under the wide mango trees and shady palms. Swallows dived, chasing insects above an ornamental pond. The delicate, sweet-smelling, rose-tinted flowers of a frangipani tree had been knocked down on to the coarse grass by a downpour during the night. The earth smelt cool and fresh. The squeals of happy children in the distance drowned out for a while the birdsong of a new morning. I too felt content.

I had a swim alone in the warm waters of the blue pool. A little kingfisher with a long orange beak and grey chest dived into the water. It then flew up to perch on a lamp where it stretched out, showing the full splendour of its turquoise wings. It wiped its beak before flying down to the water again. It did this several times. It seemed so full of health, poise and beauty. I was reminded once more of my seagull in Lisbon, and felt that my kingfisher too was a good omen.

As I was swimming sheets of lightning lit up the grey horizon. Black clouds slowly rolled in from the sea across the awakening city. Then there was a huge clap of thunder followed by a torrential downpour. The kingfisher shook its plumage. A monkey jumped down from a tree nearby me and took off across the grass. Wafting from the verandah by the bar, I could just make out the words of a song: '*C'est si bon!*', which the female singer, in keeping with the country's bilingual policy, repeated as 'It's so good!' With the cool rain pouring over my upturned face, splashing into my mouth, and coursing down my naked body, I could only agree.

Although I had to wait several weeks for my next ship, I no longer felt 'stuck' as I had done in Morocco. During the last three months a change had come over me. I now liked the leisurely pace, the inevitable delays. I sowed a few seeds here and there, and then stood back and waited to see what would grow. I wanted to be like the kingfisher by the pool, quietly alert, aware of what was going on, but not focusing on any one thing in particular.

Later in the morning, I took a taxi to visit Delmas shipping agency to find out the latest on the long-waited *Tilly*. Mr Tsanis had some good news for me. *Tilly* would be arriving on 7 May in the late evening and would be leaving for Libreville the following day. On her outward voyage from Durban, she had called at Cape Town, Walvis Bay, Cabinda, Abidjan, San Pedro, Tema, Lomé and Cotonou. She was now returning via Libreville, Pointe Noire, Matadi and Cape Town. She was expected to arrive in Durban on 20 May after a two-week voyage. She was an old ship carrying general cargo, with a German captain and chief engineer and a Filipino crew. Perfect.

Chapter Seventeen

The Unicorn

I WAS delighted to come across *Tilly* moored in a quiet corner of Douala dock. After my last two modern container ships, it was great to be joining an old cargo ship, with old-fashioned derricks and rounded lines. She was about 150 metres long, painted black above the water-line, and reddish brown below. Her bridge and accommodation quarters aft were painted white. On her funnel was the head of of a unicorn, a mythical creature which can only be caught if a young virgin is placed in his haunts; with its horn of truth, it was in the Middle Ages said to represent Jesus Christ. She was registered in Panama, a well-known land of justice.

As I approached the ship, I noticed that the stevedores were loading trunks of *azoumé* wood with 'Wellington' painted on them, presumably their destination. I went up the gangway and was welcomed on board by the Filipino crew. One of them took me up to the bridge where I met captain Fritz Witts a handsome man in his early forties, with thick white hair and piercing blue eyes. He was slow of speech, as if carefully choosing the right word in English. He was polite, formal and helpful.

The captain took me to my cabin which was next door to his. It had *Lotse* over the door, German for pilot. It was a spacious cabin on the starboard side of the ship with a desk, day bed, and large porthole. The fittings and cupboard were made from mahogany in an age when tropical hardwood was cheap and plentiful. He also showed me the dining room, again with dark wood panelling. On the wall was a faded photograph of an old German businessman with greying hair and pointed beard in a dapper suit.

'That's Ernst Russ, the owner of the shipping company. The ship is named after one of his daughters.'

'Ernst Russ? I was told the ship was owned by Tropic Lines and yet I see that it has a Unicorn on its funnel.'

'It's a complicated business. Ernst Russ Company owns the ship but it has been registered as Unicorn Lines in Panama and it is being chartered by Tropic Lines in South Africa. Our present home port is Durban.'

'But I thought South African ships were boycotted along the West African coast because of sanctions.'

'They are officially. To get round it we had manifestos made up in Maputo, Mozambique, and they were flown into Durban. On the ship's documents the destinations of the cargo is given as Yokohamo in Japan or Wellington in New Zealand.'

So that was what Wellington was all about on the logs I had seen.

'The politicians and big businessmen know all about it but turn a blind eye. They want the trade. For fifteen years, I've been sailing up and down the coast without any trouble from the African authorities. The only problems are the pirates.'

'So now that sanctions against South Africa are soon to be lifted, you can trade more openly?'

'Yes. It's okay. We can be open now. We are happy now.'

The captain showed me around the ship and gave me some more details of her past. She had been made in Hamburg in 1966, a very old ship by today's standards when many are scrapped after six years. Her total dead tonnage was 10,616 tonnes; width nineteen metres, draught eighteen metres. She had always been a general cargo ship, loading and unloading her holds with her sturdy derricks festooned with greased wires. But in order to adapt to the new age of the container in the mid seventies she had been cut in half in the shipyards in South Shields and been lengthened by fifteen metres. She had been painted countless times, but it had not stopped the sea from rusting many of her working parts on deck. It was strange when walking amidships to think that metres of British steel were holding the stern and bow of the German ship together.

'What cargo do you usually carry to the west coast of Africa?'

'From South Africa, we take steel products, paper, chemicals and also fruit.'

'Fruit? I can't imagine other African countries wanting fruit.'

'Fruit from Cape Province, like apples, pears, plums and grapes. They only grow in a temperate climate.'

'And on the homeward voyage?'

'Logs, timber, cocoa, coffee, cotton, and palm oil.'

It was the classic terms of trade between industrial and agricultural countries, Europe and the Third World: manufactured goods out, primary products back.

At five o'clock that night I joined the German captain and chief engineer in the dining room. The rest of the Filipino officers ate in an adjoining room. We sat at the end of a long table, with the captain at the head. It was very different from the *Delphine Delmas*. The young Filipino steward, on his first voyage, was so nervous that he often got things wrong, much to the annoyance of the captain. Being English, I was always served a pot of tea with my food. It was invariably cheese and ryebread to begin, followed by some meat or fish. We never had fresh vegetables except salad and rarely a desert.

The captain and the chief engineer had been sailing together for a long time and had exhausted most topics of conversation. There were long, though not uncomfortable, periods of silence at table. Over the next few days I learned that captain Fritz Witts had been born in Lübeck, the birthplace of Thomas Mann, the son of a fisherman. He grew up near the border with East Germany, a physical as well as a psychological barrier. He was used to divided nations. He had worked hard to become a navigation officer, and been master of the *Tilly* for fifteen years, but he had few illusions:

'When I was a young man, a captain was a king in Germany but now it means nothing. I would like to live in South Africa but my wife does not like it. I go back to Germany every six months for my three months leave. Unfortunately in Germany merchant seamen retire at sixty-three, not at fifty-five as in France. I've still got a long time to go.'

The chief engineer's name was Helmuth Anderfuhr. He was an efficient, affable man in his early fifties, a little plump with small eyes and a quiff of white hair. He skipped lunch with the captain in an attempt to keep his weight down, which was difficult since he liked to quench his thirst after the engine room with beer. He came from Hamburg and showed me photographs of his comfortable house with a large garden in the country. His two sons were now grown up. This was his last voyage after thirty-three years with the same company, and he was bitter about being made redundant.

'I have given my life to the company, and now they get rid of me because I am too expensive. For me, it's *finito la musica*. They get Filipino crew for half the price. They know not how to work. If I not go after them, they leave tools all around.'

'What does your wife think of you being away?'

'I have much care with her. A seaman has much experience, but you have to keep quiet with your wife or she's fed up with all your experience of the world.'

That night Fritz and Helmuth invited me to join them at the German seaman's mission in Douala. It had a fine interior courtyard sheltered by tall palm trees. We sat at one of the many tables on the grass by the pool and were served cool beer with plates of roasted peanuts.

That night a German brass band which was touring Cameroon had come to play for their compatriots. It was being sponsored by the 'Anglo-German Friendship Society' in Cameroon and both the British and German consuls were there making a lot of noise and swilling beer with a party of friends. The British consul was a huge mountain of a man with a beard, he was sweating profusely in the heat but seemed quite at home.

Compared to all the African musicians I had heard, they were incredibly stiff, seated on the edge of their chairs and reading music on special stands they had brought with them. They soon began to sweat in the sultry night. The music was beautiful, nonetheless, silvery as the stars in the dark firmament above and soft as the sea breeze passing through the swaying palm trees.

A German at our table told a story – a plain, old-fashioned Afrikaner story:

'In Lusaka, the capital of Zambia, there's a statue of a black man breaking chains. One day, it was covered with a tent.

"Why?" asked a passer-by to a workman.

"It's nothing important," he replied. The passer-by lifted the tent, and underneath read the words sprayed on the statue: "You kaffirs break everything."' Laughs all round.

'Now that Kaunda's gone, they're inviting white farmers to buy land in Zambia,' he added. 'The place's collapsed. There's not a lift working in Lusaka. They now realize they can't do without the white man.'

The chief engineer had an even lower opinion of Africa.

'All shit in Africa now. Thirty years ago Zaïre a good place. But Africa go down with the white man.'

'Maybe things will get better with the wave of democracy passing through the continent,' I suggested.

'The black man only knows how to obey orders. With dictator, he tells the people what to do and they do it. With democracy in Africa, the black man says "I'm the boss now" and they start discussing – all think they are bosses and nothing is done.'

'It can't all be like that.'

'It is so. Take Luanda. It was a beautiful port with black and white mosaics on the dock. Now all destroyed. It's gone back to the beach. You have to anchor off shore now in the lagoon and one in two ships are pirated by people in canoes with AK 45's. Africa is bankrupt, all bankrupt.'

When it was time to go, the German pastor took us back to the ship in the mission's minibus. Outside, there were many prostitutes in the shadows, ready to waylay the tipsy sailors on their way back to their ships.

'Don't go with them,' the chief advised, 'too much disease.'

We set sail from Douala at midday on 8 May, a month after my arrival. It was wonderful to be at sea under the open sky again and good to get away from the sultry, menacing atmosphere of Douala. Even the dock where *Tilly* had berthed was strewn with litter and rotting garbage, foul-smelling and rat-infested. Standing on the wing of the bridge, sea-breeze on my face, I breathed deeply and let out the stale memory of the city's fighting and despair. The engines thudded away. Mangrove swamps slipped by as we floated down the green, eddying waters of the river and out into the grey-blue sea. *Tilly* turned due south heading to our next port, Libreville.

It was only a short distance from Douala to Libreville, about twelve hours in all. I arrived in the capital of Gabon for the second time during the night. I went ashore and spent the following day with Michael Fanguinoveny; his brother Eugène was away at the time.

Since Michael was a director of the port, we had no trouble passing through the dock gates. I had lunch with his family, wife and three children, in a beautiful round bungalow by the sea. Their teenage sons remained silent at table, speaking only when spoken to, showing great respect to their father.

After lunch we drove north to Cap Estérias about an hour away along the coast. After some rolling countryside, we travelled through a beautiful rainforest, with magnificient stands of towering trees. Although the road had been repaired six months before, it was already beginning to crumble in the sandy soil because the contractors had failed to provide a proper base. 'Like building a palace on a marsh,' Michael commented.

Cap Estérias was a peaceful fishing village. We visited a compound where a group of women, young girls and babies were chatting and playing together under a palm-leaf awning in front of their wooden house. The men's nets were drying in the sun. One of the older girls was plaiting the hair of her younger sister, a complicated and enjoyable process which would last for several hours.

The palm trees sloped right down to the beach of the little bay. I came across a couple of young children playing in the ruins of an old fisherman's hut, the lush vegetation pushing its way through the rotten boards of the verandah. Just above the high water mark on the sand, was a large tree trunk being cut to form a dug-out canoe. Several others had been washed ashore from the passing ships and lay half-buried in the sand. On the beach left by the ebbing tide, a little girl in an orange dress played with the wet sand, letting it flow between her fingers, digging shallow holes and patting it into pies. She was completely at one with the deserted beach and when I said hallo she got me to join in with her play.

From out of the dense vegetation suddenly appeared an immaculate Frenchman, cartridges in a belt around his waist and rifle slung over his shoulder. He seemed completely out of place, not only by the cleanliness and expense of his hunting clothes, but by his wish to end the gentle balance of the afternoon for the children and birds. He disappeared around the headland in the shimmering heat, a white figure in shining boots and khaki hat.

'These fishermen lead good lives,' Michael observed. 'They can earn enough from their fish which they sell in town and their children go to school. Their fathers had no choice but to follow their fathers, their children can decide for themselves.'

'But can't that create problems. What if the children decide to go to town to find work, despising the fisherman's life?'

'That's true. The rural exodus is a great problem throughout Africa. The young think they'll be happier in town, with electricity and running water and bright lights, but when they get there they can't find work. Then they get very frustrated and turn to banditry, theft, delinquency. The answer is not to stop education, but to educate people to realize the value of village life and to make living in the country more attractive.'

The next morning, Sunday, I went with the captain and the chief engineer to the local German seaman's mission set in beautiful gardens with a swimming pool and bar. At the door, there was a painting of a vicious dog to frighten away intruders, but inside the German pastor and his wife were very welcoming. A few French couples and an Indian family were around the pool but no Africans.

Renate, the pastor's wife, had been living in Africa for eighteen years and was looking forward to returning to work in Europe. I asked what it was like living in Libreville.

'The Gabonese are not very friendly. They do not mix. They all want the French way of life. There are enough doctors in town, but none want to go and work in the bush like Schweitzer.'

That certainly had not been my experience, but then I had only been in Gabon for a few days with some Gabonese friends. I'm sure the lack of contact was as much the fault of arrogant expatriates as wary locals.

After a swim, we had a few beers and were joined by the German captain and chief engineer of a tramp ship in port. They were heading north to Cotonou, Lomé, Conakry and Casablanca. After several rounds of good, cold German beer with beaded bubbles winking at the brim, the conversation turned to the Second World War.

Helmuth turned to me and said. 'My father was captured by the English in North Africa and spent four years as a prisoner-of-war in a camp in Egypt. It was very difficult.'

I didn't tell him that my father had been a Spitfire pilot and been shot down three times. Instead I said: 'I think we should go beyond the Second World War. It wasn't our fault: the sins of the fathers can't be passed down to the sons.'

'Ya. It was ze English who had concentration camps first in South Africa during ze Boer War,' Helmuth reminded me.

'Hitler was Austrian, not German, anyway,' added the tramping engineer.

'You're a writer,' said his captain. 'I wonder who has the copyright to *Mein Kampf*. It's selling many more copies now because the East Germans want to read it. They say that the KGB have many of Hitler's works in Moscow.'

'Perhaps Hitler and Eva Braun are buried under Lenin – yes, and they can bury Gorbachev on top!' added his shipmate, taking another long draught from his Bavarian beer.

'All in past,' said Helmuth. 'In former times, Germany make big mistake but all over now. Why must Germany still help paying for that all?'

Fritz suddenly looked at his watch and jumped up. It was three o'clock and *Tilly* was due to leave in an hour's time. We downed our beers, grabbed a handful of peanuts, and and took our leave of our fellow mariners. There were strong handshakes and smiles between the sole Englishman and the Germans, implying that the past should be forgotten, whatever our fathers did to each other.

We left Libreville on 10 May, heading for Pointe Noire in the Congo where we were to pick up two passengers and some more logs. As we left the estuary, and the ship turned its bow into the oncoming waves, the ship began to pitch and roll a little. My heart surged with pleasure. For the captain and the crew, it was just part of the old routine, yet another day on the inhospitable coast of Africa. For me, it was deeply exhilarating. There is something very special about the first mile from the land.

Two and half hours after our departure, at 19.35 hours, I crossed the Equator for the third time. The captain presented me with a certificate, signed by the chief mate and third officer. It showed Neptune with his trident at the bottom of the sea, next to a wreck, a bottle of rum, and a treasure chest. On one side, mermaids were sporting with a tender youth while on the other a sailor played the accordion. I had been rechristened 'Octopus'.

'Why Octupus?' I asked.

'Because you have many arms holding all your pens, books and cameras!' the captain replied. 'You also produce ink to write with!'

After dinner, I went up on deck to smoke a cigar. It was a beautiful balmy evening. The air smelt fresh and salty. The moon was a crescent, gliding through the scattered clouds in the star-studded sky. Seeing my cigar glowing red in the night, the captain shouted down from the bridge deck just above me:

'Do you want a light on?'

'No, I love it like this.'

He continued pacing up and down the deck, up and down, at a brisk, never-ceasing pace. He did it every night for a couple of hours during his watch, turning every fifty yards, and over the years had walked thousands of miles. At first, I thought he was like a caged animal and he reminded me of a hyena I had once seen in a zoo desperately walking up and down behind its bars. But after a few nights, observing him under the stars, I had the impression that the captain felt free walking along the narrow deck of his ship, rising and falling on the wide silver sea, with the steady vibration of the engine below his feet and the reassuring splash of the the wake all around.

I too began to pace the upper deck when the captain was not there, and liked the feeling of being completely lost in the dark night somewhere off Africa in the Atlantic Ocean. I did not want to be anywhere else but there: alone and yet at home; being still and yet going somewhere; on the circumference and at the centre.

*　　*　　*

A day out from Libreville, I had one lovely surprise and two disappointments. The surprise was the sighting of two whales at dawn. At first they looked like dark logs in the distance, but they slowly dived and then came up and blew spouts of water close to the port side of the ship. They did not vary their speed or direction; they knew where they were going and were not going be disturbed by yet another noisy monster, hard and graceless, carrying those strange upright creatures who caused so much havoc on sea and land. They glided on, joyfully gentle, in the still grey waters.

Ever since I had read *Moby Dick* as a boy, I had always been fascinated by whales, and instinctively felt they were highly intelligent whatever the scientists might say. 'There she blows!' What excitement that cry evoked! When reading the exploits of the whalers, I revelled in the chase and envied the courage of the men hurling their harpoons from their narrow boats, too young to realize the full horror of a great whale spouting thick blood.

The first disappointment was the captain's announcement at lunch that we would not be calling at Pointe Noire in the Congo as planned. He had received a telex from head office in Durban saying that there was a dock strike, and that he should continue his voyage. The second bit of bad news, announced later in the day, was that the ship would not be calling at Matadi in Zaïre, twenty miles up the river Congo. She was due to take on a cargo of palm oil but the order had been cancelled. We would have to sail directly to Cape Town.

'The Congo is an amazing river,' the captain observed. 'The sandbacks are constantly changing. I can remember eight years ago steaming up the river to Matadi seeing a particular sandbank. It's now covered in trees and vegetation. In the rainy season, in November and December, there can be currents in the river up to seven knots. It's very difficult to navigate.'

I had been looking forward to sailing up Africa's greatest river to see what light shone in Conrad's *Heart of Darkness*. In the original manuscript of 'The Wasteland', T.S. Eliot had taken as an epigraph from the novel the last cry of the 'civilized' hero Mista Kurtz before he died – 'The horror! The horror!'. It summed up what most people thought of the primitive savagery of Africa at the height of the colonial era.

The tangled wood, the wild moor, the dark jungle have always been full of dread for city dwellers. They have tried to tame and push back wild nature as much as possible. It stands as a symbol of the unconscious, with all its instincts and passions, which rational man must suppress. Civilization – the culture of the city – must win over the wilderness. And just as the wilderness was considered the abode of the devil, so the people living within its dark realm were felt to be less than human.

Interrupting my musings on Zaïre, the captain said: 'I'm happy not to go to Matadi. Zaïre has Mickey Mouse currency. It's the ash bin of Africa'.

That evening, while we were sitting in the dining room, I asked Fritz what he thought of the Filipino crew.

'At first, they worked less hard, but now they are more reliable.

'Do they go ashore?'

'Not much outside South Africa. They like not African women. They go with the ugliest white prostitute in Durban or Cape Town rather than with a black woman.'

'By the way, do you know why kaffirs have white hands?'

'No, why's that?'

'Because when God painted them black they were on all fours!'

Helmuth, the chief engineer, had much less time for the Filipino crew, understandably for they were about to take his job: 'They know not how to look after the tools. They use screwdrivers as chisels, and take heads of nuts by using ze wrong spanner. Ship *kaput*!'

After a siesta I would usually go up on the bridge, and spend some time with the third officer, Paterno Pasaquian. A short man in his early thirties, he was clean-shaven and completely bald. He had been on board for three years without leave, renewing his contract each year whenever it was time to go on leave.

'Don't you miss your family?'

'Yes. But I want to save money to get married.'

'Do you have someone in mind?'

'Yes. I have a fiancée. We are in constant communication.'

'Do you mind getting half the wages of a European sailor?'

'Yes. But my country is very poor. I come from a good family, I work hard at school, but no jobs. So I come to sea. I get paid in dollars and can buy plenty back home. Many Filipinos want to become seamen.'

Travelling on the *Tilly* down towards South Africa, I felt I was seeing the end of an era. Not only were the days of European colonialism over, but the European Merchant Navy was being destroyed by competition from the Far East. I was on an old cargo ship which had been kept going because it was able to break sanctions. It had been modified to carry a few containers and its expensive German crew had been reduced to a miniumum, but its sailing days were numbered. Soon new container ships would be doing this run, running on time like a bus service, registered under a flag of convenience so as not to have the inconvenience of high safety standards, with a skeleton crew of cheap sailors from the Orient. Now the Filipinos were all the rage, because they were so cheap; before long it would be sailors from Red China who were even cheaper. The sun had well and truly set on the British Empire and soon it would be setting on Europe.

On 12 May we passed the Pointa de Padrão on the southernmost point of the Congo estuary which marked the beginning of the sprawling country of Angola. Since we were not calling at Luanda I would not be able to see the country of birth of my Portuguese friend Hugo Ferreira or make use of the contacts Brigadier General Correia-Pezarat had given me in Lisbon. Even if I had, I would not have seen a great deal. I had been told by the Oxfam representative in Luanda that foreigners were virtually held prisoner in the main hotel Presidente Meridien. But what was going on in the country had important repercussions for the whole of South Africa.

Although the Portuguese had established a settlement as early as 1575 in Luanda on the coast, they left the interior to its own devices. Settlers came in large numbers at the turn of the century, but they still neglected the rest of the country. The Portuguese were the first and last colonial power in Africa and ironically it was the War of Independence in Angola and Mozambique which triggered off the Portuguese Revolution in 1974.

When independence was granted unexpectedly to Angola in 1975 the worst was not over. The country became the cockpit of the cold war and superpower rivalry. The new Marxist MPLA government not only faced the military invasions of regular troups from South Africa and Zaïre, but also an uprising by US-backed UNITA rebels, mainly Ovimbundu people from the central highlands. To counterattack this onslaught the government sought help from Cuba. Together, they checked the South African incursions; in the famous battle of Cuito Cuanavale in 1988, their pilots won air superiority. It was the beginning of the end of the apartheid system in South Africa. For the first time, the South African government realized it could not win against the front-line States. Not long after Namibia won its independence and now South Africa was painfully moving towards a multi-racial democracy.

Passing off Luanda along the Angolan coast, the air and sea temperature at midday was still 27° centigrade but the air was noticeably less humid. The ship was moving easily, pitching slightly in the long south-easterly swell. For the first time since I had left Agadir, I opened my porthole to let in the cool evening air. It was lovely to lie in my bunk with the light off, listening to the swishing of the water as it glided past our vibrating hull, watching the moon sail through the clouds to bathe my cabin in silver.

While travelling down towards the Cape of Good Hope, I would spend hours looking over the handrail into the bubbling and eddying waters as our ship sailed steadily on. I had once read that sailors of old thought it dangerous to look too long into the foaming sea. At first they would see dim pictures of the ship and themselves but eventually some unholy thing would appear and lure them to their death. Certainly, I felt many times the desire to jump overboard, breathe the warm sea waters, and descend to the flowing depths. But it was not an evil feeling and I was not beckoned by evil spirits. I wanted to open my soul to the rising wave. I had always empathized with those divers who one day went over the blue edge and never returned.

On 13 of May, a Wednesday, it suddenly turned colder. The sea had turned from grey to green and there was smell of seaweed in the air. The air temperature overnight had dropped four degrees to 23°, and the sea temperature eight degrees to 19°. I saw some black and white seabirds, which I could not identify, for the first time. I had woken up to find that the ship was surrounded by a cold heavy mist, so thick that I could only just make out the derricks amidships. It seemed we had entered a world of betwixt and between. The sea was silent, mysterious and threatening. Looking over the side, I saw occasional clumps of seaweed slipping along our hull.

We were now off the Skeleton Coast whose very name would send shivers up the spines of ancient mariners. It stretched from Rio Cunene to Walvis Bay, so-called because of the innumerable wrecks along its uninhabited shores. Here the desert came straight down into the cold waters. If a mariner went overboard, he would soon die of exposure; if he made it to the coast, he would die of starvation and thirst. It was one of the most inhospitable – and unspoilt – regions on earth.

The *Africa Pilot* issued by the British Admirality warned great caution, because of the imperfect nature of the surveys. We were in the Benguela Current, a north-west current which sets in the opposite direction of the prevailing south to south-east Trade Winds. The current is associated with upswellings when the surface water is replaced by cold water from below. The currents can also set onshore, taking unwary ships towards the coast. Another hazard is sea fogs which can appear at any time of day, especially during winter.

That night I shivered with cold for the first time since I had left Lisbon three and a half months before. With a heavy swell and thick cold fog, which the ship's lights only penetrated a few metres, we seemed to be on a ghost ship voyaging towards a limbo of ice and snow. Was that the screech of seagulls or the cries of drowned mariners condemned to follow the sea until they had paid for their sins? Even the steady thud of the engine came to sound like the drums of the devil. It was eerie and I turned in early.

During the night we passed Walvis Bay, the only deap-sea port along the Namibian coast. Because it was one of the world's most barren and inhospitable regions, it had been largely ignored by the early European mariners. The Portuguese, on their way to the riches of the East, merely erected stone crosses as navigational aids. In the eighteenth century American whalers used Walvis Bay as a base, disturbing the flamingos in the nearby lagoon. The enclave was secured by the British in 1878 for the Cape Colony. It was only in the scramble for colonies at the end of the nineteenth century that the Germans arrived in force and annexed the territory for the Kaiser.

At the end of the First World War, the country became a mandated territory first under the League of Nations and then the United Nations, but this did not stop South Africa from taking it over and introducing apartheid and homelands. Ever since the arrival of the Germans, forced labour had been the lot of the Namibians. It took the guerrilla war mounted by SWAPO to force the South African government to grant Namibia independence, although it still held on to Walvis Bay.

At dawn the next day, we were so close to Namibia that I could make out the sand mounds and barren hills of the low-lying coastline. The fog had lifted during the night. The chief engineer turned off the air-conditioning and turned on the heating. The ship was still moving steadily, pitching moderately in the south-westerly swell. The forecast was for wind of up to twenty knots with fog patches.

The sea had now turned an olive green, due to the plankton nourished by the cold upswelling of Antarctic waters. I saw a large dark brown gull perch on a derrick for the first time: 'An African,' the captain commented. And then two seals leapt out of the water, with watery eyes and bristly whiskers, as if to remind me that I was still in the land of the living.

In the early afternoon, it was warm and sunny on deck with a clear blue sky overhead, but by three o'clock a cold mist descended, again turning the green sea grey and forcing me to return to my cabin for a thick pullover. The wind picked up soon after, whistling in the wires of the derricks. The swell grew heavier, the ship began to roll and pitch as its bows crashed through surging waves with white foam crests. Spray was whipped across the ship's decks and hurled against the windows of the bridge, running down in salty tears. It was the first really bad weather since my passage from Portugal to Morocco. I thanked God I was not in a yacht or a small trawler.

The seabirds, species I had not seen before, revelled in the wild elements. White gulls, with pointed beaks, soared over the forecastle of the ship, sometimes half a dozen together. 'They accompany you south to the Antartic,' the captain said. Dark brown birds with white pointed wings skimmed across the white caps of the rough waves. By now the ship was rolling and pitching heavily on the south-westerly swell. The sea and air temperature had dropped to 14°, and a force seven wind was blowing. There was steam on my breath when I went out on deck.

'Wonderful weather!' chuckled the captain, as he paced up and down the bridge wing, the collar of his thick coat up around his ears.

The next day, the mist lifted temporarily and I could make out the low-lying cliffs of Namibia ten miles away. The names of landmarks were a mixture of German and English, reflecting the tempestuous history of the country. The first was Dolphin's Head; we then passed Hottentot Point, Douglas Bay, and Marshall Rocks, all clearly marked on the chart. 'We mustn't go aground on Marshall rocks!' joked the captain, but they were no joke, a series of jagged rocks breaking the surface, with the sea boiling around them. I could think of better places to end my days, and hoped my namesake had not come to grief on them. We kept a steady course of 160° into the high winds and the southerly swell.

During the day the ship's clock was moved an hour forward, two hours ahead of Greenwich Mean Time. When we passed Lüderitz, I could just make out the buildings of the German-style town huddling in the barren, windswept coast of the Namib desert, one of the oldest and driest in the world. Fritz and Helmuth felt good about their compatriots who still remained in the country, third-generation settlers, who had their own German newspaper, Lutheran churches and coffee shops. 'Very goot place, very goot place!' said the chief engineer. They were pleased to think that some Germans still had their place in the African sun.

I had got my sea legs by now, and felt none of the sea-sickness of my first voyage, but I still felt a little melancholy in the late afternoons. I had come to the conclusion that this was partly a bodily reaction to the movement of the ship in rough weather. The thought of my family no longer made me feel anxious; I imagined them enjoying the early summer and I felt happy to think that they were all well. When I would see them again was another matter.

On Sunday 17 May we were at last due to arrive in Cape Town. I got up well before dawn. The fog had lifted, but it was still cold. The night was bright with the full moon which transformed the sea into a swelling and swaying expanse of mercury. I could still see the Southern Cross in the sky overhead. A few lights twinkled along the dark coast.

At first the horizon was red in the east and then slowly turned orange. Suddenly the yellow tip of the sun rose out of the low-lying coast. The whitish globe of the full moon, as if caught unawares like an intruder, fled into the west.

I had been told how beautiful Table Mountain was but I was not prepared to see it from the sea betwixt moon and sun, night and day. The flat top of the mountain, which must have stretched a mile and a half, came and went in whirling white cloud. I could make out a steep, stony gorge in its green middle and an outcrop which looked like a lion's head. Below, dwarfed by the mountain, but thrusting towards the sky, rose a series of skyscrapers which turned pink in the rising sun.

We passed Robben Island on our port side, low and flat and fringed with reefs. It was fairly densely wooded in parts. This narrow strip, cut off from the mainland by strong currents, had become notorious throughout the world as the Prison Island where Walter Sisulu, Nelson Mandela and other members of the African National Congress had spent much of their adult lives for having the folly to call for democracy in their land. Confronted with the splendour of Cape Town and the desolation of Robben Island, I had already seen the two faces – black and white – of South Africa.

Chapter Eighteen

The Wild Almond Tree

ARRIVING in Cape Town, I immediately felt I was in familiar territory. The pilot who came on board to guide the ship was dressed in whites and shorts, wearing the kind of gold-braided cap which was considered essential in the grand old days of the British Merchant Navy. He looked entirely out of place amongst the casually dressed Filipino officers on board *Tilly* in their T-shirts and flip-flops.

The immigration officer said I did not need a pass and I could come and go as I pleased. I walked across the clean wharf of the main Duncan dock and passed through the gates which had no security guards.

Cape Town, in its natural setting, was amazing. It was not only one of the largest ports in the southern hemisphere but one of the great cities of the world. The streets were immaculate, clean and wide. The shops were full of the world's consumer goods; sanctions clearly had not made any inroads here. In the centre was, the Golden Acre, a huge sprawling shopping mall, a temple to Mammon if there ever was one. Alongside the broad streets rose office blocks, fancy shops and luxury hotels.

But there was something strange and eerie about it. Then I realized what it was. It was Sunday afternoon, but there was nobody in the streets! It was a dead city, a phantom city, a city hit by a neutron bomb which had left the buildings intact and destroyed all the inhabitants. It was a great white city built for whites by black labour, a city after office hours only inhabited by phantoms.

I read scrawled on one wall the slogan: 'Viva People's Education', but where were the people?

I managed to find a taxi to take me up to the Table Mountain; I wanted to take a cable car to the top in order to survey the bay. The driver was light-skinned – classified as 'Coloured', I soon learned, in the crazy racial categories of South Africa.

'So apartheid is over?' I said.

'That's what they say, but it aint, man.'

'How's that?'

'Well, officially they might have got rid of petty apartheid but it's still there. Only the other day, I went into a pub downtown for a couple of Harps. A white guy comes over and says: "Hey, man, what you drinking in our pub? I don't go down to yours." No, it will take at least a generation before apartheid is over. Maybe the young will be able to think differently.'

As we were talking we were travelling along a highway through a wasteland which had a few isolated buildings here and there which looked like churches or mosques.

'This used to be District 6,' my driver went on. 'I grew up here and used to play downtown in the streets. Those were the days.'

'What happened to it?'

'The Group Areas Act. The apartheid policy of the National Party government meant that people from different racial groups had to live in different areas. Because it was a mixed race district in a designated white area, the government in 1982 demolished the whole of District 6 and moved all the people out to Cape Flats – 60,000 of them. They didn't want any Coloureds living in their white town. Okay, it may have been a bit rough with all the clubs and bars, but it was alive, yes, man, really alive. You should have seen the "Coon Carnival"; you'd never forget it.'

'Why was it called District 6?'

'That's the name the police gave it. Its real name was Kanaldrop; "*kanalla*" in Malay means "please". If a friend or a neighbour asked you for something, you couldn't refuse. It was that kind of place. Now it's all gone and been replaced by a "freeway"!'

With the flattening of District 6, the white city fathers had finally killed the soul of their city. All that was left was a beautiful shell. *Sans* heart, *sans* soul, *sans* life, *sans* everything.

Just before we climbed the slopes of Table Mountain, I could see a district with many white houses huddled close together.

'That's the Malay quarter,' my driver pointed out. 'At least, they did not destroy that. The Malays were brought over by the Dutch East India Company from Indonesia. Most of them are still Moslems; there's a mosque there which is a couple of centuries old.'

The taxi driver dropped me at Signal Hill, some 350 metres above the docks and at the foot of the final escarpment of Table Mountain. Even from here the view was spectacular: on my left was a large outcrop called Lion's Head and below me was the wide sweeping bay. On my right I could just make out the flats which linked the Cape Peninsula with the rest of the African continent.

Looking at the modern city stretching around the bay, I tried to imagine how it must have been when the Cape Peninsula teemed with wildlife, when lion, rhino, hippo, zebra, antelope of many kinds and the now extinct quagga roamed freely. Humans too had lived here for at least ten thousand years, decorating caves and using stone implements. When the Portuguese arrived five hundred years ago, they discovered the San, light skinned hunter-gatherers without material possessions, and the Khoikhoi, pastoralists who knew how to smelt metal and make clay pottery. The settlers called them Bushmen and Hottentots.

The early Portuguese mariners landed to collect water and food, but they soon clashed with the Khoikhoi, and did not settle. They were followed by the Dutch: Cape Town was founded by Jan van Riebeeck in 1652 as a depot for the Dutch East India Company which sent ships from the Netherlands to the spice islands of Asia. It became known as the 'Tavern of the Seas'.

The original Dutch settlers were joined by Protestant Huguenots fleeing persecution in Catholic France. These people formed the basis of the Afrikaners or Boers, the tribe of white Africans who by the end of the eighteenth century had developed their own distinctive language and culture. The Cape Colony came under British rule from the end of the eighteenth century, and it was not until 1910 that it joined up with Natal Colony and the Boer Republics of the Transvaal and Orange Free State to form the Union of South Africa. A key Afrikaner event in history was the Great Trek to escape the rule of the British in Cape in the nineteenth century. Some fourteen thousand Boers had set forth in 1837 with their wagons and slaves and oxen into the hostile hinterland. They had been preceded by settlers who had more or less disappeared into the African bush for two centuries slowly extending their control over the land, knowing no law except the Bible which they found increasingly difficult to understand. What sustained them was their guns, their fanatical Calvinist religion, and their ferocious attachment to the land. After six generations they emerged with their own language, an ingrained sense of racial superiority and a deep-seated conviction that they were God's chosen people.

Ironically, the Afrikaners who spread across the veld in their wagons, led a semi-nomadic life, little different from the black tribes they pushed back one on top of another. They preferred cattle ranching to agriculture and lived in partnership with the land. The paradoxes did not stop there. The Afrikaners went on to develop strangely contradictory traits: devout Christians, they could be cruel and aggressive; wanting to be liked, they could not accept criticism; with their puritanical consciences condemning luxury, they enjoyed great material ease. Because of their blind self-centredness, they were ready to destroy the country they loved.

Although their attempt to create separate states for themselves was defeated by the British in the Anglo–Boer War, the Afrikaner tribe eventually came to power in the 1948 elections. Making up sixty per cent of the white population, the National Party which represented them ruled until 1994. At first their policy of *apartheid* (literally, separation or being apart) amounted to little more than old-fashioned segregation, but by the late 1950s laws were passed to undo as far as possible any integration which had taken place. The Group Areas Act of 1950 further promoted the residential segregation of various groups. And in its long sleep of reason, the Afrikaner mind created a monstrous state.

Apartheid was a poisonous dye which ran through the whole fabric of South African society from birth to death: whites and blacks henceforth had separate living areas, jobs, schools, social amenities, political institutions, courts, prisons, doors, toilets, benches, pavements, trains, buses, taxis, post offices, ambulances, hospitals and even cemeteries. The pass laws restricted the freedom of movement of blacks in white areas but not vice versa. The government claimed that eighty per cent of the land 'historically' belonged to the 'White Nation'; the rest of the population had been herded on ethnic lines into scraps of land scattered all over the republic called 'homelands' which they pretended were sovereign states. It was an attempt to creat white rule for eternity in a country where they formed only a small minority.

I turned from meditating on the tragic history of South Africa, to admire the beauty of the Peninsula. Although it was May, autumn in the southern hemisphere, where I stood there were still some flowers lingering on under the great pine trees. The original hardwood forests had long been cut down, but the area still has one of the richest variety of plants found anywhere in the world. In an area of less than 500 square kilometres, it has more than 2,500 species of flowering plants, more than the whole of Great Britain.

But even the plants have taken on a special meaning in South Africa's past. On the eastern slopes of Table Mountain, in the famous Kirtenbosch Botanic Gardens there stands a scraggly line of entangled trees. They are wild almond trees, the remnants of a hedge planted in 1660 by Jan van Riebeeck. It was the first act of apartheid, intended to keep the indigenous peoples – the stinking black dogs, as he called them – apart. They have remained ever since on the other side of the hedge and eat its bitter fruit.

The superior weapons of the first settlers enabled them to defeat the local population. But despite the attempt of the settlers to plant a hedge around their homesteads to keep out the rest of Africa, many, driven by the thorns of the flesh, crept through the gaps and lay with the daughters of Ham, cutters of wood and hewers of water.

The result was the 'Coloured' population who dwelt in a kind of limbo land. Practising the religion – the Calvanism of the Dutch Reform Church – and speaking the language – Afrikaans – of their oppressors, they have been caught between the white world in which they would like to be accepted and the black world into which they did not wish to sink. The passing of the immorality Laws, which outlawed sex across the colour line, implied that their very existence was a crime and a sin. Under the apartheid system, morally and legally, they had no right to be.

Turning my back on the wasteland of District 6 and the Malay quarter below me, I decided to take a ride in the cable car to the top of Table Mountain. At its summit, 1,067 metres above sea level, the cloud closed in and it was cold and damp. No one was about, apart from a 'Coloured' couple huddling at the station waiting to descend to warmer climes. I strolled to the highest point and saw a few crows leap about on the rocks. But then suddenly the cloud lifted and I saw the bay stretch out below me and a shaft of light lit up Robben island which looked more foreboding than ever in the grey sea.

It was called Robben island not because it tried to rob the souls of prisoners, but after the *robben* or seals which used to flourish on its beaches. Its bleak shores washed by the cold Benguella Current sweeping up from the Antartic have witnessed some of the great crimes of South Africa's colonial past. Muslim leaders from Dutch Indonesia, such as the princes of Ternate and Madura, were banished here.

Makanda, who led a mighty Xhosa army against Grahamstown in 1819, was exiled on the island after giving himself up, wrongly thinking that he would be treated in the chivalrous way he treated others. He drowned in the cold surf trying to escape. Another famous prisoner was Nongqawuse, a Xhosa child who was placed on the island – as an official guide puts it – for 'her own protection' because her visions led to the 'national suicide' of her people in 1857. She prophesied that if the Xhosa killed all their cattle and burned all their grain, the graves would open and give up the great warriors of the past and a great wind would help drive the white invaders into the sea. When the day of reckoning did not take place, the disaster which befell the Xhosa people marked the end of organized resistance to the white settlers.

During the Second World War, the island was used as a naval base, but then reverted to a penal settlement. When Walter Sisulu, Nelson Mandela and Oliver Tambo and their comrades from the African National Congress (ANC) were brought to the island in the sixties, they were in a long line of rebels who had given all they could to check the destruction of their land and their people.

It was a pleasure to leave the cold, cloud-capped Table Mountain and to go down to the older parts of Cape Town. I strolled through the beautiful botanical gardens of the former Dutch East India Company. I was back into a temperate zone where my body felt most relaxed. The Cape Peninsula has a Mediterranean climate of temperate winters and warm dry summers. Many of the shrubs and trees in the garden were from different parts of the world, especially Australia, reflecting past trading ties. There was a wonderful smell of damp earth, a smell I always associate with Britain, and the brown leaves fallen from the imported oaks (planted to commemorate the wedding of George V) danced along the paths in the cool breeze.

I walked back to the ship through the deserted streets of Cape Town, meditating on the disaster that had happened to this country, one of the richest and most beautiful in the world. The original wild almond tree hedge still produced its bitter harvest. Because of a crazy notion of racial purity, the first and most important category of a South African is not his or her personality, talent or work but the colour of their skin. And to what absurdities had the ruling Afrikaner Nationalist Party sunk in order to pursue its policy of separate racial development!

If I had come to South Africa with my family, in what category would they fall? My wife dark brown, my son light brown, and my daughter white? Would a civil servant, employed by the racist state, run a pencil through my daughter's hair, judge its wiriness, and put her in a racial category which would determine all her relationships?

The Separate Amenities Act would have meant we would have sat on different benches and travelled on different buses. The Group Areas Act would have meant that we could not live in the same house or district. The Immorality Act, which had only recently been abolished, would have meant that I could not have shared a bed with Jenny or held her hand in public.

The deserted streets of the city centre, the empty wasteland of District 6, the absence of quaggas and elephants were all eloquent testimony to the white city fathers of Cape Town who had iron in the soul and dollars on the brain.

As I passed some of the great shops full of imported consumer goods, an elderly black man came up to me. He gave me a puzzled smile. He did not ask for money.

'Hey, man, what are you doing here?'

'I'm just walking back to my ship.'

'Hasn't anyone told you? It's dangerous for a white to walk alone in this city. Take care.' He shuffled up the hill, dwarfed by the towering skyscrapers.

Before returning to the ship, I went to hear a concert in the City Hall of Prokovief's 'Peter and the Wolf'. I got the last ticket of the whole auditorium and was let in after the first movement by a young man with a black bow tie who kept calling me 'Sir'. In the whole of the audience, there was only a handful of black faces, and none in the orchestra. If official apartheid was over, cultural apartheid had a long way to go. I settled down and let the music from the Russian steppes flow over me at the other end of the world, dimly aware that I too would soon have to confront the wolves of the regime in this frozen land.

I woke up next day to find that Table Mountain and Lion's Head were lost in cloud. It was cold and wet and drizzle swept across the grey docks. Not a very nice day to continue my exploration of Cape Town. Fortunately, I got a message from Steve Shapiro, a friend of a friend, who came down to the ship to collect me in his battered old car and to show me around.

Steve was a potter who lived in Houtbay on the other side of Table Mountain on the west coast of Cape Peninsula. He took me along the coastal road past Sea Point, Bantry Bay and Clifton, seaside resorts which had merged together to meet the housing needs of the wealthy whites who commuted during the week to Cape Town. The Atlantic rollers crashed on to the beaches sheltered by rocky headlands. We also passed the fashionable suburb of Llandudno, nestling round a cove with a fine sandy beach and a wreck washed by the waves. The Welsh, as well as the English and Scottish, had clearly been at work in the Cape Colony.

Houtbay had a long rocky headland sheltering it from the south and was surrounded by the foothills of Table Mountain. It had a fine harbour for yachts and fishing boats, and smoke belched from a fish factory.

As we entered the well-heeled town with its bungalows and well-kept gardens I noticed a several black men lay asleep or lounging around on the public lawns.

'They're waiting to be picked up for work,' Steve said. 'They're lucky if they can get a few days casual work here and there.'

'Where do they live?'

'There's a squatter camp at the foot of the mountain. The local residents are trying to get them moved, but they're digging their heels in. Most of them have family members working for the whites and they don't want to travel all the way from the Cape Flats. Besides, life is better here. It's less violent and overcrowded.'

Steve made pots from African clay; he believed in functional pots, not fancy bric-à-brac. He had been shaped himself by the continent but as a Jew he did not feel that he entirely belonged to the land.

'I grew up here, but I've been detribalized. Half of the Jews – there were about a quarter of a million – have left in the last couple of decades. I'm worried too that the ANC might be anti-Semitic: because of the close links between Israel and white South Africa, Mandela has been friendly with Gaddafi and Arafat who support the Palestinians.'

'What do you think are the chances of a multi-racial, democractic South Africa coming soon?'

'It's going to be very difficult. There's a real clash of cultures. The blacks are so different, so poor; they have no education and no skills. It's not their fault but they're virtually unemployable.'

Steve introduced me to Chaim and Jeni Rabinowitz, who lived in a beautiful house in Constantia set in a wooded estate in the hills south of Table Mountain. Chaim too was a potter. In his late sixties, he had grown up speaking Afrikaans in the Karoo, a semi-desert region which in spring was carpeted with flowers. He had never lost his love of the bush. As a boy Chaim had been sent to an English public school in Cape Town where he acquired a clipped English accent. Like all white South Africans, he had been brought up to think that his ilk were innately superior to blacks, but he told me that he had learned about equality during the Second World War when he had served in East and North Africa. For years he had supported Helen Suzman and her Democratic

Party, the lone liberal voice in parliament. Now that it was legal and the Communist threat was over, he backed the ANC.

'You know, after the war, I came back to South Africa wanting to build a better country, but we were stopped by the National Government. I've now lived all my life under the National Government, a government of neo-Nazis.'

'What do you think of the coming democracy?'

'It depends what they mean by democracy, whether it is the will of the people or the power of the people. Trouble is, all politics are bad. They cause the problems of the world!'

At dusk, we walked up to his pottery along a steep path which meandered through giant pines and oaks and great granite boulders. The wind from the south-west whistled in the high branches.

'It's not too bad this evening. The worst are the north-westerly gales in the winter, which bring heavy rain and bend the trees.'

We passed solid cottages which Chaim told me had once been slave quarters on the estate in the early nineteenth century. In the distance smoke arose across a flat plain which stretched as far as the eye could see. It was like the other side of the moon, at least for me who so far had been viewing South Africa from the verandah.

'That's the Cape Flats where the blacks and Coloureds live. It's a sprawling shanty town which goes on for miles. The smog is from their coal and wood fires. There's over a million people living down there. Life is cheap and the violence is spilling over into the white areas.'

Despite a starry night, the next morning the cold fog closed in again, hiding Table Mountain. *Tilly* was moored at Duncan Dock, the large dock opposite the town centre. At one time, freighters and passenger liners from some of the world's great shipping companies – P & O, Shaw-Savill, Blue Funnel, LLoyd-Triestino, Holland-Afrika, Deutsch-Ost-Afrika – would crowd the quays. But with the opening of the Suez canal, the collapse of empire in the East, and the coming of the aeroplane, the docks had grown quiet. Even the weekly mail and passenger service of the Union Castle Line had long ceased. In recent times, the imposition of sanctions had made matters worse. Only the Royal Cape Yacht Club at the south-east of the dock looked busy, with its yachts jostling at their moorings.

I decided to explore the old docks in the area now called the Waterside, the only area of the city which had some life after office hours. It formed part of the Alfred Basin which had been built by convicts in the second half of the nineteenth century in order to replace the old wooden jetty. It was now being developed into a tourist centre, with the old warehouses turned into museums, pubs, hotels and restaurants. Noisy high-powered pleasure boats had replaced the graceful old sailing ships.

In the afternoon, families, mainly white, though there was a smattering of Indians and 'Coloureds', strolled around the quays of Waterside. A few years ago they would not have been able to enter the area, and they now came tentatively, ready to rebuffed, but also ready to assert their rights. I suddenly heard some New Orleans Jazz and round the corner came a marching Dixie band which was greeted with great enthusiasm. That was fine, except that the black musicians were dressed up as black-and-white minstrels, with exaggerated white lips, white gloves and fancy uniform: the ultimate parody. A black busker, playing a guitar, looked on with contempt and then slipped away as I did.

Later I went to a jazz club in Waterside. At the bar, a German started talking to me in English with a South African accent. He worked as a sales representative for a pharmaceutical company. He was well aware that multi-national drug companies do not get a very good press, especially in Africa. I asked him how he was getting on.

'Everybody hates us. I don't care!'

And what did he think of the black majority being in power?

'The blacks can't even run a bath, let alone a country!'

Returning to the ship around eleven, I saw fairy lights lit up in the crew's mess and heard pop music blaring through the open portholes. A party was on. I was warmly welcomed by the Filipinos, given a bottle of local Castle beer, and two girls came and sat next to me. There were about half a dozen there, representing the whole beautiful racial spectrum of South Africa. I was besieged on my left by an Indian girl who was tall and slim, and on my right by a white girl who was petite. I remembered the captain saying that girls often came on board *Tilly* in Cape Town for a party. They weren't necessarily prostitutes, but teachers, nurses, clerks, often single parents, out for a good time.

The girl giving me all the attention was called Serena. Her mother was from Mauritius and her father was Spanish and she had grown up in St Helena. She now worked in an office in Cape Town, lived alone and had two young children. The Indian girl was called Deborah; she worked as a salesgirl, giving out cards welcoming sailors to the Manila Club, the main night spot for the Filipinos. We joked and laughed. The Filipinos sat at their tables, beer in hand, swathed in smiles, while the other girls gyrated to the music in the most provocative way. Everyone seemed to be enjoying themselves. When I explained to the Serena that I was not from South Africa, she was astonished.

'Not South African? But I was sure you were South African? Take me to your cabin,' she insisted, nibbling my ear.

The Filipino cook slipped me a condom, beaming. Everyone seemed pleased that the passenger was going to get laid. Another bottle was placed in my hand, and everyone drank to 'The Seaman's Life! The Seaman's Life!' The music, American disco music, was turned up.

Serena was a very pretty girl, full of energy and fun. I would like to have learned more about her and her world. But after another dance and a beer, I decided to call it a day. She made me promise to look her up next time I was in Cape Town; I said I would try.

The next day, I went to see a philosopher whom Chaim had recommended I visit. His name was Martin Versfeld; he had been Professor of Philosophy at Cape Town University. I discovered his house down a leafy lane called Chapel Road. It was a roomy solid Victorian building set in a large overgrown garden. The old philosopher came to the door; in his early eighties, he was still hearty with a twinkle in his eyes under their bushy brows. He wore an old pair of corduroys and a thick brightly coloured pullover. He had a white goaty beard which made him look impish.

Versfeld was no mere scholar or specialist: he had translated Plato's *Symposium* and Lao-tzu into Afrikaans, was a leading exponent of the thought of his fellow African St Augustine, and had written witty and profound books about *Our Selves* as well as *Pots and Poetry*.

He invited me into his study. He had been working that morning on a review of the latest autobiographical offering of his old friend Laurens Van der Post. Discussing St Augustine, Versfeld told me he was an anarchist at heart because he believed that the only thing necessary for society to hold together was to develop right relationships.

'The state has always been a burden. If there is to be any peace in South Africa, it will only be achieved on the principles of decentralization and regionalism. Otherwise one political group like the National Party will take over the state and use it in their own interest.'

It was the most sensible thing I had heard so far.

'South Africa also needs a positive metaphysical mind to solve its problems.'

That might prove more difficult.

After tea, Versfeld made a fire, a task which he did slowly and methodically and in silence. When it was ablaze, he took up a piece of wood and cut strips off it and put them in the fire. They gave off a wonderful, fresh piney smell.

'It's cedar. It's from our farm. I built the house there on some land I discovered long ago when looking for cave paintings. I always consider that house to be my real home. You know, God is Home.'

Versfeld was living in his spacious house with his wife Barbara. Their eight or so children had long left home, but they had a nephew and a fellow black student at the university staying with them. He asked me to stay on for dinner and I readily agreed; there was such a homely atmosphere in the relaxed household.

Sitting at the head of the table, Versfeld said grace as he had done for more than half a century. Eating in this household was a spiritual as well as physical process. I savoured the vegetables from his garden, and the fine apple pie made by Barbara. One of his works was called *A Philosopher's Cookbook* which developed the ancient Chinese view that you are what you eat and that food is divine. It was typical of Versfeld's mischievous wit to describe the universe as the soup of God and to urge us all to have a go at cooking the marvellous. When you eat bread, he believed, you also eat reality; at one with your food, you are at one with the universe.

'The true anarchist,' Versfeld asserted emphatically, 'is the cook allowing the ingredients in his soup pot to be. He is the priest of mutual arising.'

While Versfeld had directed his libertarian energies to teaching – and counted several famous radicals amongst his former students – his wife Barbara had worked in the Black Sash Organization, a liberal women's movement intended to help blacks. She told me how when Sisulu and Mandela and their comrades were first imprisoned on Robben Island, their wives, who came by train to visit them, were unable to catch the ferry because they could not get a taxi from the railway station to the quay. The government refused to help, so the middle-class ladies from Cape Town's branch of Black Sash filled the breach and provided the transport. It was a small drop of good in the vast ocean of suffering in South Africa, but it had meant that their family came under surveillance from the security forces.

When it came time for me to leave, Versfeld gave me a piece of cedar wood from which he had been cutting strips for the fire and half a dozen beans – large, flat and piebald – from his vegetable garden.

'When the slaves were first given them, they called them "Governor's Beans". The name's stuck.'

He shook my hand firmly, looking at me intensely from beneath his bushy eyebrows, and said 'Go Well'.

Back in my bunk, I pondered on Versfeld's phrase 'Home is God'. The phrase had struck a deep chord in me. For him, it appeared to mean that God is most present in the hearth, in the most menial of domestic tasks. But I preferred to extend the notion of home to embrace the whole of the Earth House Hold; for me, to say that Home is God meant that everything on earth is sacred. After leaving my family home in North Wales, I had during my voyage tried to feel 'at home' wherever I was on land or sea. I had started the voyage off-centre, emotionally and metaphysically ill-prepared, but by now, half-way through my voyage, I had achieved a degree of equilibrium. I had passed through a kaleidoscope of peoples, cultures, and languages in a pitching and rolling world and had not been thrown over. I had been able to keep my balance while all around me was at sea. In a strange way, I felt at home and a sense of the holy was not entirely absent.

171

* * *

After visiting Versfeld, I contacted his friend André Brink in Cape Town, because I knew him to be one of the most outspoken Afrikaner critics of apartheid. He was also a novelist and Professor of Literature at the university. I had an indirect link with him as the Martinician director Euzhan Palcy who had made a film of Jenny's father's autobiographical novel *Rue des Cases Nègres* (Black Shack Alley) had also directed the film of Brink's novel *A Dry White Season* which starred Donald Sutherland, Janet Suzman and Marlon Brando.

I met Brink in his office at the university, a fine ivy-clad building with long steps overlooking Cape Town. He was a tall, fit-looking man with curly hair and glasses, serious but not without warmth and humour. He told me how he had grown up in a strict Calvinist Afrikaner family in a small village in the late thirties in the Transvaal. Like all his schoolfellows, he knew so little of the life of his black neighbours that they might have been living, to use one of his telling phrases, on the dark side of the moon. He did well at school and university and went on to study languages in the Sorbonne in Paris. It was here that he had an experience which undermined his whole world-view.

'I had always considered myself to be intellectually superior to blacks, but for the first time I came across some black students from Francophone Africa who were more intelligent than me. It came as a great shock!'

'But do you think your fellow Afrikaners will also be able to throw off centuries of prejudice?'

'I have a stubborn faith that they can. I think that inside South Africa as a result of apartheid and especially abroad there has been a perception that Afrikaners are a granite-like, monolithic, very dour people. Unfortunately a very real aspect of the Afrikaner psyche has not been illuminated as well as it ought to have been, that is, its ferocious attachment to Africa. During three and a half centuries of living here, they learned to understand the continent in very basic terms – the seasons, the drought, the floods – and they learned to live with the indigenous people who could tell them a lot about survival. Of course, they exterminated a lot of blacks, of course they subjugated them, they took over the country and very violently raped it, but at the same time a very strange kind of coexistence emerged.'

172

'But are the Afrikaners prepared to give up their privileges without a fight?'

'It will be difficult, but I believe they will make a deal. They will have to. Many of the English-speaking whites can get up and go but the Afrikaners have nowhere to go. This is their land.'

'What makes you feel so sure?'

'You know, when South Africans are at a party in Europe, you will often find them at the end of the party huddled together in a corner talking Afrikaans. What unites black and white South Africans is greater than what divides them. That's why I am confident that there will be a future for this country in the long run.'

'In your novel you quote from a poem by the black writer Mongane Wally Serote:

> it is a dry white season brother,
> only the trees know the pain as they still stand erect
> dry like steel, their branches dry like wire,
> indeed, it is a dry white season
> but seasons come to pass.

Will the dry white season in South Africa come to pass?'

'That's the small bit of hope, the little flickering of light in our pretty dark situation which has kept me going as a writer and an individual. Indeed, we have seen seasons come to pass. One of the distressing aspects of the situation at the moment is the perception of the outside world that apartheid is over and done with, is dead, and one can move on to the future, whereas the real problems are only just beginning now. The changes we are going through right now are so convulsive and so unpredictable and so dangerous and so bloody depressing that one sometimes wonders whether one is ever going to get out of it. The discrepancies in the distribution of wealth in the country, the discrepancies in education, are so staggering that it may well take generations to overcome them unless there is a massive involvement of the rest of the world.'

I spent a week in Cape Town before sailing on to Durban. While *Tilly* had her cargo unloaded and loaded, I tried to track down a yacht which would take me around the Cape of Good Hope. I had started under sail in Lisbon, and wanted to sail around the Cape like Bartholomeu Dias and Vasco da Gama had done 500 years or so before me.

With this in mind, I went to the Royal Cape Yacht Club where I met the commodore. He introduced me to 'a world-class racing yachtsman' who said he would only take me around the Cape in a yacht for 2,000 rand – about £400 – a day. So much for the love of the sea and international brotherhood of yachtsmen! My faith was restored by Steve Shapiro, my potter friend, who put me in touch with the False Bay Yacht Club on the other side of Table Mountain. The commodore there, Alvin Kushner, said he would be delighted to take me out in his yacht to round the Cape – for free.

We travelled by car due south under the shadow of Table Mountain to False Bay, and then drove along the coast through Fish Hoek to Simon's Town where the yacht club stood next to the naval base which the British Navy had used until 1975. We set sail in a sturdy catamaran with the commodore's wife, son and a friend. His wife had recently lost a finger which had caught in a rachet while tightening the sails. The sky was overcast and the sea grey, but there was a good wind and we made reasonable headway tacking towards the Cape. The coast was rocky, with jagged cliffs rising to a sweeping expanse of heathland. As we neared Cape Point, I could make out two white columns with crosses on top which stood out of the rocky coastline about a mile away. They were to Vasco da Gama and Bartholomeu Dias, the mariners who first put the Cape on the world map.

As we rounded Cape Point, there was a heavy swell and the Cape rollers threatened to throw our small catarman on to the jagged rocks at the foot of the lighthouse. The waters were boiling. Eric Fry, the commodore's friend who had once been the town clerk of Fish Hoek, was not perturbed. He was a large, affable man who had represented South Africa in 1972 in the World Power Boat Race and had come seventh.

'You know, it can be very dangerous here,' he said.

'Dias originally called it the Cape of Storms, but the Portuguese king changed the name afterwards to the Cape of Good Hope because it promised a passage to the riches of the Indies. The original name is more apt. You've probably heard of the *Flying Dutchman* – it's a phantom ship often sighted here in bad weather.'

As we rounded the Cape, a bottle of fine South Africa sherry was brought out, and everyone drank to my health, and to Cape Point.

'In the old days,' Eric went on, clearly a man who liked a good yarn, 'if a sailor rounded the Cape he was entitled to wear an earring in one ear; if he rounded the Horn he could then wear one in the other ear.'

'Is that the same for women?' asked Alvin's wife.

'You've been round at least ten times,' her husband said, 'which means you can wear ten earrings!'

Running home in the late afternoon towards Simon's Town, the freshening wind behind us, a school of seals joined our yacht, dozens of them, leaping out of the water in graceful curves, only to splash nose first into the grey waters. We passed one rugged outcrop in False Bay which was called Seal Island.

'We also get whales coming to breed in the bay', Eric said, 'and great white sharks.'

I saw some cormorants, gannets, black-backed gulls and a large petrel. Three species of albatross sometimes could be seen soaring in the sky. Just looking at the gulls wheeling in the spray by the cliffs was inspiring. They were entirely at one with the raging sea, exulting in the wild elements.

The next day I returned to the Cape of Good Hope and Cape Point, but this time on land. I walked along the rocky promontory of the Cape of Good Hope, where the long Atlantic swell crashed over the rocky shore, with spray flying high in the onshore wind. It was very cold, and despite wearing pyjamas under my trousers and a thick woollen pullover, gloves and hat, I still shivered in the damp wind.

I was standing on the most southern point of Africa. The coast reminded me of Sagres in Portugal where Henry the Navigator spent the last years of his life and where I had begun my voyage. I had come from the most south westerly point of Europe to the most south westerly point of Africa. There was a wooden board which reminded me that I was standing 34° 21' 25" south latitude,

18° 28' 26" east longitude. I was 6,000 miles from home – as the seagull flies.

I climbed the rocky cliff above it and lay down on the rock under the blue sky, out of the wind. I closed my eyes and felt the earth turn in the universe. Many a time during my voyage, I had thought of turning back but at last I had reached the Cape of Good Hope after four months. Despite all my trials and tribulations, it was certainly worth the effort. I was half-way round my voyage; from now on, I would be homeward bound!

Chapter Nineteen

Cape of Storms

Aᴄᴛᴇʀ a week in Cape Town, it was time for *Tilly* to leave for Durban. My stay in Cape Town had left me in a confused state of mind. I had met some fine individuals, had been overwhelmed by the natural beauty of the peninsula, but the constant theme of race, race, race depressed me. Is it too much to ask for human beings simply to be humans without constantly referring to their race or country? While I was there President de Klerk had issued a plea for reconciliation, and for a new South Africa to be like a tree with many cultural branches, but the endless stories of the division, hatred, and cruelty between the races which filled the media gave me the impression of a country self-obsessed to the point of madness.

In the event *Tilly* did not depart until the evening. Because of the fog which had persisted all day, the pilot ordered up two tugs to help manoeuvre us out of the harbour. One ship had recently crashed into the long concrete jetty, and he did not want a recurrence. The pilot looked like an old sea-dog, with his white beard, peaked cap and smart uniform. He was gruff and efficient, clearly not impressed by *Tilly* with her rusting derricks, countless coats of paint and casual Filipino crew.

We left Cape Town at dusk in a fog, the very opposite of our magnificent arrival in the morning sunshine. Table Mountain and Lion's Head were hidden in the thick fog and night was setting in. The whole place seemed unreal and I wondered for a moment whether I had dreamed the whole stay in Cape Town.

When we passed the Cape of Good Hope, the fog had lifted a little. I could make out a few lights along the coast. This was the most southerly tip of Africa, a place I had dreamed about ever since I had left Lisbon. I could make out the lighthouse flashing on Cape Point a little to the east.

Although the local fishermen and guidebooks claimed Cape Point to mark the division between the Atlantic and Indian Oceans, strictly speaking the dividing line was drawn from Cape Agulhas more than 90 miles to the south east. As we rounded this cape in the early hours, I was suddenly woken up by crashing and banging in my cabin. All my toiletries had fallen in the bathroom, and my books, pens and papers were strewn all over the deck. The ship was pitching and rolling on a long swell. We were in the Agulhas current which brings warm water down from the Mozambique Channel from the Indian Ocean, before mingling with the cold waters of the Benguella current which sweeps up from the Antarctic. We were entering a region which experiences some of the largest waves in the world.

I went up to the bridge and found the captain keeping a close look out. He was well aware of the dangers. He had travelled the coast for fifteen years and had some close shaves with large waves. He recalled how in 1968 a 28,000-ton ship, SS *World Glory*, encountered such a wave and was broken amidships and sunk with considerable loss of life. I remembered reading before the start of my voyage about a 7,500-ton Greek cruise ship, *Oceanos*, which had sank off the Transkei Wild Coast 200 miles south of Durban in roaring gales with thirty-foot waves and thirty-five-knot winds. Even on her outward voyage, *Tilly* had experienced extremely bad weather in this area.

The reason why the waves of the southern ocean are so big is that they are not destroyed by breaking on a beach. They form part of the great swells produced by westerly winds which roll around and around the world. But what makes the waves off South Africa particularly dangerous is the very steep leading edge of the crests which come after the very deep troughs. They move fast in a north-easterly direction, apparently caused by a combination of swell in the Agulhas current and the passage of a cold front. If a ship steering south west is unlucky enough to encounter such a wave, she will find her bows dropping into the trough with increasing speed until she meets the steep-fronted face of the oncoming wave. As the *Africa Pilot* of the British Admiralty notes, the wave will eventually break over the fore part of the ship with 'devastating force'.

During the day the swell gradually increased and waves grew larger. Foam was whipped by the wind across them as their tops crashed over in a cloud of white water. The bows of *Tilly* dipped steeply into the waves and sheets of spray crashed over her forecastle. It was rough all day. I ate only a little soup, bread and water in an attempt to settle my stomach. I walked up and down the pitching and rolling upper deck, gulping down the cold air whipping my face, and delighting in the stinging sea spray. It cleared my head wonderfully.

Poseidon must have had mercy on us for the rough weather slowly abated the next day. I awoke to find the ship sailing due east, directly into the warm rising sun. We were rolling slightly in the gentle swell of the blue Indian Ocean. The Agulhas current was running at two knots against us, but the wind was behind us and we were making a steady 13.5 knots. After breakfast I could make out East London on the coast. Since it was Saturday, pleasure boats were out early and a few yachts sailed in the light haze which was being burnt off by the strengthening sun. In the distance, I could make out sandy beaches and a few rocky outcrops.

We passed groups of two or three laid-back seals – literally laying on their backs, front flippers and heads out of the water, lolling in the gentle swell. They turned a watery eye to us as we glided past, refusing to budge unless we were almost on top of them. In mid morning, I saw another whale. It rose, blew a spout of water, and then dived, only to re-emerge several hundred yards away in our wake. The captain had seen many whales along this part of the coast.

'Once I was sailing in these waters when suddenly the ship lost speed. I couldn't understand why. Everything was running normally in the engine room. Then one of the crew reported that we had caught a whale across our bow. It was badly injured and could not get away. The only way to clear it was by increasing our speed.'

As we were talking some seagulls circled around the bridge wing on which we were standing.

'You know,' the captain said, 'there's a story about some fishermen who caught a seagull and bound its beak with tape. After that, everything went wrong – there was no fish and a great storm blew up. The fishermen were sorry that they ever did it. They said "never again".'

'I've heard tell that every seagull has the soul of a dead sailor.'

'I don't know about that,' Fritz replied. 'Seagulls are no good to you. If you're shipwrecked in a lifeboat, they come and pick out your eyes . . .'

We arrived off Durban at 06.00 hours on 24 May. We were all itching to get ashore at the end of our voyage but because of congestion in the port we had to anchor four miles off its golden beaches in a queue with half a dozen other ships – tankers, containers, and general cargo vessels. The ship rolled moderately at anchor in the long swell and current. The great benefit was that it was warm, and at midday the temperature reached 22° centigrade. Durban was in a sub-tropical region which made it ideal for all-year-round holidays.

We stayed at anchor all day long. I could see the blue surf crashing on the twenty-eight miles of Durban's golden beaches and could make out the high-rise hotels along the west end. When yachts came out for an afternoon race, it was doubly frustrating to be hanging around, so near and yet so far. I wondered what the first settlers must have thought of the place when they splashed ashore among the reeds of the bay, disturbing the hippos and scattering the wildebeest.

The captain lent me a travel booklet about Durban which was full of white girls in bikinis, white men in suits, but not one black face. I could be excused for thinking that it was Miami, not an African city on the Indian Ocean. Of the things I could look forward to was a visit to a night club called Mrs Thatcher (advertised with that lady's warm face), to lose my money in a casino (only recently allowed), buy endless furs (no animal liberationists here), book a date with an escort agency (leggy white girls on show) and have a massage. I could also go on an 'Oriental Walkabout' in the Indian quarter and see the largest mosque in the southern hemisphere, relax in the Japanese gardens, have a ride in a gaily coloured rickshaw along Marine Parade, spend a moment of silence in St Paul's Church, and go on a historical tour of Durban's colonial past and 'relive the city's exciting days, when courage and human endeavour in face of incredible adversity was a way of life'. There was even a Vasco da Gama clock to see in Victoria Embankment erected in 1897 to commemorate the Portuguese explorer's discovery of Port Natal.

But what about the real Africa, the Africa of black Africans and wild animals? That too could be arranged. Not only were there Game Hunting Ranches to try out your skill at close range but also tailor-made Zulu Kraals overlooking the valley of a 1,000 hills where one can savour African tribal life in the raw. There was no mention of Chief Buthelezi and his Inkatha Freedom Party, whose members were fighting the comrades of the African National Congress and threatening the slow tortuous move towards democracy.

As the day wore on, the captain grew increasingly impatient, pacing the decks, working mechanically the muscles on his square jaw as he chewed hard into his gum.

When Helmuth came up on the bridge from the engine room, he said:

'What I tell you, Peter, nothing is certain at sea. The seaman's life is always waiting. Waiting for something to happen.'

'Waiting for death,' observed the captain, who did not cease his pacing.

This was a good lesson for me. I had started the voyage wanting to keep up a certain pace and feared getting stuck. Now out of necessity I had grown more philosophical; I had realized that there is no point getting impatient if one cannot change things. It wasn't just a case of accepting stoically the inevitable. I had learned that by pushing too hard, one can often make matters worse, like the child who pulls down the table cloth and ruins everything while reaching for the big cake.

I had learned to take things more easily; after all, one day was not necessarily any better than the last or the next during my voyage – or during the voyage of life, for that matter. Breathing the fresh sea air, I gave thanks for having reached the Indian Ocean. I no longer felt disorientated, a stranger on a strange shore. A deep sense of peace descended on me and I hoped it would pass through me and spread in all directions.

I returned to my cabin and wrote home on a post-card of the Cape of Good Hope:

All my love from a lovely old cargo ship which has taken me all the way down the West Coast of Africa, from Douala to Durban, from above the Equator to near the Antartic. The seals, dolphins, whales, flying fishes and soaring birds have been all my friends on the way. I've watched the sun set in the sea and rise out of the sea like a great ball of fire. I've listened to the wind whistling in the rigging. I've seen the rainforest reach down to the shore and the sands of the desert flow into the surf. I send my love from the Indian Ocean to the Irish Sea – the one part of the other, as I am part of you . . .

In the end we had to wait two days at anchor off Durban because of the congestion in the port. Fritz observed:

'This is Africa! This wouldn't happen in Europe!'

The immigration officer did not turn up so I unpacked my bags and decided to stay on board another night. When the young immigration officer, dressed smartly in white uniform and white shoes, came on board he was very accommodating. I had no visa for South Africa, but he said not to worry. I asked him not to stamp my passport since it could prevent me entering other African countries. Again, no problem: he gave me a stick-on visa which could easily be ripped off without a trace. He also offered me a lift into town.

'People say we're racialist,' he said as we drove past warehouses and factories towards the city centre, 'but the blacks are not educated here as elsewhere. They have babies all over the veld. We give them schools and they burn them down. That's why the country is run by whites.'

As we emerged into the city centre, it reminded me of a mixture of Miami and an English provincial town. In the comfortable suburbs on the surrounding hills, there were neat detached houses set in spacious gardens in tree-lined avenues. In the city centre, there was an old Tudor-style building and a solid municipal town hall. Down towards the seafront, high-rise hotels and broad highways evoked Florida again. The weather was much warmer than Cape Town and there were palms trees and sub-tropical plants in the public gardens. The grass itself was parched, hinting at the terrible drought further north.

Author contemplating his coming voyage at Sagres, Portugal, the most
south-westerly point of Europe.

A vendor gives the final touch to his wares
in the souks of Marrakesh, Morocco.

A villager and baby in Senegal,
West Africa.

Drummers warming up in
Casamance, Senegal.

Ganvié, a village on stilts on Lake Nokoué, Benin.

Roger Milla, Africa's greatest football
player, Cameroon.

Cape of Good Hope,
South Africa.

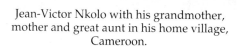

Jean-Victor Nkolo with his grandmother,
mother and great aunt in his home village,
Cameroon.

General cargo ship *Tilly*,
built in Hamburg in 1966.

A boy with coconuts
on the coast of Tanzania.

Swahili sailors on a dhow off the East African coast.

The author's family enjoying breakfast in the Old Stone Town, Zanzibar.

Rhino and baby in the Ngorongoro Crater, Tanzania.

Masai warriors in East Africa.

Author sailing a felucca on the Nile at Luxor, Egypt.

Camels taking it easy by the Giza pyramids, Egypt.

Author contemplating the wreck of Ozymandias, Luxor, Egypt.

I made two visits. The first was to the office of South African Airways where I booked a ticket to Johannesburg where I hoped to meet an old friend of mine, John Schlapobersky, who was flying in from England with the TV crew. I then headed for the main office of the Mediterranean Shipping Company (MSL), an Italian-owned company based in Geneva. I had already telephoned them from Cape Town about the possibility of taking a ship up the East African coast. The girl in the travel section of the huge, futuristic glass building confirmed that I could get a passage on the *Barbara D*, a small cargo ship sailing from Durban to Dar es Salaam via Maputo, Beira and Mombasa in a couple of weeks' time.

Once again, I could not believe my luck. I had tried countless times to contact Zim Lines of Israel and the America Lykes Line based in New Orleans but had got nowhere. The MSL seemed the only chance and I managed to get a ticket, even though it was going to cost me $100 a day.

Wandering about Durban I noticed that English was the main language. Durban was in fact the capital of the only predominantly English-speaking province in South Africa. After the first two waves of Dutch and Huguenot settlers in the seventeenth century in the Cape region, the British came in their thousands two centuries later. A large group was sent to settle along the Natal coast and Durban grew because of its fine natural harbour. Where the Afrikaners were content to make a reasonable living for themselves, loving their independence more than comfort, the British were keen to develop the economy as part of their wider empire. What united them was a desire to carve out their own place under the African sun and to get the Africans to do the dirty work. By the the middle of the nineteenth century, the British had imposed a comprehensive system of racial segregation on the colony of Natal.

Because they could not find enough Africans to work the sugar plantations of Natal, the British brought indentured labourers over from India in the 1860s. The community had grown to almost one million and now out-numbered the whites in the province; to add insult to injury, they were often better at business.

I found it particularly interesting to be in Durban because of its associations with Gandhi. It was after being thrown out of a first-class carriage from Durban to Pretoria in 1893 that the British-trained barrister decided to stay in South Africa and fight racial discrimination. During his twenty-one years in the country he developed his strategy of passive resistance and non-violent civil disobedience which eventually helped liberate India and shook the British Empire to the root. He also helped inspire the formation of the African National Congress in 1912.

But what about the original inhabitants? Before the whites' arrival, the Eastern coastal plains of Southern Africa were occupied for centuries by the Nguni, a people related by language who include the Tembu, the Xhosa and Zulu. While hunting and cultivating, they were predominantly herders whose cattle were their primary source of wealth. Like all pastoralists they lived in small, mobile settlements in relative harmony with their environment. Their extended families formed clans, but the chiefs at their head consulted their councils of elders and their authority was of a conditional, not an absolute kind. The exception were the Zulus amongst whom, from early in the nineteenth century, a central authority emerged which organized a powerful military kingdom over which their royal family held despotic power.

All Nguni peoples, including the Zulus, were bound by highly evolved kinship ties which precluded slavery and supported those in need in their societies. They maintained a rule of law, and practised codes of hospitality and land use. The chief could allocate land but he was its steward and not its owner for there was no concept of private property or title. It was a country of relative abundance.

The steady advance of the frontier wars changed all that. Afrikaner settlers, as they came north and east from the Western Cape, introduced slavery, private property, and the exercise of arbitrary and unconditional authority. As the pastoral society was attacked from without, it was also being undermined from within as the Zulus colonised neighbouring tribes and developed a war-like nation organized on Spartan lines. Until these events, wars rarely went beyond local conflicts or cattle raids. If one group did engage another, the conflict was usually ritualized and one side would withdraw before much blood was shed. The Zulu's newly acquired military might made their territories too inhospitable for the Boers who established their republics in the hinterland of South Africa, across the Orange and Vaal rivers (hence their names Orange Free State and Transvaal). But the Zulus were also a threat to British settlement in what was to become Natal so it finally fell to the British army to vanquish the Zulus at the Battle of Isaldwhana near Ulundi, the Zulu capital, in 1879. Thereafter the British Governor and his administrators helped to redirect the Zulus' military prowess into regimented labour on behalf of the growing white economy.

The trappings of Shaka, Dingaan and the other great Zulu warlords of the nineteenth century were now being exploited by Chief Buthelezi who had built his capital in the ashes of Ulundi in the KwaZulu 'homeland'. His warriors marched like the *impis* of a bygone era with shields and *assegais* (short spears) at the mass rallies of the Inkatha Freedom Party where they tried to intimidate other people and parties. The white right wing were using them to divide and rule the black opposition and yet, of all the homelands KwaZulu was the most surreal, scattered all over Natal, interspersed by large 'white' areas, including Richard's Bay, the only natural seaport. The whole arrangement made a mockery of the National Party's idea that the homelands were sovereign and independent states.

I mulled all this over in the bus on the road to Durban's airport, twelve miles from the city centre. It was difficult to imagine Shaka's well-disciplined warriors pouring over the hills. I passed many factories which showed how South Africa was now a major industrial country and could easily become the powerhouse for the development of the whole of Southern Africa. There was of course a down side to this. It was based on the exploitation of cheap black and brown labour. And as the philosopher Versfeld had pointed out to me, the second industry of South Africa was the manufacture of weapons. The country was even reputed to have nuclear bombs.

At the airport, the canteen mirrored the nature of Durban society itself: the kitchen staff were black, the girls on the till Indian, and the manageress white. Observing this as I took a reassuring cup of tea and piece of cake (again I could have been in England), I cursed the apartheid system which made one think in racial categories and not in terms of human individuals. I had this contradictory feeling many times in South Africa: I felt at home there, was overwhelmed by the beauty of the coast and land, yet I could not really enjoy it all because of the country's confounded race relations and its organized system of injustice. It was similar to liking a person who has a terrible streak in his make-up.

As I settled in the immaculate Airbus made in Toulouse (what happened to sanctions?), I noted that the only non-white passengers were a young black man in a baseball hat, an Indian couple, and two Chinese businessmen. Once we had taken off and veered towards the interior, I could see where the labour force of Durban lived – in endless shanty towns with corrugated roofs which clung to the hills surrounding Durban. We then headed north-north-west towards the town of Ladysmith and then passed over the parched veld of the Orange Free State and the Transvaal before landing in Johannesburg. Under the beating sun in the deep blue sky, the reddish plain stretched for miles and miles until it was lost in the blue haze.

Looking through the window of the aeroplane, I suddenly felt a sense of awe in the face of the vastness of Africa. It was a familiar feeling. However much I tried to cast a net around Africa, I knew it would escape me.

Chapter Twenty

Live *and* Let Live

WAITING to meet me at Smuts airport in Johannesburg was Felicity Potter, the companion of David Schlapobersky, my friend's brother. She drove me to her comfortable villa in the northern suburbs. I hardly saw a black face; we had kept to the rich white ways of this surreal city, the largest in Africa south of Cairo.

John and David Schlapoberksy had been born in Johannesburg but had grown up on a farm in Swaziland, where they had run bare foot and developed a lasting love of the African bush. Their grandparents had come to South Africa at the beginning of the century to escape pogroms against the Jews in Lithuania. David had become a successful potter and had stayed in South Africa while John had left as a student for England to be followed by another brother and sister.

John had not left of his own free will. As a student at the University of Witwatersrand studying psychology in the late sixties he had been arrested on suspicion of having contacts with subversive organizations. Although he was opposed to apartheid and supported the aims of the Freedom Charter of the African National Congress, he was not in fact working underground or a member of a political organization at the time. After being imprisoned and tortured, he was eventually deported and had made his way to England where he had become a psychotherapist. He also worked for the Medical Foundation, rehabilitating tortured refugees from all over the world.

As we unlocked the complicated locks of the car gates to Felicity's house, I realized how security conscious the white citizens of Jo'burg had become. 'Only the other day one of our neighbours was burgled,' she told me. 'The thieves nowadays are armed and don't hesitate to shoot. It's so dangerous here now that few dare walk out in the street after dark.'

In the afternoon, David took me on a tour of Johannesburg. We started off in the leafy avenues of the northern suburbs, which had familiar English names likes Sandhurst, Hyde Park, Saxonwold and Sandown. The Afrikaners held political power in the country but the English still controlled most of the wealth. They had built themselves grand palaces set in beautiful and immaculate gardens. The streets were empty except for the carefully cut grass verges and spreading trees. I noticed that the high walls of the houses all had barbed wire on top, with boldly displayed security systems.

We went up to a vantage point on a hill overlooking the high-rise buildings of the city centre. In the distance, I could see the ridge of man-made hills made from some of the deepest gold mines in the world. It was here on the Witwatersrand – Ridge of White Waters – that one of the richest gold reefs in the world was discovered in 1886. 'South Africa still has fifty per cent of the world's gold reserves; it's the government's main source of revenue,' David informed me.

Literally five minutes away from some of the richest homes I had ever seen, we came across the township of Alexandria, which was surrounded by a few factories. I knew that Johannesburg was strictly segregated and that there were huge differences in wealth, but I had not expected what lay before me. By now the night was drawing in and Alexandria seemed like a city in a nightmare. Within a square mile, cut off from the rest of Johannesburg by wide roads, a golf course and wasteland, I could see a few crude apartment blocks surrounded by row upon row of makeshift huts. The whole was lit by the huge arc lights used in football stadiums which cast a ghostly white glow. The rough streets, littered with rubbish, were patrolled by armoured cars. There was an eerie silence in such a dead city, made all the more frightening by the occasional barking of scavenging dogs.

'Where else do the blacks live?'

'In townships especially to the south of the city where the main factories are. Over a million people live in Soweto. Officially the blacks are guest workers, since they are all meant to be citizens of a homeland and not the Republic of South Africa. They therefore have no rights here.'

'I should imagine that such a place can only breed violence.'

'Yes, the violence is getting worse all the time.'

We then turned away and headed into the city centre, where modern office blocks towered over the few turn-of-the-century buildings left. The whole city was built on a rectangular grid pattern which reflected the mechanical thinking of the town planners during the gold rush. Passing some fine shop fronts with Indian-style decorations, David observed:

'The Asians used to live here but they were resettled in the town of Lenasia on the southern outskirts at the time when the Group Areas Act was applied.'

By this time, night had fallen. The Johannesburg Stock Exchange, symbol of white aspirations, was lit up by a thousand lights against the orange sky. By contrast, the nearby Market Theatre Complex was deserted; nothing was happening there that night. Money in South Africa had always come before culture. At the pavement level, Johannesburg, like Cape Town, seemed a dead city after dark. The only hint of night life was a few tawdry escort agencies where white girls sat in brightly lit parlours waiting for clients.

We headed back home through Hillbrow and Joubert districts. Here at last there seemed to be some action. I was surprised to see quite a number of young black people on the streets.

'This is the only part of the city where you can sense that apartheid is coming to an end', David said. 'For the first time, blacks can rent apartments here. Our maid has got one with her son. But they still have to get a bond from whites to guarantee payment of the rents to the white landlords.'

As we returned to his home, I asked David to tell me more about the aims of the ANC.

'They want to overcome the economic injustices and racial differences in the country. At the moment, anyone classified as black in South Africa has no political rights at all.'

'And what kind of society would they like to see develop?'

189

'A non-racist, non-sexist democracy based on "one person, one vote" in a unitary state. That means getting rid of all the homelands.'

'And do you think that the government and the opposition will ever resolve their differences?'

'I think so. In a couple years, there could well be majority rule in this country. But it isn't going to be easy and it could easily be postponed if the violence continues.'

Not long after my arrival in Jo'burg David and Felicity took me to see an acquaintance who lived nearby in a lovely house in the northern suburbs. Her name was Ardree Fritz. She had lost her husband who had been a mining engineer and friend of Harry Oppenheimer, the mining magnate.

Over tea by her swimming pool, Ardree Fritz recalled how the wives of the mining managers were trained in the use of firearms in case of an uprising during the periodic strikes of the workers. Although from an ancient Huguenot family, she was on the liberal wing of white high society. She recognized that democracy would eventually come to South Africa, but insisted that there had to be some qualification:

'If you're turning over a hundred rand a month or ten thousand a month, I think the person turning over ten thousand should perhaps have more votes. I think a person like Harry Oppenheimer who started a tremendous empire here and has given lots of people job opportunities should get more votes than a person who sweeps the streets, whether he is black, white or khaki.'

It was an argument put forward by the nineteenth-century British liberal philosopher John Stuart Mill, who believed votes should be distributed according to education rather than the ownership of property. It had also been put forward in recent times by that old African hand, Ian Smith, who had tried, Canute-like, to hold back the rising tide of black aspirations, in Rhodesia.

'Did you know any educated blacks when you were young?'

'When I was at varsity, there were some blacks at Fort Hare. We used to mix at certain times and at certain cultural levels. My mother and father were horrified. They said "Did you drink tea with them?". I said I didn't even think about it; I never thought about them being black or white.'

Earlier in the afternoon, I had met her daughter in the living room of their house and had played with her little blond, blue-eyed baby. I asked his grandmother the fifty-thousand dollar question:

'Would it worry you if your daughter married a black man?'

Ardree Fritz was not a woman to be flustered and she replied calmly: 'I think it would probably would, because they would be marrying out of their cultural norms. But only for that reason. In the future, probably not; there will be a melting pot for all the colours in South Africa. I've said so all my life.'

As we left, she said to me with a half-smile: 'You won't take the mickey, will you?'

When David and I went to the airport to meet John, he came through the customs and immigration beaming and gave me a bear hug.

'You know, it's the first time I've been allowed to enter without special permission. They didn't even hold me up at immigration. The regime must really be changing!'

Soon after John's arrival, I returned with him to the place where he had been tortured in Pretoria, the headquarters of the South African security police. On the way we visited the Vootrekker Monument, on a hill which dominated the rolling veld for miles around. It was built to commemorate the centenary of the victory of the Boers over the Zulus during their great trek to the interior.

'This is the holy of the holies for the Boers,' John said. 'It was inspired by the fascist architecture of Nazi Germany. When they lay the foundation stone a crowd of 200,000 gathered in 1938 in a South African equivalent of the Nuremberg Rally.'

The square brown granite monument had statues of trekkers holding a rifle at its four corners. It was surrounded by a circle of wagons cut in stone relief, a symbol for me of the laager mentality which tried to keep all black Africa out. On the inside walls was a frieze commemorating the Day of the Vow and the Day of the Battle of Blood River.

In 1938, the Voortrekkers' leader Piet Retif had gone to negotiate a treaty with the Zulus, but was killed on the orders of Dingane, Shaka's half brother and assassin. The Zulus then massacred the unsuspecting

191

encampment of men, women and children. Andries Pretorius – who gave his name to Pretoria – returned with a band of 530 Voortrekkers, who formed a laager with their ox wagons, and vowed that if God allowed them to triumph they would celebrate the occasion like the Sabbath. On 16 December 1838, they beat back 10,000 Zulu warriors until the river ran red with their blood. More than 3,000 Zulus fell and only three Boers were slightly injured. God was on their side. Revenge was sweet and brutal. Never again would a black man's word be trusted. The myth of the Zulus' betrayal became a central feature of the Afrikaner's psyche

In the dim light of the crypt of the Voortrekker Monument, I could make out the flame of a small oil lamp in a niche accompanied by the sign: 'The Light of Civilization'. It was written at the time without irony, the self-same light of Afrikaner civilization which brought guns which cleared the people and wild life off the high veld, the light which made sweet rivers run red, the light which buried black miners in the gold-giving earth, the light which reduced brave warriors to kitchen boys.

In the cavernous centre of the monument was an empty marble tomb inscribed with the words from the national anthem: ONSVIR JOU SUID-AFRIKA – 'We are for you, South Afrika'. At noon on December each year – the Day of the Vow – a ray of sunlight shines through the dome and picks out the inscription. I felt I was looking at the mausoleum of apartheid.

As we approached Pretoria, John revealed how he had been in a state of shock and confusion travelling along the same road after being arrested twenty-three years earlier.

'I can remember seeing some workmen shovelling soil at the side of the road into a heap. I could see the dust rising up and time seemed to stand still in the smoke.'

We went along the wide streets of Pretoria – wide enough to enable an ox wagon to turn around – and pulled up outside a solid neo-classical edifice called the Compol Building. It was here that John and countless others had been interrogated by the security forces. Its history symbolically linked the Boer republic with gold and oppression.

It was formerly the Bank of Paul Kruger, the President of Transvaal elected soon after the Boers had beaten a superior British force at Majuba Hill in 1881. It still had heavy metal safe doors made by Chubb of London.

It had now been made into a Police Museum, but the section where John and other suspected 'subversives' had been interrogated was closed off with the sign: 'South African Police Historical Archives. No Admission'. We left the building and walked down a side road to talk outside the barred room where John had passed the most harrowing time of his life.

'I must tell you that my heart's pounding now. You can be sure that we're under surveillance.'

Sure enough up the road stood a black policeman.

'I was taken here on Friday 13 June and held just under a week, from Friday to the following Wednesday, in that tiny room behind those bars. It contained just a desk, a bare light and a washbasin. During that period, a team of six security police officers interrogated me around the clock for twenty-four hours. They kept me entirely without sleep but they fed me well to make sure I could have enough stamina to withstand the interrogation. They kept asking me for names, but since I didn't know them, I couldn't have helped them even if I had wanted to. After some time, one of the interrogators threw me a brick and said:

"Here's your brick. Stand on it!"'

'That must have been agony to stand on after a while.'

'It was no joke. But it's important to bear in mind that as a white I was to some degree protected by reason of my colour. There were a large number of other black prisoners who were subjected to electric torture, beatings, and a wide range of atrocities. There's no way of knowing how many people were interrogated in this building.'

'It must feel strange to be standing here, on the other side of the bars.'

'Many people lost their lives during police interrogation here. The regime was frightened of any dissent, and the red peril was considered one step away from the black peril. I was one of the lucky ones for I survived. But in a sense, all the people of this country who have withstood and struggled against apartheid are also standing here as survivors on the other side of what was a prison for most of the population.'

'In what ways was it a prison?'

'The apartheid system was a system of contrived malevolence. It was based on a racist ideology which incorporated many tenets of European fascism from the twenties and thirties, in which the world was divided between *untermenschen* and *übermenschen*, the sub-human and the master race, only they were called blacks and whites.'

'Where did you fit in?'

'As a Jew and from a Jewish community in South Africa I was in an anomalous position, somewhere between the two. During my interrogation, which was in English, I managed to convince the policemen that I couldn't understand Afrikaans, so they allowed themselves to speak freely. I was able to understand a great deal about their thinking and their approach to me and to the others they were interrogating me about. They referred to me between themselves as *die klien Joodkie*, the little Jew. It was a way of diminishing me, to add this kind of endearment, the little Jew.'

'Do you feel revenge or can you forgive your torturers now?'

'I don't feel revenge nor do I have anything to forgive. The torture and beatings may have stopped in this building, but they continue elsewhere. But it's very important for me to come back here. The next step is to meet my interrogators.'

'Given its history of oppression and violence, do you think the country will ever be able to heal itself?'

'I'm astonished by the magnanimity and generosity of the black leaders and their call for reconciliation. If there's going to be recriminations, then the whole country will be torn apart. We need to face these things, but only to leave them behind and get on with the task of recreating a human order in this uniquely beautiful country where one group has created a nightmare for most of the others.'

John, as he said, was one of the lucky ones. After his week of interrogation, without sleep and on his brick, he was taken to the prison on the outskirts of Pretoria. After two months, he was suddenly presented with the stark choice: 'Either you stay here and never get out, or else you leave the country and don't come back'. He chose the latter and the next day he was put on a plane. Since he had been living in the British protectorate of Swaziland, he had a British passport; his case had been raised in the British parliament and diplomatic pressure applied to the South African government. He went into exile like thousands of other young people.

*   *   *

John was one of countless opponents of apartheid who had suffered. But had anything changed since his time? Was the National Party really up to dirty tricks while telling the rest of the world that apartheid was over? I went to see Brian Curren who was director of Lawyers for Human Rights, an organization run by a multiracial staff in a small office in the centre of Johannesburg. Although apartheid legislation had made a mockery of the administration of justice in South Africa, Curren and his colleagues still tried to use the legal system to oppose the worst miscarriages.

Curren was no rampant radical but a soft-spoken lawyer in striped shirt and tie and sports jacket. He insisted that since the judiciary was written by the racist South African state and controlled by white judges it was inevitably loaded against the blacks. The judiciary, which implemented the most racist legislation of any existing state, was inevitably compromised.

I asked him whether the state had been involved in trying to undermine the anti-apartheid movement?

'I am certain that there's ample evidence to demonstrate the existence of a "third force" which is trying to create havoc in the country. I also have well-documented evidence of state-sponsored terrorism.'

'It seems to me that the legal system in South Africa has little regard for black life.'

'You're right. The state consistently considers black life to be less important than white. Only recently there was the case of fourteen children being burnt to death in a church in Pretoria. The police the next day ordered the demolition of the church which, of course, destroyed any possible evidence of arson. Had it been white children killed in a fire of that nature, I can assure you that the area would have been cordoned off for at least three or four days and every stone would have been turned over.

'Do you think you'll ever be able to change this state of affairs?'

'Well, it'll have to change; if it doesn't change, the country's not going to survive. It will mean a fundamental change of attitude, and that's very deep-seated. We're going to have to undergo a phase of massive education, of people setting an example; we're going to have to rise above ourselves.'

Brian Curren was a courageous English-speaking white liberal who had received many death threats. To get a view from a radical Afrikaaner opposed to the apartheid system, I visited the office of the only independent Afrikaans daily newspaper, *Vrye Weekblet*. The editor, Max Du Preez, was dressed casually in jeans, with longish hair, beard, and round John Lennon glasses. He too had been persecuted by the authorities.

'We are the most persecuted newspaper in the history of the country,' he announced proudly. 'In the first few years, I was in court thirty-seven times and I've been interrogated by the state security police many times. Whenever I go to the United Kingdom, I have to fill out a form with details of my criminal record and I say: "But please, this is political because we have these funny acts in South Africa!" What we didn't bargain for when we started were the physical threats. This office was blown up by a large bomb eighteen months ago.'

'Have you changed your line over the years?'

'The last President of the National Party called us media terrorists; I prefer to call ourselves media guerrillas. Our paper was the first to disclose the existence of military hit squads which assassinated opponents of apartheid. It was certainly front-line journalism. Because Afrikaner nationalist rule had been in power so long, we had to kick their arses a bit to open things up. Now we're more professional journalists.'

'What are your main aims now?'

'On the one hand we try to expose the evils of the apartheid system, and at the same time to tell our readers that we have seen the future of non-racialism and democracy and it works. We try to bring people together and to introduce black people, black society and black aspirations to the whites because they don't have any idea about them. There are more non-whites than whites speaking Afrikaans now and they need a voice.'

'And after the abolition of apartheid . . ?'

'Even if legal apartheid is abolished, there will be a long haul to end economic apartheid through a massive redistribution of wealth. At the moment in Johannesburg, a hundred people control most of the wealth.'

'But do you really think the Afrikaners will ever be able to change their spots?'

'They're in the process of discovering that they have a lot in common with those people they hated and feared so much. For many generations, they were divided into Africans and Europeans, but they're beginning to realize how much they have in common with their black countrymen, like a passion for the soil, like a loathing for Europe – even negative things. I believe in the next ten years, unless something dramatic happens in the transition during the next two years, we will build a non-racial society in South Africa where Africans and Afrikaners will share a common loyalty. Even if they don't love each other so much, they will at least tolerate each other.'

As we were talking, blaring music from the other side of the road threatened to drown our conversation.

'It's a shebeen – brothel,' Du Preez chuckled. 'We've agreed to live and let live. We won't report them, and their clients won't break into our cars!'

To get an official view of the changes, I trekked back to Cape Town to see the Deputy Minister of Foreign Affairs Renier Stephanus Schoeman. The Foreign Minister Pik Botha, who had recently claimed that a refusal to accept change was tantamount to a 'death wish', was abroad at the time. I met his deputy instead in the legislative capital.

He was a smooth, middle-aged man whose greying hair was carefully combed with a little wave over his forehead. After losing his seat in the last election, he had been 'indirectly elected' National Party MP for Natal and appointed by President de Klerk to his post. As a former Captain in the South African Defence Force and Chief Director of the Federal Information Service of the National Party, he was a good man to have around. According to his CV, his hobbies included walking, tennis and listening to classical music. He was clearly a humane, civilized man – with a knowlege of hard weapons and the wiles of party politics.

On the wall of his office, there was an illustration from the French magazine *Le Petit Journal* depicting a Boer bull with President Kruger's face sticking its horns up a British Lion's arse. 'I like to show it to the British ambassador when he comes here!' the minister joked.

I asked why in the history of the National Party, every shift in policy had been described in terms of its opposite?

'The exclusion of blacks from university was called the "Extension of University Act". The denial of education to blacks was called the "Bantu Education Act". The introduction of petty apartheid, which barred blacks from public amenities, was called "Separate Amenities Act".

With such a history of doublespeak why should the non-white population of this country believe you when you say that apartheid is over?'

'I would submit that the National Party has always been a party which has proved itself capable of renewal. What I can testify to you is that at this moment in time the National Party, its leadership echelons, its leader President de Klerk, are totally committed to that which they say in public every day, to a truly democratic, non-racial dispensation with room for all, participation for all. They mean it, we mean it, and I mean it.'

'So it is the end of doublespeak? Justice will no longer mean injustice?'

'Doublespeak and apartheid died together.'

'It may be the end of legal apartheid, but what about economic apartheid? Are you going to change that?'

'I personally feel great sympathy and empathy for hardship wherever I encounter it. When on the occasion I travelled with our Finance Minister and stayed at the Savoy Hotel in London and I walked down the Embankment and saw all the tramps sleeping under cardboard it really touched me. It hurts me to feel that there is so much deprivation in the world. In our own country, I represented a constituency in Natal on the northern coast and I made it my business to go often to the squatter areas. I find it totally unacceptable that – let's say for argument's sake – a white home should have ten taps, while there are a thousand black people for one tap. There's something wrong, drastically wrong, there. But there are many countries in the world where you have a clear-cut and tragic distinction between the extremities of poverty, between the haves and the have-nots. The whole of the African continent is a classic example of this. It is the major challenge of this country to try to uplift the people who have less.'

'Do you really think, given your past record, that you will ever be able to negotiate a multiracial democracy in this country?'

'I think it was Woody Allen who said that if ever the lion and the lamb lie down together, the lamb will not get much sleep. In that respect, nobody has illusions to the extent and complexity of the problem facing us. The imperative in South Africa for finding a peaceful solution is tremendous. If the government and the ANC had continued as before it could have reduced the county to ashes. If we can find a constitutional arrangement which can accommodate our diversity, it will serve as an example for many other places. But our own situation is unique in complexity and we have no imperialist intentions of exporting our solutions. We need a home-grown solution acceptable to all of us in this country.'

Despite his devious manner and tortuous reasoning, I felt that the minister like other members of the National Party government had seen the writing on the wall. Deep within them, they knew that the days of apartheid were numbered and there was no turning back. It was now a question of postponing the day of reckoning and of salvaging as many privileges and powers as possible from the shipwreck of the grand Voortrekkers' dream.

At the end of our conversation, Renier Stephanus Schoeman said to me: 'You English always have a sting in the tail!'

Chapter Twenty-One

Seasons Come to Pass

THE ANC building was a huge skyscraper in the centre of Johannesburg. Only a couple of years before the African National Congress had been a banned organization; now it had white security guards. It was to all extents and purposes a provisional government-in-waiting. In the lobby, dozens of people were milling around, many of them banned until recently.

My first meeting was with Walter Sisulu, the Deputy President of the ANC, who was flying in from a homeland specially to see me. While I was waiting for him to show up, I saw two white veterans of the anti-apartheid movement: Joe Slovo, the white-haired general secretary of the South African Communist Party who had been in exile since the sixties, and whose wife, Ruth First, had been killed by a parcel bomb, and Albie Sachs, also from the Communist Party and an ANC activist who had his arm blown off by a car bomb while in exile in Mozambique. The bombs in both cases had been despatched by South African government agents but both were now committed to negotiation rather than armed struggle and accepted the need for a multi-party democracy. Slovo even suggested that the opposition should agree to interim power-sharing with the white-minority government to speed up constitutional change.

I took the lift to the top floor, twenty-two stories high. While waiting for Walter Sisulu to arrive, I met his wife Albertina. Like Mandela's wife Winnie, she had suffered much while her husband was twenty-six years in prison on Robben Island, but she had never tried to seek power for herself. Despite often being under banning orders in Soweto, she had worked as a nursing sister and made sure all her five children had as good an education as possible. She was ebullient and friendly despite her long struggle to keep her family together. I asked her about her husband's eightieth birthday which had taken place a few days before.

'It was a a very happy occasion. He had many wishes from all over the world and we had a big party with all our friends.'

'How does he feel at eighty?'

'Very well, except the other day he had a fall and hurt his back. It's giving him a lot of pain.'

At that moment Walter Sisulu turned up. He was short and stocky, with completely white hair. He looked fit and alert, with a sparkle in his eye behind dark-rimmed spectacles. His wife called him affectionately 'Papa'. We went into his simply furnished office where he sat under a painting with the words *Mayibuye*. I asked him what it meant:

'To come back to Africa, to come back to its people, and Africa to come back to itself after colonialism.'

The ANC was founded the year Sisulu was born in 1912. He was once the best-loved national figures in South Africa, and one of the most influential figures in South African politics in the twentieth century. Mandela called him the 'Father of the Nation'. Where many of the leaders of the ANC, including Mandela, had moved into posh white suburbs of Johannesburg, he still lived in the same small home in Soweto where his mother used to take in other people's washing.

Although he had a lower profile than Mandela, he was four years his senior and very much his mentor; he even gave him his first suit. The son of a white foreman who came to his village in the Transkei to supervise road workers and a woman who took in washing, Sisulu was largely self-educated. He had worked in mines, factories and domestic service. The 'cheeky kaffir', as the whites called him, knew all about exploitation and discrimination.

After the landslide victory of the Afrikaner National Party in 1948, he had worked with Nelson Mandela, Oliver Tambo and others to form the Youth League of the ANC. They drew up a radical Programme of Action advocating civil disobedience, strikes, boycotts and stay-at-homes.

It not only called for 'national freedom' and 'political independence', but committed the ANC to a new strategy based on mass action in defiance of the law. As the apartheid legislation poured out, Sisulu was tried under the Suppression of Communism Act for leading the Defiance Campaign and served with banning orders to prevent him from attending meetings.

It did not prevent him from participating in the congress in 1955 which drew up the Freedom Charter which still forms the basis of the ANC's demands. In a remarkable spirit of reconciliation, it declares 'that South Africa belongs to all who live in it, black and white, and that no government can justly claim authority unless it is based on the will of all the people'. It then goes on to list the usual human rights to be respected, with the controversial appendage that 'the mineral wealth beneath the soil, the banks and monopoly industry shall be transferred to the ownership of the people as a whole'.

The Charter did not win the support of all black activists. It was attacked by the Pan-Africanist Congress precisely because it included whites and blacks. The PAC believed that liberation should be carried out by blacks alone and that any future should be 'of the Africans, by the Africans for the Africans'. Their message for the whites was 'one settler, one bullet'.

In a single raid on a farmhouse in Rivonia in 1963 the government arrested the entire ANC clandestine leadership, including Sisulu and Mandela, before it had time to develop an underground network. At the Treason Trials which followed, they were sentenced to life imprisonment. I asked Sisulu what he felt when the sentence was announced. With typical understatement, he replied:

'Great relief. We were expecting to be condemned to death for treason, but life imprisonment was a reprieve.'

'What did you most miss on Robben Island?'

'Most of all I missed seeing my own children. I saw the warden's children but I couldn't touch them. Now I can touch my grandchildren and I am happy.'

It was President de Klerk's decision to release Sisulu and six other members of the ANC leadership in October 1989 which led to the virtual unbanning of the ANC. They immediately began talking in its name and organized mass rallies. Mandela's release soon followed early in 1990.

I explained to Sisulu what I was trying to do by circumnavigating Africa 500 years after Vasco da Gama rounded South Africa.

'You've arrived at a most appropriate moment', he declared. 'The talks we are having for a democratic South Africa are a very great achievement in the history of our country since the arrival of the colonists. It was remarkable how we managed to bring together various parties so hostile to each other and that they could be discussing jointly the future. Although there are differences, sharp differences in some cases, there is a definite acceptance of the fact that the only way is that South Africa must negotiate a peaceful solution.'

'Do you see any dangers ahead?'

'As far as the left is concerned, I don't think so. Those who do not accept our line of peaceful negotiations are a comparatively small group and are not likely to upset the situation. On the far right, that is where the danger lies – although it has been flattened by the success of the talks and by the fact that the white population here voted for negotiation. Usually on the far right you have elements that are not guided by logic and reason but by blood and feeling. People like that are in a sense not quite normal and therefore anything is possible; others can be deceived to follow suit. I don't think the danger is as sharp as it has been before yet we can't rule it out.'

'You've just celebrated your eightieth birthday. After a lifetime devoted to the struggle to liberate your country from oppression and racialism what is your vision of a new South Africa for the twenty-first century?'

'Well, I've no doubt that South Africa is going to play a very important part in the next century. We can't help but democratize. We have been the last but we are fortunate in one way for we can learn from others before us. I'm quite hopeful that a great future lies ahead and that our people will with pride take their rightful place in shaping not only South Africa but Africa as a whole. We have been helped by Africa and by the world, and therefore we have an obligation to help Africa and to help the world in whatever manner we can.'

As I left Sisulu, I felt I had been in the presence of a man of great strength and courage, who had devoted his life for a cause of justice but had not in the process lost his humanity. Whatever the white world had done to him, Sisulu had remained gentle, kindly, forgiving and lucid. His belief that racists are morally inferior people and his dedication to the ideal of a non-racial society had stood him in good stead.

While totally opposed to apartheid, I was not an uncritical supporter of the ANC. I disagreed with the need for armed struggle, preferring the strategy of non-violent direct action and civil disobedience which Gandhi had developed in the country. Winnie Mandela and her followers who wished to liberate South Africa through necklaces of burning tyres would only continue the spiral of injustice and cruelty. The ANC had not been exempt, according to Amnesty International, from trying to cover up the torture and killing of opponents in detention camps outside South Africa during its years of exile.

There was also the danger that the ANC's proposal of a strongly centralized government based on permanent black majority rule in a unitary state could lead to new tyranny. Although clearly an advance on the fascist trappings of apartheid government, the British-style parliamentary system is by no means the political ideal. More than most countries, it seemed to me that South Africa would benefit from a radical decentralization of power and regional autonomy within a loose federation. It could well draw on the older African traditions of popular participation and communal solidarity which apartheid had largely destroyed. If the tragic experience of South Africa proved anything, it is that racism destroys human affection, power corrupts, and violence breeds violence. They may be clichés, but they are profoundly true for all that.

Before leaving the ANC headquarters in Johannesburg, I called on Morgane Wally Serote, the director of the ANC's department of cultural affairs. While a young writer, he had been closely associated with John Schlapobersky, then a student. John's arrest followed Serote's in 1969 but, where John had settled in London, Serote had returned from exile with his family to continue the struggle in South Africa. He had become an uncompromising writer and had once written 'Black men, you are on your own'. He gave me a warm handshake and friendly smile when I met him. Where the 'Father of the Nation' was dressed in a suit, he wore a mustard-coloured, open-necked shirt with his sleeves rolled up. He had large sad eyes. I asked him whether the traditional view of the ANC that 'art is a weapon of the struggle' was now too narrow.

'That has been our view, but now that we need to move from the politics of resistance to the politics of reconstruction the landmarks are less clear. South African literature will be judged by how it portrayed the struggle of our people for liberation, but literature does not only have to have a political theme. It can be about flowers and children and whom you love.'

'But given all the divides in the country, will a common South African culture ever emerge?'

'We need to encourage all the languages and cultures in this country. We must encourage Africans to use their mother tongue. I speak Tsawna though I write in English. In South Africa, we have people from three continents – Africa, Europe and Asia – each can be a source of wisdom.'

'Has it been a long struggle for you to get as far as you have?'

'The struggle which we've waged for eight years up to now has mobilized black people in this country to the point where they are absolutely not prepared any more to be ruled under apartheid. It's been a long way to come to that. We've had to go through underground work, we've had to wage armed struggle, we've had to organize mass actions, and we've had to mobilize the international community. I would say the twenty years or so that I've been in the ANC have been the most valuable education for my life.'

'And the future? Will you ever be able to overcome the legacy of hatred and violence?'

'We need to let a culture of tolerance evolve in this country. We have been people that have lived like animals. We tolerated no different view. If you did not agree with apartheid, you were a Communist and you belonged in jail, or in exile or you were killed. This is the culture we've had for forty years. Now we want to create a culture of tolerance. To do that we have to heal lots of wounds, allay lots of fears, and reassure lots of people.'

Before I left, Wally Serote read out his poem 'Alexandra'. He had been born in the township and it had become an inescapable knot in his destiny, an object of love and hate:

I cry Alexandra when I am thirsty.
Your breasts ooze the dirty waters of your dongas,
Waters diluted with the blood of my brothers, your children,
Who once chose dongas for death-beds.
Do you love me Alexandra, or what are you doing to me?

The next day David Schlapoberksy took me down to Alexandra where he worked one day a week in the arts centre giving pottery classes. When I had first visited it with him late at night, it was like a ghost town in a nightmare. Now as the sun was beginning to rise in the cold morning on the veld, it was transformed: everyone was on the move. People milled around the private minibuses to go to work in the white city. I saw several armed groups of black policemen sauntering through the garbage-strewn lanes and an armoured car cruising along the grid of main streets. One stopped and three men and a white officer entered a shack. Violence was a daily problem for the inhabitants, and the security forces only exasperated it.

I met some young ANC 'comrades' who showed me around the square mile. We started off in the northern slope where the emerging black middle class had built small villas in neat gardens overloooking the squalor below. Smoke from a thousand coal fires hovered over the valley as women prepared the meagre breakfasts for their men and children and tried to warm themselves in the freezing air. On a nearby wall I read the slogan: 'Salute the fallen comrades'. Someone had added: 'May many more fall'. This was a town swept by revolution, where the services were provided by the people for themselves.

In 1986, there had been about 150,000 people living in the square mile of Alexandra; now there were more than a quarter of million. After the scrapping of the Group Areas Act, not only people from the homelands had moved in desperately searching for work in Jo'burg, but refugees from Mozambique had flocked to the township. They were living in makeshift huts in the worst quarter near the cemetery and the main open sewer, or donga. Two or three families had to share one tap and an outside toilet which was only emptied once a week. Cows, goats and chickens rummaged in the rubbish dumps alongside the roads, bringing the country into the city.

'The main problem is the Madala hostel at the moment,' my guides told me. 'They house migrant workers from Kwazulu homeland – about two thousand of them, four to a room. There's also a woman's hostel. Before 1980 the hostel workers were well integrated into the resistance, but they have been ousted by supporters of Buthelezi's Inkatha Freedom Party. They have occupied several rows of houses around the hostel and forced the residents out. We call it the 'Beirut area' and try to keep away. Inkatha wants to destroy the talks between the ANC and the government.'

'Do the security forces do anything about it?'

'When Inkatha attacks, the police do nothing; when the ANC attacks back, the police take the side of Inkatha. The army is not so bad as it used to be and sometimes helps.'

'How are things with the other residents?'

'We're very together. After the 1976 student uprising and Soweto riots, we broke through the wall. Now there's a real sense of community, and we know we're going to win.'

'What were the students' demands in the uprising?'

'We wanted to change the whole of the education system. It was a disaster. Afrikaans was the language of oppression; we didn't want to learn Afrikaans and we didn't want the Afrikaner version of history. We just weren't allowed to discover ourselves or develop self-awareness. If the teachers told the truth, they would lose their jobs. We want to learn about Shakespeare and chemistry, not just gardening and practical things.'

They took me to visit Realogile High School, one of the few schools open. I quickly realized the enormity of the problem. A young teacher told me that the school had 1,600 pupils, often a hundred to a class, but no staff room, no science laboratory, a handful of books in the library. Not surprisingly the drop-out rate was high. Few pupils got beyond primary level. Although the schoolyard was well kept with beds of shrubs and flowers beds, I saw for myself that the windows of the crowded classrooms were broken.

'There's not one school which has a proper library in Alexandra. We have no text books?'

One of the young teachers told me that he still had to struggle against the idea that blacks are intellectually inferior to whites:

'I am a product of Bantu Education. The whole system of education made you feel incompetent and inferior to white students, even though you had higher grades.'

'How did you change that attitude?'

'Within the Black Consciousness movement. Only by discussing and acting within the movement were we able to free ourselves from the prison mentality which says that the whites are superior. The trouble is that there's a new generation of whites who still think in the same old way. The whites have been locked in their own mental prisons. They don't know what goes on in the townships. They never come down here. The whites in the suburbs don't know and they don't care.'

I had my reservations about the Black Consciousness movement, just as I had about black power in the United States, because it often came over as an inverted form of racism. But I could see how after generations of indoctrination it was psychologically important for those who had been brought up to despise their own colour and to undervalue their talents. It was for them to define themselves, not the whites who oppressed them. In a white world, black is evil. In a black work, white is evil. Perhaps it was a necessary stage for some black people to pass through before they could assert their humanity regardless of race or colour.

Before I left Alexandra, I met a large lady in a woollen hat who had just built a tiny shack on the edge of the main donga. If the rain fell heavily, it could easily be washed into the open sewer. Several children had already been drowned there in a recent flood. She had four children but her parents and mother-in-law were bringing them up in the Venda, one of the poorest homelands. She preferred to live here, she told me, to be with her husband who worked as a cleaner. She put her faith in the Zion Christian Church. Her single room was immaculate, with one single bed, table and a kerosene cooking stove on which she boiled water in an old tin.

'How do you feel about not being with your children?' I asked her.

'It's bad. But there's nothing you can do; only here can you find any work.'

'How often do you see them?'

'The smaller kids come here in June during the holidays, and I go and see them in December.'

This was how the apartheid regime in South Africa treated the people who ensured the whites one of the highest standards of living in the world. Ten minutes way from this woman's shack next to the sewer, I had seen at the gates of a vast mansion a new Porsche gleaming in a glass garage. It sparkled like a palace of diamonds. Perhaps that woman's husband cleaned it.

I left Alexandra depressed by its terrible squalor and horrified by its atmosphere of violence. At the same time, I was impressed by the ability of its residents to organize their lives in the constant presence of a hostile police force and under the crushing burden of an oppressive state. A whole network of self-help and mutual aid had evolved. It was a triumph of the human spirit in face of organized evil and systematic tyranny. Against overwhelming odds, the residents had managed to retain their dignity and sense of worth. When they were thirsty, they could cry Alexandra.

As with the ANC leaders, all the people I met expressed forgiveness, forbearance and tolerance towards those who had done them so much wrong. They still believed in the ultimate triumph of truth over falsehood, love over hate. None of them wanted revenge; all wanted to live in peace with the peoples and races of South Africa. It was the closest example of the Christian ideal of turning the other cheek I had ever witnessed. If there is any hope for South Africa, it lies with the youth of Alexandra and the other shanty towns of the country. Whenever someone tells me how flawed human beings are, I shall remember the people I met in Alexandra.

Before leaving South Africa, I was determined to visit the heartland of Afrikanerdom in the Orange Free State. To call the 'Orange Free State' a 'Free State' was the ultimate irony. No state is strictly speaking free, but this one was the most racist state in the history of the world. It might have been free for the small minority of whites who ran it, but not for the mass of impoverished and oppressed citizens. I had come to the land of the supporters of the extreme right-wing Conservative Party and of Eugene Terre-Blanche (White-Land) and his neo-Nazi Afrikaner

Resistance Movement. When President de Klerk had visited the town not long before me, he had been pelted by the whites.

Generally speaking, the further north one goes in South Africa, the greater the racial prejudice. The Boers had moved north into the hinterland to be free from British interference, to shape their society as they saw fit. They feared the loss of their possessions, the loss of their superiority, the loss of their whiteness. But they had created a prison not only for the people they conquered but for themselves. No more could they walk freely under the starlit sky or linger to watch the setting sun turn the veld red with fire. They had turned their hearts to the stone of the hills, and eroded their feelings like the deep gullies on their farms. Their only response to the rising river of black aspirations was to call for higher banks, heavier sentences, and deeper apartheid. If they were not careful, they could well drown when the banks burst, dragged down by their own self-centredness. Then the white tribe of Africa might share the fate of the peoples they exterminated, the Khoikhoi and the San.

At the time of my arrival in Bloemfontein, the capital of the Orange Free State, the rains had not come for more than two years in some places. It was the worst drought of the twentieth century, affecting two-thirds of the territory of South Africa. In the Transvaal alone half the maize crop had failed. Civil war in neighbouring Mozambique had only made matters worse, and refugees and drought victims were steadily travelling south. It promised to make the famine in the Horn of Africa in the mid eighties look mild by comparison.

I had flown in with Judith Mokhetle, regional director of Operation Hunger, an organization founded to combat rural poverty. She was a short, stocky, determined middle-aged lady from Soweto. Like everyone else there, she had got up at five o'clock to see her children off to school.

Judith was used to taking 'celebrities' to see others suffer. Not long before me, she had taken the wife of the former Vice-President of the United States, Mary Quayle, to peer at starving black babies. She had just accompanied the American actress Joan Collins. She had not been very impressed.

'She was with a much younger man and kept asking him: "Am I doing all right? Am I doing all right?" "You're gorgeous, gorgeous," he would reply. She took no interest in the children until the photographers wanted some pictures, and then she picked one up and gave it a hug.'

On the plane from Johannesburg to Bloemfontin was the Traansvaal rugby team heading for a match with the Free State. In their immaculate blazers, they were well-fed, broad-shouldered, red-necked, and slow-speaking. In a country which treated sport like a religion, these were the high priests of white South Africa. No famine there.

As we drove from the airport, I noticed some beautiful horses in the peak of condition being exercised by a well-kept race track. No famine there.

Bloemfontin had the feel of a mid-west town in the United States, with wide, open streets, pick-up trucks and low-rise houses. Its reputation as a cultural desert was belied by a fine park – King's Park – and a fancy modern opera house, the largest in South Africa. In one street a 'Whites Only' sign was still up.

On the outskirts, a mile and ten minutes from the spotless city centre where all the world's consumer goods were on sale, we arrived at a squatter camp at the end of a dirt track. Dotted on parched land all around were makeshift shacks. The squatters were queuing up at a soup kitchen where a huge cauldron was boiling on an open fire alongside a great pot of maize meal. Children were first in line, many with stick legs and swollen bellies, the tell-tale signs of malnutrition.

As soon as the food was served a group of women started ululating, and a few broke into a dance. I looked at the dishevelled men with their woollen hats, wrapped in blankets and old dirty overcoats to keep warm. Queuing up and waiting their turn in the women's world of the soup kitchen, they looked completely demoralized. Some had only a plastic bag to eat from.

Outside a rough hut made from two rusty pieces of corrugated iron, a man stood stooping like a scarecrow. One of his hands was crippled from an old injury. Judith spoke to him in Xhosa to get his story.

'He was thrown off a farm when the farmer didn't want him any more. He grew up on the farm and when he was laid off he was given only fifty rand [£10]). Government compensation is only for white farmers, not black farmers. But he's one of the lucky ones; he's got no family and is on his own.'

Knowing how important the family is to African society, that seemed the ultimate injury.

I asked Judith whether the citizens of Bloemfontein were doing anything for Operation Hunger.

'White society in Bloemfontein doesn't care. We get our money from the large towns like Johannesburg and Pretoria, but the whites in Bloemfontein, forget about them. Poor whites are helped here by the white whites, but in other parts of the country we're feeding 20,000 whites now.'

We then went to visit a 'school' which had been set up temporarily in the abandoned bungalow of a white farmer. All the windows were smashed and it had no furniture or fittings. The teachers, two women and a man, were in their early twenties; they slept on the bare ground. The school consisted of an empty concrete room with a blackboard. It was packed with pupils, ranging from about eight to sixteen. Many were coughing badly from TB; others had scurvy. There were no books, no paper and no pens for the 200 children who came in shifts.

The voluntary teacher, a small smiling man wearing a tie, went laboriously through some sums, explaining in Sotho when their English failed. He then pinned up on the board a chart showing the basic rules of hygiene, how to prepare food, how to wash one's hands after going to the lavatory. He may have been talking about the other side of the moon: none of the pupils had access to fresh water and their stomachs were empty. Just as they were about to leave, they shut their eyes, put their hands together, and sang the Lord's Prayer, a bit ragged at first, unsure of the English words, but ending together in a deeply moving melody. I noticed one girl, her eyelids tightly shut, swaying to the music. They then got up, picked up the battered tins which served as seats, and filed out in silence.

I climbed the top of a nearby hill and below stretching for miles on the treeless, baked veld under the pitiless sky were thousands of makeshift huts. If there were one tap for three families in Alexandra, here there was only one for 100,000. In the distance, I made out a well-fenced-off reservoir.

'Why can't they use that water?'

'It's owned by a white farmer. He will shoot anyone who goes near it. There are no wild animals here, except Boers.'

'Who are all these people?'

'They're mainly refugees from the war in Mozambique.'

From my vantage-point, I could see close to the outskirts of town women and children turning over the garbage on a huge tip. They were joined by cattle, knee deep in broken bottles and rusting cans, who had given up searching for grass on the parched veld. Their bones would soon be mixed with the rubbish.

As I looked on in disbelief, ringing in my mind were the voices of the children who had sung: 'Give us this day our daily bread, and forgive us our trespasses'. What trespasses had these people committed? Why had God, if he existed, punished these people in this way? Why in South Africa had he given white children everything and black children nothing?

We decided to go and visit the homeland of Bophuthatswana a few hours north of Bloemfoentin. Following the Group Areas Act, it was created out of a small area of poor and eroded land to be the sovereign and independent state for the Tswana people who would then be guest workers in the rest of South Africa. The government had installed a puppet chief in the tin-pot state, a man called President Lucas Mangope who lived in Mafeking where the Boers had once besieged the British.

Although all citizens of Bophuthatswana were meant to have passports, we were not stopped at the 'border' and drove to the small town which was the capital. We did not linger: it was so full of furniture shops that it was nicknamed 'Furniture Town'. Instead we drove on through parched rolling hills to visit a black farmer.

It was hot by now, in the twenties. The blue autumn sky was cloudless and the sun was baking the brown earth. Although this was the season when the whirlwinds change direction and the ants block up the holes in their hills, there was no sign of the expected rain.

Clements Seyape's farm was in rolling countryside. His farm buildings nestled under a rocky hill covered with heather, with a fine view over the surrounding fields. Africa stretched out in the shimmering haze. As we arrived, we came across some young boys riding bareback on thin horses: both had their ribs sticking out. A wind blew dust across the empty yard, and a water windmill creaked and sighed.

Mr Seyape was a formal gentleman in a sports jacket with old-fashioned manners. He had been a teacher in Botswana and had semi-retired to his farm. He showed me what was once a beautiful garden: the fruit trees had died and the shrubs were no more. What was left of his once well-tended lawn crackled under foot. I picked up some grass and it turned to powder in my hands. The bright sun poured down but a cold wind blew down from the hills.

'It hasn't rained here for two years. For two years I haven't been able to plant anything. The seeds are in the ground waiting for the rain. If it doesn't rain this season, I'm finished. We're just keeping going with the water from the borehole, but when that dries up, there's nothing else.'

'How are your labourers getting on?'

'They aren't doing too badly, as I continue to pay them their wages and their rations. I can't send them off just like that; I'm morally obliged to keep them. But it's getting more and more difficult every day. I just have to increase my overdraft at the bank. I just hope it will rain one day.'

Before we left the farm, I wandered about the yard. A few emaciated cattle stood listless. I walked over a brow and almost fell into a hollow which had several half-eaten carcasses of calves. When the cold night fell, the jackals would return.

We set off at dusk, dust trailing behind our car on the bone-dry track. In the parched soil of the surrounding fields, the seeds waited in the darkness. They had been waiting for two and a half years in the place where they had fallen, passing through freezing nights and burning days. Would the rains ever come? Would they ever burst into life and turn the veld again into a rolling sea of green?

After our long day we returned to the capital of the Bophuthatswana and had dinner at the Sun Hotel, the best hotel in the homeland where the whites still got out of the pool when the blacks got in. On the same day, I had seen malnourished children queuing up for a small bowl of soup and calves dead because their mothers could produce no milk. We were now offered a huge meal with the best wine from the Cape vineyards. I could not enjoy it.

At a neighbouring table, Judith pointed out the son of the chief of the homeland, wheeler-dealing with a white businessman.

'I hate him,' she said. 'He doesn't want black people to touch him. He doesn't even like his own father.'

'How do you cope living with apartheid?'

'The whites who support it are sick. I just try to forget about them.'

'Do you think there's any chance of a peaceful solution?'

'I don't think so here. The whites are afraid of the unknown. In Jo'burg most whites have accepted the need for change, but in Bloemfontein they won't accept it. They're going to fight it out. It's going to be very, very violent.'

After dinner, I visited the casino adjoining the restaurant. In a huge room full of flashing lights and loud pop music, flushed middle-aged men and women pumped money into fruit machines. They came here for sex across the colour bar and gambling forbidden until recently in South Africa. It was like a vision of hell. I closed the door fast and went out into the starlit night and breathed the crisp, cold air of the veld. Groups of men were trying to keep warm around open fires in the wind-swept street. It was now freezing. I thought of the man with the injured hand, alone, under his piece of corrugated iron.

Chapter Twenty-Two

Born Under a Dark Star

WHEN John and the film crew flew back to London, I flew back to Durban. I contacted the Mediterranean Shipping Company to confirm the booking on the *Barbara D* I had made in Cape Town a couple of weeks earlier only to be told that the vessel had been overbooked: 'The only accommodation available,' a girl called Michelle tried to joke, 'is a hammock on the third deck!'

When I went round to see her at the great glass monstrosity of a head office, the news was even worse: '*Barbara D* has been delayed several days and I'm afraid there's no room for you on her now. Three stewardesses – one from Poland and two from Madagascar – have taken all the available cabins.'

This was devastating news. As far as I could see, the *Barbara D* was my only hope. I refused to be put off and demanded to see the chairman. I took the lift to the seventh floor and went into his large office overlooking Durban and demanded an explanation. Captain Salvatori Sarno was not amused.

'No problem,' he said. 'We'll just have to move all the Malagasy stewardesses in with the captain!'

Turning back to Michelle, he demanded: 'Why are you so frightened of me? Borrow a director's car and take Dr Marshall to the *Rosemary* in the dry dock where he can stay until the *Barbara D* arrives. *Barbara D* is the smallest ship in our fleet 3,784 tons, but it's got character!'

As I was about to leave, the chairman of MSC said: 'This is the last paradise on earth. But not for long. The blacks will be taking over.'

The *Rosemary* was festooned with gear and crawling with workers painting and repairing her. There was incessant crashing and banging. The dock was covered in oil. It was not very pleasant.

I was welcomed on board by the captain who had flown out specially from Italy while the ship was in dry dock. We had a drink in his cabin. A steward was then called to show me to my cabin. It was not very clean and smelt of a mixture of must and cheap perfume. Two Malagasy girls had been sharing it and on the bulkhead someone had scrawled a heart with a piece of chalk. There were some empty bottles that suggested there had been a party there recently. The worst of it all was when I opened the bathroom: the place was crawling with cockroaches. The steward sprayed them with poison. As they writhed in agony, the steward observed, shrugging his shoulders: 'It's an old ship! They do not harm.'

After lunch, I chatted with the steward who came from Naples but spoke good English, with a strange accent. While working on a ship bound for Australia, he had met a girl from Rochdale who was travelling with her parents; he jumped ship to elope with her when they got to Sydney. The lovers had married and they had a daughter who was living with her grandmother in Naples. Now he was stuck in Durban on a filthy ship where all the officers expected him to look after them. He was particularly unhappy about doing their washing.

'I am a man,' he said, pointing his hands to his chest. 'I can wash my clothes in a bucket. They have two hands; so can others. I am a man. I do not iron for others.'

He preferred it on British ships where there were stewards for cabins and stewards for the dining room:

'It is not good to wash toilets and then serve at table,' he observed.

That night in my bunk, I was suddenly woken up by something on my face. I put on the light and found the whole place crawling with cockroaches, bigs ones and little ones. I went into the bathroom and it too was crawling with them. They had come out of the ventilation holes. My principle of reverence for life took a knock as I sprayed their entrance

217

holes in the bulkheads, hoping to deter them. Africa can dent the most honourable ideals!

After a restless night, dreaming that I was being eaten by huge insects with long antennae, I got a lift into the city centre of Durban. I visited the Victoria Market Centre in the Asian quarter where everything from videos to ivory tusks were for sale. An Indian kept following me, saying 'special pictures, sir, special pictures!' Stretched out on a filthy cloth on the bonnet of a new Toyota were spread animal skulls – including a monkey's – and bits of rotting animal and bird corpses, together with small phials of yellowish liquid. The carrion, swarming with flies, stank in the hot sun. I assumed they were for the purposes of witchcraft or 'alternative' medicine. A couple of blacks were sitting in the back of the car, and a fat, dissolute white man was at the wheel.

After my night of the cockroaches, it was the last straw. I walked straight down to the beach and dived into the cleansing surf of the Indian Ocean. I wanted to wash away the smell of the oily docks, the coakroach spray, the musty cabin, the rotting flesh, and that taste of death. The sea was beautiful: clear and cool, with blue sky above and white sand below. But I came out spotted with tar from a tanker which had been wrecked in the Mozambique Channel.

In the late afternoon, I went to a café on the seafront and had a pot of tea – with fresh milk. In a local newspaper, I read an interview with Ian Smith, the former president of Rhodesia, who was visiting South Africa. 'Every country in Africa is a dictatorship,' he had told the reporter. 'Africa is in chaos, bankrupt . . . I don't know a black man in Africa who wouldn't like to live in South Africa where there's so much more freedom and justice.' Could he be sane?

I could almost have been in Brighton except that sea mist was swirling off the beach and creeping into the town. Nearby I saw an Indian vendor on the beach help a fat old white lady to her feet. Further away small black and white figures were diving through the surf. Out at sea, half a dozen ships were queuing up to come into port. 'I shall be on one of them before the sun sets twice,' I said to myself.

It was then that I saw the only mixed couple in public during my three-week stay in South Africa – a middle-aged white man with a young

Coloured girl. Otherwise all along the the promenade, it was whites with whites, blacks with blacks, Indians with Indians. Birds of a feather flocked together. The most despicable regime ever to be devised had had its way. Apartheid had triumphed. The legislation might be abolished soon, but it had poisoned the souls of South Africans for generations to come. In a moment of despair, I thought it might take centuries to erode the deep-seated racist mentality of this country.

But despite all I had seen in South Africa, despite the organized madness which made people think in racial categories instead of individuals, despite the crippling discrepancies in wealth, I left the country with a glimmer of hope. Two individuals, born on opposite sides of the wild almond tree hedge, had inspired me in particular. They were both writers and both involved in the struggle to end apartheid. One was born in the narrow cage of a small town in the high veld, the other in the urban hell of Alexandra. The first was André Brink and the second Wally Serote. From Brink, I took the idea that while many of the problems were only just beginning in the long run what united the whites and blacks in South Africa – their ferocious attachment to the land – was greater than what separated them. From Serote, I took the calm reassurance that whatever had befallen his people over the last five bloody centuries, they wanted to create a culture of tolerance in which all could find their place and reach their potential. Perhaps after all the Cape of Storms could really become the Cape of Good Hope.

The captain on the *Rosemary* told me: 'For a ship and a lady, you must always wait.' I waited and waited and the *Barbara D* eventually arrived. I went on board as soon as I could. She was indeed a small ship, old and rusty. She had a black hull and green decks and was registered in Panama. Her wooden handrails were rotten and her metal superstructure badly corroded.

I was given the owner's cabin next to the captain's. It was large with two separate bunks but it had seen better days. There was no seat or desk, the bath was stained, and the water pipes leaked. The toilet did not work: I had a bucket to flush it out by hand. The few light bulbs left had no shades. The doors of the cupboards did not shut. There were also cockroaches. On the pillow was a thick beige towel embroidered with my name. All for $100 a day.

The captain and the chief engineer of the ship were Italian, but the first officer was Croatian and the rest were from Poland and Mauritius. East European crews, like Filipinos, were paid in dollars, but they got half the wages of their Western European counterparts. It was still worth it for them since hard currency could buy so much in their countries. The world was not a just place.

We left Durban at 08.00 hours on Sunday 7 June. It was good to be at sea again after three weeks and after so many contradictory feelings. After passing by the skyscrapers of downtown Durban, we sailed through the harbour entrance and turned north towards Maputo, our next port of call in Mozambique just over the South African border. There was a long swell and the ship began to roll heavily. I was not bound for Tanzania as was planned: at the last minute the schedule of the *Barbara D* had been changed and we would have to double back to Durban before sailing up the East African coast.

The two Malagasy stewardesses – Sylvie and Anita – were sick the first day out. Sylvie was the oldest and most capable, with a round figure and long wavy hair. Anita, a tiny girl with a shy smile, still bravely served the huge engineers and deckhands at lunch. They couldn't keep their eyes off her. She looked like a schoolgirl but wore a T-shirt with the words '*Le Sexy Express*' below a picture of a couple making love. She was far too delicate and intelligent a flower amongst these tough seamen. Like her friend she looked more Indonesian than African, with straight black hair and light brown skin – which was not surprising since Madagascar was settled by Malay and Polynesian migrants from the sixth century. She spoke French. When I asked her what she thought of South Africa, she replied: '*C'est trop civilisé!*'

The atmosphere at table was not gay. There was a general air of depression and the Polish and Yugoslavian crew ate in silence with their heads down. The Yugoslavians – or Croatians and Serbians to be precise – were understandably worried about their families as their country drifted into civil war. The Italian captain at the head of the long table seemed as depressed as his drooping moustache. He only spoke to me to answer my practical questions about the ship's movements. He seemed to be ashamed of his ship and to resent the presence of the stewardesses and the passenger. When I asked what he thought of Africa, he replied:

'I do not like Africa. There's nothing here. The people do not work.'

The only exception to the gloom was the chief engineer, a short, round, middle-aged Italian with a few white strands of hair standing out of his large bald dome. He was from the Adriatic port of Bari which he called 'Paris by the sea'. Where everyone else was taciturn, he talked non-stop; while the others were miserable, he had a twinkle in his eye. He had been in Africa for thirty years and still seemed to enjoy life. He told me he had a wife and two children in Italy and a second family in Reunion.

The Polish stewardess came to clean my cabin. She seemed quite out of place on the decrepit ship, dressed in a tight leather mini-skirt and Yves St Laurent shirt with padded shoulders. I told her not to bother to clean my cabin but she insisted on going through the motions. Afterwards she lit a cigarette and told me a little about her life. Her name was Irena and she was twenty-eight years old. She had a degree from Warsaw university and had been a history teacher in a school in her home town but found that she simply could not make ends meet. Teaching after hours in a prison did not make up the shortfall. When her boyfriend decided to go and make a new life in Canada, she followed him. She had hoped to get married but it did not work out. Instead, she worked nights in a supermarket and after two years returned home to Poland.

'I was born under a dark star,' she said.

She could have returned to teaching but she preferred the drudgery and humiliation of cleaning out seamen's cabins to make some money. She had become a member of the world's underclass of migrant workers.

'If I do two more voyages I will have enough to pay for my small flat. My friends say I should meet someone old, rich and ill, but I haven't yet! I hate my job and cry in my cabin every evening.'

'What do you think of Africa?'

'It's very beautiful.'

'And Africans?'

'I'm scared of them. When you hear their music, you feel the animal inside.'

She told me she also had trouble with the captain because she was not trained properly. But I suspected it was more than that. Later in the morning, I saw her at ease smoking in the captain's cabin. He seemed tired and irritable since leaving Durban and I was sure it had something to do with Irena.

I asked him at lunch what he thought about having women on board.

'Maybe it's because I'm Italian, but I think a ship's crew should be all men. Women cause difficulties. They cause many fights; people get jealous. We are only men. That's life!'

It took only a day to reach Maputo, the capital of Mozambique. We arrived in warm sunshine at ten o'clock in the morning. There was a dusty haze over the city. As we sailed up the estuary, on our port side mangrove swamps came down to the water's edge while handsome buildings of the former Portuguese quarter rose on the headland to our starboard. Palm trees had been planted along the attractive corniche. Half a dozen hulks lay half-submerged in the grey, greasy water.

The Portuguese pilot who came on board in casual dress blinked heavily and his black assistant immediately asked for breakfast. They tucked into newly baked bread, cheese and ham and drank the piping hot black coffee as if they had not eaten properly for a long time.

Sailing into Maputo, I saw the first dhows of my voyage, a wonderful sight with the breeze filling their white lateen sails. Their graceful design had not changed for thousands of years. I had sailed off the East African coast from near the border of Mozambique to Dar es Salaam in a dhow ten years before, and down through the archipelago of the Maldives three years ago. For me, the dhow evoked all the ancient mystery of the Indian Ocean.

When Vasco da Gama first arrived off Mozambique, he was impressed by the dhows he saw, describing them accurately as of good size and decked, held together by coir rope and with sails of palm matting. He also noted that they had 'Genoese needles' – the mariners' compass – by which they steered as well as quadrants and navigating charts. They determined relative latitude by observing the altitudes of certain stars.

At this time, there were already Swahili people – a mixture of African and Arab – well established along the Mozambican coast who had already seen big ships like Vasco da Gama's. He called in at the island of Mozambique. They traded with 'white Moors' – Arabs – whose vessels in port were laden with gold, silver, pearls, rubies, cloves, pepper and ginger. The Sultan was so proud that he treated all that the Portuguese gave him – hats, wool dresses and corals – with contempt. Faced with the flourishing Swahili civilization of east Africa, the Portuguese were only superior in guns and ruthlessness.

The Swahili thought at first they were Turks or Moors, and gave them two pilots. They told them about India to the east and the Christian country in the north – Ethiopia – which the Portuguese took to be the fabled land of Prester John. But things did not turn out well. When Vasco da Gama and his men returned to the mainland to take on water, they were met by hostile villagers. Their response was to bombard the defenceless village for three hours, killing some of the inhabitants. 'When we were weary of this work we retired to our ships to dine,' wrote one of the crew. They then took some African prisoners, flogged the pilot, and proceeded up the coast to Mombasa. The first encounter between the Portuguese and East Africans set the tone of the subsequent history of conquest. The Portuguese were called *afriti* – devils – for good reasons.

After *Barbara D* moored in Maputo, the representative from the Shipping agency took me to the immigration office in the docks where I had to pay $20 for a temporary visa to land. Walking through the docks I read the slogans daubed on the side of the warehouses: '*Abaixo apartheid*', '*Abaixo imperialismo, enemigo permanente*', and '*Viva socialismo cientifico*'. The Marxist orientation of the government was pretty clear.

Coming out of the dock gates into a large square, I immediately had the impression I was in an old colonial town in Latin America. It had the same Portuguese–Spanish feel about it, very different from the North American-style of Durban. In front, handsome tree-lined avenues stretched up the hill, although some lamposts had fallen and not been cleared away.

On my left there was a beautiful old marble railway station built by the Portuguese with well-kept gardens in front. An old man swished a machete, cropping the grass as close as he had done when the Portuguese were here, when the Russians were here, and now when no one was here. The marble floors were brushed clean but the old tobacconists was closed down and there seemed to be no passengers or trains around. Two old steam locomotives kept in good condition were on display, dated 1895–1940, left-overs from the bustling days when the direct line from Pretoria to what was then Lourenço Marques would have taken a few hours. I was ninety kilometres from South Africa's border and eighty-four kilometres from Botswana's. Over the entrance to the station was the faded slogan: 'A Producao o liberta o poyo' – Production, liberty and duty.

The Portuguese who followed Vasco da Gama on their way to the Indies first set up forts and trading posts along the Mozambican coast and it was not until the late seventeenth century that private agricultural estates were established. With Salazar's coming to power in Lisbon in the 1920s, there was an attempt to tie the economies of the African colonies closer to Portugal, but very little was done for the development and the education of the Mozambican people. In the mid sixties the Marxist FRELIMO liberation front launched its military campaign, but as in Angola it was not until after the Portuguese Revolution that Mozambique won independence in 1975. In an act of revenge, the Portuguese settlers, who had taken so much and given so little over the centuries, deliberately destroyed the infrastructure of the country, leaving only forty doctors for a population which was ninety per cent illiterate.

FRELIMO had a huge task of reconstruction to undertake. Its opposition to apartheid and colonial rule in neighbouring countries meant that South Africa expelled Mozambican mine workers – an important source of foreign currency – and the profitable road and rail link between Rhodesia and the coast was closed. The attempt to collectivize the land failed miserably when workers on state farms could buy nothing with their wages; they preferred to return to subsistence farming. If this was bad, Ian Smith's forces in Rhodesia then invaded the country and South Africa armed and supported the small opposition group RENAMO. The result was serious disruption of the economy.

The country became so crippled that its first president Samora Machel felt obliged to sign an accord with South Africa, expelling the ANC in return for its withdrawal of support for RENAMO. Things began to look up when Zimbabwe won its independence and the Beira to Harare road and rail link was re-opened. But South Africa continued to support RENAMO and at the time of my arrival, prolonged civil war, dire poverty and drought had reduced a beautiful and potentially rich country to ashes.

All around was the tragedy of a revolution which had gone wrong. The once resplendent shop windows were empty except for a few paltry and tawdry goods. Many of the windows had been broken and boarded up. I spoke to one shopkeeper who joked:

'When the government took over the foreign exchange shops, the only thing available was locally made toilet paper and that hurt! Now they've freed the economy up a little, there's more goods around, but no one can afford them. They're three times more expensive than in South Africa.'

Children were sleeping in doorways, while others were selling old boots with holes in them or single cigarettes or sweets on a piece of cardboard. Few cars were on the road, and it was virtually impossible to find a taxi. One small dirty poster on a wall said: 'Learn English at the British Institute'. Nearby on the side of some workers' flats a huge red one declared: '*Beba Coca Cola*'. Allegiances were clearly changing.

It did not seem like it, but Mozambique was in the grip of a terrible drought, the worst in living memory. It was a rich country and normally could feed itself, but it had not rained properly for two years, the civil war raged, and the people were powerless to do anything about it. Even the 'great, grey, green, greasy' Limpopo river had dried up. Ten per cent of a total population of fifty million were threatened by famine.

I telephoned the United Nations Development Programme from the Monica Shipping Agency opposite the railway station. While I was waiting there to be picked up, I noticed a quote from Gandhi in English pinned up on the wall: 'When your heart is not pure, and you cannot master your passions, you cease to be an educated man'. Someone had added below: 'My friends know they must take me as I am'.

At the UNDP headquarters, I met Mr Masago from UNICEF who took me to see some of the refugee camps which had sprung up around Maputo. My companion was a young man in tinted glasses with a hint of a beard on his chin. He was well-educated and spoke good English as well as Portuguese and several local languages. He told me that in the seventies Mozambique was exporting rice, sweet potatoes, citrus fruits and bananas.

We came across an old woman at the side of the main 'Luis Cabral' highway into the capital. Huge lorries constantly rumbled by. She had built a makeshift hut along with thousands of other refugees in the mosquito-infested swamps. She sat exhausted next to the only remaining member of her family, a little girl of about five, who held tightly a small dry orange in her tiny hands.

'She comes from Gaza province where it hasn't rained for three years,' Masogo interpreted. 'She left a year ago, running away from the violence with her daughter. RENAMO came to her village and killed her mother, son and husband.'

Much further out of Maputo, we visited another refugee camp near the village of Machara. There was more space between huts here and artisans had set up a few workshops. An unofficial economy was already developing. I spoke to one man who was cutting a neighbour's hair with a rusty old pair of scissors and a piece of broken mirror. His wife was carefully watering some seedlings which were just surviving in the scratched dirt. RENAMO had looted everything in their village and they had no choice but to stay until the war was over.

Returning to Maputo, I asked Masago what RENAMO stood for.

'They claim to be national, but they have a base in only one area. They argue against socialism, but they have no political line. They are just living with bullets. They now control much of the rural areas, so it's very difficult to get food to the provincial capitals.'

'Are the talks between FRELIMO and RENAMO getting anywhere?'

'They're trying to arrange a ceasefire, but I don't think it will last. All we need is peace and confidence and rain, and in two years of harvest, there'll be enough food for all. We can wait for things like salt, soap and kerosene.'

'It's as simple as that?'

'Yes. Without rain and peace, it's disaster.'

We were due to leave Maputo the next day but there had been a delay.

'It's Africa', said the chief engineer. 'Even in Durban with whites they take longer than in Europe. They may be white but they're Africans all the same!'

'The dockers have only unloaded three containers during the night. They go slow to get more money', said the captain.

'If they get money', said the engineer, 'there's nothing to buy with it.'

I decided to return to downtown Maputo with my camera. There was nothing to do except wander the streets. It was difficult to find even a café open. To hell with it, I thought, this may be a police state but I'm fed up with treading carefully. I'm going to do some filming, whether they like it or not. I ostentatiously took out my tripod and set it up opposite the main railway station. I put on the camera and started to do a slow pan of the square but before I had finished, two shadows had fallen over my shoulder. I had expected them. They were security officers with Kalashnikovs.

They spoke to me in Portuguese.

'It is forbidden to film the railway station. It is a strategic building. You must come with us to the police station.'

I pretended not to understand.

'How do you do?' I replied in English in my friendliest manner. 'You have a magnificent railway station here. I was just filming it.'

'It is not permitted to film here. It is against the law, strictly prohibited. Can we see your papers?'

'Papers. Of course. Here you are.'

I took out all the papers I had – British passport, temporary visa, and a letter from the United Nations introducing me to the representatives in Maputo.

'I'm here with the United Nations, you know, *Nacioes Unidos, Nacioes Unidos*'. I pointed out the words at the top of the letter.

Now is the time for action, I thought.

'I must be going now. And with that I swept up my tripod and shook each of my interrogators firmly by the hand.

'*Obligado*, thank you very much! *Bon dia!*'

I then stroded away towards the Shipping Agency, expecting them to call me back any second. But the shout didn't come and I disappeared up the stairs into the air-conditioned building. I was sweating, but safe.

After dinner that evening, I went for a stroll along the docks. I gave an orange to a boy in rags who had been waiting at the bottom of the gangway all day. There was enough moonlight to bathe the grey docks in silver, and the stars stood out pure and bright in the sky. I shivered. It felt cold after the heat of the day, and mist swirled across the wide oozing river.

As I walked, I asked myself why I liked Africa. Perhaps I didn't. Perhaps I romanticized it. But I did like its closeness to nature, its wild landscapes, its vast expanses, its huge rivers, its sun rising and setting all afire with raw energy. I liked its people, their warmth, their classlessness, their laughter in adversity, their feel for the flow of life and death, their readiness to lend a hand, their hospitality to strangers. I had benefited from them all.

But Africa was dying. Its great cities had only a foothold along the coast. Its people were losing their identity, living in a land of betwixt and between, overawed by technology but unable to maintain it, playing with weapons but unable to control them. They were losing their wisdom of living with the land, forgetting the ancient stories told around open fires under the stars. They had been self-sufficent before the arrival of the white man, changing, adapting, in harmony with their environment. But now millions were dependent on outside aid, now the tank and money ruled, now honest criticism of dictatorship was called racism, now the voice of the peasant was silenced, now the heart of Africa was dying.

And what could I do about it? Nothing, except witness, nothing, except call for an arms embargo, nothing, except let them return to the quiet and simple life.

Chapter Twenty-Three

Night and Day

A FTER leaving Maputo I was disappointed about doubling back and returning to Durban. I wanted to head north to the Equator, not south to a tortured land. But it was a moment of taking stock during the voyage. Walking up and down the deck for an hour before the sun set, I felt good about having come so far relatively unscathed, depressed and inspired in equal measure by what I had seen. I felt centred there and then, not wanting to relive the past or anticipating the future. I was aware of death, but felt the pull of life, I could face squalor and see the good. I knew the darkness but looked towards the light.

When we berthed in Durban the following evening, I walked over to Dolbyl's Shipyard to see a family whom I had briefly met when boarding the *Barbara D*. They lived on a beautiful schooner called *Dwyn Wen* which had been moored next to us. Built in Dartmouth in 1906 she was 106 feet long with two masts, constructed of teak and Canadian rock elm. She had the elegance and grace of the grand epoch of sailing.

John Guthrie, the English skipper, had been at sea with his French wife Nanou and three young children in the Far East for several years, but had now decided to explore the Mozambique Channel and the Indian Ocean. They had just returned from the island of Mozambique to take part in a film called *The Golden Samurai*, an epic about the wrecking of a ship at the turn of the century off the Natal coast which was bringing a golden statue of a Samurai warrior from Japan to South Africa. The producer of the film wanted to use their schooner, a good break since they usually had to earn a living chartering the ship three months each year.

I was invited on board the *Dwyn Wen* for dinner. I set off at dusk from the *Barbara D* in a taxi and asked the driver to drop me off in Dolbyl's Shipyard. It was only five o'clock, but the orange sun was disappearing fast behind the Durban skyscrapers in a greyish blue sky. A cold chill sent shivers through my body. I came to an Indian guard who said that I had to go the next dock along. As there were no taxis, I set off walking fast. I had been told by several people that it was dangerous to walk around the Durban docks at night, especially for a white man, but I had no choice.

By the time I had reached the gates of the next dock it was completely dark, the moon hidden by clouds. The containers, stacked like so many giant matchboxes, created a labyrinth through which I blundered. I came across a man with a rifle by an open fire; I assumed he was a nightwatchman and I asked him the way.

'Down this road, man, turn left at the bottom, and right again. Be careful! You never see a white man walking here at night! There're thieves around.'

After walking down for some time, I suddenly heard footsteps on the other side of the road. All I could see was the dark silhouette of a black man. As he passed me, I could just make out the whites of his eyes and teeth. There was no light here, only the white glow of ships in the distance behind the stacked containers. I walked on with a determined air as if I knew where I was going. In fact, I was lost. The footsteps grew quieter; I breathed a sigh of relief and slowed down.

But then they grew louder again, this time behind me and getting nearer all the time. I quickened my pace, but I could not run because of all my camera equipment. I decided it would not be a good idea anyway: all my experience of going on safaris and underwater diving warned me that flight only encourages predators. I felt the sweat run down between my shoulder blades. Was he friend or foe, mugger or guide? Just as he was about to catch up with me and I was determined to turn round and confront him, I saw two white lights of a car in the distance approaching fast.

'Hello, Peter!' came a warm English voice from the dim interior of the van. It was John Guthrie! I could not believe it. My pursuer disappeared in the shadows. John had come to look for me after visiting the *Barbara D*. It was a huge coincidence that he had found me at that moment – as lucky as finding a pin in a haystack.

'You have to be careful around here,' he said, as we drove trough the docks towards his schooner. 'I know someone who was with a friend in a car and they ran out of petrol. My friend hitch-hiked to get some petrol and when he returned his friend was gone. After a long time looking for him, he eventually found his decapitated body by a railway line. Perhaps the man who killed him tried to make it look like the train had cut his head off. Let's go and have some supper,' he added imappropriately cheerily.

When I climbed on board *Dwyn Wen*, I realized that she had shifted her moorings. I would never have found her in the maze of the docks that night. God only knows what would have happened to me if John had not turned up at that crucial moment.

I was introduced to John's French shipmate Nanou and their children Daphne, Cecile and Paul. I could see a small aqua lung for the children on the schooner's teak deck, and asked the eleven-year old, bilingual Daphne what it was like living on a ship all the time.

'It can be very nice; it can be quite awful!'

'Do you mean the weather?'

'Yes, I get very seasick sometimes. Sometimes I like it at sea, sometimes I wish to be on land.'

I thought it must have been difficult for her mother to bring up three children at sea.

'No, no,' Nanou said. 'It's just in your head. If you're anxious, then the children will be nervous and they won't be very happy on board, but if you're happy, they're happy.'

John who had been listening said: 'They have a tough life. But they learn a vast amount just travelling the seas.'

The next day I did not have enough time to visit Durban and stayed on

the *Barbara D* because we were due to sail at noon. I stayed in my cabin
and wrote a poem:

The darkness of Africa is
the carrying of water for miles on the head
the young tree crashing in the equatorial forest
the red earth rushing down a gully in a flash flood
the stick child dying in her excrement
the elephant enraged by poisoned arrows
the mercenary lighting the thatched roofs of a village
the man standing on his brick behind barred windows
the yellow armoured car patrolling the township
the killing of a gorilla to give strength to a baby
the official who delays entry and awaits a bribe
the driving of machines until they break down
the man beating his woman and sending her to the fields
the labourer dismissed after a lifetime's service
the woman sitting by the pool who says her conscience is clear
the guide who abandons the stranger at the centre of a maze
the man who stones to death a woman who sleeps with another man
the woman who would liberate her land by burning rubber necklaces
the police who run brothels and cut the hands off garage mechanics
the imported white marble of the presidential palace
the open sewer where the children splash and play

The lightness of Africa is
the forgiveness of the downtrodden
the Southern Cross rising in the darkening sky
the peace of evening fires in lost villages
the third pot of tea shared under a full moon
the quills of a porcupine on a sea cliff edge
the wave of a fisherman from his dug-out canoe
the smiles of children jostling in front of a camera
the singing of the Lord's Prayer in an abandoned school
the dancing of a big woman with a baby at her breast

the little girl standing with a new blanket around her shoulders
the old philosopher who doesn't say where the rock paintings are
the woman who gives an extra orange after haggling over the price
the smile of a young man as his football star steps out of a car
the smell of maize grilled over charcoal at dusk
the white salt lake which turns rose pink in the sun
the crazy baboon who pulls one over the warden
the running of two ostriches down a valley towards the sea
the dried flowers on a mountainside waving in the cool breeze
the surfer who has no money and says all men are equal
the family man who crosses the continent to see his friend.

Is there more light than darkness?
Is the sun stronger than the moon?
Can the night defeat the day?

I left Durban for the last time at dusk on 13 June. A cold wind blew up, sending flurries across the still waters of the docks and flapping the canvas covers on deck. Whatever African leaders, especially from the front-line states, might say about sanctions for South Africa, *Barbara D* was loaded with containers for Mozambique, Kenya and Tanzania. She was so low in the water, that amidships the deck was only a few feet above sea-level. As we left the protection of Durban harbour and turned north towards the Mozambique Channel, *Barbara D* began to roll and pitch in the freshening winds and heavy swell.

We anchored off Maputo the next morning. The sky was grey and squalls brought cool showers which swept across the grey-green sea. It seemed more like the Irish Sea than the Indian Ocean. The pilot came on board at nine and we docked an hour later. He was a cheery Russian who mistook me for the chief mate. He told me that there used to be eight Russian pilots but they were now down to two. The harbour master was an Englishman. Another sign of the times was a visiting French destroyer which was moored in Maputo downstream from *Barbara D*. The cold war was well and truly over.

I went ashore with the radio officer, Abdulla, a small man in his late fifties. He had a hooked nose and light brown eyes. His bald brown dome was encircled by short white hair while black tufts grew out of his large ears. He told me that his ancestors came from the Yemen – hence his Arabic looks – but he was born in Mauritius. Whilst studying for his radio certificate, he had met an Indian Muslim in South Shields in England and they had made it their home for years. In his slightly cockney accent he confessed: 'I used to love drinking a few pints of Watney's Red Barrel in the pub with the lads on a Sunday morning'.

We went to one of the few café-restaurants open in Maputo – the Continental – and as we leaned on the empty bar, we saw the captain and the Polish stewardess jump out of a battered black taxi in the pouring rain.

'Excuse my language, doc, but you see what I mean. The captain's fucking around with the stewardess. That's why he's so jumpy.'

For some reason we began talking about horses. When he saw my name on the crew list he had wondered whether I had any connections with the trainer Bill Marshall. He also told me that the bosun had asked him whether I was a jockey. The bosun was a powerful man called France Ng Hung Woo from Mauritius who had recently worked on the North Sea oil rigs.

It so happened that my father was Bill Marshall, one of Britain's top race-horse trainers.

'Do you remember that horse Raffingora?' Abdulla said excitedly. 'Over five furlongs, he won every race. I remember going to the races on a lovely summer evening in the early seventies and betting on him and Lester Piggott who was riding him with top weight. He won in a photo finish and was pelted by Irish punters who had lost their money!'

Partly because I was the only person who could speak English fluently on board and partly because of my family connections, I became a close friend with Abdulla throughout the rest of the voyage. For my part, I enjoyed his humour, his enjoyment of African ways, and his original turn of phrase.

After lunch, Abdulla wanted to go back to the ship, a little expansive with his whisky and water which he drank with his meal:

'I think you will acquiesce if I go back to the ship, doc,' he said. 'I want to retire now to kip.'

I decided to wander around Maputo on my own. By chance, I came across the old Governor's Palace which was a heavy, dark neo-classical building overlooking Independence Square. Nearby was the other wing of the Portuguese State, an ornate white Roman Catholic cathedral. Both looked as if they had been closed for some time. Many elegant buildings, including a hotel with fine wrought-iron work, had been burnt down, no doubt during the closing days of the war of independence. Some of the wide avenues had been renamed under Marxist leaders, such as Karl Marx, Mao Tse-tung, and Ho Chi Minh.

At the entrance to the botanical gardens, a large forged statue of the first president after independence stood out against the sky with his finger outstretched. Samora Machel was famous, like Fidel Castro, for his four or five hour speeches.

'Do you know what he's saying?' a Maputo resident asked me.

'I suppose he's telling the people about the advantages of Communism and the great future ahead.'

'No. He's waving his finger to tell them that they can have only one mealie a day!'

Despite the failure of his collectivization programme, and his banning of any opposition, Machel had at least tried to increase literacy and encourage racial harmony in Mozambique. But he was a fanatical Leninist. While he wore military fatigues and expensive boots, he had ordered his 'popular vigilance groups' to shave long-haired young men and banned women from wearing tight jeans and shirts because he thought them too much of a temptation. He aimed to create the New African Man – an educated nationalist who worked for the common good. Unfortunately, his chosen means was a rigidly centralized state and party dictatorship: 'When a class imposes its will,' he once said, 'those who refuse to accept this imposition must be forced to conform. Those who oppose this will be repressed'. He kept his word: dissidents ended up in 're-education' camps. Not only did he alienate many by his methods, but South Africa by arming the opposition group RENAMO made sure that the Communist experiment would not succeed. The outcome of Machel's revolution was a seventy per cent drop in agricultural and industrial production, civil war, and now millions of Mozambicans were threatened with famine.

Walking back to the ship, I noticed how many barefoot, ragged, filthy street urchins there were. Many must have been orphans from the civil war still raging in the bush and were living on the streets. They played, they begged and they offered services: shining shoes, finding taxis and selling a few cigarettes. They did not know the beauty of the setting sun over the savannah, the screech of the parrot in the jungle, the green shoots of crops after the first rains. Their horizon was the grey houses of Maputo and the cars, oil, garbage, hunger and hardness of the streets. I wondered what kind of world they would grow up in. The problems of the country seemed insurmountable.

Leaving Maputo next day, we sailed passed a French destroyer and two ships registered in Panama which were unloading wheat and maize. There were also a few Russian trawlers, with the new Russian flag, still benefiting from the past links between the Soviet Union and Mozambique and scooping up the fish that the local fishermen were unable to catch in their dhows. Our wake rocked a few of them under sail as we made for the calm open sea under a blue sky. *Barbara D* pitched gently: it was a good feeling to be at sea. We had two clear days ahead of us until we reached Beira, our next port of call.

The next day I joined the captain on watch. He was a competent navigator on his first command and was naturally concerned about keeping his old ship together when there were so many centrifrugal forces at work. It was a very warm and sunny day, and in mid morning I saw a large black shark swim by. The sky gradually became more cloudy turning the sea from blue to greyish green.

I had read somewhere the coastline of Africa is 18,900 miles long, but I asked the captain if he could work out roughly how many miles I might expect to travel before returning to Lisbon. Taking out his nautical tables and calculator, he reckoned – 'like a shoemaker', as he put it – the distance to be some 13,300 nautical miles, that is, about 16,340 statute miles. I had only passed the half-way mark and still had a long way to go.

The night before we arrived in Beira, there was magnificent sunset. The perfectly round sun passed through huge black clouds, turning their edges to red and gold. The sea was calm and there was a warm breeze. Just after the sun had dipped below the horizon, its golden light still fanning out across the sea and sky, I saw a small whale jump out of the water. It made a big splash – twice.

I felt like diving into the water too. I felt I had come a long way spiritually as well as physically since the beginning of my voyage. I had then felt emotionally at sea, having brusquely torn myself away from my home and family. At first, I had clung to my ego like a life raft, fearful of letting go. But now, four months on, I felt a loss of personal ego. I no longer laid claim to 'my' book, 'my' home, or even 'my' family. I no longer wanted to conquer time and place, to arrive at a certain point on a certain day. Like the fish in the sea and the birds in the sky, I did not care for the morrow. I had glimpsed the truth that we are already what we must be. I felt the stream of life flowing through my body. I felt part of the whole, a strand in the cosmic web, a drop of wine dissolving in the ocean of being. I was the flying fish, the phosphorescent plankton, the reeling gull, the diving whale, the Southern Cross.

Chapter Twenty-Four

Sailing North

WE arrived in Beira just before midnight, and anchored off shore. After breakfast on Wednesday 17 June, the pilot came on board and we sailed past a lighthouse along the sandy coast where dozens of rusting ships had been beached. Beyond some shacks, the drab buildings of Beira rose above the palm trees. It had once been the beautiful and prosperous Swahili city state of Sofala at the time of Vasco da Gama's arrival, grown rich on the gold trade from the ancient capital of Zimbabwe. I saw some dhows with square sails, a rare sight these days in the Indian Ocean; most had long been replaced by the more efficient triangular lateen sail.

We docked in a brand-new container terminal. Giant gantries were unloading ships full of maize and wheat for drought-stricken Mozambique, Malawi, Zambia, and above all Zimbabwe. Beira was the key trading port for land-locked Zimbabwe.

As soon as we had moored, half a dozen officials came on board – the usual mix of immigration, customs and health – and immediately started asking for bottles of wine, cigarettes and frozen chickens. While their country was undergoing famine and civil war, they were all large and well-fed. They sat down in the officers' mess, and only started shifting papers after they had glasses and several bottles of wine on the table. It was still early in the morning but the wine worked its way and with a certain largesse they allowed me ashore without the visa demanded in Maputo.

I had been given the address of the representative of the UN Development Programme in Beira, an Ethiopian called Admasu Haile, and I went ashore to track him down. The whole town was in a terrible state of neglect. Fine old Portugese buildings had been left to collapse and the only new ones were horrible concrete blocks. The sewers had broken in many places; children played amongst the litter and filth in the streets. There was no electricity in the main town, though the wealthy international aid community living behind high wire fences had their own generators. Once chic stores now stocked a few shoddy goods.

The UNICEF and UN office was on the fifth floor of a building opposite the *Diario de Mozambique*, the unique, government-controlled newspaper in the country. By a stroke of luck, I met in the UN office both Admasu Haile and Nancy Barnes, the director of the famine relief programme in Mozambique, who had just flown in that morning from Maputo. They were going by car to visit a refugee camp along the Beira corridor and invited me to join them.

Nancy Barnes was a short, energetic American, with grey hair and blue eyes. She wore big earrings and had an ivory ring on her finger. No UN careerist, her primary interest had always been the welfare of Mozambique. In the United States, she had served on the Committee for Freedom in Mozambique during the war of independence in the 1960s when the Portuguese were using napalm against the guerrillas.

She was an open supporter of FRELIMO and the ANC. During his exile in Mozambique, she knew Albie Sachs, the ANC leader whom I had met briefly in Johannesburg. She may well have saved his life in April 1988:

'I drove past him in my car and turned to wave. When I was fifteen seconds away there were was a huge explosion. It was a car bomb. The driver in the car behind him was killed, and he had his arm blown off. There was blood everywhere. A TV team nearby who were filming Women's Day came and filmed the scene and took him to hospital. Fortunately the hospital was only ten minutes away.'

With experiences like that, no wonder Nancy Barnes bit her nails.

We set off in a four-wheel drive Toyota in the early morning. It took about seven or eight hours to travel the 600 kilometres along the Beira corridor to Harare, the capital of Zimbabwe, but we were going only a third of the way to Nhamatunda. The road was in good condition outside Beira as we sped through the well-cultivated fields, where vegetables, maize and rice were surrounded by coconut and mango trees. But the effects of drought were soon apparent after leaving the coastal strip. Young maize plants were already wilting in the hot sun, having been germinated by a short spell of rain some weeks earlier.

The road and railway along the Beira corridor, Zimbabwe's lifeline to the sea, were being kept open by 18,000 Zimbabwean troops. They protected a strip three kilometres wide; the rebel organization RENAMO controlled and terrorized the bush beyond. Refugees had flocked to the security of the corridor where they had became entirely dependent on aid.

'Peasants are not interested in politics,' Haile said. 'They want a quiet life. But they've been caught up in a war where they have been forced by the soldiers to take sides.'

We stopped for lunch at a 'Safari Lodge', a run-down collection of thatched buildings which advertised gazelle meat at a dollar a kilo (hard currency only) and Black Label beer (America's 'lively and lusty' beer brewed in South Africa). We were soon invaded by flies. When I went off into the dry, spiky bush for a pee, I returned with my trousers covered in tics. Haile bought a lump of meat for his supper and we moved on. Children by the side of the road risked death picking up some of the grains of maize falling from the passing convoys destined for Zimbabwe.

The constant stream of huge lorries were escorted by armoured cars of the Zimbabwean army. At the bridges, gun emplacements on each bank were well dug in. I saw women carrying wood along the road to the military bases; some of them no doubt served the Zimbabwean soldiers in other ways too.

'We're in RENAMO territory now,' Nancy observed. 'The rebels still cross here and come up to the road.'

'It must be nerve-wracking being in a war zone all the time.'

'You get used to it. But you know Trevor McDonald, the black British TV newsreader; he was here last week reporting on the famine. We had to take him past some dead bodies and he was terribly upset by it all! For us, it's part of everyday life.'

We had been travelling for several hours by now and the landscape had changed from fertile plains to rolling hills with scrubby bush. There were few signs of cultivation or villages until we reached Nhamatunda.

We then travelled another twenty kilometres to the railway halt of Siluvu where a new refugee camp was being established. A makeshift school had been set up in the old railway shelter, without books and pencils. Free food – maize, beans and oil – were distributed each day. Some children, with swollen bellies from malnutrition and flies playing around their eyes, were playing with model lorries made from old cans which they pushed in the dust at the end of a stick. The sights of the Beira corridor were already changing their culture.

As we arrived, new refugees were queuing up under a spreading tree to be registered in a big book. They were just a fraction of the 3.5 million peasants who had been displaced by the war. Those who had come earlier had already built themselves round huts from palm leaves. A few had even tried to grow a few maize plants in the sandy soil – the habit dies hard. They had lost all their worldly possessions, seen close relatives killed, witnessed atrocious acts of cruelty, and were reduced to a pitiful state of dependence. At least here they could sleep safely at night without fear of RENAMO attacks.

'What is the solution to all this?' I asked the local administrator.

'The ending of the war,' came the simple reply.

We left late in the afternoon to drive back to Maputo. There were few convoys and armoured vehicles now and we drove much of the time on our own. About a hundred kilometres from Beira, Nancy said in a matter-of-fact way: 'A Brazilian agronomist returning home about this time was recently ambushed here and killed'.

I asked her why the Mozambican Revolution under President Samora Machel and now Joaquim Chissano had failed.

'Because of the war, there was no chance. It's incredible that everything hasn't yet completely fallen apart. The FRELIMO government still has some support. There's emergency relief but the World Bank and the IMF haven't allowed the funds for reconstruction to take place. The EEC is prepared to subsidize the famine, but not Mozambique itself!'

'Is there any help from Portugal?'

'The Portuguese government sends no food. But there are many

Portuguese in South Africa who dream of the good old days when an illiterate white mechanic could live like a king in Mozambique. Unlike the French and the British, the Portuguese did not even create an élite to act as local administrators. FRELIMO had to work from scratch after winning the war of independence.'

'Will democracy ever come to Mozambique?'

'There's no democratic country in Africa, except perhaps Botswana,' Haile observed lugubriously. His own Ethiopia had a poor showing on the democratic scale.

'Maybe parliamentary democracry is not relevant to Africa,' Nancy added. 'Traditionally in Africa, you have the chief system. The political system needs to evolve.'

'What about the future then?'

'It's very difficult to predict anything at all. Even if there is a peace settlement the big question will be what to do with the armies. They will have to be disbanded but many of the soldiers have only known war all their lives. Reconciliation, rebuilding the material infrastructure and the social communties will be a much more complicated process.'

By the time we arrived back in Beira, it was half past six and already dark. I had been assured in the morning by the agent that the *Barbara D* would not be leaving until the following morning, but when I returned to the Manica Shipping Agency I was told that the time had been changed to 17.00 hours that afternoon. I must have missed my ship! How on earth would I get out of Mozambique to Tanzania where my family and the film crew were expected to join me in a week's time?

Now, if ever, my new philosophy of detachment was to be tested. I tried to keep calm as Haile raced through the dock to the berth where *Barbara D* had moored. The only way to get to Dar es Salaam, he told me as we skidded between stacks of containers, was to fly from Maputo to Johannesburg, Johannesburg to Nairobi and then from Nairobi to Dar. That still left me with the problem of getting from Beira to Maputo.

At the immigration office, I returned my seaman's shore pass and grabbed my passport. I ran through the gates looking for the empty berth. I could not believe my eyes: the *Barbara D* was still there! As I rushed up the gangway, it was pulled up behind me. I had made it by the skin of my teeth!

I turned and waved to Haile who was standing by his car smiling. The bosun told me that an awkward container had held the ship up for a couple of hours. It had been my saviour.

The radio officer said: 'I waited for you for two hours in the Arcadia restaurant. I had many cups of piping hot tea. I thought you had been mugged or arrested!'

The chief engineer said: 'All's well, that ends well!'

I was not upset to leave Mozambique where war and drought and famine and harsh politics had turned a beautiful country into hell. There seemed no obvious reason for the civil war to continue. It was colonialism in its death throes, still lashing its victims with its tail. Only when peace came to South Africa would things begin to settle down and that might take years rather than months.

When I woke up the next day, there was a thick sea mist but the rising sun soon burnt it off to reveal clear blue sky. The sea was calm and azure. It was perfect sailing weather. I was lucky enough to have just missed the wet period on the East African coast, from November to March, when the north east monsoon wind prevails and it can be very sultry. The south west monsoon was now blowing. In the old days, the great large trading dhows would now be heading towards the Persian Gulf or across to India.

For the next three days, the ship settled down to its regular routine, the day marked by the changing of the four-hourly watches and the meals. At lunch, I would mainly talk in French with the chief engineer who sat opposite me. The captain next to us at the head of the table would occasionally answer my questions in stumbling English. I also spoke French to the chief officer. The common language for the rest of the crew – the Yugoslavs, Poles, Malagasies and Mauritians – was English, although the Malagasies and Mauritians also spoke French to each other.

On the second day at lunch as we sailed up the Mozambican Channel, the captain suddenly exclaimed: 'My God, look at that!' pointing towards the wide porthole in the officers' mess. On our starboard side, a huge creature leapt out of the water. It was a whale, bigger than any I had seen during the whole voyage, yet it had leapt out of the water like a dolphin. As he came down again, he rolled sideways to show his flipper and then dived, slapping his great flukes several times against the surface of the water, whether annoyed or joyful one could not tell. He was about a hundred metres from the ship but seemed to pay no attention. He dived, rose again in our wake, blew a fountain of water into the air, and made the same movements as before.

I woke up the next day in my cabin to find water pouring out of the deck head above my door. I called the chief engineer who got a fitter to dismantle the wood: behind the asbestos insulation, an air-conditioning vent was completely eroded. My cabin soon became stifling hot. With the monsoon wind behind us, there was no cool breeze coming through the open porthole. Lying on my bunk, the sheets soon became damp with sweat.

'You know, the ship is called *Barbara D* after Barbara Davis – the wife of a director in the UK,' the chief engineer told me. 'She was bought for very little five years ago. She had been lying in a wharf in Marseilles for a year because the Indian owner did not pay the crew. MSC bought her but she was in such a bad condition that several companies refused to insure it. In the end it was insured in South Africa.'

'They'll probably try to keep *Barbara D* going for another five years,' the chief engineer went on. 'A Germany company will then arrange for it to be taken to Chittagong in Bangladesh where it will be broken up by labourers on one mark a day. The scrap metal will then be sent back to Germany to be recycled.'

It was a good idea to keep old technology going but not by exploiting cheap labour and neglecting safety precautions.

The Italian officers on board were as right wing as the French and Germans had been, and both the chief engineer and the chief mate admitted that their fathers had supported Mussolini. When the subject of race came up at lunch, the chief engineer said: 'Arabs are worse than blacks. Blacks are more honest and sincere but with Arabs you don't know where you are.'

'Isn't that a bit racist?' I said.

'The worst racists are the blacks between themselves. I can remember when I was on the West African run, the Liberian Kroumen we took on used to be beaten by the other blacks on board. When I asked one of them "Why do you do this? He's your brother." He replied: "No, he's not my brother, he's a Krouman. My brother has the same skin as me, from the same tribe." You know in Liberia, there are tribes which still eat each other.'

I had come to expect this sort of thing from the white officers, but I was surprised to find that the Mauritian cook, who seemed to be of Indian and African descent, also had little respect for his fellow countrymen:

'Africans are poor because they're lazy. They don't want to work.'

'Maybe that's because they're not paid enough,' I suggested.

'Africans have no initiative. In Mauritius people buy food from the market in town and then sell it more expensively in the countryside. They're prepared to work hard but the African isn't. He always wants something for nothing. If you leave something outside your cabin door in port, the Africans will steal it.'

'Maybe it's a question of education.'

'When they're given schools, they don't work in them.'

'What can I say to all this?' I wrote in my journal. 'It's the same old racist talk I heard from the whites in South Africa. Even if Africans are lazy and don't want to educate themselves, perhaps they are being wise not to go down the road of Western "civilization" where time is money and the devil takes the hindmost. If you work hard enough to get by, why not sit under a tree and spend the time chatting and drinking with your friends? Why should you work for the state, growing cash crops for a few pieces of paper which can't even buy anything in the empty stores? If anything, the so-called African reluctance to work is a virtue rather than a vice. It shows they value leisure and social life more than wage slavery. Slaves to the clock and money, we in Europe cannot understand people who think and act differently.'

During the voyage from Beira, I would usually spend an hour or so in the prow of the ship watching the sunset. The sea was calm and peace descended with the night. The stars came out bright and clear. I would sleep in my bunk with my porthole open, enjoying the warm salty breeze and the swish of the water running along the hull. After a sound night's sleep, I would be woken by the orange rays of the morning sun which played on the bulkhead of my cabin.

We had reached the tropics once again. The ship rolled moderately in the south westerly swell. We passed the islands of Zanzibar and Pemba; I knew them well and felt I was back on home ground for the first time since leaving Senegal four months earlier. It was wonderful to be sailing north, sailing home, in the Indian Ocean.

Chapter Twenty-Five

Guns *and* Crosses

*A*s we arrived in Mombasa, the Mauritian bosun France Ng Hung Woo said on behalf of all the crew: 'Mombasa very good! Good girls, good night clubs. No trouble for seamen!'

Kenya was the principal tourist destination for Europeans on the East African coast. After becoming a British protectorate in 1893, the highlands were cleared of local peoples for white farmers who tried to recreate a little England, complete with fox hunting and tea at four. With only seven per cent of the country receiving enough rainfall for cultivation, land was at a premium. As Jomo Kenyatta, the first president of independent Kenya, put it: 'When the missionaries arrived, the Africans had the land and the missionaries had the Bible. They taught us to pray with our eyes closed. When we opened them, they had the land and we had the Bible'. African resistance against British rule culminated in the bloody Mau Mau rebellion which led to independence in 1963.

At the time of my arrival almost thirty years later, memories of the atrocities of the Mau Mau period (13,500 Africans killed to ninety-five Europeans) had given way to images of *Out of Africa*, of white high society living in a colonial Garden of Eden or of tourists lounging under coconut trees on coral beaches in the tropical sun. But while a rich African élite had emerged in Kenya thanks to Western support for its unbridled capitalism and pro-Western stance, most Kenyans were having a difficult time to make ends meet. The country was riddled with tribal rivalries, especially between the Bantu Kikuyu people, the main entrepreneurs and the Nilotic Luo. With agricultural production dropping and with one of the highest birth rates in the world – on average every Kenyan woman has eight children – the country could not feed itself.

President Daniel arap Moi continued the tradition set by the first president of giving jobs for the boys. In 1982 he introduced a one-party state and banned the freedom of assembly. His suave appearance, including the inevitable rosebud in his buttonhole, went with an autocratic style. He interfered with the judiciary and tried to silence the boisterous opposition by muzzling the Press and jailing and torturing dissidents. Most visitors loved the taste of colonial life still on offer and turned a blind eye to the daily violation of human rights.

The recent killing of some tourists in the northern park of Masai Mara – stabbed with spears by tribesmen – had tarnished the image a bit and the rise of AIDS had checked the general sexual exuberance. Social and tribal tensions, exasperated by economic recession, were beginning to undermine Kenya's reputation for stable prosperity. While the South African state was reforming itself, Kenya's was becoming more authoritarian and dictatorial.

In Vasco da Gama's time, Mombasa, Lamu and Malindi were all part of a string of Swahili city states which stretched a thousand miles along the coast from Sofala (Beira) to Mogadishu in Somalia. The Swahili people lived where two worlds met, the land and the sea, Africa and the Orient. Centuries before, people from the interior had drifted down to the coast where they intermarried with sailors and traders who had been blown by the monsoon winds from Arabia, Persia, India and Madagascar. They developed a common lifestyle, language and Islamic culture. Their main interest was trade, fishing and navigation. Their sense of travel and adventure, coupled with their Islamic religion, gave them a strong sense of fate: every event in life was determined by Allah. They were also strongly superstitious, believing that evil spirits – *djinii* – were sent to test them.

The Swahili traded with Arabs, Persians and Indians by dhow across the Indian Ocean. Eighty years before the first appearance of the Portuguese, the sultan of Malindi had sent a giraffe to China as a gift which overawed the imperial court in Peking. It prompted the Chinese emperor to send his admiral Chêng Ho with a huge flotilla to escort the Swahili ambassadors back to East Africa. The wealth of the Swahili city states, based on gold, ivory, slaves and spices, was far greater than Portugal's at the time. Mombasa had about the same population as London.

What the Portuguese lacked in wealth, they made up for in ruthlessness. The sultan of Mombasa was rightly suspicious of them. When da Gama cast anchor off Mombasa in 1497, he saw a low-lying fortress with many fine multi-storeyed houses. Large dhows, decorated with colourful flags after the fasting month of Ramadan, came out to meet him.

Suspecting trouble da Gama weighed anchor and sailed on to Malindi further up the coast. The city which lay in a bay and extended along the shore reminded the Portuguese of Alcochete on the left bank of the estuary of the river Tagus, above Lisbon, with its lofty, white-washed houses which had many windows and its surrounding groves of palm trees and fields of maize and vegetables. The sultan's wealth and sophistication were reflected by his dress: he wore a robe of damask trimmed with green satin, and was seated on two cushioned chairs of bronze, beneath a sunshade of crimson satin attached to a pole.

In return for the Portuguese gifts of coral-beads, wash-basins, little bells and pieces of cloth, the sultan gave cloves, cumin, ginger, nutmeg and pepper – the fabled spices they had been seeking. They were also given a pilot whom they thought to be Christian but who was none other than the famous Arab geographer El Masidi who directed them safely to Calicut in southern India. The Portuguese were to return the favour by crippling the trade of the Swahili states along the East African coast.

Five centuries after da Gama, I entered Mombasa harbour in the late afternoon of 22 June on board the *Barbara D*. We passed through a gap in the coral reefs and steamed up the estuary into calm waters. Mombasa was originally an island, although it had sprawled over the mainland to which it was connected by a causeway. Dhows still moored past Fort Jesus built by the Portuguese opposite the old town. We berthed in the modern container terminal in Kilindini Harbour on the western side of the island. Mombasa was now the largest port on the East African coast, with a population of nearly half a million. Its climate was hot, humid and sultry.

The pilot who came on board was a Kenyan, but he had studied his ticket in South Shields, lived in London and served in the Canadian Pacific Company.

'Mombasa used to be full of ships, but now there are sometimes only five in port,' he complained. 'A lot of the traffic is now going to Dar es Salaam. It's because of the bureaucracy and high costs; all the dollars paid in Mombasa end up in Nairobi!'

I obtained a shore pass without any problem and caught a new London taxi cab waiting by the ship, one of many which had recently been imported into Mombasa. They were owned by – who else? – the president. The spacious womb of the black cab was a delight after all the clapped-out taxis I had used in most parts of Africa. We crossed over the causeway and made for the centre of town. I asked to be dropped off near the two huge artificial tusks forming an arc over Nkrumah Street, the commercial and shopping centre.

Mombasa fortunately had still retained its intimate feel of a provincial town, with only a few high-rise buildings to mar the skyline and dwarf the palm trees and luxuriant foliage. I managed to trace down a neighbour's friend whom I had met in Wales – Dipan Shah – whose family had a textile factory and owned the Kilimanjaro Boutique. He was a descendent of the Asians who had come as merchants voluntarily or had been brought over as indentured labourers by the British from India, especially Punjab and Gujarat, at the end of the nineteenth century. They had helped build the 'lunatic line', the railway from Mombasa to Kampala in Uganda, which cost hundreds of deaths, some to man-eating lions. After independence, many had stayed on to form the main business community; they made up about a quarter of Mombasa's population. Dipan had thrown in his lot with the country and was a Kenyan citizen. If another Idi Amin arose in Kenya, he would have nowhere else to go.

'Is it you, Peter? I can't believe it!' Dipan exclaimed behind the counter of his shop when I made my way through the counters of safari clothes. He was a tall man in his early thirties with a round, smiling face. He immediately sent one of his African staff to fetch some delicious spiced tea. I learned that his family – like many in Mombasa – were Jains and strict vegetarians. Unfortunately, his mother was visiting relatives in London and was unable to prepare a meal for me. He was very open to new ideas, and took a keen interest in Kenyan politics, yet he was still sufficiently traditional to accept an arranged marriage which was in the offing.

After my chat with Dipan, I wandered like a mad dog out into the midday sun down Nkrumah Road towards Fort Jesus. On my way, I cashed some money in a British bank in a mock-Tudor building and had a beer on the verandah of the famous Castle Hotel. Although it was only about two-thirds of a mile, I was sweating profusely in the steamy heat by the time I reached the massive walls of Fort Jesus.

The name summed up the two elements the Portuguese brought to the coast: guns and crosses. After the town had been destroyed by marauding Zimba cannibals, the Portuguese built Fort Jesus in 1593 on a coral ridge dominating the entrance to the harbour. But it only brought further turmoil to the coast. At the end of the seventeenth century, it was captured by Omani Arabs who were a rising power in the Indian Ocean, and the Sultan of Oman eventually moved his capital from Muscat to Zanzibar in 1832. His red flag fluttered over Fort Jesus until it was bombarded by two British men-of-war. The Imperial British East Africa Company then administered from 1888 the territory that was to become Kenya.

Walking along the high walls of the fort I could see the rusty tin roofs of the old town of Mombasa, interrupted by the minarets of mosques. I saw a large dhow sailing out through the harbour entrance into the swell of the open sea, while a white schooner with a red ensign sailed gracefully by. Only recently a wreck had been excavated of a Portuguese forty-two-gun frigate which had sunk in front of the fort three hundred years before while attempting to relieve an Arab siege.

After leaving the fort, I wandered down to the shore where children were swimming and playing in the clear blue water of the creek. Along the shore, palm trees gently swayed overhead and bougainvillea flowers tossed their pinkish paper heads in the refreshing sea breeze. An old man was mending a net nearby in the shade. The blood on the grey walls of the fort had long been washed away by the monsoon rains.

Wandering down the first alley opposite Fort Jesus, I entered the rabbit warren of the old town. Nearly all of the old Swahili houses with their beautifully carved wooden doors had disappeared. Few houses were much more than a hundred years old, although some had ornate Indian balconies and reflected the British colonial style with their shady verandahs and shuttered windows. The people milling around in the alleys mirrored the past far better: Arabs, Persians, Indians, and that special mix of African and Arab which make up the fine features of the Swahili people of the East African coast. Muslim women wore black *bui-bui* shifts over their colourful African dresses, while men walked by in embroidered caps and white flowing *kanzu* robes. Many Indian women wore saris. Kiswahili was the most common language, but English, Arabic and Hindi were also spoken.

Sitting in a doorway, quite out of place near Ali's Curio Market (formerly Mombasa's first police station), was a Masai warrior. He wore the traditional short red toga, sandals, plaited hair, and carried a spear. He should have been roaming with his cattle in the highlands of the interior, but instead he was waiting to be photographed by the tourists who were few on the ground.

A short middle-aged man wearing a Muslim hat introduced himself in good English as Soulemayne Guido – a good name for guide. He offered to show me around the old town.

'I miss midday prayers to show you Old Town,' he insisted. 'You pay what you like.'

We walked down Mbarak Hinaway Road (formerly Vasco da Gama Street) where the main government offices and banks used to be, and passed the sixteenth-century Mahndry Mosque, the oldest in use in Mombasa, with its fine carved doors and phallic minaret. We then came out into Government Square with its Customs House, Old Post Office, go-downs and old trading houses opposite the dhow harbour. For over a thousand years, the harbour had been one of the major ports of the triangular dhow trade between East Africa, Arabia and India. As late as the 1840s over 200 dhows would call, carrying passengers, carpets, chests, mangrove poles and other goods.

'No photography!' declared a large notice in the dhow harbour.

'An American some years ago took photos here of the men unloading a dhow and said that slavery was still practised in Kenya. The government did not like it.' Souleymane explained. But he was a resourceful man, and took me down some narrow back streets to the Leven Steps which had been built by freed slaves under the direction of the British Lieutenant James Emery in 1824. Owned by the Sultan of Zanzibar, Leven House – now demolished – once welcomed the German missionary-explorer Ludwig Krapf and his wife and the the British explorers Richard Burton and John Hanning Speke before they set off looking for the source of the Nile.

At the top of the Leven Steps, in the shade of a crumbling house, some men were carving wooden chests. Souleymane slipped them some shillings to let me take some film of the old harbour. There were only about a dozen dhows there, a few from Somalia, Yemen Oman and Dubai. A man soon came up shouting and waving his arms; he was shabbily dressed and seemed touched by the sun. I ignored him until he drew a knife, when Souleymane decided that retreat was the better part of valour. I returned to the ship.

That evening I went with Abdulla, the ship's radio officers, into town.

The captain had been indecisive again about letting him go ashore; he still felt sore about it:

'Excuse me, doc, I don't want to be uncouth, but he's a bastard!'

After a curry at Singhs, Abdulla suggested:

'If you acquiesce, we can go to the Florida night club. I surmise it is time.'

We waved down a taxi – a clapped-out one which had springs coming out of the back seat, but no springs on the back wheels. The driver introduced himself as Tony and said he would look after us for the evening.

'Me good boy, you pay what you like,' he said.

As he drove, he chatted away, looking round at us without slackening his speed. The streets were narrow, potholed and busy.

'My friend, you're talking too much.' Abdulla said. 'Concentrate on your driving.'

Tony paused for a while, but was soon holding forth on how he could take us to the beach, or to see girls, or to do anything we liked for whatever price we liked.

Abdulla replied: 'My friend, you are a good boy but stop talking. Concentrate on your driving. Silence is golden!'.

The Florida was in full swing, with black, shining London cabs queuing up outside in the taxi rank like fat whales amongst the hungry, rusting sharks. I had seen the bright neon lights of the club as we had sailed into Kilindoni harbour the night before. We went through the lobby, missed out the casino, and went straight down to the main bar and dance floor. It was dark and cavernous, except for the flashing lights which focused on the dancers. They all seemed to be beautiful young black girls in the latest fashions. The music was funky and sensual; the atmosphere, intense. Before I could even order a drink at the bar, I was accosted by a beautiful young woman in a tight white mini-dress with great locks of hair piled high on her head.

There were a number of white faces in the night club with short back and sides; they were from the *Boxer* of the British Royal Navy which I had seen moored in the harbour. They were drunk, having a great time, and dancing with as many girls as possible.

The Croatian electrician from the *Barbara D* was also there, and he came over to our table with a bottle of beer in his hand. He proudly announced that he had beaten a girl down to 500 Kenyan shillings for her services:

'I paid 500 for short time and a 100 for the room.' That meant about a fiver in all, the cost of a meal. The girls had to pay 120 shillings to get into the Florida and only a few would be able to get a man each night. Times were hard, and there was little other work.

The noise was too much for Abdulla and we went out on to a terrace under the stars. I could hear the sea crashing on the wall along the back of the garden. We were joined by two girls. The one next to me was a Kikuyu girl of twenty who had come from the interior to look for some work; she had been in Mombasa for three months but had not yet found any. She called herself Mandy. I noticed that while I was sweating, her skin was very cool; she even shivered in her thin dress.

Next to Abdulla was a Somali girl, with a strong plump body. Her name was Halima. She had a long scar on her forehead:

'Girl there hit me with bottle. Head broken. Plenty blood,' she explained. The girl in question was scowling in a far corner with a young British sailor from the *Boxer*.

Abdulla questioned Halima about her origins: she was from Kismayo, and had come down to Mombasa because of the war.

'No disrespect, but how old are you Halima?'

'Twenty-five.'

'Are you a Muslim?'

'Yes.'

Abdulla seemed satisfied and soon afterwards announced that he was going back to her flat. I decided to return to the ship so we all piled out of the Florida and found Tony still waiting for us. He was having a row with a driver of one of the London taxi cabs who did not appreciate his presence.

On the way to Halima's flat, Tony chatted to her in Kiswahili. She offered to show me around Mombasa the next day – with Tony of course as our driver. I dropped Halima and Abdulla off in a back street and they disappeared down a dark side entrance – solid young Halima with small, frail, middle-aged Abdulla. Tony took me back to the ship.

When I saw Abdulla next morning on board, I asked him how things had gone.

'Very well. Very good fuck. She made me some piping hot tea afterwards. It was A1.'

'Are you worried about catching anything? Did you wear a condom?'

'No. She's a very clean girl. Her flat's clean and she washed herself with fresh water. The only trouble was that she demanded twice the normal rate. I paid her to avoid any trouble.'

The ship was leaving for Dar es Salaam that evening, but we went to the seaman's mission for some beers at lunch just outside the dock gates. Tony was waiting by *Barbara D* for us. As usual he had to slip the armed soldiers at the gates fifty shillings to be allowed in and out.

The seaman's mission had a comfortable bar and some well-kept gardens. I rang home from the special cubicles and spoke to Jenny and the children who confirmed that they would be flying out with the film crew to meet me in Dar es Salaam in a few days' time. It seemed surreal.

Back in the bar, I got speaking to the minister who ran the mission, an Englishman who had previously worked in Hull. He was very worldy wise and tolerant but was concerned about the welfare of the seamen who passed through his hands.

'You know, in a recent survey it was found that eighty per cent of the hookers in Mombasa – that means the girls of the Florida and the Istanbul – were HIV positive. Their average age is fifteen to twenty-five and they don't always take precautions – they can't afford to as they would lose their customers. The ship's doctor on the *Boxer* is terribly worried. He can't stop the sailors going ashore and the temptation is great because the girls look fit and beautiful!'

There were several Englishmen drinking in the seaman's mission, which was a little like a yacht club. I mentioned that I was trying to contact a Captain Simon Dyer of Mackenzie Maritime Ltd to see if he could help with a ship from Dar es Salaam to Port Said. I had read in the *ABC Shipping Passenger Guide* that this shipping agency had several ships doing the run and had faxed them from Durban.

'Captain Dyer?' the chaplain said. 'This is Captain Dyer.' He was behind me, half a pint of beer in hand, a trim, dark-haired man with a brisk nautical air.

'You're Peter Marshall? What an amazing coincidence! I've just contacted your people! We may have a Greek ship for you leaving Dar on 7 July calling in at Mombasa, Djibouti and Port Said, but I shall have to confirm it. Contact our agent Mr Patel in Dar.'

Barbara D left Mombasa mid morning on 25 June. We were now doubling back on our wake, sailing into the south-west monsoon winds. The ship began to pitch in the heavy swell. The air conditioning in my cabin had finally broken down, and water was rationed to only two hours a day. It was very hot and very humid. Although we were in the period between the long and the short rains we passed through several squalls. When the sun came out, the rain quickly evaporated from the deck and the grey sea turned to a deep azure. In the afternoon, between the squalls, I could make out the familiar coast of Zanzibar. If all went well, it would be a matter of hours before I joined my family in Dar es Salaam – the Haven of Peace.

Chapter Twenty-Six

Haven of Peace

WE entered the harbour entrance of Dar es Salaam between the coral reefs in the late afternoon and sailed along the deep channel into the wide natural harbour. Fishing dhows and dug-out canoes bobbed up and down in our wake as we swept up the palm-fringed creek. Despite its population of one and half million, Dar was still largely a low-rise city of red-tiled roofs. I scoured the balconies of the Kilimanjaro Hotel on our starboard bow with my binoculars, knowing that Jenny, Emily and Dylan should be staying there.

The bosun saw me and warned: 'Be careful in Dar. There're lots of thieves. Pirates come on board with guns even if we're anchored offshore. Dar is the most dangerous port on the East African coast. I once saw the police shoot the arm of a stowaway.'

That had not been my experience a decade earlier. I had found the Tanzanians throughout the country remarkably friendly and welcoming, with few hang-ups about Europeans. But things could change rapidly along the African coasts. In the nineteenth century, Dar es Salaam had been a little fishing village until the sultan of Zanzibar turned the creek into a safe port and trading centre. It became the capital of German East Africa after the Germans moved their headquarters from nearby Bagamoyo in 1891. After the First World War, Tanganyika, as it was then called, became a British protectorate until it gained its independence in 1961 without a shot being fired.

Its first president had been the remarkable intellectual Julius Nyerere. Educated at Edinburgh University, he had translated Shakespeare into Kiswahili. He had also written many essays on African socialism, claiming that it drew on ancient traditions of mutual aid and self-reliance. Soon after the unification of Tanganyika and Zanzibar to form Tanzania in 1964, *Mwalimu* (Teacher) Nyerere launched the policy of *Ujaama* (familyhood) in order to create an egalitarian commonwealth in which all would hold their head up but none would rise too far above the crowd. While his aims were idealistic, his means were disastrous.

At the end of the sixties, Nyerere forcibly moved the scattered population into communal villages, using the army to impose his will where necessary. The plan was not properly thought-out – villages were often established far from water and fields – and the use of force only alienated the farmers. Agricultural production dropped; factories closed down. Although Tanzania continued to receive the largest amount of foreign aid in Africa, especially from Scandinavian countries, it became one of the poorest countries on the continent.

While capitalist Kenya had prospered, socialist Tanzania floundered. In frustration Nyerere closed the border between the two countries in 1977, thereby destroying the East Africa Community. Corruption in the state-run enterprises became rife. The costly invasion of Uganda in 1979 to depose Idi Amin further crippled the country's economy. Tanzanians found an empty pot of maize meal at the end of the rainbow. And despite Nyerere's rhetoric of freedom and opposition to apartheid, he allowed no free Press or opposition in his own country. There were more political prisoners in his one-party state in the seventies than in South Africa.

At the time of my arrival, Nyerere had resigned – the only African president apart from Léopold Senghor of Senegal to do so. He had been replaced by the former president of Zanzibar, Ali Hassan Mwinyi who was busy introducing political reforms and loosening market forces. Nevertheless the difficult socialist years had left some benefits: unlike Kenya, the 200 or so tribes in Tanzania were welded into one nation with a rare sense of common purpose. By establishing schools throughout the country – even if they had few books – it meant that every Tanzanian understood

Kiswahili. While countries in Central and East Africa were falling apart, Tanzania appeared united and stable.

Barbara D moored in the new container terminal beyond the main quay. The agent agreed to give me a lift into town. My trunk was taken down the gangway and camera equipment placed on the wharf. I said goodbye to the radio officer, chief engineer, and the captain. I felt most sorry for the delicate Malagasy stewardess Hanita and urged her return to Madagascar to continue her studies before it was too late. She promised me she would. At our last meeting, Irena said: 'The reason Peter, why I came to sea is because I have a baby at home. I have to work here to pay my mother to look after her.'

I wished her well, knowing what it was to be away from a child you love.

Dar looked much more run down than I remembered: the potholes had multiplied and grown deeper, the traffic was more congested, the corrugated iron rustier. A few new buildings had gone up, but the old ones were shabbier, their walls grey and their paint peeled off in the tropical heat. At the same time, there were some new cars which suggested at least some fat cats were benefiting from the economic reforms. I noticed many young men selling goods in the street which was new.

The state-owned Kilimanjaro Hotel – the main one in town – was as busy as ever. The receptionist said I was expected and gave me the number of my family's room. Jenny was the first to open the door and give me a big hug. Then I saw Dylan, much bigger than his ten years, a handsome and strapping lad with olive skin, dark brown eyes and dark wavy hair. Emily, who was now fourteen, had blossomed into a beautiful young woman with blue eyes and a light-brown curly mass of hair. Everyone was excited about being in East Africa for the first time, especially after hearing my travellers' tales on winter nights at home around the fire.

The children were pretty tired but full of energy. They had arrived on an overnight flight from Europe and apparently had not slept a wink.

'It was amazing,' Dylan said. 'At dawn we flew over Kilimanjaro. I could see its peak covered in snow. It seemed to be floating above the clouds.'

Jenny looked much better than when I had left. Her jaw was no longer giving her trouble and she was sleeping well. She had managed to survive the winter in our remote cottage in the Welsh mountains, look after the children, continue her radio work and do some French lecturing in a nearby college. Despite her early worries, she had been able to cope magnificently. We both agreed that it would have been disastrous for me to have given up in Senegal. That had been a difficult moment for both of us but we had got through it. Reunited once again, it all seemed to have been worthwhile.

It was good too to see the TV film crew again who had come out with Jenny and the children. David Williams was pleased to have got through customs unscathed but still had his mysterious headaches. Elayne the sound recordist was enjoying the steamy heat and munched away on fresh *mange-touts* secretly imported from her organic garden. David England the cameraman was raring to do what he had always dreamed about: filming African wildlife in their natural habitat.

I went to bed late that night after catching up with all the news from home. I woke at first light, expecting to be on a ship. When I realized that Jenny was next to me and that Emily and Dylan were asleep in an adjoining room, I had to rub my eyes to make sure it was true. I went out on to the balcony and saw the sun rise over the palm-fringed harbour. It had been raining during the night, but already puddles were beginning to evaporate.

We all went for a walk along the busy waterfront before breakfast, mingling with the crowds of people walking to work, the women in colourful dresses and headscarves and the men in trousers and shirts or in long flowing robes. We stopped at one of many stalls selling delicious, fresh, juicy oranges and mangoes. We, a mixed family in Western clothes, were an object of interest in return. Dylan wore a shirt I had bought him with the words 'Africa' printed under two friendly warthogs. He was in his element.

We decided to visit the island of Zanzibar and at lunchtime we clambered on one of the daily ferries. It was seething with passengers who sat on their parcels and bundles wherever they could find some space on deck. The ferry was a Greek ship called the *Apollo* and it still had a map of the Greek islands in its main lounge. At least they had changed the name of the ship to *Muungano* on her bows.

The passage from Dar to Zanzibar took four hours. There was quite a strong swell running and the ferry pitched moderately. Rain clouds dispersed as the afternoon wore on, and the sea turned from grey to blue. I went up with the children into the bow of the ship, sitting on the thick mooring ropes, enjoying the fresh sea-breeze and spray.

We first saw land in the late afternoon when the declining sun was turning the shallow waters around the coral reefs of Zanzibar to a deep turquoise. The Old Stone Town of Zanzibar came into view with its multi-storeyed houses made from coral rag and mangrove poles and corrugated iron roofs. The main waterfront was dominated by the House of Wonders, a neo-classical palace built for the sultan of Zanzibar by British marine engineers. In order to make sure the sultan of their choice came to power in 1896, the British Navy bombarded it for forty-five minutes in the shortest war in history. Next to it, I could make out the brown walls of a fort built on the ruins of a Portuguese chapel. Some way beyond rose the Ithnashiri dispensary, a delicately fretted and ornate building in the Indian style. Children played and splashed in the water below the Old Town where a little more than a hundred years ago the dismembered bodies of rebellious slaves would be left for the sharks, their limbs and heads bobbing in the water and their bones whitening on the beach.

We moored near the old dhow harbour and went through customs and immigration. Although Zanzibar and its large neighbouring island of Pemba had joined with Tanganyika to form Tanzania, Zanzibar still ran its own economy and was jealous of its independence. It had been a largely self-sufficient settlement for over a thousand years, since the first visitors from Arabia had intermarried with the local inhabitants. Their descendents were called Swahili after *swahil*, the Arabic word for coastland. Their own language Kiswahili was mainly Bantu but with Arabic words and phrases.

We made our way into the Old Stone Town along narrow sandy alleys through which only a hand cart could pass. In a little square opposite a small mosque where the muezzin was calling the faithful to prayer, we came across a white building called the Spice Inn. A sign over the door announced that it was 150 years old and offered a 'relaxive and peaceful atmosphere'. After checking in, we were shown to our spacious rooms which had coloured glass windows with shutters, old-fashioned sofas and chairs, and solid beds under mosquito nets. There was a comfortable lounge with a cabinet full of yellowing English books from the thirties and forties.

That night we had dinner on a long table on the balcony overlooking the square. The inn more than lived up to its name. From our vantage point, we watched the goings – on in the little square below: men with embroidered Muslim hats and white *kanzu* robes striding purposefully across; women, their heads and colourful dresses hidden under their black *bui-bui*, lingering as if reluctant to return to the chores of the house; little boys in shorts and girls in skirts playing in the sand until they were shooed home by elder sisters. Opposite the mosque an old man sat under a hurricane lamp by his small shop, his exotic fruit laid out on a stand. One small boy sidled up and snatched an orange and ran off into the dark.

We slept that night under our mosquito nets, listening to the soft whisper of the breeze in the palm trees and distant murmur of the sea. Next morning, I was woken up by the dawn chorus. The whole sky seemed to be filled with bird – song and the noises of the wakening town: shutters being opened, babies crying, children shouting in the street below. It was not long before the morning sun, climbing in the deep blue sky, turned us out of bed.

We spent the morning wandering through the dark maze of the narrow streets and alleys of Zanzibar. Turning a corner, we would suddenly come out into a small sunlit square surrounded by high walls and shaded by a towering palm tree. We marvelled at the beautifully carved doors with their metal bosses, said to keep elephants out but more likely to impress the neighbours. Swahili family life looked inwards, and the grander houses gave on to inner courtyards.

The sandy streets were clean and tranquil. It would have been very different in the nineteenth century when Zanzibar was the capital of the Sultan of Oman who controlled the coastal trade in slaves, gold, ivory and spices. Its 25,000 inhabitants would swell to 40,000 during the dhow season and the place became so filthy that the British explorer Richard Burton nicknamed it 'Stinkibar'.

It was tragic to see such a historic and beautiful town in decline. Many of the buildings built from coral rag and mangrove polls were crumbling; some were reduced to a pile of rubble. Many of the unique carved wooden doors had been taken away to Mombasa where they were sold on at great profit to antique collectors in America and Europe. Zanzibar was the last of the great Swahili city states along the East African coast still functioning, little changed for two hundred years; if some restoration work was not undertaken soon, it would disappear forever.

I came across odd reminders of the British presence from the turn of the century: an old red Royal Mail pillar box and a milestone giving the distances to local villages on the island and 'London 8064 miles'. There was even a billiard table with a base made from slate taken from the mines of Blaenau Ffestiniog near where I lived in Wales; it was in the former British Club, now the Africa Hotel owned by the Afro–Shirazi Party. Some of the street signs were in Kiswahili, Arabic, English and Hindi. I noticed that a hospital which had been called the V.I. Lenin Hospital during my previous visit had changed its name to a Swahili one. The revolution led by the Afro–Shirazi Party in 1964 which had massacred the ruling Arab élite had largely been forgotten.

Everywhere we went were smiling and friendly faces. In a warm and casual way people would greet us in Kiswahili with '*Jumbo*' (Hallo) and '*Karibu*' (Welcome). No one hassled us or begged, something unique in my experience of Africa. The wise Swahili people knew the dangers of over-exertion in a tropical climate and followed religiously the principle: *Haraka haraka heina baraka* – more haste, less speed. They were laid-back people, practising a tolerant form of Islam, hospitable to strangers, valuing above all their families and social life.

There was no drought or famine in Zanzibar. The market was bursting with rows upon rows of neatly piled fruit and vegetables, everything from aubergines to spinach, limes to dorians. The latter was considered a particular delicacy but not by me: the size of a cannonball with sharp spikes it smelt and tasted like rotten camembert.

After visiting the market, I took my family to see the Cathedral Church of Christ built over the old slave market. The Swahili traders, collaborating with local chiefs, brought the slaves from central Africa along the old caravan routes. Many died on the long trek, tied together with chains and yokes. If a mother could not carry her load, a spear would enforce the rule: 'Ivory first, child afterwards!' Those who reached the coast were shipped by dhow from Bagamyo ('Be quiet my heart') to Zanzibar. Here they were washed, dressed up in jewels, and led in procession through the streets. Any prospective buyer would examine them as if they had been cattle. Over a million slaves were exported in the nineteenth century, about half to India, the Gulf and Arabia. The saying was no exaggeration: 'When you play the flute in Zanzibar, all Africa as far as the lakes dances'.

It was along the slave routes to the interior that Richard Burton and John Hanning Speke travelled in search of the source of the Nile. Henry Morton Stanley went the same way in search of Livingstone whom he met, he presumed, at Ujuji on the shores of Lake Tanganyika. The British eventually persuaded the Sultan of Zanzibar to prohibit the slave trade in 1873 and to commemorate the event the Anglican Bishop of Zanzibar built the Cathedral Church of Christ on the old slave market.

It was a grey, drab building built of coral stone and Portland cement, but inside it had some fine stained-glass windows and massive marble pillars at the entrance placed by mistake upside down. A member of the local congregation pointed out a small cross over the pulpit which was made from the wood of the tree under which Livingstone died in Chitambo, Zambia. His servants James Chuma and Abdulla Susi buried his heart under the tree and carried the rest of his dessicated body 1,500 miles to the coast in eleven months, one of the great unsung journeys of the age of exploration. Before he died Livingstone declared that he thought ending slavery, the 'open sore of the world', was worth the discovery of all the Niles in the world.

In the afternoon, we went to visit a spice plantation out of town. It was owned by a Shirazi, whose ancestors like many Zanzibaris came from Shiraz in Persia. His light-skinned teenage boys showed us around. The cloves were just ripening and ready to be picked and dried in the sun. Cloves provided the economic backbone of Zanzibar and had made it even after the abolition of slavery one of the richest countries in Africa. A large workforce was still necessary to pick the buds from the three and half million trees every five months. Zanzibar and Pemba remained the world's largest producers of cloves.

Before we left the plantation we bought a variety of spices: cinnamon, chilli, cardamon, pepper, cloves, ginger, nutmeg which filled our bags in the hotel with their heady aroma. With our 'relaxive' curries at the Spice Inn, we began to exude the exotic fragrance of Zanzibar.

In the evening after dinner we strolled through the narrow streets down to the moonlit waterfront by the House of Wonders. Families were on their balconies talking quietly with neighbours or each other. On the waterfront young people gathered to chat, drinking coffee in the small cafés on the green, playing cards under oil lamps, or eating maize grilled over open charcoal fires under the palm trees. Whole families came out to enjoy the warm evening air. Several young men said politely to Emily: '*Ginarako nani?*' (What's your name?). Whatever may have been Zanzibar's bloody past, no where else in Africa did I feel more secure.

The next morning, we went dhow sailing. For centuries these graceful boats were the principal means of transport along the coast and across the Indian Ocean, sailing down with the north east monsoon and returning with the south west monsoon. The large ocean-going dhows – up to 400 tons – would engage in triangular trade between East Africa, India and the Persian Gulf. There were many more in the harbour than in Mombasa. They were mainly of the *jahazi* variety, about sixty feet long, weighing up to twenty tons. We clambered over a couple to reach one which we had arranged to take out. The owner was a business man in Zanzibar who used it for transporting building materials from the mainland. Dhows were coming back into fashion because they were easy to maintain and used no fuel; his had already doubled in value in a couple of years and been twice to Somalia. Its name was *Wshikamando*, meaning 'solidarity' in Kiswahili.

In the old days, the dhows were sewn together with coir rope, possibly from fear – mentioned in the *Arabian Nights* – that a lodestar would pull out all the nails of a ship. Nowadays the rough planks of the hull were nailed together, but still caulked with cotton and a greasy substance made out of fat and lime. Fish oil was rubbed on the upper part of the hull. The deck and gunwhales were made from plaited coconut fronds spread over mangrove poles as they always had been.

The *Wshikamando* had one mast and a large rudder. At her stern on her port side was a kind of barrel slung over the side which served as a toilet. I took my shoes off before climbing on board, remembering the Swahili saying that one should not take the evil of the land on to the sea.

I had once sailed in a similar dhow from Kilwa, the site of an ancient Swahili city state near the Mozambican border, to Mafia Island near Zanzibar. The crew had consisted of about eight men, with the skipper or *nahoda* having earned his position of authority through his seamanship. They navigated by the sun and stars, having no charts or compass, taking their bearings from familiar landmarks along the coast and its small islands. Life on board was spartan: maize meal porridge – *ugali* – had been the menu for the day: with a little sugar at breakfast, salt at lunch, and dried fish in the evening. Drinking water was carried in an old oil drum lashed to the deck. At night we anchored and slept in a pile on deck under the sail.

Sailing on the *Wshikamando* off Zanzibar was much more pleasant. As we shoved off from the other dhows in the harbour a young ragged boy was sent up the shrouds to unfurl the lateen sail which hang from a long slender yard at the top of the mast. When the triangular sail filled with a moderate wind, the dhow leaned and began to surge through the turquoise waters at the harbour entrance. The skipper brought in one end of the yard and fastened it tight. Another sailor shifted sacks of sand in the hold which acted as ballast and helped with the trim.

I went up forward with Dylan and leaned out to watch the bows of the dhow cut merrily through the rising waves. Unused to the heat and still recovering from his long plane journey, Dylan soon felt queasy and was eventually sick over the side. He went back afterwards to sit amidships by the mast on the coconut matting. Jenny and Emily were there discussing with a young man.

'So Swahili women have to stay below decks when at sea?' Jenny was saying.

'It's for their own good, if they stayed on deck they would get in the way of the sailors' work. It would also be difficult because of mistaken nudity.'

'But what if they wanted to come up sometimes to get some fresh air?' Emily insisted.

'On a dhow, the women remain in the hold. It's always been like that. We Muslims believe that men and women have different duties and responsibilities. It's part of our tradition of respect for our women. No one complains.'

'I think I would if I were a Swahili woman!'

'You're not. But don't worry, you can stay on deck!'

When we sailed back to Zanzibar, smaller *mashua* dhows were coming in after a day's fishing. Further inshore there were several *ngalawas*, small dug-out canoes equipped with outriggers, a design probably introduced by Indonesian mariners who settled in Madagascar fifteen centuries ago.

The next day we returned from Zanzibar to Dar es Salaam in a Russian-built hydrofoil. It took half the time of the ferry, but was far less pleasant. Locked inside its fuselage, cut off from wind, sun and sea, we were jolted all the way; it felt like clinging to an angry dragon's tail. We arrived battered and tired. Give me a slow, graceful, seaworthy dhow any time.

Chapter Twenty-Seven

A Cold Place

O N our return to Dar we set off for a safari. We had to first fly to Arusha in the foothills of Kilimanjaro, half way between Cape Town and Cairo. We had no choice but to go by Air Tanzania Corporation, the national airline, otherwise known as Air Maybe or more accurately by its initials ATC – All Time Cancelled. In the old days, it would only accept cash, but now travellers' cheques were acceptable. The whole top management had recently been sacked for corruption, part of a process sweeping through the government-owned enterprises.

When we landed the largest mountain in Africa, which I had climbed a decade earlier, was covered in cloud. But the sense of space on the wide open savannah as we got off the plane was stunning. Unlike Europe, there are vast tracts of Africa still unfenced, where animals roam free and know no owner. In some places, the horizon is so far away that it seems as if you can see the curvature of the earth's surface.

Travelling into Arusha the countryside became more undulating. We passed through lush green countryside with coffee plantations, wheat estates, and *shambas* of ripening maize. After Mozambique, this part of Tanzania seemed like the golden age restored: there was no drought or war going on and people were well fed and relaxed. At the foot of Mount Meru, Arusha was a bustling town, the commercial and agricultural centre for the northern region of Tanzania and the springboard for organizing climbs up Kilimanjaro and safaris to the great northern parks of Lake Manyara, Ngorongoro Crater and the Serengeti.

We organized a safari through the State Travel Service and set off in a Volkswagen van with our driver Gerald Msuya, and our guide Silvester Dilli. Gerald was a small stocky man, with incredible powers of concentration and the eyes of a hawk. Mr Dilli for his part was friendly, polite and a good fixer.

For an hour or so the road was good, but when we turned north west towards a volcanic range of mountains, it became a dirt track. We bounced along in a cloud of dust until we reached a town at the foot of the escarpment of the Great Rift Valley which runs down East Africa from Ethiopia. In the distance we saw our first zebra and wildebeest on the rolling savannah with scattered flat-topped acacia trees. Some men in red togas carrying spears walked along the side of the track.

As we struggled up the hairpin bends of the escarpment, the savannah gave way to rocky ground with huge boulders. A few fat baobab trees, looking as if they were growing upside down, rose out of the rough bush. Once over the top of the escarpment, a thousand feet higher, we travelled through rolling hills covered in fields of ripening wheat and maize and dotted with villages with red mud houses and thatched roofs. Away from the dusty road, the air was beautifully fresh and cool in these fertile highlands.

In the late afternoon, we eventually reached the gate to the Ngorongoro Conservation Area which adjoins the vast Serengeti plains. Ngorongoro means 'A Cold Place'. The earth was reddish and the vegetation much more lush; we were entering some of the last remaining equatorial rainforest which used to stretch thousands of miles across central Africa. An hour later we pulled up at our lodge for the night, the Ngorongoro Crater Lodge, 5,500 feet above sea level, the highest point so far in my voyage.

It was the view which people came for. The lodge was perched on the edge of the Ngorongoro Crater, the largest unbroken caldera in the world, which stretched below us like a lost world. I could just make out in the setting sun the crater rim on the other side eight miles away. With the use of powerful binoculars, the black specks in a clearing near a small lake turned out to be buffalo.

We got up early next morning and set off with a packed lunch in a Land Rover. It was still cold and misty, with water dripping from the lianas and lichens in the rainforest on the rim. We then bumped down a steep track, negotiating dizzy bends, to the crater floor some 2,000 feet below. The sun soon broke through, burning off the remaining mist and warming our bones. Muscles relaxed in the gentle breeze. I could not imagine a more idyllic place in the world.

At the bottom of the track there was a group of young Masai dressed in all their beaded finery waiting to be photographed. Two girls had their faces painted white, a sign that they had recently undergone clitoridectomy, or female circumcision, which marked their passage to womanhood. Some young men with shining bodies and braided hair carried spears – they had also passed through painful rites although they were no longer allowed to kill a lion to reach manhood.

The Masai long ignored the border between Kenya and Tanzania. But even their strong culture – they consider themselves to be God's chosen people who own all the cattle in the world – has been unable to resist the forces of the modern world. Their days as independent people are numbered: warriors without a war to fight, nomadic pastoralists in an age of settled agriculture. The once feared *murran* are now reduced to begging from tourists at the side of the road, their carefully braided hair and oiled bodies for sale. Their fathers believed that a photograph stole their soul; they were right.

On the crater floor, we drove quietly through herds of grazing zebra and wildebeest. They live permanently in the crater, but just over the rim to the west their cousins in the vast Serengeti Plains – some 8,000 square miles – join in the last great annual migration of large mammals on earth. Every year several million wildebeest and zebra come to calve in lush green pastures from November to May, but when the grass became exhausted they migrate in a headlong rush to the northern western Masai Mara on the other side of the Kenya border. Thousands each year drown crossing the rivers in their way, many pulled under water by the waiting crocodoiles. Other predators – lions, hyenas, cheetahs, hunting dogs – follow picking off the weak and injured and ensuring that only the fittest survive.

As I was telling the children about the migration, we suddenly came across a kill on the edge of the large soda lake in the middle of the crater. We disturbed a pride of lionesses who had just had their fill, ambling a few yards from the carcass of a wildebeest, their necks red with blood and their stomachs bloated with fresh meat. They flopped down in a line in the cool mud for their siesta, some slowly rolling on their backs or their sides, panting with exhaustion. Flies settled on their necks, attracted by the smell of warm blood. At the same time, a frenzied pack of hyenas moved in to what was left of the lions' feast. Vultures, next in turn, hopped around impatiently in a wider circle. A silver-backed jackal sloped by trying to get a morsel left over in the squabble, and a couple of Egyptian eagles flew in hoping to pick up a morsel. Nothing is wasted in nature's economy.

We were only about a few yards away from the lions and the hyenas but they paid us no attention, one set because of their contentment, the other because of their blood lust. The hyenas fought each other for their share, crunching with massive jaws through the rib cage and severed head of the wildebeest. They let off blood-curdling giggles and grunts. One hyena ran off with a black leg dripping bright red blood on the white shore of the soda lake, laughing like a maniac. It was pursued by a couple more who soon gave up the chase and returned to the bloody melée.

Near by other wildebeest grazed nonchalantly, loping along in their comical way, sensing that they were in no danger for the time being at least. Little devils – whirlwinds of dust – skimmed across the white gleaming soda flats. Along the shores of the lake thousands of pink flamingos moved to and fro on their long stick-like legs, dipping their heads in shallow water for the algae and shrimps which managed to live there.

Not far off we met a lumbering old bull elephant, his ears ragged at the bottom edges. His thick, grey, wrinkled skin hung off his great backside with its ridiculously small tail. His guts rumbled and he suddenly gave a loud fart. He then proceeded to suck sand and dust up his trunk in order to give himself a dust bath by blowing it over his back and wagging his ears. I was pleased to see that he still had a fine yellowing pair of tusks.

The elephants in East Africa had been massacred in recent years for their ivory, especially by Somalis who came down in fast four-wheel drive vehicles with automatic weapons. I had also read reports that hundreds of elephants were being shot in Zimbabwe because of the drought. Since they feed largely from stripping bark off trees, they can cause immense damage to a small area and need a wide range in order to allow trees time to regenerate.

I had visited the Ngorongoro Crater many times, but each time was special. For me it was the most beautiful place on earth, the closest I could imagine to the Garden of Eden, even though I recognized that all life lived off each other and nature was red in tooth and claw. I felt completely at home here, maybe because as a species we had come from this part of the world. An hour or so away was Olduvai Gorge, where the Leakey family had found the 1.75 million-year-old remains of early man, *Australopithecus boisei*, nicknamed 'Nutcracker Man' because he had large teeth and was probably vegetarian. Humanity had first emerged in East Africa and then spread out to populate and pollute the planet. In nearby Laetoli, Mary Leakey had also discovered, embedded in solidified volcanic ash, the first known footprints of an early human and a child, made some 3.6 million years ago.

The highlight of our safari came in the late afternoon when our driver spotted in the far distance a rhinoceros and her baby. All I could see was swaying grass. After some difficult manoeuvres, we managed to get within a few yards of them. The mother was careful not to let her baby get between her and the Land Rover; otherwise, they just carried on grazing as if we did not exist. Their long pointed top lips worked constantly as they chewed the long grass entwined with flowers. The mother had a fine horn. It was an incredibly rare sight to see them so close in the wild where they had naturally evolved.

It was tragic to think that these creatures were being wiped out throughout East Africa by the same poachers with their automatic weapons and high-speed cars who killed the elephants. In the rhino's case, they were after their horns of matted hair which were made into dagger handles in the Middle East or grounded down for medicine and aphrodisiacs in the Far East. Despite well-trained wardens in the parks of Zimbabwe, Tanzania and Kenya, the poachers were still winning the war, and the rhino population was threatened with extinction.

Before I left Ngorongoro, I met the chief conservator Paul Mshanga. He was a mild-mannered man who was deeply concerned about the well-being of the Conservation Area. I asked him what its aims were.

'The Area was established to conserve the natural resources, wildlife, soils, forests, and water. Another aim was to develop the interests of the 26,000 Masai pastoralists who live here. It is a difficult job, but we keep trying.'

'What about the impact of tourism on the area? I saw young Masai posing for photographs alongside the tracks.'

'In a way, where you encourage tourism, you have to sacrifice some things. Of course the Masai wait to be photographed as a way of getting money; it's not traditional in their culture. But that is how tourism influences culture everywhere in the world.'

'And the poaching? I was disappointed to see so few rhinos . . .'

'The rhinos are a sad story. There used to be a lot – in 1966 there were between 100 to 150 in the whole of the Conservation Area, but in the late seventies and early eighties there was a lot of poaching which brought the population down to about thirty animals. Elephants so far are not a problem. After a nationwide campaign, poaching for ivory and game trophies has gone down.'

'But are you getting the support of your people?'

'Of late we are considering the possibility of allowing tribes living in the peripheries to hunt and kill for the pot. If they are allowed to use bows and arrows and to kill a certain number of animals, it will do little harm where there are 1.7 million wildebeest! It will ensure that they will be with us in the spirit of conservation.'

The conservator was right. The only way to ensure the well-being of wildlife in Africa is to ensure the well-being of those humans who live amongst it as part of a living, fully integrated ecosytem. Africans will not support conservation wholeheartedly until they become active, willing participants, until they appreciate that by caring for their environment they are caring for themselves. Only if they feel that conservation is in their interest will the policies of the international wildlife organizations succeed. Otherwise fenced game reserves will be seen as playgrounds for rich foreigners and conservation as a foreign plot to deprive Africans of their right to manage their own affairs. Europeans and Americans might be righteous about conserving the animals now, but it was they who wiped out the big game of East Africa in the first place. Africans had lived with the wildlife for centuries and only killed what they needed to eat.

At the same time, I can see no defence for the World Wildlife Fund's strategy of 'sustainable utilization' by killing crocodiles for their skins, lions for trophies, and elephants for ivory. Such a policy encourages a fashion for such products and it seems a strange way to preserve wildlife by making it glamorous to kill it. Moreover, to find pleasure in blasting a lion from the safety of a vehicle not only degrades the killer but fosters the kind of macho morality which was mainly responsible for killing most of Africa's wildlife. It was not all that long ago that lions in Tanzania and Kenya were considered 'vermin' and shot by white hunters in their hundreds. To kill an elephant was also considered manly: a photograph taken in 1925 shows the Queen Mother and George VI proudly reclining on the still warm flanks of a huge elephant – like an exotic sofa – which the king had just shot. By comparison, the attitude of a local poacher – now shot by wardens – was much more understandable; at least he killed game for his family's survival.

This is not to say that some culling might be necessary in carefully managed small parks where natural rhythms are unable to operate because of previous human interference. Ideally parks should be big enough to allow nature to find its own balance. This is the case with the Serengeti ecosystem, which includes Ngorongoro, and for that reason deserves to be defended at all costs.

As we left Ngorongoro the mist lifted and for a tantalizing few seconds we saw the vast Serengeti plains below us. They stretched for hundreds of miles to Lake Victoria. We did not have time to visit the Serengeti this trip but I felt sure that I would return one day with the children.

On our way out, I stopped on the crater's rim at a famous viewpoint where there was a plaque to commemorate Professor Bernhard Grzimek, who had dedicated his life to care for the wild animals and to defend their place on earth. Below the plaque I read in the morning mist: 'It is better to light a candle than to curse the darkness'.

We spent the next night in a lodge perched on the edge of the Great Rift Valley, a thousand feet above huge Lake Manyara.

The Lake Manyara National Park is a 'biosphere reserve' of special scientific interest, famous for its tree-climbing lions. No one knows for sure why the lions sprawl on the horizontal branches of the umbrella acacia trees. Perhaps it is to escape insects, to catch a breeze in the heat of the day, or even to enjoy a view. The most probable reason is to escape the herds of buffalo and elephant milling around on the ground.

As the shadows began to lengthen and the sun descended towards the escarpment of the Great Rift Valley, wave upon wave of flamingos came into land along the shores of Lake Manyara. There were millions of them and they turned the bluey white waters into swathes of moving pink. Sitting on an old tree trunk, I watched the last rays of the sun illuminate the gnarled branches of a spreading acacia tree. I thought that I would happily lay down my heart in this corner of Africa.

Chapter Twenty-Eight

Oranges by the Road

ONCE back in Arusha we learned what I had half expected: the Air Tanzania Corporation flight to Dar es Salaam had been cancelled and the next one was not until after the weekend. It looked like we were stuck and the film crew would miss their flight home. Silvester Dilli came to our rescue. After long negotiations with the local manager, he persuaded Ethiopian Airways to take us to Dar, something normally not allowed as Air Tanzania had the franchise for internal flights. But in Africa, where there's a strong will, and some wheeler-dealing, there's a way.

'The customs officer is a friend of mine,' Mr Dilli said. 'We play tennis together.'

On our return to Dar, the film crew left for the UK; I would meet up with it again in Cairo, Allah willing. Jenny and the children had planned to fly home later so that we could have a leisurely time together on the coast. I contacted some friends of Dave and Maggie Burke whom I had met in Agadir and they invited us to stay with them in their beautiful house at the end of the harbour creek in Dar.

Jan van Liere was a Dutchman who had worked on oil rigs but who was now in charge of the Dar es Salaam Port Development Project financed by Finnish aid. His companion Chanel Croker was an Australian teaching English at the International School. They rented their house with its garden full of bougainvillea, frangipani, palms and orchids from one of the 7,000 Germans still living in Tanzania.

'He's a real cowboy,' Jan said. 'When we arrived here he had an arsenal of guns and hand grenades. Neighbours say he would let off a gun from time to time to deter any thieves. His wife was the one who did the garden.'

Jan's companion Chanel was one of eleven children and had been sent to a Catholic boarding school in Australia. After university, she had practised self-sufficiency on a hundred acres in the outback, but in her late twenties decided to go to Africa. She had taught in Uganda during the civil war which followed the Tanzanians' toppling of Idi Amin:

'It was very difficult. Shots rang out in Kampala from dawn to dusk. A friend of mine had to hide in the pit of a garage for three days while fighting was raging all around him. I also had a neighbour whose head was blown off when he came across some thieves in his house. There were sixteen-year-old kids with AK 47 rifles who would stop cars and trucks on the road and demand money. No one could control them. Some came round to my house one night; I thought they might rape me or even kill me but they left empty-handed. People are less predictable than the wind. I decided soon after to come to Dar.'

Her great passion was hang-gliding. With some friends, she had built a hut high in the Usumburu mountains which she used as a launching pad. She told us of a recent adventure there:

'It takes about ten hours to climb the 2,000 metres up the mountain to get to our hut. I got some porters from a village in the valley below, three young Masai. They set off with one gourd of water between them and no warm clothes. I told them that they weren't coming into my sleeping bag or having any of my water! They replied: "No problem. We're *murran*, warriors!"

'As we started climbing the mountain, I soon realized that they weren't used to it. Towards the summit, they started saying "Let's go back down." I refused and we eventually made it. They were shivering in the cold and I had to give them all our spare clothes and hats. By the time they woke up next morning at dawn, I had already assembled my glider outside my hut. I was trailing some paper at the end of a Masai stick to check the direction of the wind. They started muttering that the *musungu* is crazy. As I geared up, they were fascinated by the strange headgear. But when I picked up the glider and leapt off the mountain top, they started shouting: "Aaaaah, Mama! Aaaah!", pounding the earth with their sticks. It took me twenty minutes to get down. When I met them seven hours later in their village, they were still wearing the ski caps in the sweltering heat!'

I asked why she liked doing it.

'It took me a long time to overcome fear, fear of heights. You're totally alone, a small speck in the vast sky, but in a positive way. You're weightless and when you glide, the birds come and fly with you. Being up there, I have a sense of total freedom. It's only for those who know how to enjoy life.'

During our stay with Chanel and Jan, they lent us a four-wheel drive Susuki; we made good use of it. The morning traffic meant that a ten-minute drive into town could often take over an hour, and then it was very difficult to find anywhere to park. The *mutatus*, great smoke-belching buses, blocked up the narrow streets of the city centre. It called itself a 'struggling bus service'. The adjective summed up Dar as a whole: everything was a struggle, to get around, to get a job, to make ends meet.

The centre was packed with young men on the pavements trying to sell anything from watches and shirts to umbrellas. Plush new private *bureaux de change* had opened up, but the shelves in the few old bookshops were almost bare. The paint was peeling off the houses, and telephone and electricity wires coiled down their walls like spaghetti. Sand was moving into the town and blocked drains ensured that after heavy showers the roads became flooded. No one seemed to be doing anything about it.

My first call was the Egyptian embassy in Ghana Street, an old colonial building with a wide verandah, where I hoped to get a visa. I was told to leave my passport and come back the next day. I then with great difficulty traced down the shipping agency of WEC Lines, whose name had been given to me by Captain Dyer in the seamen's mission in Mombasa. It was situated in a small office in an alley with no visible name.

After waiting for some time on a bench in a dark corridor, we were eventually ushered into the small office of the agent, Mr Anil Patel. He was very warm and friendly. Over some delicious spiced tea, he confirmed that I could join the MV *WEC Rotterdam* chartered from

Southern Steamships Ltd by the Dutch WEC Lines for no fee. She had a Greek crew and I was to be their guest. She was leaving on 7 June, calling in at Mombasa and Djibouti and expected to arrive in Port Said on 23 June before proceeding to northern Europe. I had fallen on my feet.

Mr Patel came from an influential Asian family in Tanzania. He told me that his father had been an adviser to the British governor in Zanzibar and had been awarded an OBE for his services. With his four brothers, Mr Patel had business interests throughout Tanzania, from shipping, export–import, engineering, photography, boutiques to plantations. I asked him how he had got on during Tanzania's socialist years.

'You know, whatever they say about him, Nyerere brought unity and stability to the country. At the top level at least, there was very little corruption. He was respected and visited almost every village. That's more than you can say about most African leaders.'

Before we left, he invited us to stay anytime at his coffee plantation overlooking the Ngorongoro Crater:

'You'll find a cook there and all the drinks you need. The British ambassador stays there sometimes.'

We spent the following days visiting the beaches to the north of Dar along the Bagamoyo road. It was just as well that we had a four-wheel-drive vehicle because they could only be reached by a wide, potholed road with a severe cam. Just before arriving at the Bahari Beach Hotel, an enterprising seven-year-old boy waved us down with a red flag. He had half filled in a big pothole with sand. I gave him a couple of oranges but he was clearly disappointed; he was after money not food. I hoped one day he would enter the highways department and begin to sort out the other potholes.

Since times were hard and there was no public welfare, most people were intent on survival. I noticed that some squatters from makeshift huts nearby were cutting down a huge baobab tree for firewood. Its branches had been lopped off, but its trunk was too big to tackle. A few leaves were trying to burst out of its confines. Such a tree could live for two thousand years but the people cutting it down could hardly think two weeks ahead.

We decided to go on the beach by a hotel because of the danger of being mugged. My Agadir friends Dave and Maggie had been mugged just wandering a little way off a hotel beach; some youths had stuck broken bottles in their necks and faces. The experience had shaken them and speeded up their departure. We were lucky. Under the palms of the luxurious Bahari Beach Hotel, we enjoyed the warm waters of the Indian Ocean. The monsoon winds made the water cloudy, but it was great fun splashing and playing with the children in the surf crashing on to the white coral sand.

The next day we went to the Kunduchi Beach, a run-down hotel in Swahili style nearer Dar. We managed to hire a boat to take us to a deserted coral island where we spent the day swimming, picnicking and lazing under the swaying palm trees. It was the closest I got to lotus-eating on a sea-girt isle. Unfortunately, our ferry man returned to pick us up at dusk.

On the way back to Dar, we stopped to buy food and drink for Jan and Chanel at the well-stocked stores at the side of the road. Closer to town, we also came across a huge pile of oranges which were for sale. They cost virtually nothing; no wonder the young road repairer had been disappointed. I thought the oranges must have fallen off the back of a lorry, but then I remembered that wages for a casual labourer in the capital of Tanzania were 200–300 shillings a day, about thirty pence. Jan paid his gardener 12,000 shillings a month, about twelve pounds sterling.

To reach his house we had to cross a railway line. It had been built by the Chinese in the sixties and was the main link for Zambia to the sea and the outlet for its copper. Known as the Tazara line, it passed through some of the most remote areas in Africa, including the vast Selous Game Reserve. As usual the lack of maintenance meant that it was often breaking down and schedules were erratic. As a railway buff, Dylan was fascinated to see the huge diesel locos shunting up and down the railway lines outside our house in the shimmering heat.

After ten days, the time came for Jenny, Emily and Dylan to return to Wales. I drove them in the evening to the airport in order to see them off. It was a painful wrench as we were just getting used to being together again after our four-month separation. For Emily and Dylan it was their first time in Africa and every day had brought new discoveries and delights. They would go home with an idea of the roots of some of their ancestors and a sense of the relaxed and hospitable African way of life.

Dylan cried as we said goodbye. I felt my heart choking in my throat as I saw my family disappear through the immigration barrier. As I drove back to our little bungalow in the beautiful gardens, tears clouded my vision and I almost crashed into a broken-down lorry abandoned on the highway without any lights in the pitch black. People were moving along the sides of the road like shadows or sitting still around small flickering lamps. My hosts had told me that, as a rule of thumb, they never drove at night unless they had to; I could now see why.

I said goodbye to Chanel the next morning. She was packing a four-wheel drive vehicle for a safari to a remote part of Western Tanzania. She was going with a German girl; if they broke down, they might well have to wait days before getting any help. Looking from the kitchen window, Chanel's young Tanzanian cook smiled and shook his head at her folly:

'Africa women don't do that.'

'They might like to,' I said.

'Nature is for white peoples.'

Jan took me down to the port in the afternoon to see me off. His work at the port was coming to an end, but he was not very optimistic about the future.

'We've put a whole new container terminal in, with new gantries, and trained the staff to work it. In two years, it will probably break down. No one bothers to maintain anything.'

'What can be done to change things?'

'At the moment when things go wrong, they just rely on experts from abroad. The only answer is to give proper wages, get rid of corruption, and train the workforce – otherwise nothing will change in Africa.'

Jan accompanied me to my cabin on board the *WEC Rotterdam*. It was a medium-sized container ship, about ten years old. I was given the owner's cabin next to the radio officer's just below the bridge. It had a spacious day room, with a separate cabin and bathroom. For me its best feature was the splendid view in three directions.

The crew consisted of Greek officers and Filipinos. The captain introduced himself as Georgios Kastis – 'call me George'. He was a large man with curly, swept-back white hair and an aquiline nose. Captain Dyer, the agent I had met in the seamen's mission in Mombasa, was also on board travelling from Dar to Mombasa.

We left Dar es Salaam, the biggest port on the East African coast, at 16.00 hours on 7 July. As we sailed out of the harbour entrance and turned north, the *WEC Rotterdam* began to roll in the waves. With the south-west monsoon blowing behind us, and a four-knot current helping us on our way, we were soon averaging a fast twenty-two knots, the fastest I had travelled on my voyage so far.

The captain told me more about the ship I was on. 'It's managed by Southern Steamships based in London but owned by a Greek magnate who has business interests in South Africa. He's got seven ships which he charters out. He always buys new ones.'

George seemed the first really contented captain I had met during my voyage. On his last ship, he had stayed for two years before taking leave and he had already passed nine months on the *WEC Rotterdam*.

'I'm like a gypsy,' he confessed. 'I like always to be moving. Every day is new and every day is different. I've visited thirty-two countries in the world and still enjoy being at sea.'

When Captain Kastis met Captain Dyer, he embraced him in the warm Greek way. Captain Dyer was an old P & O man who had become a captain as early as thirty-two. Now a fit and trim fifty-one, he was regional operations representative for Beacon Lines (British East African Lines) which had formed a consortium with Ellerman Line, Harrison Line, P & O Containers, and WEC Lines.

A few hours out of Dar, the crew discovered three stowaways on board.

'It's a regular problem here,' Captain Dyer said. 'They come without papers. I've known some who were refused entry in Mombasa and had to be taken to Europe before being returned to Dar. One even went

282

on a three-month voyage to Los Angeles and Honolulu and complained of the service!'

'Why do they stow away?'

'Those coming from Tanzania are mainly looking for a better life in Kenya. But in the north of Kenya, hundreds of thousands of refugees are coming over the Somali border to escape the war and famine up there. They're also coming down the coast in old boats, dhows, even on rubber tyres. Normally, they're interred on arrival.'

As we were steaming towards Mombasa, I asked Captain Dyer why the British Merchant Navy had shrunk in the last couple of decades. So far. None of my ships had been British-owned.

'Two things, mainly. Firstly, the ships are much larger. A large container ship can now carry 4,000 twenty-foot containers, probably the equivalent of 50–60,000 tons. Secondly, red-ensign tonnage has been vastly reduced by people placing their ships under flags of convenience. There's been a large run-down of European tonnage, and the UK has suffered more badly than most.'

'All the ships I've been sailing on except this one have been flags of convenience. What's the advantage?'

'Flags of convenience have been used mostly for tax reasons and also because it's a fact that operating with crews under flags of convenience is a cheaper option than under the United Kingdom Seamen's Agreement. Some of the regulations, it would be fair to say, are not quite as stringent.'

'One other thing still puzzles me. Why are so many ships under charter around the coasts of Africa?'

'For anyone to invest in this part of the world their own tonnage would be an extremely expensive capital investment. A new container ship like *WEC Rotterdam* can cost between $40 and $70 million, a very high capital investment for a trading route for which frankly there are very few returns. WEC Line choose to charter their tonnage rather than own it on the basis that they can divest themselves of that tonnage at any time.'

Two small incidents irritated me during my voyage from Dar to Mombasa. When I joined *WEC Rotterdam*, I let someone carry my camera for the first time up the gangway. When I tried to use it at sea, I found that the lens was jammed. I blamed myself for not carrying it myself. The second incident was the result of a misunderstanding and a clash of values. On a small table at the side of my bunk in my cabin, I placed a piece of cedar wood given as a momento by the philosopher Martin Versfeld in Cape Town and some sprigs of bougainvillaea and franjipani flowers picked by Jenny in our friends' garden in Dar. The young tall Filipino steward who came in the morning to clean my cabin swept them all away and placed some Coca Cola cans in their place. He knew no better and I couldn't blame him.

Chapter Twenty-Nine

Big Trouble

*I*T took only a day to travel from Dar to Mombasa. The sky was heavy with clouds and warm rain swept across the sea, which was unusual for the back end of the rainy season.

On arrival, Captain Dyer's number two, Captain Mohamed Hatamy, came on board, a tall handsome Swahili. 'He's a good man,' Dyer said. 'Totally hard-working, totally trustworthy and proud to be Kenyan.'

When I met him he said: 'Welcome to Africa. Africa is all the same: too much talk and too little work!'

Using Dyer's office as a base in the new building of Mackenzie Maritime Ltd opposite the seamen's mission, I booked myself a return air ticket to Nairobi in a nearby travel agency. The girl warned me about walking back to the office: 'You should be very careful going under the railway bridge near the mission. A girl was mugged there this morning by a gang of eight youths; they pulled the rings off her finger with their teeth.'

Captain Dyer drove me along Moi Avenue to the Moi International Airport where I handed over money printed with Moi's portrait. Dyer was meeting his wife who was flying from the UK to join him. It turned out that her flight from Nairobi had been cancelled and mine was three hours late. Kenya Airways did not seem much better than Air Tanzania.

Fortunately, my plane turned up and I settled down in a window seat next to a young Muslim woman. I could see in a corner of the airport three Hercules transport planes painted with a red cross which were flying regularly to Somalia with emergency rations. They were costing millions of dollars while road transport would do, but the Red Cross had to satisfy its donors that it was doing something immediately. It was difficult to imagine that Somalia had collapsed into total disorder with warlords being the main beneficiary of international aid and attention. The West and the East should have been more careful before backing with arms the former President Siad Barre whose overcentralized and tyrannical state had largely caused the present turmoil.

The Muslim woman next to me on the plane was intriguing. She was dressed from head to toe in black. She had black shoes, black stockings, black dress, black head scarf, black veil and black gloves. The only thing I could see of her was her eyes which were dark brown, nervous and beautiful. She appeared very anxious, constantly twitching her knee and drumming her gloved fingers on the arm rest. I waited to see what would happen when the food was served: would she take off her gloves, would she take off her veil, would she say anything?

No, she did none of these things. She lifted her veil with one gloved hand and pushed the paltry cheese sandwich we were served with another gloved hand into her invisible mouth. As a good Muslim, she left the ham sandwich. But how was she going to drink her coffee? She first darted a side glance at me, and then lifted her veil as before and cup and hand disappeared into a black hole. 'What a rigmarole!', I thought. 'Why on earth should this young woman impose this on herself just to please the man at home paying for her ticket?'

Nairobi Airport was named after Kenya's first president Jomo Kenyatta. At 6,000 feet above sea level it was noticeably cooler than on the coast. The city had grown up around a Masai watering hole at the turn of the century. Its skyscrapers, surreal hybrids, sprouted from the bush.

As I drove in a taxi to the city centre, I passed a golf course and parks. Banners advertising Coca Cola supported a 'Clean Up Nairobi' campaign, although old cans from the same company were strewn about the lawns and streets. I noticed that the traffic lights worked, the only ones in a major city during my voyage except in South Africa to do so. My taxi weaved its way through the heavy traffic past the famous Thorn Tree Hotel to Chester House, the headquarters of the foreign Press who liked to cover the events of Africa from the comfort of Nairobi.

I had come to see my old colleagues, the photographers Duncan Willetts and Mohamed Amin, whose photographs illustrated two books I had written on Tanzania and Maldives. I found Duncan, a large, expansive man with blond hair and bristly moustache, in his studio taking photographs of a beautiful Kenyan model. He had just flown in from Mogadishu in Somalia where he had been covering the war.

'It's hell out there. It's the ultimate folly. Mogadishu is bombed out, blown to pieces. Along the waterfront, it's like Dresden. There's a Roman arch which stands out of the rubble. It's very eerie.'

'Was it very dangerous?'

'Gunfire was all around us at night. We crossed the line between the northern and southern parts of the city and drove like mad through no man's land. I slept in an old prison which is now a hospital. I was lucky for I had a nice cell to myself! Trouble is that I had to keep stopping to shit in the desert. Everybody's sick there.'

'You still seem in pretty good shape . . .'

'In fine fettle, battling on, a man of steel!'

'Why are the Somalis killing each other?'

'God only knows. I can't see any reason. They have one race, one language and one culture. It must be some form of collective suicide.'

During my previous journeys with Duncan, he had caught a tapeworm and dengue fever; now he had just returned from Somalia with giardiasis. As an old African hand, he made light of it. He had started out in advertising in London, but after a stint organizing a studio in Sudan, he had settled in Nairobi where he had consolidated his international reputation as a travel and wildlife photographer. He had been a great frequenter of night clubs but age and the AIDS scare had calmed him down. He now had a lovely Kenyan Asian friend Arundhati Inamdar, an environmentalist, whom he subsequently married. He rarely returned to England.

Duncan was a warm-hearted and amusing man who had little time for corrupt bureaucrats and officials. To some he appeared a little eccentric, a man who had lived in the bush too long or been through too many war zones. But he loved Africa and had made it his home.

I asked him why he had settled here.

'If you're born in Manchester like me, you'd probably want to come here very quickly! Being a photographer, I was stuck in a rut in London; always the same photographs. It paid a lot of money but who cares? Whereas in Africa I can do wildlife, I can do the odd war, famine relief, I can do underwater photography which is my great love, I can do all that in a day's work.'

I went later to see Mohamed – Mo to his friends – in his office in Chester House. As a talented photographer, he had come a long way since his early days in the streets of Dar es Salaam. His father had worked for the East African Railways before the war and from the age of eight Mo had grown up outside Dar in Kusuni where lions still roamed in the *shambas*. As a young man, he had been expelled from Tanzania by Nyerere's government for photographing Russian soldiers in Zanzibar after the revolution there. I had in fact helped him get back into Tanzania ten years earlier when we collaborated on a travel book on the country together. He had settled in Nairobi where he had become Africa bureau chief of Reuters, established a successful publishing company and had become one of Africa's best-known photographers and cameramen.

It was thanks to his filming and Michael Buerk's commentary that the news of the famine in Ethiopia hit the world's headlines in 1984. He had been in Addis Ababa again in 1991 to film the rebels entering the capital. While covering an exploding ammunition dump in the early hours, his left arm had been blown off above the elbow. His camera, which took most of the blast, probably saved his life. Not long after, Mo was given the MBE, an ironic twist since the British government had brought his forebears from Pakistan to East Africa as indentured labourers at the height of the British Empire.

Not long after the accident Mo had sent me a moving photograph of himself and his stump sitting with his shirt off in a doctor's surgery. He also sent one with an artificial arm which enabled him to hold a camera again. He was not a man to be put down. He had broken one of his legs about six times, but we had climbed Kilimanjaro together without too much difficulty. Each time I met him he seemed more and more like an old pirate. He was a hard man to do business with but his saving grace was his honesty about himself and his wry sense of humour.

As we chatted in his office, Mohamed hooked the stump of his arm over the back of his chair and gesticulated with his right arm. I asked him what it had been like after the accident:

'It's been difficult but not impossible. I consider myself extremely lucky that I survived the blast and all the bits of ammunition and rockets that hit me. My only regret really is that our sound engineer John Mathai was killed on the spot. But I've come to terms with my life and I've got back to working just as effectively. In fact in the last year since my accident I've probably been twice as busy as ever before!'

'Has it really been that easy?'

'Well, you've got to keep going. I've always thought there's no point feeling sorry for yourself, sitting in the corner hoping that people will feel sorry for you. They'll only feel sorry for a few days and then you'll become a bit of bore for them. So I just keep going.'

'What's your main interest now?'

'My main interest has always been covering the big stories in Africa, usually the disasters – wars, famines, coups or whatever. That's what I long to cover. Whenever there's a big story around, I'll cover it myself.'

Since he was in a good position to know, at the centre of news gathering in Africa, I asked him what he thought of the future.

'If I was to put it in a nutshell, the problem with Africa is its corruption, bad politics, bad management. Whatever the government – obviously there are some exceptions – their interest is in how much they can make for themselves, right from the leaders to the lowest level of the bureaucracy you can get. Unless people begin to realize that the wholesale stealing has got to stop, I'm afraid there's not going to be a lot of hope in the next ten years or so. Africa is in for big trouble!'

When a nervous young man entered to clear up the tea things, Mohamed said brusquely: 'What's your name?'

Turning to me, he said: 'I can't remember the names of my staff any more.' He then turned back to the nameless underling and ordered:

'Clear up after this British pig!'

I had spilt some tea on the corner of his desk.

I left Chester House with Duncan who put me up in his house during my stay in Nairobi. It was rush hour. The overtaxed traffic cops only just kept the cars moving. Although Nairobi was one of Africa's largest cities, with over one million people, the centre was very compact and could be crossed on foot in fifteen minutes. The small élite lived in the beautiful leafy suburbs of the old colonial quarter on the hills while the vast majority subsisted in endless shanty towns from which they occasionally emerged and went on the rampage.

After extricating ourselves from the jam, we drove up Haile Selassie Avenue and turned right into Cathedral Road. We stopped on Community Hill and got out of the car to admire the view. Below was the green of Uhuru Park and beyond that Parliament House, dwarfed by the great skyscrapers of the big international companies which had made Nairobi their headquarters for their African operations. The highest and most futuristic was a blue, glassy Lonrho building.

'There's no town planning anymore in Nairobi,' Duncan complained. 'Politics has taken over. Moi, for instance, planned to build a sixty-storey building named after himself in Uhuru Park, with a thirty-foot statue of himself with the names of the subscribers on it. That way everybody would know who to condemn for the monstrosity! Nobody wanted it. The government guaranteed millions but eventually the World Bank pulled the plug on its loans.'

Duncan lived in a quiet estate off Milmani Road. The next day we drove round the wealthy suburb, and he showed me the flower-decked gardens and spacious mansions of the colonial era now occupied by the fat cats of the new order. On Railway Hill we stopped to look at the oldest house still standing in Nairobi, called H 1, built by George Whitehorn, the chief engineer of the railway from Mombasa to Lusaka which put Nairobi on the map. It took 32,000 indentured labourers from Gujarat and Punjab as well as the local workforce to build it. The solid brick walls and fine old fireplaces of the house were typical of English architecture of the solid middle class in 1900. Thanks to the railway, five years later Nairobi had replaced Mombasa as the capital of the British East Africa Protectorate.

Near Chester House, where the foreign Press holed up, stood Nyayo House.

'It's here,' I was told by a journalist, 'that old MacMoi had his main torture chamber for some of the 10,000 political prisoners. Moi hates the intelligentsia and would like to bump them all off. He's surrounded by arse-lickers. One of them has even compared him to Jesus. By the way, what's the difference between the Presidents Moi and de Klerk?'

'You tell me.'

'Only one of them wants to give blacks the vote.'

'What can be done?'

'I don't know. Greed's the trouble. They're eating the goose that laid the golden egg.'

'And the police? Are they under control?'

'They shoot first and don't ask questions afterwards. Recently a Finnish girl returning from a party after her exams got out of a car for a pee near a government building. The police told her to move on but as she turned back to the car, they opened fire and put three bullets in her back. In court, the policeman said: "I didn't mean to hurt her." He got off lightly. She's crippled for life and may never walk again.'

'How does the president fit in?'

'Moi's been in power for fourteen years. He's been a tribal broker of power, dishing out posts according to loyalty. The whole system is based on Big Man patronage. If a region is pro-government, it gets some services; if not, it gets none.'

'What are the other politicians like?'

'There are MPs in parliament who are illiterate, who can't speak English or Kiswahali. Amongst the ten million voters, only about a million understand the issues. Moi likes to present himself as a good Christian, a lover of children, and champion of the poor but he has a compulsion for total control. The parliament is just a rubber stamp for his policies. He abuses human rights with a drop of a hat. Kenya used to be the shining knight of Africa but now it's becoming another pariah nation.'

'What's gone wrong?

'Misuse, mismanagement, misappropriation, any "mis" you like!'

'And the future? What kind of future can Kenya expect?'

'A bleak one. The population growth is way out of control. Kenya has the highest birth rate in Africa and probably the world; women expect to have eight or nine children. At the same time, despite the increase in land brought under cultivation, overall food production has dropped. If Kenyans fail to bring their birth rate under control they will have to either live permanently on foreign food aid or face famine.'

Wandering around the city centre of Nairobi, it was sometimes difficult to remember that I was in the middle of Africa near the Equator. Europeans still maintained a colonial style of life, despite the growing political repression and economic decline. I took a London black cab (Moi's fleet are in Nairobi as well as Mombasa) to the Norfolk Hotel which was a mock Tudor pub full of white faces.

In the evening I went with Duncan and Mohamed to the luxury Serena Hotel where a fashion show was held around the illuminated pool. A pukka English compere provided the vacuous commentary as the black, brown and white models sidled along the cat walk over the water, swaying to Zaïrean music against a video backdrop of African wildlife. Very chic, very swish, very boring.

The black as well as the white élite of Nairobi were there, most of them wearing dinner jackets and black ties. I sat at a table by the pool with Duncan and Mohamed next to Stuart and Evelyn Briggs, an English advertising director and a cookery book writer from Penang. She told me how she had once bought a severed horse head covered in flies in a market in Marrakesh: 'It was delicious!' They invited me to join them for lunch the next day at the Muthaiga Country Club, the most exclusive in Kenya.

The following morning they picked me up and we drove out to the club on the outskirts of Nairobi. It was the heartland of the white Kenyan settlers and until recently the last bastion of their aristocratic and racist values. Stuart pointed out to me the men-only bar in which Karen Blixen, author of *Out of Africa*, had broken all protocol by bursting in and downing a whisky in one.

'You know,' Stuart said, 'the club is so set against any photography that when they filmed *Out of Africa* they had to build a special set.'

The club however had been forced to make some concessions. Black Africans from the country's sixteen ethnic groups had now been allowed to join. The day I visited the only black faces were those of the servants. I strolled through the lounge, library and billiard room where old men and one or two of their grandchildren talked quietly. The waiter in immaculate whites served classic English fare: fish pie, roast pork and bread-and-butter pudding.

After lunch I said goodbye to my hosts. They were going up to Nakuru in the rich farming area half-way to Lake Victoria, and then to the Aberdares for a spot of trout fishing. Stuart was determined to experience the old colonial privileges and way of life before they disappeared for good.

When I returned to Duncan's and told him about my day, he observed: 'The Muthaiga club is wasted on you!'

The next day he took me on safari in a Land Rover to Nairobi National Park where one can view rhino in the bush to a backdrop of Nairobi's skyscrapers. It was small, only forty-four square miles, but it was unfenced on one side so that the animals could migrate to the Amboseli Park and beyond. In the dry season, they came to the park because of the water holes. As soon as we entered by the Eastern Gate, we spotted a herd of zebras, some of whom had lost their tails in skirmishes with lions. Within the first half an hour of our bumpy drive along the winding and undulating track, we saw impala, Grant's gazelles, wildebeest and hartebeest as well as some ostriches and secretary birds with their quill-like head feathers.

We pulled up by a creek, and accompanied by a warden with a loaded rifle, went on a foot safari, disturbing colobus monkeys and baboons with their long canine teeth overhead in the thorn trees. In the browny green water, the hippos dozed, sinking lazily, only to reappear a few minutes later for air. Crocodiles lay still in the mud – proverbial logs. Monkeys scampered in the bushes on the bank but kept their distance. On the lower branch of a fever tree, I spotted a rare Battler eagle.

It is only on foot in the bush, amongst the dust, the dung, the sounds and the smells, that one can experience the real Africa.

'This is what's it is all about,' Duncan observed.

I asked him what he liked about Africa.

'It's the openness, the wildness and, really, you're left alone. The sort of thing I do, we all do, you can't do it in Europe. It's not necessarily against the law, but you're totally left alone to do it. It's the wild spirit!'

On our way out of the park, we saw two rhinos grazing on a hillside. A privilege indeed, as there were only about forty left. I asked Duncan about the elephants in Kenya.

'The warning's still there. The encroachment of humans on their property continues. Elephants destroy their environment, humans destroy their environment, both do, they have that in common.'

Before I left Nairobi to return to my ship in Mombasa, I visited the Kariakoo Market in the suburbs, so called after the British Carriers Corps which once had its headquarters there. Outside its broken and grimy walls women were sitting on the earth with their finely woven baskets and printed cloth. Inside, men worked in many workshops, some recycling old tyres into shoes or selling rough-hewn furniture. I paused to see one old man in rags playing with puppets of a man and woman made from wire and some sticks; the male puppet had a big erection and danced and copulated with the female to the accompaniment of crude singing. When I got my camera out the hostility of some young men was so great that I had to beat a hasty retreat.

On my return to the city centre, I went by the sprawling shanty towns of Nairobi where the cheap labour bred, brawled, and died. Rows and rows of rusting corrugated roofs stretched out into the distance, separated by filthy tracks where naked children played. Big trouble was brewing up in these suburbs which one day would erupt and engulf the city centre. And you can be sure that the boys of Chester House will be there to record it.

Chapter Thirty

Plenty of Money, No Power

I FLEW back to Mombasa to catch the WEC *Rotterdam* only to find that the departure had been postponed by a day. The cargo of coffee, tea, cotton and hides was still being loaded. Passing through the gate to the container wharf, my taxi driver said to the policeman with a rifle:

'Can I go with my cab to ship?'

'By arrangement only,' came the reply. The driver slipped him a note and we were waved through. It summed up Kenyan society.

We left Mombasa at 02.00 hours in the early morning on 14 July. As we turned northwards towards the Horn of Africa, the ship pitched in the south-west monsoon. The current was running with us at four knots and we were steaming at seventeen knots. The wind was already a force 5 and at this time of year, from July to August, it was not uncommon to have gales up to force 9. It was also extremely hot.

The day broke cloudy and rain showers swept across the rough grey sea. Some dolphins joined us in the afternoon, running and leaping across our bows.

'If dolphins swim with you, good weather,' the captain said. 'If they cross you, bad weather.'

I asked him what he thought of the sea.

'Remember what I say,' he replied. 'First you have to respect the sea. Second, do not fear the sea. Third, be prepared for its sudden changes.

Fourth, know when to attack: in a storm or typhoon, you must know when to go ahead.'

During the night, at 22.50 hours, I passed the Equator for the fourth time on my voyage off the coast of Somalia, just south of Mogadishu. Mogadishu was the most northerly Swahili port that Vasco da Gama visited during his return voyage from India. It had flourished in the thirteenth century when its Great Mosque was built and trade with Persia and India was at its height. I said goodbye to Vasco da Gama and the southern hemisphere at the same time. His ghost had not been a pleasant one to accompany me on my voyage: the Portuguese arrival in the Indian Ocean brought havoc along the East African coast and swept in the racism and cruelty of European colonialism.

I was now entering a world which was known to Europeans more than a thousand years before Vasco da Gama and the Portuguese. A Greek merchant from Egypt had written a naval and commercial guide called *Periplus Maris Erythraei* (Circumnavigation of the Erythrean Sea) in the second century AD which described the East African coast and mentioned an island called Menouthias which was probably Zanzibar. I was also probably off the coast of the Land of Punt, the farthest point reached by the great expedition of Phoenician sailors sent by the Egyptian Queen Hapshepsut in the fifth century before Christ. They saw hippos and elephants and returned with ivory and myrrh.

As with my previous ships, I was invited to sit at the captain's table next to the chief engineer and first mate. The other officers sat on an adjoining table. The captain, George Kastis, seemed to appreciate my company and we often lingered on after meals or went up to his cabin to continue our conversation. He had some firm views on most subjects. He was so used to being the supreme authority on board that he did not like anyone interrupting him when he was holding forth. On one occasion, when I expressed surprise on hearing apples were grown in Greece, he said slowly and firmly: 'Let me finish, my friend. You owe me that for my age.' He was fifty-six and I was forty-five.

I could find no fault with his hospitality. When I asked him the usual hour for lunch, he replied: 'When you ask what time is lunch, we say "No time. Anytime you want." We do our best for you as our guest.'

Next to my cabin under the bridge lived the radio officer, Hrisostomos Manias, a handsome man in his later thirties with white hair. He came from the island of Ithaca, the birthplace of Ulysses, and had adapted to a life of wandering the high seas. On my arrival, he offered me a bottle of ouzo shaped like the Acropolis and did his best to make me feel at ease. In his neat cabin, he had a yellow canary which would fly around when the ship was not in port. It was lovely to hear it singing in the morning sunshine. When off duty, Hris would often play Greek folk music which filled the passageway with a sense of joy and vitality. He had a certain lightness of being and the members of the crew who came to speak over the radio to their families and sweethearts would often linger on to chat.

I was still a long way from home, but he told me that when Greeks approached the Suez Canal in the Red Sea or the Strait of Gibraltar, they felt they were approaching home – the Mediterranean. Looking at my map I realized how close Greece, especially Crete, was to Egypt and Africa – far nearer than to northern Europe. Like north Africans, with whom they had constant contact for thousands of years, the Greeks were a Mediterranean, sea-going people.

'We Greeks are born with the sea in our blood,' Hris told me. 'The sea is all around us. Many go to sea because there's no work at home.'

A message came through on the radio that there was a man – a Pakistani fourth engineer – reported overboard near the island of Socotra off the Horn of Africa. Had he slipped? Been pushed? Committed suicide? I imagined the poor fellow struggling in the wake of his ship, crying out until falling back exhausted into the cold water, knowing that he would soon go under for ever.

I had looked over the railings of my ship for hours during my voyage and had often imagined what it would be like at that moment when you breathed in and filled your lungs with water. It did not horrify me. If anything, I was drawn to the idea of being absorbed into the whole, dissolving like a drop of wine in the vast ocean.

There was genuine concern on the *WEC Rotterdam* about the man reported overboard. I reflected that all sailors, whatever their race, creed or nationality, form a universal brotherhood, united by the incomprehension of landlubbers and a common fear and love of the sea. Men have long tried to control the elements: they have tamed the land; they have changed the atmosphere of the planet; they have confined nuclear energy. Yet the sea continues to escape them. The surface of the moon is known better than the bottom of the sea. The sea remains untamed and untameable; it is the ultimate wilderness, the experience of eternity, the fullness of being.

On 16 July at 22.00 hours we rounded the Horn of Africa and entered the Gulf of Aden. It was not a cornucopia, but a horn of sand, bitterness, blood and dried bones.

The captain had been right about the dolphins: the sea grew rougher, with force 8 winds blowing. He reduced speed but the ship began to roll as well as pitch. The sea was no longer a deep blue but grey and the sky a hazy white. Waves broke over the bows of the ship, spinning spray across the salt-encrusted containers. The thermometer on the bridge deck at noon read 35 centrigrade. We were entering one of the hottest places on earth.

As we entered the harbour of Djibouti at 10.00 hours on 18 July, I noticed several motor-driven dhows heading out towards Yemen.

'They're smuggling whisky to Saudi Arabia', I was told by the Greek bosun. 'If you added up all the bottles of whisky imported into Djibouti, it would work out that every man, woman and child would be drinking two bottles a day!'

We passed a moored French frigate, with a red, blue and white *tricouleur* flapping in the hot desert air, a reminder of the large French military presence in Djibouti. It was not only the last place in Africa with a camp for the Foreign Legion, but had been used by the French as a base in the Gulf War.

There were also a few small rusty warships, remnants of the Ethiopian Navy. Now that Ethiopia had lost Eritrea and the port of Mitsiwa, Djibouti was its only link to the sea.

We moored at the container wharf, and from the bridge I had a fine view of the low-lying, palm-fringed town dominated by a mosque and minaret. By the shore was a new Chinese mission and the white presidential palace. Beyond stretched the sand, flat, brown and featureless, disappearing into a dusty haze. It could sometimes reach as high as 50 in the shade. At least the *khamsin*, the 50-day long desert wind, was not blowing.

I had once anchored offshore in Djibouti in 1966 when sailing on a P & O ship from Australia. It had been rerouted to the French enclave at the entrance of the Red Sea because of troubles in the former British base in Aden on the other side of the Bab el Mandeb Straits. The French had occupied the region in the middle of the nineteenth century to offset the British presence. They had forced agreements out of the nomadic sultans of Obock and Tadjourah and started to build Djibouti in 1888. Their land became known as the French Territory of the Afars and Issas.

At the time of my arrival the government of Djibouri, controlled by the Issas, who identified with the Ethiopians, were oppressing the Issas, who had ties with the Somalis. Every storm which broke out amongst its huge neighbours sent shock waves through the mini-state, bringing new surges of refugees escaping the war and famine. The artificial state, which was given independence in 1977, only survived because of French military and economic aid.

After mooring, I went ashore to visit the representative of Inchape Shipping Service, a Frenchman who happened to be the acting British consul. He offered me a car and a driver but the Greek captain was shocked when he demanded payment. It did not square with his admiration for all things British.

'You British do everything well', he confided in me. 'What was India or Africa before the British? The British Admiralty charts are the best in the world!'

Then he remembered that the honorary British consul was in fact a Frenchman; no wonder he had demanded payment.

Our driver's name was Said Mussa, a Muslim. I asked him what it was like during the Gulf War in Djibouti.

'Very tense,' he replied. 'A bomb went off in the middle of town. It killed two sailors. It was meant for the French soldiers.'

I saw many of them wandering the streets and squares, their crew cuts, straight red necks and brightly coloured shorts marking them out from the foreign, slovenly sailors in jeans. We could have been in a

French Mediterranean town, with its cafés and restaurants, except for the dark faces, sandy streets and palm trees.

I asked the driver who owned all the bars and nightclubs we went past.

'Muslim men have the bars. Girls are Ethiopian. Christian. Somali girls no good. Muslims. No drinking. Police catch Somali girls.'

'How much do the girls cost.'

'One night, $5. You want?'

'Does AIDS worry them?'

'She has plastic. When she go to mate, she give you.'

The streets of Djibouti were drab, grey and dirty. There was a clear demarcation between the old European quarter and the sprawling filthy alleyways of the shanty towns where no European dared set foot. Apart from the fruit and vegetables in the central market, the only colours were the brightly dressed women, many of whom boldly gave me the glad eye and smiled as I walked by. In the market place, men seemed to be selling the fruit and vegetables, women the grain. The men were much more hostile and threatened me with sticks when I got my camera out opposite a mosque. I was in no state to argue: the temperature was 42centigrade and the slightest effort brought beads of sweat to my brow.

In this frontier town, money could buy anything – a melon, a body, a rhino horn: you name it, they had it. Near the market was a long line of wooden shops selling curios to the visitors. Carved ivory tusks, ostrich eggs, leopards skins were all on open display, no doubt brought up from East Africa by the Somali poachers. I was astonished to find that I could buy an antique Ethiopian parchment Bible for $20, a leopard skin for $80, and a beautifully carved Ethiopian warrior in ivory for $100. Even these were the asking prices which the seller expected to be halved during bargaining. Much of what was for sale was probably booty from the wars which had been raging in neighbouring Ethiopia and Somalia.

In the evening the honorary British consul invited the captain, the radio officer and me for dinner. At first we went to the city centre in search of a small restaurant which he insisted had the 'best sea food in town'. It was closed.

George insisted on going to the Sheraton, the best hotel in Djibouti

– and the most expensive. A can of Coca Cola cost the same as an Ethiopian girl for the night, such was the distorted values of the place. During the meal, the consul, who sat at the head of the table, became very excited as he recounted his experiences under President Musevini in Uganda after the fall of Idi Amin.

'You know, Museveni killed more men than Amin, 7,000 once in forty-eight hours. The bodies were left to rot for a week. The stench was terrible. I can remember going to a party at a friend's who had his house fortified like an arsenal on top of a hill. He would let guns off just to annoy his neighbours – bum, bum, bum. It was great fun in those days!'

'How could such killing be "great fun"?' I asked him.

After dinner, George was all for going to the casino and the radio officer and I reluctantly joined him for a while. George sat at the roulette wheel in the large dark room where groups of men were crowded around brightly lit tables playing cards. He had changed a hundred dollars and insisted that fifty was for me. He wanted us to play together. Out of politeness, I joined in, telling him what numbers to place his bets on. He won steadily, slowly increasing his stake. After half an hour, I had had enough and agreed with Hris to go down town to visit some of the nightclubs. Just before I left, the captains said:

'Give me a number.'

'Twenty five,' I said, the first figure I could think of.

He put half of his chips on it, and by enormous luck it came up, paying him many times his stake.

'Give me another number,' he said.

'Thirty four,' I said. The number won again. From the original $100, he now had made more than $2,000.

'Half of them are yours, remember!' he said as I left. 'Don't forget to come and collect me before you go back to the ship.'

Hris and I took a cab and went back to the centre of town to sample the night life. In the red light district, there were clubs and bars enticing the passers-by – almost entirely French soldiers and foreign sailors – with flashing neon light and loud music. A jeep with French military police cruised up and down the streets.

There were clubs to cater for all tastes and nationalities. In bright neon lights, the exotic names shouted their style: Penelope, Clemestra, Florida, Montparnasse, Bar St Cimon, Tropicana, Flamingo, Bar la Lune, Video de Carnival de Rio. The music ranged from Elvis Presley, Greek folk, Arabic and America disco to Jamaican reggae. As soon as you entered a bar, girls would come up and ask for a drink and dance, rubbing their bodies seductively against yours. If you sat down, they would come and sit next to you and put their hands on your thigh. They were all ages, from young teenagers to mature matrons. As my driver said, they were mainly Ethiopians.

There were not many clients the night we were in town, so some of the clubs were almost empty. Since it was a question of survival for the girls, many of whom were refugees from the civil wars in the Horn, they tried their hardest. It was sad to see the young men of the Foreign Legion trying to find fleeting comfort with girls who had lost everything and dreamed of being whisked away by a lover for ever out of the hell-hole of Djibouti.

About two in the morning, we went back to the casino to collect the captain. He was still at the roulette wheel. His chips had been reduced to a few hundred dollars. His hands were shaking slightly. I eventually persuaded him to jack it in for the night. He had won a lot of money and lost it all but he was well content with his evening.

'I don't do it for the money, but for the fun. I shall give you your half share.' As we said good night back on board, he said:

'When you're young, you have plenty of power and no money; now I'm fifty-six I have money to buy what I want but no power.'

He was like Djibouti itself.

Chapter Thirty-One

Marlboro Country

WE left Djibouti the next day, 19 July, at 09.00 hours and passed soon after through the Bab el Mandeb Straits into the Red Sea. On the starboard side, I could see an island and a shipwreck. The good ship *WEC Rotterdam* sailed into a force 6 wind and pitched moderately as she cut through the white horses of the greyish green sea. There was a very strange atmosphere which the captain called 'sick' but I felt was eerie. Fine dust settled everywhere and a dust haze covered the sea. We were passing through one of the hottest places on earth where it never rained; like the North Pole, it was not a fit place for humans to dwell. It was reassuring to hear the steady thump of the engines below my feet.

There had been a chance that we would call at Port Sudan for empty containers but head office had instructed the captain to press on; important cargo was waiting in Europe. George was spending more time on the bridge now, sometimes missing a meal. I asked what the trouble was.

'The agent in Djibouti delayed the ship for three hours. Now we are having to go as fast as possible to catch up with the convoy for the Suez canal. If we miss it, we shall be delayed twenty-four hours and that will cost my company thousands of dollars. I have calculated that we must not go slower than 14.8 knots if we are to reach the convoy on time. I don't like to go without breath.'

The race was on.

Sitting in my cabin mid-morning on 21 July, I was suddenly jolted by the sound of the ship's siren. I rushed out to see the radio officer next door who announced calmly: 'It's all right. It's practice. Lifeboats.'

I thought this unusual since I felt sure the captain would have warned me in advance. I went out on deck and saw below most of the crew – including the Greek cook, Filipino stewards as well as the chief officer and cadet – struggling on the main deck to lift a huge hatch above the engine room. Acrid smoke billowed out from the gaps. It was no practice.

I quickly went up to the bridge. The chief engineer arrived at the same time, walkie-talkie in hand, panting, pale and sweating. After a long conversation in Greek, the captain turned to me and said calmly:

'Everything's okay. One of the generators has caught fire but it's under control. It's 42 centigrade in the engine room. We need not reduce speed. We can still catch the convoy.'

Soon after a stowaway was discovered on board hiding under a bag of sawdust in the forecastle. He was very thin and very dark, with black curly hair and dark brown eyes. He had no papers, but gave his name as Danhil Kassa Mehari, born in Addis Ababa, Ethiopia, in 1953. His deceased father had been a colonel. Having graduated from a technical college, he had become a radio officer in Mengistu's army for seven years and supported the Ethiopian Revolution. Now that the regime had fallen to the rebels he was seeking political asylum in Europe, preferably Italy, but if not Germany or England. He had a brother in California and knew his address by heart.

The captain ordered him to be kept in a cabin and given as much food as he wanted. The Greek seamen enjoyed watching him tuck into a huge pile of food in their mess. It was his first good meal for months. Afterwards the cook gave him a cigarette. He was so happy that when the chief mate came to take him to the captain, he was beaming.

When the captain interviewed him, I was asked to be present. He had to draw up a detailed document in English for his company.

'How did you get on board?'

'I living seven months in Djibouti, sleeping in street, stealing food with knife. All the time, very danger; my life is very danger. Me make mischief, come on board, nightwatchman sleep, hide in front of ship with water and bread.'

'Have you done this before?'

'Three times. Last time on Messina ship.' As he talked, he played nervously with a plastic necklace of white flowers wrapped around his slender hand.

'You're not only poor, you're stupid. Without papers, we can't help you. Why did you leave your country?'

'Ethiopia now two countries. I say one country. I support the revolution, now civil war. I not want go back to my country. If I go back, they kill me. If you send me back, I jump overboard. Better you kill me now!'

'My friend, I will help you if I can.'

As the chief mate took the stowaway back to his cabin, he pleaded: 'Me work'. He replied: 'You can't work, if you have no papers.' Catch 22. He was returned to his cabin where he would have to remain until his case was decided. It could mean travelling to Rotterdam and coming back to Djibouti in a couple of months time. His story was only one of tens of thousands.

That evening a party was arranged for me, the other guest on board. A long table was set up on the deck below the bridge wings and a barbecue was brought out for king prawns. Greek dishes were laid out on the linen table cloth as well as several bottles of ouzo, wine and boxes of beer. Coloured lights were put up and in pride of place Hris played Greek folk music on his stereo – music which had such a strong dancing rhythm that if Zorba had heard it, he would have risen from his grave. With liberal splashings of ouzo, we clashed our glasses together under the starry, black night.

Some of the other crew, led on by Hris, soon began to dance. The captain sat at the head of the table, preoccupied and unusually quiet. He did not drink and looked on benevolently like a village elder at the excesses of youth, confident that his word was law.

It was not long before the music and dancing drowned out all possibility of conversation. These men without women, steaming up the Red Sea, danced with Dionysian passion, arms held in the air, eyes closed, stamping

305

and leaping to the ancient rhythm of their sun-splashed islands. As they danced the moon slowly rose out of the sea, casting a golden light across the calm waters, gilding the dancers. The great white ship sailed on, towards the Mediterranean, towards home.

We knocked our glasses together, linked our arms, and threw back the ouzo as if it had been water – until it hit the stomach and sent fire coursing through the veins. By this time, the second engineer had began to balance his glass on his head while dancing. When it fell to the ground and smashed, Hris picked up a handy broom and swept the broken glass into a corner. That was the general signal for all to try, some dancing on the top of glasses, others balancing plates on their heads. The pile of broken crockery in the corner grew larger by the minute.

'You see how we have a party, Greek way,' said the second engineer. He had the head of a laughing lion. 'We always like to break plenty of things. We show our happiness in this way.'

I began to understand why. They had an excess of energy, a superabundance of life, which burst out of the careful planning of a miserly routine. They showed a disregard for material possessions and objects by smashing them; however poor in worldy goods, they were rich in spirit. In their dancing and music, they revealed the destruction of order at the heart of creation, and enacted the sublime union of Dionysius and Apollo.

In the early hours of the morning, when music, dance, ouzo and the intoxication of the desert air had exhausted all our energies, Hris and the engineer gathered up the two ends of the table cloth on the long table and hurled the remains of our feast overboard into the Red Sea. The bottles and plates and knives and food splashed in the swirling water. The cloth fluttered away in the wind, disappearing like a white bird in the darkness of the warm night.

After breakfast the next day we passed Jedda and Mecca. The sea grew calmer as we made our way between Saudi Arabia and lower Egypt at a steady sixteen knots. The wind dropped, the sky became deep blue with bright sunshine, and the air was splendidly clear. The temperature too dropped from over 40 in Djibouti to a pleasant 30. Since the Red Sea was so salty, no dolphins were to be seen.

After entering the Gulf of Suez brown slicks on the surface of the still sea showed that earlier cargo ships had washed out their holds regardless of the damage in such an enclosed waterway. The coastline of the Sinai desert was rugged, an austere and barren emptiness. A few wrecks and the occasional off-shore oil rig were dwarfed by a high escarpment rising to some 500 metres – not a good place to be abandoned without water.

In the afternoon a white pleasure boat leisurely crossed our bows, ignoring the blasts on the horn ordered by the captain. We heard on the ship's radio a US aircraft interrogating a ship about its cargo in the Gulf of Aqaba as it sailed towards Jordan, a reminder that we were in a war zone. I also heard on my portable radio that President Rabin of Israel was going to visit President of Mubarak of Egypt in a few days in Cairo – another round in the endless 'peace process' between Jews and Arabs.

It took us almost three days to pass through the Red Sea to the town of Suez at the entrance to the canal. We arrived at noon on 22 July. Suez was a bustling town with a fine mosque by the canal front and some well-kept gardens. After the wilderness of the surrounding desert, boundless and bare, it felt like an oasis. There was a rich smell of the earth, of oil, and of sweet decay. We had just made it on time to join the convoy to go through the canal.

George had achieved his aim but he was unable to relax: 'Going through Suez for a Greek seaman is like hell,' he told me.

The officials clambered on board. George observed: 'Here the comedy begins.' I had reached Marlboro country. He was armed with sixty packets from his special stores to appease them: 'If we run out of Marlboro,' he said morosely, 'they demand twice the number of Greek cigarettes.'

When the Egyptian pilot came on board, he ordered a large plate of pasta. 'I not eat,' he said. 'I is hearing all the time. Only my bag eats.'

Mr F. Sharaky was short, round, bald, youngish and sweating. He chain-smoked, and hissed his orders to the helmsman from the corner of his mouth. He could not resist worry, tobacco, sweet things and his new wife. He proudly showed me a black and white photograph of her: like himself, she was exceedingly well-proportioned, all dressed out in white frills and fancy lace. 'She's a ladies' doctor,' he declared proudly.

The captain did not know Arabic, and the pilot's English could have been better, so the Egyptian quartermaster was on the bridge in case of a linguistic emergency.

The pilot coughed every few minutes: 'Wife always saying, no smoke, but smoke not too bad. I have cold.'

'Are there any problems, on the way?'

'No problems. *Hamdillulah*. Port 5!'

'Do you like your job?'

'Yes. But all time tension, all time tension.'

'Have you ever had an accident?'

'No accidents. *Hamdillulah*. Midships!' While chatting away and issuing orders between mouthfuls of pasta, he had to make sure that the *WEC Rotterdam* travelled at exactly 7.7 knots in the convoy and was at all times 1.2 miles and three minutes away from the container ship ahead. It was no easy task, and required constant concentration. The bends had also to be negotiated in the canal, which at its minimum was only sixty metres wide.

As we slipped into the canal, I could see huge earthworks on the west bank thrown up in 1967 during the Israeli–Egyptian war and several burnt-out vehicles and guns rusting under the sun. There were a few children swimming in the canal. Their parents sat on small stools in the shade of a few date palms. An old man was leading some donkeys along the side path. They all ignored the great ocean-going ship gliding by.

'Ship like a woman,' the pilot said. 'Jump, no good. Easy, easy, okay.'

The ancient Egyptians had planned a canal from Cairo to the Gulf of Suez but it was not until 1869 that the French engineer de Lesseps completed one linking the Mediterranean Sea and the Red Sea. It was an enormous feat of engineering: including the approaches, the canal was 174 kilometres long, with a minimum depth of ten metres. It was level throughout and therefore had no locks. It took about thirteen hours to get through. Its strategic nature made it the source of conflict as soon as it was completed. Having been nationalized by Nasser in 1956, it was now one of Egypt's principal sources of foreign exchange, earning about $6–8 million a day. At the time of my passage, about sixty ships were passing up and down the canal. There were two northbound convoys, the first consisting of seven container ships and a tanker. Our convoy contained thirteen ships.

After travelling along the canal for a few hours, we came out into the wide Great Bitter Lake. Its salty water was a milky light green. A strange silence hung over the lake, only disturbed by the steady swish of our hull cutting through its still surface. As we picked up the narrow canal again, a sweet water channel on the west bank irrigated the carefully tended fields of sugar cane and maize bordered by palms. The temperature was a bearable 32 and the movement of the ship created a pleasant breeze.

The pilots changed over at Ismaili in Lake Timsah. I said farewell to Mr Sharaky, who was eager to return to the plump arms of his new wife. Before he left, he gave me the names of some hotels in Cairo, but warned that the capital was 'hot, crowdy, noisy, with every kind of pollution'. His last words before he gathered up his bag and hat were: 'Nice journey here, good luck, best for everything.' I wished I could say the same in Arabic.

The next pilot was a dour man who kept himself to himself. It would have been difficult for anyone to follow Mr Shakary's act.

Ismaili was a popular resort, with children playing on the beaches of swanky hotels with brightly coloured umbrellas. After passing one of President Mubarak's palaces, the canal continued as far as the eye could see. Beyond its steep stony banks, the lone and level sands stretched far away.

As we approached Port Said, another long irrigation channel on the west bank watered green fields. Cars went fast along the parallel road; it was dead straight and totally flat. An electricity line also reinforced the sense of approaching city life after the barren wilderness of the desert. At one point, part of our convoy, including the ship ahead, veered east along a new canal which by-passed Port Said and went straight into the Mediterranean.

As I was standing in the prow, the young cadet came up to me and said:

'You are a lucky man. I like to come with you to Cairo.'

'Why's that?'

'It's terrible for me. We go so near Crete and my home. But no stop!'

In the corridor outside my cabin, members of the crew queued up to talk to their families on the ship's radio. The first engineer had a heart-rending conversation with his son aged five, who according to Hris was saying: 'You come home. I love you, I love you. Why you leave us? Why you not come home?'

We arrived in Port Said at dusk, with the setting sun turning the low-rise buildings of the town a rosy pink. It had taken nine hours to pass through the canal. A couple of tugs came to help steer *WEC Rotterdam* into the narrow space between two moored ships; the pilot did not aim well, and the ship crashed and juddered into the wooden piles of the wharf. George was not amused. I could see why passing through the Suez canal could be hell for him.

Mine was about to begin. If the navigation was difficult, the bureaucracy was impossible. Officials swarmed on board like pirates as soon as the gangway was lowered and invaded the officers' mess. The problem arose from the fact that there were two agents, a private one employed by the shipping company and a state one which was a hang-over from the time when Nasser nationalized the shipping agencies along with the canal. They not only duplicated work, but seemed to be at loggerheads most of the time.

Aware of the potential difficulties, I had obtained a visa to enter Egypt in Tanzania. The captain opened the negotiations by saying:

'Professor Marshall is a very important guest. He is going to see your president's wife and I hope you will give him your full co-operation.'

I had been upgraded from Dr to Professor, but the reference to Suzanne Mubarak – who came from Wales – was partly true as I had asked to see her.

The state agent replied: 'Professor Marshall is on the crew list. You must pay $450 US to cover expenses of his disembarkation and for being responsible for him until he is repatriated.'

'I pay no money!' George insisted, looking his fiercest. 'Only for visa.'

This was getting worrying. On one hand, I had no intention of being repatriated back to Britain; on the other, I already had a visa. I thought it was time for me to intervene.

'The immigration official has already agreed to stamp my passport. I just want to get off the ship if you don't mind.'

'That is not possible, sir. He cannot stamp your passport without an authorizing letter from me. I have blanks here.'

With that, he brought out a fat envelope from his old brief case and spilled out countless forms in Arabic.

'But immigration have already agreed to let me in,' I insisted.

'If that is so, you do not need me.' Then, suddenly changing tack, he added: 'But you will not get through customs!'

Turning to George, he said: 'Captain, for you, I can do special price of $100 US.'

The captain called for more soft drinks and cigarettes and replied:

'No, no money, except for visa.' I didn't have the heart to tell him I already a visa.

'All right, $65.'

'Is that all right, Professor?'

'Okay, if they're no more problems.'

The deal was struck. The price had been reduced from $450 to $65. The captain refused to take any money from me and paid the agent cash and insisted on a receipt. 'I repay what you did for me in the casino!' he said.

'Now you go to customs,' said the state agent. 'But you will have trouble with camera video!'

I quickly collected my bags from my cabin and said goodbye to George. He embraced me warmly and made me promise to send him a card at Christmas. At the top of the gangway, I said goodbye to the cadet who was feeling homesick, and to the radio officer who said: 'Come and see me in Ithaca! Remember Ulysses!'

By now it was dark, and the private agent took me in his car through the docks to the customs shed by the gates. Beyond the armed soldiers, I could see children playing in the street under the lamps and people passing by on the pavements, a normal world of comparative freedom. I sat in the dark of the car as the agent – an old man with white hair and slow movements – went into the sheds to argue my case. After half an hour he reappeared:

'You must pay $10.'

'I don't undertstand. The captain told me not to pay any more.'

'Please pay $10,' he said wearily. 'You see, sir, a customs official must accompany you to Cairo airport to make sure you are repatriated.'

'But I'm not leaving the country by air! I'm going to find a ship in Alexandria.'

'It is regulations. Customs official must accompany you to Cairo. It costs $100. If you pay $10, the customs not come.'

I couldn't quite follow the reasoning here, but I handed over the $10.

He disappeared for another ten minutes and then beckoned me into the dark empty shed. I stood alone with my bags. Another heated discussion went on in the lighted office nearby. Eventually, the customs official appeared in his uniform, took details of my camera which he wrote in my passport, and stamped it.

'You free now. You can do what you want.'

I shook hands with everybody in sight and made my way to the bright street beyond the gates. As I said goodbye to the private agent who had helped me through the Scylla and Charybdis of the port authorities, his last words were:

'You see sir, we have our regulations. But it helps to give a tip. Welcome to Egypt!'

Chapter Thirty-Two

So M*any* M*arvellous* T*hings*

O NCE outside the Port Said dock gates, I hailed down a taxi and asked
him to take me to the Holiday Hotel which I had been recommended
by the shipping agent. It was an unpretentious family hotel with a white
lobby in a busy street. I was taken to a small, airless room. I was so
exhausted after coming through the port that I fell asleep immediately
after a quick shower. But it was not for long: in the early hours, I was
woken up by the cars below my window which seemed to sound their
horns twenty-four hours a day.

The taxi driver of the previous night had offered to take me to Cairo for
£155 Egyptian. The manager in the hotel offered £130. My young driver,
turned up with an eight-seat Peugeot 404 and came down to the same
figure. Before we left I asked him to take me on a tour of the city, and I
was impressed by its colonnades, tree-lined avenues and spacious, well-kept
gardens. There was a Russian ship called the *Shostakovich* disgorging its
round, middle-aged passengers. Weaving amongst the busy traffic, we
overtook a whole family, which included a girl and a baby, perched on
a small motorbike. The temperature soon climbed to the thirties.

As we left Port Said on the main highway to Ismaili, we had to pass
through a customs barrier. I got out of the car. A smiling officer came
up and said:

'What nationality?'

'British.'

'You smoke?'

'No.'

'Let me see your teeth.' I presumed this was to see if they were smoke-stained.

'You like President Mubarak?' A trick question? I decided to be non-commital. Perhaps this man was a member of the Islamic Brotherhood who wanted to overthrow the secular state.

'He seems okay.'

'Tell me honestly, do you like Egypt?'

'I only landed here last night. But so far, so good.'

'My wife is British. Her name is Ida. Good luck.' And with that he waved us through, without examining my bags.

The distance from Port Said to Cairo was about 215 kilometres. The road to Ismaili, eighty kilometres away, was good, flat and straight, running parallel to the canal. I was returning on my tracks, this time seeing ships pass along the canal from the land. It looked as if they were gliding through the desert sand, apparently out of water.

It was not long before we were speeding past kilometres of salt pans, with mud and thatch farm houses perched just above the water level. Wherever there was fresh water, brought by channels from the Nile, the desert burst into green: date palms swayed over fields ablaze with sunflowers, ripening maize and rice. Egyptian peasants – *fellaheen* – went about their tasks as they had done for thousands of years. At the side of the road, giant green watermelons and ripe mangoes were piled high for sale.

At the first main town El Qantara there were still remnants of the October war between Egypt and Israel in 1973: rusting trucks, tanks and armoured cars. We stopped soon after at a wayside café for a drink of mint tea and a hookah. The smoke tasted sweet and cool after it had bubbled through the water in its large transparent bowl. My driver inhaled deeply: 'It makes not sleep,' he explained, beaming.

After turning west at Ismaili – which we skirted – the road passed through rolling, light-brown desert. We passed many military encampments seemingly in the middle of nowhere, reminders that peace in the Middle East was always temporary as long as Israel occupied Arab lands. The heat waves rose from the road, which often turned into a white lake from the reflection of the sun's rays.

The occasional town rose from the sand without any apparent rhyme or reason, announced by rows and rows of advertising boards along the sides of the road which pictured everything in garish colours from trucks, fridges, sparking plugs to clothes. Beyond, the flat barren desert disappeared into a heat haze.

We entered Africa's largest city from the eastern side, past the airport and through the élite district of Heliopolis, the ancient 'City of The Sun'. Its once-great buildings had been lost under luxury hotels and extravagant villas including the president's palace. A huge billboard announced 'October War Panorama'. I stopped in to look at my first colossal statue of Ramses II which rose above the crazy rush-hour traffic of modern Cairo.

After the 'City of The Sun', we drove over a hill and down through the 'City of the Dead', a vast cemetery where wealthy Egyptians over the centuries had built houses for their deceased relatives.

To the right on a hill rose the great Mohamed Ali Mosque built in the nineteenth century next to the ancient Saracens' citadel. From the ramparts of the hill, Cairo stretched below me in all directions, dotted with domed mosques and minarets. Along the Nile, modern skyscrapers were dwarfed by the great, green river. On the edge of the sprawling city on the west bank I could just make out the pyramids of Giza and beyond the level sands of the interminable desert.

I asked my young driver to stop on the bridge over the Nile so I could take in its size and meaning. It seemed impervious to all the noise, bustle, and dirt of the collapsing city all around as it swirled down towards its great delta and the open sea. Pyramids had been raised and had crumbled, dynasties had come and gone, but the old Nile just went rolling on. The Aswam dam had tried to check its floodwaters and control its flow, but the rains in central Africa ensured that it would continue to bring life to the desert and fifty million Egyptians.

After crossing the Nile, we headed out along the Pyramids Road to Giza. I had the address of the Oasis Hotel on the Cairo–Alexandria Road. Old women dressed in black darted between the endless traffic to brush

315

up sand and litter. Old carts got in the way of ancient lorries belching black smoke and new air-conditioned tourist coaches with darkened windows. What threw me was to see the pyramids rising out of the suburbs of Cairo. No town plan had stopped the westward expansion of the city into the desert, and only the need to preserve the pyramids for the tourists stopped them becoming entirely engulfed by the brutish concrete of modern Cairo.

At last, I saw along the shady road the sign 'Oasis Hotel', appropriately set in well-watered gardens. I booked in, paid my driver with a handsome tip, and was shown to my chalet room. I ordered tea which I took in the garden under a palm tree. As the sun set a bright orange, the cries of the muezzin from a local mosque soared over the singing of the birds and the trill of the cicadas. I had well and truly arrived in Egypt, the spiritual centre of Africa, the heart of the Islamic world, and the cradle of Western civilization.

During my first morning in Cairo, I decided not to go to see the pyramids but to visit the Cairo Museum. I had been told that it was always best to explore the pyramids in the late afternoon, when the the blinding light of the desert softens and the coaches have departed. It was going to a be a special occasion, and I did not want to dilute it.

Before I left the hotel, I tried to contact Mr Khalil of Mesco Shipping Agency in Alexandria. George had given me his name. After many attempts, I eventually got through and he said he would do his best to see if there was a ship sailing to Tunis. I asked him whether it would be possible to call in at Tripoli in Libya, but he thought it very unlikely.

I took a bus into the centre of town which set me down outside the Cairo Museum, one of the great museums of the world. It stood in Tahrir Square on the east bank of the Nile next to the Hilton Hotel. It was overcrowded, gloomy, musty and incredibly hot. I felt as if I had stumbled into the warehouse of a museum where a great jumble of exhibits were waiting to be sorted. The explanations were usually given in Arabic, French and English, reflecting the country's colonial past, but they were often mispelt, sometimes mixed up or only in one language.

Most guards in museums are as impassive as the statues, but not in the Cairo Museum. In their white uniforms, they hissed at me as I went past, not as I thought, wanting *baksheesh*, but to point out an interesting or famous exhibit. The informal atmosphere meant that little children could play amongst the statues and sculptures, bringing the pharaohs down to size. I saw a black cat rub itself against a massive sculpture and then slip away silently into a dark corner.

I kept returning to the museum during my stay in Cairo, and found it a treasure trove of unexpected delights. Though little is known about the ancient Egyptians, they undoubtedly left some of the greatest and most lasting monuments ever raised by humans. Even the Greek historian Herodotus, writing about Egypt in the fifth century BC, acknowledged that 'nowhere are there so many marvellous things, nor in the whole world beside are there to be seen so many marvellous things of unspeakable greatness'.

Facing the entrance of the museum was the huge head of Userkaf, four and half thousand years old, the earliest example of a free-standing colossal statue. The place and meaning of the statues and symbols in ancient Egypt might never have been fully understood without the discovery of the Rosetta Stone. I had already seen the original in the British Museum in London, but a guard beckoned me over to see the replica of the black granite commemorative tablet. Broken at the edges, it was inscribed in 196 BC in three languages: ancient Greek, Egyptian hieroglyphs, and Egyptian vernacular or demotic. It had been discovered in 1799 during Napoleon's expedition to Egypt and eventually provided the information needed to decipher the ancient hieroglyphs on the pyramids, temples and tombs. It was not until 1822 that the Frenchman Jean François Champollion managed to realize the cartouche always used in Egyptian for a king's or queen's name, contained glyphs that read phonetically – by sound – and not as symbols as in Chinese. The code was cracked and modern scholars have been able to reassess ancient history and wisdom by analysing the original texts. I felt sympathy for Champollion's view that 'The Egyptians of old thought like men a hundred feet tall. We in Europe are but Lilliputians.'

I went on next to see the room dedicated to Akhenaten (1353–35 BC), the bizarre pharaoh in the New Kingdom period who went beyond the elaborate hierarchy of gods and godesses – *neterw* – and established the worship of the single god *Aten*, whose power comes through the rays of the sun disc. Religion as well as art was transformed during his reign, the earlier rigid, stylized forms giving way to more flowing designs and exaggerated features. Many of his statues show an androgynous and deformed figure. He was so controversial that his name was subsequently left out of the lists of Egyptian pharaohs. I saw the famous bust once thought to be of his beautiful wife Nefertiti, although it now seems it was probably one of their daughters. One of his sons was Tutankhamun.

Another person who intrigued me was Queen Hatshepsut (1473–58 BC) who also shared the dishonour of being left out of lists of pharaohs. Although queens could rule as pharaohs, they still had to be depicted as men. The beautiful granite sphinx statue of her in the museum had a false square beard. Hatshepsut not only ordered many wonderful buildings to be erected, but sent the first great natural history expedition to the Land of Punt along the East African Coast.

Nearby her sphinx there was a fine statue of her ward, husband, step-son, co-regent and successor Tuthmosis III. His dreamy expression belied his warlike manner and ruthless search for power. Whilst they lived together as lovers, Hatshepsut was the real ruler of the country but when Tuthmosis took over after her death, he defaced and destroyed the monuments in her mortuary temple at Deir el-Bahari. Not content with that, he went on to smash her inscriptions and break up her large statues and sphinxes, a symbolic act which could impede her journey in the afterlife.

As I searched the enigmatic face of Hatshepsut for some glimpse of her character, a muscular young Australian in a vest sat between the two paws of her sphinx to be photographed by his girlfriend. Did she blink in the flash? Nearby a shabby old scholar with thick glasses was poring over an inscription and writing down the hieroglyphs with a trembling hand.

I noticed that many of the statues in the museum had broken noses, like my own. Since the statues were intended to be 'living' representations of the deceased, it was thought that the act of breaking off the nose of a statue would deprive its subject of 'life' – the breath of life comes through the nostrils. A tyrannical ruler like Tuthmosis or a common tomb robber had good reason to fear the wrath and vengeance of the dead whose works they desecrated.

I had never been drawn by the euphoria over the Tutankhamun treasures when they came to London in the seventies, but coming across them by chance on a cluttered upper floor of the Cairo Museum, placed with wrong explanatory cards, I was struck by the superb artistry which had gone into the construction of the funerary equipment, furniture, basketware, ornaments and jewellery placed in his tomb. I also realized that they were there not to impress – indeed they were meant for no living eye to see – but all played a part in the great drama of death and rebirth on which Egyptian civilization was built. The golden head of the boy-king also glowed with perfect proportions, his eyes giving off an uncanny incandescence.

I had seen Egyptian mummies of humans in the British Museum, but was surprised to find that none were on show in Cairo. For many years the Mummy Room had been a favourite with visitors but President Sadat had closed it down on the grounds that it was like putting one's ancestors on public display. It was not decent to gawp at the the dead; they needed a rest. I could see his point. Most visitors came to indulge their morbid curiosity rather than to appreciate the symbolic place of mummification in the Egyptian cycle of life and death. At least Sadat had the good sense not to be mummified.

After a while even the most exquisite statuary wearies and I was pleased to emerge from the dark cocoon of the museum into the bright sun and rediscover the bustling life of Cairo. I would not have liked to stay overnight in the place on my own. Perhaps once the crowds had been cleared out and the guards gone home, the great stone statues would come creakingly alive and crush any intruder. As the moon shone through the dusty windows, the wild dance would begin.

What intrigued most about ancient Egypt was how it had come about in the first place. Never before or since in the world has such an advanced civilization with the art of writing, subtle religion, monumental architecture and complex society developed over such a short period of time, a mere few centuries.

Until as late as 15000 BC the trackless Sahara Desert had been a green savannah. Before 10000 BC there were a number of huge floods (the flood in the Old Testament?) which covered the land. When the water receded the desert emerged except for a long strip of very fertile soil stretching a thousand kilometres along the Nile to the broad lowlands of the delta.

A number of Neolithic cultures developed which produced rough pottery, followed by a more advanced one which left ceremonial maces and slate palettes. I saw the famous Narmer palette in the museum, probably dating from the fourth millennium BC, named after one of the last kings before the pharaohs. He was followed by the legendary 'Menes' who was said to have unified lower (northern) and upper (southern) Egypt and founded the civilization which lasted for three thousand years. He may not have been a historical figure but the king of Egypt was called thereafter 'Lord of the Two Lands'.

The sudden explosion of Egyptian civilization took place around 3000 BC, a unequalled flowering of human genius. Over about four centuries in the early dynastic period, hieroglyphs suddenly appeared in complete form, along with advanced mathematics, medicine, astronomy, mythology, symbolism and the complete texts of the *Book of the Dead*. Only in architecture and carving can a gradual evolution be discerned. The fact that a similar but unrelated development took place along the banks of the Euphrates might suggest that both the ancient civilizations of Mesopotamia and Egypt were kick-started by migrants from a third lost civilization who brought their skills and knowledge with them. Could this have been the legendary Atlantis, situated not in the Atlantic Ocean, as Plato and others claimed, but in the western region of the Indian Ocean? This seems more likely than the claims of Egyptofanatics who suggest that the migrants came from outer space. There were clearly giants in those days.

After my first visit to the Cairo museum I went to see the pyramids at Giza before returning to my hotel. It was five o'clock in the evening. The last tourist coaches were taking their harried passengers back to their hotels. The bright yellow sun was descending in the sky, gilding the pyramids and casting long dark shadows.

It was one of the great moments of my life. The glimpses from the other side of Cairo, the snatched glances on my way into the city centre, the illustrations in books, nothing had prepared me for what I saw before me. Rising out of the stony plateau and the level sands of the desert, the three pyramids were much bigger than I had imagined. They seemed to be the living symbol of Mut, the Egyptian principle of order, equilibrium and harmony in the universe.

As I approached the base of the largest, Cheops, I marvelled at the precision with which the huge blocks of stone had been cut and placed together. A small knife could not have penetrated their seams. I had read many different theories about how the pyramids had been constructed, but I was mainly impressed by the energy and vision which had inspired them in the first place. Goethe had once called architecture 'frozen music'; the pyramids formed a perfect symphony of stone in three movements.

I had entered the plateau of the pyramids from the southern side, and I now walked across the rocky ground to the eastern side to see the Sphinx. I deliberately walked until I was well in front of it before turning and opening my eyes. Although damaged by the ravages of time and men, it had a vast and profound presence, a stillness and a poise which I had never experienced before. I would not have been surprised if its vibrating atoms had produced some unearthly music. As Ra, the sun god, continued to sail in his golden boat towards the west, I sat meditating in front of the Sphinx and the pyramids until I lost all sense of time.

When I came to, I felt the need for action. Many Egyptians had arrived and were out taking an evening stroll on the plateau. Some were riding in the dunes of the desert to the south. I found a horse to hire on a hill overlooking the pyramids, a tall mare with the kind of fiery spirit and sharp intelligence traditionally associated with Arab thoroughbreds. Her owner in his white flowing robes and turban looked as if he had ridden straight out of the desert. We mounted and set off at a wild gallop, gliding over small sand dunes, sandy hollows and stony flats. It was very different from riding my Welsh cob Black Jack in the mountains of Snowdonia in North Wales.

'You ride Australian style. I teach you Berber,' my companion said. He showed me how to ride holding the reins in one hand, moving them either side of the horse's neck while deftly using one's legs. The excitable horse responded immediately and smoothly to the ancient ways of the

321

desert and we galloped up and down the dunes until rider and horse were sweating with exhilaration. By this time, Ra had almost disappeared over the horizon, his ship ablaze with red light, turning the tops of the pyramids to a pink glow. The stone and sand were still warm but the first cool breeze of the coming night swept across the plateau. I turned away, feeling a rare sense of peace and contentment. That day I had been in touch with ancient mysteries, with the stream of life at the heart of the universe which flows through stones and animals and air.

Chapter Thirty-Three

Boat of a Million Years

I return to the pyramids at Giza the next day. Through my reading, I knew that there was little historical information about the great pyramid builders, apart from the fact that Cheops (Khufu in Egyptian) built the Great Pyramid at Giza, and Chephren (Khafre) the adjoining one during the fourth dynasty of the Old Kingdom (2575–50 BC). I tried to imagine through half-closed eyes what the pyramids must have looked like encased in soft polished limestone, glinting like prisms in the sun, superb monuments of both technical precision and spiritual meaning. The more I looked at them, the larger they seemed to grow. It was somehow right that I should have spent six months voyaging around Africa to reach them.

No one has fully explained how the ancient Egyptians managed to build the pyramids without the use of the pulley, iron tools or wheeled carts, how they managed to raise in twenty years two million interlocking blocks, mostly weighing from two to three tons but some over fifteen tons, into a pyramid of perfect symmetry with an angle of slope of exactly 51° 51′. Perhaps they achieved in that short period a collective state of heightened consciousness, lost to their successors, which enabled them to build with matchless equilibrium and poise.

I was able to arrange it with the guards to enter the pyramid without the tourists. The original entrance had been blocked with huge granite plugs, so I entered via a rough hewn and dimly lit horizontal passage which had been forced by Al Mamun, Caliph of Cairo in the ninth century AD. I then

323

clambered up another narrow passage, the low ceiling forcing me to double over until I came out into the Grand Gallery, with its smooth walls and steep incline. By the time I reached the top of the gallery, I was sweating profusely. I then had to go down again almost on my knees to scramble through the entrance into the bare 'King's Chamber'. At the far end of the rectangular chamber was a broken granite sarcophagus, its lid missing. No one knew whether it had ever contained the mummified body of Cheops.

I closed my eyes and stood in the darkness alone at the centre of the pyramid. It was not a pleasant feeling. Although there were two narrow air ducts, it was difficult to breathe. The chamber had a heavy gloom which I associated with massive Victorian architecture. It was not a question of feeling claustrophobic: I was not frightened of being inside mountains and had even scuba-dived along narrow passageways in limestone caves. I instinctively felt that it was something to do with the pharaoh himself. With his monument robbed and desecrated, it seemed as if his tormented soul still hovered nearby. I felt I should not have come here and penetrated so deep. It was like violating the womb of a great living being.

Before leaving, I was still sufficiently rational to admire the labour and skill of the workers who had created the space. I noticed that the sarcophagus was bigger than the entrance to the chamber; the massive granite stones must have been placed around it. The floor plan of the chamber was a 2 x 1 rectangle, with the height one half of the diagonal of the floor, thereby expressing the golden section or the transcendental number Phi. Geometry for the Egyptians was as sacred a science as it was for the Greeks.

Needless to say, my watch did not stop nor did I suddenly grow younger. I did not have any razors on me so I could not say whether they sharpened themselves on their own. What was certain was my pleasure in leaving the gloomy place. Once out into the pure desert air and the coolness of the late afternoon, I felt as if a great weight had been lifted off my spirits and I could breathe freely again.

Looking back up at the great pyramid towering over me, it suddenly occurred to me that what was truly impressive was not so much the technical achievement of the pyramid builders but rather the level of organization which must have been required to bring together tens of thousands of people for the first time in history to raise such a stone building to the sky – not as slaves but as workers who believed in what they were doing. But while I admired the work of the craftsmen who built the pyramids, I found little to admire in the pharaohs themselves. Ancient Egyptian society formed a perfect pyramid and was both hierarchical and authoritarian. At the apex, the pharaoh ruled as an absolute monarch and the priests and scribes under him did their best to make their subjects believe in his divine right. The complex ceremony, ritual and religion all made it easier to manipulate and control the people at the bottom of the pile. The huge energies and wealth which went into the building the pyramids could have made their lives much easier.

For me, the pharaohs' desire to have their images immortalized in stone and their physical bodies preserved by mummification implied an obsessive concern with material things and their personal egos. I preferred the Buddhist ideal of losing one's ego, becoming part of the universal Self. Rather than being remembered by colossal statues, I would prefer to be dissolved into nothingness like a grain of salt in water, leaving no trace behind.

What interested me as much as the actual pyramids were the three boat-shaped pits cut into the rock on the eastern side of the Great Pyramid and the two complete cedarwood boats discovered in kit form on the southern side. One of the boats, 120 feet long with a displacement of over forty tons, had been found in 1954 and reassembled in an ugly museum on the site. A second boat, which included sails, had only recently come to light and had not yet been excavated. It amounted to the greatest archaelogical discovery in Egypt since the Second World War.

I met Dr Zawi Hawass, Director General of Antiquities of Giza and Saqqara and a powerful man in the international circles of Egyptology. He was full of the visit of Princess Diana of the Cursed House of Windsor whom he had accompanied around the pyramids the previous week. I was more interested in boats than tales of royalty and asked him why they were buried alongside the pyramids.

'The boats are of course symbolic. They're called "solar boats" so that the dead pharaoh could travel in them with Ra, the sun god, on his daily voyage, the trip of the day and the trip of the night. It was the hope of the dead to join Ra in his "Boat of a Million Years". The oars would never be used; the Egyptians imagined the stars would come and row for the king in the afterlife.'

'So boats were very important for the Egyptians.'

'We have a story about Snefru, the father of Cheops. He was upset one day and took forty ladies to row him in a boat on the Nile. One lady stopped and put down her oar. The king asked her why. "My earring fell down in the water." The high priest took the water out and picked up the earring and gave it back. This story shows how the ancient Egyptians loved boats.'

The boats at Giza were perfect examples of the craftmanship of the shipwrights of ancient Egypt. But the Egyptians were not known to be ocean-going seafarers and they usually employed Phoenicians for their long-distance expeditions. Why then should they build ships capable of sailing around the world, more seaworthy than those of Vasco da Gama or Columbus, when they used them to navigate the ripples and eddies of the Nile? Could it be that they learned their shipbuilding skills from an earlier sea-going people – from the inhabitants of the lost city of Atlantis, situated not as commonly thought, in the Atlantic Ocean, but in the Indian Ocean?

The two boats discovered next to the Great Pyramids were some 4,500 years old, and, as such, were great marvels in maritime history. But a dozen more boats, fifty to sixty feet long, had recently been discovered 400 miles to the south of Giza. They had been dated to the first dynasty, 2900 BC, which made them the oldest boats in the world. When would it ever end?

'We probably know of only a third of the ancient monuments in Egypt,' the director general of antiquities reminded me as we said goodbye. 'You cannot know what secrets the sand might hide.'

Before I left the pyramids at Giza, I took one last long look at the Sphinx. It was in the shade now, with the pyramids silhouetted against the setting sun. My suspicion of the morning that it was a solar symbol became stronger. I was struck by the beautifully balanced proportions of the face, despite the present disfigurement – probably the result of artillery target practice by the occupying Mamelukes. I noted that it had the head of a man and a body of a lion, unlike the Greek sphinxes who had the head of a woman and the body of a winged lion. For some, the Sphinx represented the power and consciousness of the spiritual. For me, the organic fusion of

326

human and animal was a reminder of the remarkable ecological sensibility of the Egyptians who could see a world in a grain of sand and eternity in an hour.

Carved out of the living rock, this first and greatest statue in history was long thought to be made in the image of Chephren, builder of the second pyramid. But in profile its head, carved from an extremely hard outcrop, has a distinctly black African look, quite unlike the pharaoh's known features. It may well have been carved much earlier. Since for most of the last 4,000 years its body has been covered by sand, its considerable degree of weathering suggests that water and not wind was responsible. If this were the case, then it would push back its date to before the flooding of Egypt which coincided with the melting of the ice from the last Ice Age from 15000 to 10000 BC.

Was this was more evidence for the idea that Atlantis was in the western region of the Indian Ocean? Perhaps after the submergence of Atlantis, some of its citizens had migrated to Egypt at the end of the Ice Age, carved the Sphinx, and then when it too was flooded, moved to the higher ground further south in Africa only to return when the waters subsided. Then, perhaps I had been looking at the Sphinx for too long . . .

After the pyramids at Giza, I was keen to go further back and visit the most ancient Egyptian pyramids at Saqqara, an hour south-west of Cairo beyond Memphis. It was the site of the oldest and possibly the finest stone complex in the world.

The film crew joined me for the last and sixth time. They brought with them a whiff of summer in Wales, memories of green hills and rushing streams and waving trees, a world apart from the dusty, noisy, sweltering, overcrowded and enthralling city of Cairo. We were accompanied by a guide called Sami Hassan, a large man in his thirties. An archaeologist by training, he had once been the representative of Egypt's Museums and Antiquities at the Arab League.

The funerary complex of the pharaoh Zoser at Saqqara dated from 2650 BC, 650 years before Stonehenge in Britain. The reconstructed walls had sparse, clean lines, but I was overwhelmed by the sheer beauty of the Doric columns within, built 2,000 years before the Greek. The complex was probably the work of the legendary Imhotep, sage, priest, doctor and architect. The fact that he is remembered is a measure of his greatness. While the megalomaniac pharaohs insisted on their 'cartouche' being carved on the buildings they ordered for themselves, the real builders – the architects and craftsmen – remained anonymous as in medieval cathedrals.

The Doric colonnade of Zoser's temple opened out into a great courtyard with the ruins of the great Step Pyramid rising to the north. Built at an angle of 55, it had once been covered in limestone blocks. Several hundred yards to the south west, connected by a causeway, I came across the blunted outline of the Pyramid of Unas, (2356–2323 BC). There was nothing left except a pile of rubble, but in its underground burial chamber the earliest Egyptian funeral texts had been discovered, chiselled on to the walls in beautiful hieroglyphs. These Pyramid texts, the most compressed and pure, were later developed into the *Egyptian Book of the Dead*, literally 'The Book of the Coming Forth by Day'.

Between the Zoser enclosure and the pyramid of Unas, there was a jumble of tombs in half excavated gullies, some dating back to the Old Kingdom. Breaking the rules, Sami took us down one of the shaft tombs, a very deep hole dug into the bedrock with a burial chamber at the bottom. It was the tomb of a man called Nefer, an overseer of singers. Inside the first chamber, there was a wonderful mural with realistic goats eating trees, an overseer represented as a baboon, and sailing boats.

I climbed down a narrow passageway dug in the rock on a rickety ladder to the burial chamber. There in the hot, dry cave, I saw in the dim light of our torches a mummified figure of a man, wrapped in sixty layers of linen, his phallus clearly visible. It was certainly the oldest I had ever seen, dating back some 5,000 years. Would it ever again rise from the dead?

Beyond the Step Pyramid, I came across the remains of some massive tombs of the Early Kingdom (3050–2575 BC.) They were called *mastabas* after the Arabic for 'bench' which they resembled. They were made from mud-bricks, arranged in neat rows, ranging from 150 to 250 feet long, and had once been plastered over with painted stucco. Nearby some boat-shaped pits had been found.

As I was surveying the *mastabas*, a group of black Americans wandered past, some in safari gear, most with wide hats and cameras. A young woman began to chatting to me; she was from California and had come to Egypt in search of her African roots.

'It's amazing what they did here,' she exclaimed in her West Coast drawl 'when you people in Europe were running around in skins and throwing spears. By the way, are you a writer or something?'

'Yes. How did you guess?'

'I saw you scribbling in your little book. You know what I think? The trouble with our so-called civilization is that we're going too fast. We're destroying more than we build. The Egyptians knew better.'

'Do you identify with Egypt?'

'For sure. Do you know that some of the pharaohs were black? Herodotus, the Greek historian, described the Egyptians as having "black skins and woolly hair" – just like me! He even says that the oracle at Dodona in Greece was black. The Greeks got most of their philosophy from the Egyptians. There you are, Africa is the source of your European civilization! Have you read *Black Athena*? It's all in there.'

She was touching on an important controversy in modern classical studies. Until the nineteenth century, most people in Europe shared the view of ancient Greek and Roman authors that the origins of Greek civilization and therefore Western civilization were to be found in Egypt. But with the rise of Eurocentric history which coincided with the expansion of empire, it became fashionable to deny the Afro–Asiatic roots of classical civilization. Recent research had gone back to the earlier view and stressed that Egyptian civilization itself was fundamentally African, especially during the Old and Middle Kingdoms.

Egypt's great achievements certainly exorcized the myth of African historical and cultural inferiority – a myth exploded for me once and for all by my travels. But in the end, did it really matter what was the colour of the pharaohs' skin? The important point was the achievements of the Egyptian people themselves and the wisdom they passed on to later generations.

Before leaving Saqqara, I went to visit the Serapeum where the sacred bulls of Apis had been worshipped as an incarnation of Ptah, the cosmic architect and giver of form. Walking on foot along a barren track in the desert, I came across a lopsided sign which said 'To the Philosophers'.

I scrambled down a sand dune to find half a dozen life-size statues in a semi-circle. They had been badly weathered and had lost their heads. Usually, philosophers are all head and no body, but here it was the other way round. Brushing away the sand at the bottom of one, I read in Greek: 'Plato'. After the conquest of Alexander, the Greeks had inserted the statues of their philosophers in an avenue of purely Egyptian sphinxes, a neat way of showing the cross cultural ties between Egypt and Greece. I could imagine Plato, who considered the Greeks to be infants compared with the Egyptians, would have been happy to be near the oldest and greatest temple in the world.

There was a side to Egyptian worship which the old rationalist would probably have not appreciated. A dig at the Serapeum had not only unearthed a blue-eyed squatting scribe but also a grotesque statue of the dwarf god Bes with protuding tongue, bowed legs, thick ears and long arms. She came to prominence in Egypt during the rule of the Greek Ptolemies. She was the anarchic, exuberant counterpart of Ptah, the creative energy behind the formal geometry. Despite her devilish appearance, she was associated with childbirth, music and the arts.

Out of the window, there was an extraordinary sight: a green swathe of land either side of a huge river beyond which stretched endless sands of the desert. I was on a plane of Air Egypt on my way to Luxor, an hour's flight from Cairo.

Luxor in Arabic is *L'Ouqsor*, meaning 'the palaces'. Half-way between Cairo and Aswan, it was the site of the ancient capital of Thebes. Although it was famed for the Valleys of the Kings, Queens and Nobles, I had come principally to see the temples of Karnak and Queen Hatshepsut.

It was in late July in the off season when the temperature reaches the mid thirties. After the invigorating bedlam of Cairo, Luxor proved to be a quiet, sandy town where one of the main modes of transport was still the nineteenth-century *calèche* drawn by scrawny horses. We booked into the Sheraton Hotel, beautifully situated on the east bank of the Nile, further upstream than the famous turn-of-the century Winter Palace, where we were welcomed by traditional Egyptian folk music played on small drums and a kind of violin. The hotel was extremely comfortable, not too big to get lost in.

I arrived in time to see a wonderful sunset from my balcony overlooking the river, with the red orb of the sun disappearing behind the reeds and palm trees on the other side of the Nile's slowly moving waters. The graceful *feluccas* caught the last golden rays in their sails as they glided through floating mats of lotus plants.

Without the Nile, Egypt would be a desert; without its waters, none of the great works of art would have been created. The ancient Egyptians depicted the river as a fat man with breasts, bearing lotus or papyrus. I was in Luxor at the time of the annual flood, when the rains in the Ethiopian mountains brought vast amounts of water splashing down the Blue Nile to join up with the White Nile at Khartoum. The united river would then rush over the cataracts until widening out and slowing down in the flat plains of the desert. Here it would flood its banks every year for several miles on either side, leaving a thick layer of fertile black silt. The original name of Egypt, *Kemet*, meant the 'Black Land'

This could all change. The Aswan dam built in 1971 to control the flood waters had improved the all-year-round irrigation and transport on the river, but in the long run it could prove an ecological disaster. The river was much lower than before, with new islands and sand banks creating hazards for navigation. More important, without the annual deposit of silt, the soil along the river banks was gradually losing its fertility, a process which could prove irreversible. In the meantime, Lake Nasser behind the Aswan dam was silting up.

I visited a farm near Luxor to see the complex system of canals, dykes and basins, which carried the sweet water to the desert and made it blossom. Tradionally the *shaduf*, a beam balanced on a pillar with a bucket on one end and a weight on the other, was used to transport the water, but here a water wheel with pots turned by an ox was pouring water into small irrigation channels. Under the dappled light of acacia trees, it was lovely to see the cool, clear water running along the small channels and slowly being absorbed by the brown earth, watering the roots of the sturdy green plants.

Nearby was a flat-roofed house with high walls which was still being built. The farmer showed me around inside, pointing out the short rafters which were made from date palm wood. Its perfectly straight walls were built from traditional mud bricks: Nile mud and wheat chaff mixed together and dried in the hot sun. Since it never rained, there was no danger of the bricks being washed away. Inside the dark rooms, it was cool and calm.

The scene outside seemed like a rural idyll. In the shade of large acacias and date palms, there was the steady creaking of the water wheel turning. A slight breeze trembled the leaves on the branches. A group of half a dozen men were sitting on their haunches, their long *galibavvas* hitched up, drinking tea around a slow-burning fire. A tethered camel and two donkeys slowly ate hay nearby in the shade. In the distance a farmer was bent over weeding his fine field of maize. The leisurely pace of life had not changed for millennia.

Just as I was about to leave, two men who had been quietly drinking tea by the fire suddenly started to shout and tug at each other's clothes. Suddenly one of them had streams of blood pouring down his face. The others in the group quickly intervened.

It transpired that the row had been sparked off by a present of an electric hand fan which we had given to an old man tending the ox which turned the water wheel.

'Giving presents is a delicate matter,' Sami observed. 'It's very important not to upset anyone's feelings. People of Upper Egypt have a strong sense of honour, like the knights in the Middle Ages. The gift's not the real problem; these two have had a long feud over land. The wounded man cut himself with a piece of broken glass just to make it look bad. Don't worry, they're from the same clan and the elders will fix it.'

'Are there many disputes over water rights? The irrigation systems are so complicated and must pass over many people's land.'

'Disputes are rare. But if there are any, they're usually solved amongst the farmers themselves. Egypt might be the oldest state in the world, but people try to keep out of the official courts!'

After each hot and dusty day of my stay in Luxor, I would hire a *felucca* in the evening and go for a sail on the Nile. They were flat-bottomed and broad-beamed boats, with a large heavy rudder. Originally the *feluccas* would have been made from cedar wood imported from the Lebanon, but in recent times they were being made from metal. They had one lateen sail attached to a long yard like a dhow.

Because the *feluccas* could not sail close to the wind and there was so little room to tack, when the wind blew from the south in winter, the skippers would wait until the wind turned to go upstream. While I was in Luxor, the winds were light and blew from the north west, enough for me to lean comfortably with my back against the tiller and glide past the Temple of Karnak, the grand hotels and the huddle of the old town on the east bank. On the west bank, beds of weeds gave way to date palms and green fields. Towards dusk, when the sun turned the buildings, trees and water a pinkish gold, fishermen came out in rowing boats. They would slap the water with long poles and rattle pieces of metal to frighten small fish the size of sardines into their nets. The famous Nile perch, who would break their nets, kept to the deeper waters midstream.

My favourite *felucca* skipper would be accompanied by his twelve-year-old son in the late afternoon who was learning some English at school. The boy would brew up some sweet mint tea for us in the bows of the boat which was served in small glasses. The skipper would call me 'Captain Cook', no doubt part of a long tradition of flattering wealthy British visitors. On one occasion, he suddenly started to clap his hands and sing a sad song in Arabic as we sailed far upstream. He offered to take me to Aswan, the ancient site of Nubia six hundred miles away, but unfortunately I did not have enough time. I said to myself that I would one day return with my children to undertake the voyage, sleeping on deck under the desert stars, learning more of the ancient wisdom of the Nile and its people.

Despite the call of the Nile, my main interest in Luxor was the Karnak Temple. It had been erected during the New Kingdom period (1550–70 BC), when the pharaohs had abandoned pyramids to build temples to the gods and to carve eleborate tombs into the living rock. They were not only great builders but also warrior kings who pushed the borders of Egypt far into Nubia to the south and to the Euphrates in the north-east.

I entered by the western gate past a long row of ram-headed sphinxes, each with a tiny statue of a king placed between its paws, and then went through a mighty pylon, a ceremonial gateway which once had great cedar wood doors.

At first, I had the impression that the building was not quite symmetrical: the first courtyard and colonnade were set at a different angle to the rest of the temple. On closer inspection I realized that the temple was constructed harmoniously around three axes. It was almost as if the architects, masters of harmony, had deliberately done this to give an organic feel to the temple.

I then passed through a second pylon which gave onto the grand Hypostyle Hall with its enormous pillars, the real gem of Karnak and one of the world's greatest masterpieces. The original stone slabs on top of the pillars were missing and the sunlight filled the maze of towering capitals with dancing light and delicate shade.

Sami pointed out the cartouches of Rameses II. Although his father had started the Hypostyle Hall, he had superimposed his own signature to take all the glory – another example of his megalomania. I noticed that one 'John Gordon 1802' had also carved his name crudely on a pillar in order not to be forgotten.

Going deeper into the Temple, I next came across the single remaining obelisk of Queen Hatshepsut, standing almost ninety feet high against the deep blue sky. It was the tallest obelisk in the world standing in its original position. The carved hieroglyphs on its sides were in perfect condition, although the gold and silver covering at its tip had disappeared. Its twin was now suffering from the noise, damp and fumes of the Place de la Concorde in Paris: Mohamed Ali in the last century had given it to France in return for a clock which had never worked.

After passing through yet another courtyard, I eventually reached the inner sanctuary, the holy of holies, dedicated to the god Amun-Ra, the sun-god and creator of all. He would have been represented by a small statue, probably made of wood covered in gold, placed in a barque on the altar. Each year the priests would sail up the Nile with it so that the people could pay homage. By carefully guarding their secrets, the priests were able to acquire enormous power for themselves.

When I entered the holy of holies, I had a rude surprise. Alexander 'the Great' had been there before me. Alexander knew how to sanctify his rule over the people he conquered and even had himself painted being presented with the ankh, symbol of life, by Horus, the Egyptian god of the sky who had a falcon's head and the body of a man. The Romans had followed in his footsteps and had left a painted recess in which they had put their own gods. Beyond the inner sanctuary was a festival hall, a kind of stone tent, built by the warrior pharaoh Tuthmosis III.

Before leaving Karnak Temple, we visited the sacred lake on its south flank. It symbolized the waters of the Nun, the primordial ocean from which the earth emerged. On its north-west bank there was a large carved scarab beetle. A young girl in Cairo had once slipped a little blue stone scarab, crudely carved, into my hand as an amulet, demanding *baksheesh*. I had also seen a live one rolling its eggs in a ball of dung in the sand. It would do that for forty days, until its offspring emerged as winged creatures. It was for good reason that the scarab represented the sun, the light which emerges out of darkness.

The following day, I visited the temple of Queen Hatshepsut on the west bank of the Nile. It took us an hour and half to cross over on the ferry, such was the queue of donkeys and carts, clapped-out cars and modern taxis. On the road to the sandstone cliffs where the sites were, we passed lush fields of sugar cane and maize, and mud brick houses with flat roofs. Men strode by in long white tunics with turbans agains the sun. After passing two seated figures over sixty feet high – the Colossi of Memnon – we stopped at the 5,000-year-old village of Korna to have our papers checked.

I wandered off into a nearby field where a little girl in ragged red dress was tending black sheep and two hobbled donkeys. She came up to me and said: '*Allez, monsieur, baksheesh*' and held out her little hand. Although generally taken to mean a tip, *baksheesh* means 'alms', literally 'share the wealth'. As I scribbled something as incomprehensible to her as the hieroglyphs on the temple ruins, she absent-mindedly rubbed the hard palm of her hand with her forefinger. She wore a gold bracelet which shone against her dark skin. For a moment, her dark liquid eyes looked straight into mine. When I got up to go, she said quietly '*Salaam*'. I replied '*Male kum salaam*': 'May Peace be with you'.

I passed by at 8.30a.m. on 30 July 1992. I wonder if she will remember me as I will always remember her.

It was not long before we reached Queen Hatshepsut's temple at Deir el-Bahari, which in Egyptian means 'The Most Splendid of All'. I could easily see why. It had a long causeway leading up to two storeys of colonnades, situated at the foot of a rugged escarpment which seemed to enclose the temple with sheltering arms. With its clean, delicate lines, it was a harmonious work of art rising out of the spontaneous order of nature. Its spare geometry marked the zenith in Egyptian architecture. It had been created by Hatshepsut's lover Senmut, the ultimate labour of love.

I wanted to see the Punt frieze on the southern colonnade. An inscription declared that it was the god Amun who ordered the expedition and it was Hatshepsut was carried it out. Its aim was to travel to the Land of Punt to get precious goods, myrrh, incense and trees to plant in the Temple 'to establish a Punt [Holy Land] in his [Amun's] house'.

Although shallow and faded, the reliefs were amazingly life-like. They depicted seven ships sailing southward as well as the sailors landing in a part of Africa, the land of Punt. It contained bee-hive huts with ladders built over water surrounded by plants, coconut trees, birds, cattle, animals and even a small dog. There were large realistic pictures of the marine life of the Red Sea, including a turtle, squid and lobster carved underneath a beautiful ship.

The exact location of Punt remains a mystery, but it probably was along the East African coast below the Horn. Hatshepsut's expedition undertaken in *c.* 1500 BC was the first great natural history expedition in the history of the world, an early version of Darwin's voyage on the *Beagle*. According to another inscription, on their way they came across: 'All goodly fragrant woods of God's land, heaps of myrrh resin, of fresh myrrh trees, with ebony and pure ivory, with green gold of Emu, with cinnamon wood, with incense, kohl [for make-up], with baboons, monkeys, dogs, with skins of the southern panther, with natives and their children.'

It sounded like a description of the market in Djibouti. What was remarkable was the absence of scenes of war; unlike the Portuguese, the Egyptians and the Phoenicians who sailed down to the East African coast were interested in opening up peaceful trade routes to the benefit of all.

Any temple would have been a disappointment after Queen Hatshepsut's, but before leaving Karnak I was determined to visit the fallen statue of Ozymandias in the funeral temple of Ramses II.

Rather than having the 'sneer of cold command' of Shelley's famous poem, the huge head had the kind of quiet inner smile I had seen in statues of Buddha in Sri Lanka. But the colossal statue, wrecked in an earthquake, was still a symbol of what would happen to all tyrants, and a reminder that however humans might like to impose their will on earth, nature would have the final say.

Clambering up what was left of the ceremonial gateway of the temple, I could see the rugged escarpment to the west already in the shade. To the east carefully tended fields stretched across the flood plain to the Nile. Ozymandias, surrounded by acacia trees and fallen masonry, was exactly on the border between the barren and fertile, the desert and the oasis.

An old man with sunken cheeks, dressed in a dirty robe and turban, brought some delicious mint tea. He sat crouched with his knees bent, smoking a cigarette, a popular Egyptian brand called Ramesses. By now the night was closing in. I could hear in the distance some singing from the village – a wedding. A pack of scrawny dogs ran across the dusty sand amongst the ruins, barking and chasing each other. Up on the escarpment, the misshapen rocks began to crack in the cool air after the heat of the day. The children of the peasants were coughing, huddled around their fires in their mud brick houses. The stars came out in the moonlit sky, casting an ethereal light across the desert stretching far away. With their tombs pillaged and empty, their magical spells broken, I wondered if the pharaohs voyaging in their 'boats of a million years' ever asked themselves whether their earthly labours had been worth all the trouble.

Chapter Thirty-Four

A Lyrical World

A FTER the tranquillity of Luxor and the calm contemplation of Egypt's ancient civilization, it was a shock to come back to the hustle and bustle of bursting Cairo. I checked in at the Oasis Hotel again and decided to get to know something more of modern Cairo. I use the word 'modern' in relative terms. Cairo is as old as the Bible, where it is called 'On'. The Greeks and Romans called it 'Heliopolis' or 'City of the Sun'. All that remained of that time was an obelisk which once stood at the entrance of a Sun Temple in the now wealthy district of Heliopolis.

In my wandering around Cairo, I had the impression that a third of the city was standing, a third collapsing, and a third half-built. There were some fine buildings in the fashionable centre along the Nile, but there was also another side to Cairo, the hidden city where most of the fifteen million inhabitants who have migrated from the countryside live. In the Imbaba district on the east bank, the main thoroughfare just allowed the occasional car to lurch over the gullies and ruts amongst the garbage and cess-pools and chicken coops. These were crossed by filthy passageways where the sun never shone and the state rarely reached. This was the City of the Night. Suburbs like Imbaba were the breeding-grounds for flies, diseases and Islamic fundamentalism. Thousands of people even lived by turning over garbage on the great fetid tips of the ancient city.

I went to visit Old Cairo early one morning in search of one of the world's first Christian communities, the members of the Coptic Church. I wanted to visit the fifth-century Church of Abu Serga. Situated in a maze of alleyways above the ruins of the fort of Babylon, it was a gem of its kind. Built in the Basilica style, its timber roof was being repaired, and a flapping tarpaulin suddenly revealed the deep blue sky above and filled the church momentarily with sunlight and fresh air. Inside the crypt, there were some worn steps going down to a cave. It was here that Joseph, Mary and the baby Jesus hid for three months during their flight to Egypt. Because of the rising water table of the Nile, it had become flooded with clear, still water. People had thrown small coins into the water, and I noticed a small leaf floating on the still surface.

I had been alienated from the Christian religion by years of muscular Christianity at boarding-school. I did not believe in the Christian God as a personal being nor that he had sent his son down on earth to save us. Nevertheless, I felt strangely moved to be so close to Jesus of Nazareth and to walk on the same ground that he had once trod. What had always seemed remote characters and events in the Bible suddenly became real.

I tried to remember the Lord's Prayer which I had repeated countless times as a boy. I was not sure whether I got it right. I hoped we would all get our daily bread, forgive those who trespassed against us, and be delivered from evil. But I did not wish for power and glory in God's kingdom anymore than in the pharaohs' empire. Over the centuries, power and glory had been two of the main sources of trouble on earth.

I had no god to pray to or worship or plead with; for me, God is Nature in the sense that everything that exists is of value. I expected no personal afterlife except absorption into the living whole. But I was thankful for having been preserved so far in my travels and I lit a candle before leaving the church, as I had done in Lisbon, in memory of all the mariners who had lost their lives at sea around the coasts of Africa.

Although during my stay in Egypt the Christian Copts were under threat from the Muslim fundamentalists, they were a much older community. It was not until the Arabs invaded the country in AD 641 that Islam was established. Egypts's first Islamic capital emerged from the military camp of the Muslim leader and it was during the rule of Salah Al-Din (Saladin) – a Kurd from Iraq – that Cairo took on its recognizable shape. It became the greatest cultural centre in the Islamic world: so many mosques were built during the period of Mameluke and the Turkish occupation that it came to be known as the 'The City of a Thousand Minarets'.

Next to Saladin's citadel, Mohamed Ali Pasha had built a huge mosque in the Ottoman style which dominated Cairo. I preferred the simple mosques made from coral to be found along the East African coast, but with its cool, dark interior illuminated by coloured windows, it provided a welcome respite from the noonday sun. Ali Pasha had founded the Farouk dynasty which Gamal Abdel Nasser overthrew in 1952 with his military coup.

Although hated by the West, Nasser was the first to win Egypt's independence after nearly 2,500 years of foreign conquest and set up a secular state in which Muslims and Copts had equal rights. His successor President Sadat had been assassinated by the Muslim brotherhood, a sect dedicated to the overthrow of the secular state. Just before my arrival the more radical Muslim Associations had gunned down yet another intellectual who had defended the separation of church and state. They had also fired on tourists and murdered thirteen Coptic Christians. They were gaining support amongst the unemployed graduates and illiterate masses by providing minimum welfare services and a sense of purpose. But Sami insisted that Islam was not by its nature an aggressive or repressive religion: 'It's for peace and brotherhood, generosity and tolerance. The fundamentalists in the Muslim Brotherhood are politically motivated; they want power for themselves to create an Islamic state as in Iran. But Egypt has always been a very flexible society, allowing Christians to live alongside Muslims. Don't forget the Gate of Babylon was opened by Christians to the Muslims!'

Before leaving Cairo, I went deep into the Bazaar of Khan Al-Khalili which dated from the fourteenth century and was reputed to be one of the greatest in the world. I took a taxi from the hotel into town which weaved in and out of the lanes, the driver with his hand permanently on the klaxon. Despite the smoke and din, I noticed a couple of young children asleep in a hammock tied under a horse-drawn cart. A large, beaten-up lorry then went by, carrying a camel. Water-sellers dressed in baggy black trousers also dodged between the traffic, carrying great urns on their backs.

I paid the taxi driver off, a portly middle-aged man, gave him a reasonable tip and then set off for the bazaar. A couple of minutes later he was running after me, carrying something in his hand. It was my camera. I had left it in the back of the taxi.

After the traffic, the bazaar was a comparative oasis. The first delight was the absence of hassle: unlike Morocco, the sellers let me browse and ponder without a hard sell. And what a marvellous collection of brassware, textiles, and other Oriental products to see!

With the steadily rising temperarature, it was a pleasure to find a little recess at El Fishaway's Coffee Lounge. It was an old building with wooden tables spilling out on to the narrow passage where middle-aged men sat with their round stomachs, pots of mint tea and *nargileh* or hubble-bubbles. I ordered one for myself and the smoke of the tobacco, mixed with a little molasses, apple and spice, wafted gently through my mind. The benevolent Mr El Fishaway looked down on us in a faded picture in a heavily ornamented frame.

A few tourists wandered by amongst the surging crowds. I had now been in Africa for six months and felt more used to seeing black faces rather than white. Having been for so long in Islamic culture, I could also appreciate the shock of the orthodox and the passion of the young when a couple of sunburnt Italian women walked by, their hot pants revealing their buttocks and pubic hair and their flimsy cotton shirts the outline of their nipples. The Egyptian women, by contrast, were covered from head to foot.

In my local Egyptian guide – the cover stapled on back to front and upside down – I read that 'Night-time in Cairo is a lyrical world, bathing in a dreamy lake of lights and inspiring shadows. Night-time in Cairo combines the magic of the East with the arts of the West . . .' To test this out, we went one night to have a meal at the Sheraton Hotel on a floating restaurant on the Nile. The hotels, clubs and nightclubs along its banks were in full-swing, and the taxis were disgorging richly dressed men and women.

'The rich Arabs used to go to London for their casinos, nightclubs and women,' Sami said, 'now they come to Cairo. You see that motor boat going all over the place; it's probably a Saudi prince who has been smoking too much hashish!'

'And presumably they come for the belly-dancing.'

'Of course. For Arabs, Egypt is famous for two things: films and belly-dancing. Middle East men are crazy about belly-dancing. They spend all day sleeping in their hotels and then go downtown to the night clubs to watch the belly-dancers. At this time of year, the clubs and hotels are completely booked. It's the same in Alexandria.'

Every night at the Oasis Hotel, belly-dancing went on under the stars and date palms in the open-air restaurant until the early hours. If anything, the smart Egyptian women were more enthusiastic than the men. They were the first to be up on their feet, clapping their hands to the rhythm of the moaning music created by drums, electric guitars and violins. The dancer, a plump lady with dyed blonde hair and a bright red smudge of a mouth, wore a black bikini with gold spangles and red tassles. Her belly, the centre of attention, would twitch and roll slowly to the music until suddenly the rythm would change, sending her into wild gyrations as it reached a climax, after which she relaxed and moved her belly slowly and seductively again. This was repeated many times. When the music finally stopped, the dancer's false smile collapsed with her sweating body, and she tottered off in her high heels and fish-net stockings like a tawdry trapeze artist who had known better days.

'Does your wife know how to belly-dance?' I asked Sami.

'All Egyptian women know how to belly dance! When they want something from you, they dance very well!'

I said goodbye to the film crew for the last time next day. Being involved with television during my voyage had been a mixed blessing. It was always good to see the crew and hear their news from Britain. The two Davids and Elayne had fused into a creative and efficient team. They all agreed that their travels in Africa had changed their lives and would never be forgotten. But after spending months on my own, their sudden arrival was often a cultural and emotional shock. In the week or so we were together in six parts of Africa, it had been a mad rush, trying to squeeze out the maximum from each country in the minimum of time.

Taking film with a video camera on my own also had its advantages and drawbacks. My sense of duty made me contact people and go to places I may not have bothered to visit. Yet I often felt the camera cut me off from the reality I was filming; seeing the world through a lens is a bit like being behind a windscreen in a car rather than walking on foot. The process also got me abused – and arrested – on several occasions.

Before leaving Cairo, I went for one last look of the surrealistic city from Saladin's citadel. I felt that my visit to the sites of ancient Egypt, with their constant refrain of decay and dissolution, had prepared me for my own inevitable death. This did not make me want to withdraw from the world or to escape into the fantasy of an afterlife but rather helped me appreciate more fully the passing joys and beauties of this life. I would remain faithful to the earth in the full awareness that all good things (including my own life) would come to an end. My voyage had confirmed what I had always suspected: that the world is in constant flux, that life is always temporary, and that our lives themselves are journeys into the unknown. Reason is the chart and passion the gale, but there are larger and more incomprehensible forces at work which ultimately decide our fate.

From the vantage point of the towering walls of the citadel, I watched the great buildings, mosques and minarets of Cairo slowly disappear in the twilight, with the last rays of the sun catching the tiny pyramids on the horizon. I began to understand why so many foreigners had come to love Cairo, with all its diversity and confusion. As the lights of the great city came on and twinkled below me, I thought of South Africa at the other end of the troubled continent, a drop in the well of time compared to Egypt's ancient civilization. And as the sun finally disappeared in the darkening sky streaked with red ochre, I thought of how good it was that Cecil Rhodes had never realized his ambition of building a train from Cape Town to Cairo and of turning the map of Africa into a dull, uniform pink.

I wanted to catch the train from Cairo to Alexandria but since it was the holiday season, there were no seats. I hired a taxi instead. It had grinding gears, an ominous rumble in the back axle and no air-conditioning. The young driver in a white *galibavva* did not speak a word of English.

We set off at midday in the blinding sun for the 140-mile drive to the coast. The highway was wide, dead straight and in good repair. For miles we sped through a dirty yellow desert, the only break in the dreary landscape being the odd military encampment, garish advertising hoardings, or thin lines of scraggly casuarina trees. As we reached the delta, all was transformed: the sweet waters of the Nile turned the desert into fertile plots of vegetables, maize and watermelons, and field after field of bright yellow sunflowers.

343

Towering date palms, their roots gripping the moist black earth, reached for the sun.

Towards the late afternoon, the countryside became more undulating. We went over the crest of a hill to see a great city stretched out along the coast beyond a wide lake: Alexandria. For the first time in my voyage, I saw the Mediterranean Sea. It was light blue, shimmering in the sun, and my first impulse was to dive into its clear, cool waters.

But first we had to cross the pink salt flats and marshes and lagoons. Amongst the papyrus reeds, I saw people in flat boats out duck shooting. The calm was ruined by great juggernauts belching black smoke. The smell of crude oil mixed with the salty air.

As we swung into Alexandria, it immediately reminded me of Havana in Cuba. There were the same fine buildings with balconies and columns and the same peeling paint and dilapidated air. Both cities had been highly cosmopolitan but both had undergone revolutions which had sent the rich merchants and businessmen packing. Both had grand hotels on the waterfront which had known better days.

After trying a couple of hotels, I settled on the Windsor Hotel facing the eastern harbour and the sea beyond. Its façade had been freshened up, and the sign 'Piccadilly Coffee Shop' repainted, but it was unable to throw off its air of decadent grandeur. Its false Doric columns were painted gold while all over its walls and ceilings there were thinly veiled Rubenesque women with fat thighs and vast bosoms attended by chubby cherubims. It seemed more appropriate for an Edwardian brothel than a genteel hotel by the sea. Its clients were Egyptian families, and I wondered what the head-scarved Muslim women must have thought of the half-naked European beauties cavorting around them. As I checked in, the music playing in the wood-panelled vestibule was fifties American jazz.

I was shown to my room on the fourth floor. When I pressed the button in the lift, the light went out. When I flushed the lavatory in my bathroom evil-smelling water welled up the plug hole of the shower. At my bedside table, under a glass top, a smudged photocopied notice declared 'Dail Nummber. Continous when ring.' But whatever the idiosyncracies of the place, all was forgiven when I opened the large French windows and walked out on to the small balcony overlooking the bay.

344

A glorious sea breeze billowed the curtains and made me hanker to be back at sea.

I contacted once again Mr Khalil of the Mesco Shipping Agency to see if he had come up with a ship for the next leg of my voyage. He said: 'There's not one ship to Tripoli. There's no ship – not even tramping – to Tunis. Believe me, I've tried for you.'

There seemed no choice but to try to zig-zag across the Mediterranean, by ferry if necessary. My *ABC Shipping Passenger Guide* informed me that passenger ships called in Alexandria on their way to Italy via Greece. I came across a Travel Agency in the main street behind the hotel and its elderly proprietor – Mr Adlan – knew immediately what had to be done. He contacted the offices of Adriatic Lines and within a few minutes was able to offer me a shared cabin on the Italian cruise ship *Egitto Express* which was travelling to Venice via Heraklion, Pireaus and Bari. It was leaving on 3 August and would cost £284 sterling. I took it.

Having settled my ticket, I went for a stroll along the waterfront which curved around the eastern harbour. Boys dived into the murky waters to cool off while old men fished from the oil-spattered rocks for sardines. In the afternoon, the waterfront became very quiet as the shops closed and the citizens of Alexandria took a siesta to avoid the pummelling heat. Towards dusk, street-sellers reappeared, some carrying great bundles of balloons, others setting up their barbecues for grilling maize. It was not long before the promenade was full of strolling families and young men and women who eyed each other shyly as they went past. The men often walked touching each other, holding hands or throwing their arms around each other's shoulder.

Everyone was friendly and polite to me, the only European around on foot. 'Welcome to Egypt, sir, Welcome to Alexandria!', young men would say, smiling as they passed. I wondered what reception they would get in Britain. The number of different faces was extraordinary, ranging from dark brown to white. Many of the women had very light brown eyes, some even blue. Alexandria was clearly a racial as well as a cultural melting pot.

Apart from being the largest port in Egypt, Alexandria was also one of the major summer resorts in the Arab world. I had been unable to meet Suzanne Mubarak, the Welsh wife of the President in Cairo, because her aides said that she was on holiday down in Alexandria. The city had many well-laid-out gardens with beautiful trees and palms, particularly appreciated by a desert people whose vision of paradise was a garden with fountains. For their pleasure, the wealthy Arabs did not go into the wilderness but into man-made palaces of luxury and ease.

Alexandria also had some fine white, sandy beaches stretching along the western corniche. The names of the beaches reflected the city's cosmopolitan past: Sidi Bishr, El-Mandar, Cleopatra, but also Miami, Stanley and Sporting. Off Abu Kir, one of the calmest beaches, Nelson destroyed Napoleon's fleet in 1798.

I took a cab along the corniche and went past countless hotels, most of them featureless high-rise blocks. All the beaches were packed with Arab holidaymakers, under umbrellas if they could afford them. All the members of the large families went into the sea, including the Muslim women who remained fully dressed with headscarves on. At night, there were clubs, casino and belly-dancing galore. What had been a largely European resort when E.M. Forster had written his guide had become a Middle Eastern one. It was a reclaimed Egyptian city going the way of Brighton.

While waiting for my boat to come in, I decided to have a look at some of the archaeological and historical sites of Alexandria. For centuries, it had been the gateway between Africa and Europe, with peoples travellings in both directions as conquerors, workers and travellers. The city was named after Alexander the Great, who ordered its foundation in 322 BC in order to connect Greece and Egypt by sea. After his death his empire was divided among his generals, and Ptolemy declared himself king of Egypt. He founded the Ptolemaic dynasty which ruled the country for nearly three centuries. The final defeat of Cleopatra and Antony in 31 BC meant that Egypt ceased to be an independent country and became a Roman province.

To get a feel of the Graeco–Roman period I visited the Catacombs of Kom el-Shugafa. It was situated in a down-at-heel suburb and to reach it I had to go down a pot-holed sandy street. The smell of wood shavings, oil, perfume, coffee and rotting vegetables rose in the still air. Workers' flats overlooked the nondescript rocky site. The catacombs had been discovered in 1900 when a donkey drawing a cart fell into a pit. Dating from the second century AD, they were unique for their plan and decoration which were a mixture of Egyptian and Graeco–Roman elements.

I entered down a spiral stairway carved in sandstone rock with small chapels spreading out; the dead bodies used to be lowered down the central shaft. It was cool and damp below. At the bottom of three storeys, there was a central tomb with Egyptian motifs executed in the prevailing Graeco–Roman style. Most of it was under three foot of water and the attendant told me that the water table was continuing to rise. On the back wall there was a relief of a typical Egyptian scene of mummification, with the jackel-headed Anubis in the centre, ibis-headed Thoth, god of wisdom, on the right, and the falcon-headed Horus on the left. But the style was stilted and mannered, with Greek touches such as bunches of grapes and Medusa heads added. It was crude and lifeless compared to the great tombs near Luxor, a sad reminder of the decline of Egyptian art. It was the last construction built in the name of old Egypt and marked the death-knoll of its civilization which had lasted 4,000 years.

Not far from the catacombs, I stopped to gaze at 'Pompey's Pillar', a huge red granite column standing in the midst of the ruins of the Serapeum Temple. I persuaded a guard on the site to show me the famous library burrowed out of the rock underneath. He unlocked the creaking door, and led me through a dimly lit passage along which papyrus scrolls had once been kept in niches hewn in the rock. We ended up in a small, round, empty cavern, the dead end of ancient Egypt.

The greatest library in the ancient world had once been in Alexandria and amongst the many African scholars, poets and scientists who used it were Euclid, the father of geometry, Hipparchus, the father of astronomy, Eratoshenes, the father of geography, and of course Claudius Ptolemy whose map of the world was the starting point for the Portuguese discoverer's.

I was particularly attracted to Philo, the Jewish philosopher born in Alexandria in the first century AD, who taught that a man should transform himself into the nature of the cosmos, to become a little cosmos. The surpassing good was not the destruction of the passions but the discovery of wisdom: 'When this is found, all the people will sing.' When I looked back on my voyage, I realized that I had been groping towards this state of being.

After the Roman conquest of Alexandria, the museum and library went into general decline. Later historians accused the Arabs who arrived in AD 642 of burning the library, but by the time of their arrival, it was probably already ruined. At all events, its loss proved to be one of the greatest tragedies in the cultural history of the world.

Many relics from the Ptolemic period were stored in the modern Graeco–Roman Museum in Alexandria. The very opposite of the Cairo Museum, it was well laid-out in airy, uncluttered rooms. Amongst the exhibits, I particularly liked a simple little bust of Socrates. I wondered what he must have thought of the remnants of religions and empires all around him: he had always thought that an unexamined life was not worth living. No doubt he would have been tolerant of their folly, believing that vice is ignorance and no one deliberately wills evil.

I also spent some time contemplating the bust of Cleopatra, the last queen of the dynasty of Ptolemies in Egypt. It showed a plump woman with small lips and a slight double chin. As I surveyed her face, it was difficult to see what made great emperors fall for her. I wondered whether her delicate nose really had changed the course of history. I doubted it; the actions of the masses are far more important than the decisions of rulers. Even if Cleopatra had not come to power, Egypt would probably still have ended up a province of Rome.

During my stay in Alexandria, I became friendly with an elderly Armenian called Ara Khatchadourian who ran a dusty film shop in the centre of town. I first came across him in a busy street whilst looking for some film. A faded Kodak advert from the fifties in his window caught my eye, with an American model in a large bikini playing with a red ball on a beach.

Khatchadourian came from a family of musicians who left Armenia in 1915 to escape the Armenian 'genocide' by the Turks who occupied the country. After escaping they passed through Turkey, Greece, Syria and Lebanon before ending up in Alexandria sixty years ago. Like many Alexandrians, he was a polyglot, speaking seven languages, including English, French, Greek and Arabic, the main languages of the different communities in the city earlier in the century.

'It was wonderful here in the old days,' he told me. 'In Farouk's time, we had many cultural events, orchestras, exhibitions, debating societies. All that is gone now.'

'What do you miss most?' I asked him.

'We weep about the musical life. Alexandria used to be like a second Paris in every way. The most famous and talented musicians came to Alexandria rather than Cairo.'

As we spoke he served his customers who came for their developed prints, handing over a frangipani flower to each of them with the change.

'Why do you stay here?'

'We love Alexandria because it is a cosmopolitan place. The climate is good. We thank God for all the goodness we have had in this country.'

The evening before I left Alexandria, I took a *calèche*. The small, sturdy horse, I was pleased to see, had his balls intact and neighed at his fellows as they went by. I asked to be taken to the fort of Qayet Bai, on the northern tip of the entrance to the eastern harbour. It was a fine fifteenth-century square fort, housing a marine museum. But I was more interested in standing there on the former island of Pharos, the site of the great lighthouse built during the reign of the first two Ptolemies and finished in 279 BC. Made from limestone, marble and granite with bronze ornamental work, the lighthouse was considered one of the seven wonders of the ancient world. It was dedicated to Castor and Pollux, 'the Saviour Gods, for sailors'. Above the domed lantern (where metal mirrors reflected a fire made from wood), there was a huge bronze statue, probably of Poseidon, god of the sea. I gave thanks to them all, for they had protected me well.

Standing on the rocky shore of Pharos, my back to Africa and looking out across the Mediterranean, I felt a pang of regret. For the first time in over six months, I would be returning to Europe. I was pleased to be homeward bound and I was looking forward to seeing my family and friends. Yet, but at the same time, I had become so 'Africanized' that I was not sure that I wanted to return to so-called European civilization. Perhaps like Alexandria I told myself, I could draw on the best of Africa and Europe in the future.

Thinking about my home in Wales, I recalled the advice given by the

Alexandrian poet Constantine Calfavy to Ulysses not to hurry his journey home to Ithaca:

> Ithaca has given you your lovely journey.
> Without Ithaca you would not have set out.
> Ithaca has no more to give you now.

Chapter Thirty-Five

Lost in the Wilderness

THE *Egitto Express* was new, with red stripes painted along its shinging white hull. It had two brown funnels and a square stern which dropped down to let vehicles drive on. Its interior was designed to impress with its showy glitter. A steward led me along a passageway of metal bulkheads shining like mirrors, in which I saw myself reflected – a medium-sized, middle-aged man with a broken nose, carrying a straw hat on his tanned head, a small rucksack on his back and a great bag full of cameras on his shoulder. I saw a man who looked slightly out of place and slightly out of his mind.

The cabin was a tiny polished plastic rectangle with two single bunks and a shower. As I was stowing my gear away, a huge man burst in, covered in dust, a gold chain around his thick, deeply tanned neck. He swore in French as he threw his back pack down.

'I didn't pay all that money to sleep like a boy in a dormitory!', he exclaimed.

I thought he might be a deserting French Legionnaire, except that he had a fluffy little dog with him. He went off to find a steward to get a cabin for himself. He returned with the news:

'They will try later, once we're at sea. They better had. I'm not used to living in a tiny box like this!'

His name was Alain Muret, an engineer on contract in Egypt returning with his car and dog for the summer holidays in France. His wife had gone on ahead by plane.

351

We set sail in the late afternoon. I went up past the swimming pool to the top sundeck which was crowded with passengers, mainly Italian and Greek, leaning over the stern railings taking their last look of Africa. I bid *au revoir* to the bright continent, confident that I would soon be returning to its sunny shores.

All next morning on the public address system, the entertainments officer droned out in Italian, French and English the words: 'We are trying to organize a Treasure Hunt'. Clearly 'trying' was the operative word; most passengers were either sleeping off last night's booze or keen to get a suntan. The passengers, no doubt hard-working and responsible at home, had given themselves up to collective lethargy, overwhelmed by too much sun, too much food and too much leisure. They had been told that they must enjoy themselves on this cruise, and they were doing their best.

I had my meals with my reluctant cabin-mate. He had worked for seventeen years building dams in Africa – in Nigeria, the Congo, Kenya, Sudan, Libya and Egypt. He claimed to have always had good relations with Africans and admired their traditional skills and knowledge of their environment:

'The nomads are brilliant in the desert; they can live at one with nature. A nomad has a compass in his heart. Whereas we're lost in the wilderness, he is completely at home. But when a nomad becomes settled, he loses his identity and can't orientate himself.'

Alain was less impressed though by his experiences of Africans and modern technology:

'I can build a dam, train the personnel, but I know in a few years it will need foreign experts to put it right. Nigeria is the worse place I've been to. We built a dam and left them a camp like the Club Méditerranée but in a year it was ruined – the windows broken, goats in the gardens, frogs in the swimming pool. They were cooking in the corners of the houses on open fires. The trained personnel hadn't bothered to do the minimum maintentance. It's like that all over Africa.'

After a smooth crossing from Alexandria we docked in Heraklion in Crete the following day, only long enough to allow the passengers and vehicles to disembark and embark. I had a few hours to go ashore and strolled towards the old harbour full of colourful boats under the Venetian fort.

What struck me most was the closeness between Africa and Crete, only eighteen hours away by boat. It did not surprise me that Minoan paintings should have been recently found in a royal palace at Avaris in the Nile delta. It would have been comparatively easy for Egyptian pharaohs to mount their military campaigns to the north and occupy parts of Greece, thereby transmitting Egyptian customs and beliefs to Europe.

We left Heraklion at 22.00 hours and arrived in Piraeus at breakfast time the next day. This was the first time I had visited Greece. Since we had so little time on shore – leaving in the evening – I decided to join an excursion to visit the Acropolis in Athens.

Wandering around its ruins, I recalled Solon, the founder of Athen's democracy, one of the seven wise men of antiquity who had followed his principle: 'Nothing in Excess'. By the time Pericles came to prominence in 461 BC the Greeks had gained full independence and Athens had become the foremost city in Greece, reaching unparalleled artistic intellectual heights.

From the walls of the Acropolis – meaning 'Upper City' in Greek – I looked down to the restored colonnade of Attalus in the ancient Agora, the market place which was the centre of public life. Amongst its marble arches Socrates and Plato once strolled with their pupils, and Zeno had expounded the philosophy of the Stoics.

To the west of the Acropolis, I could also see the the Pnyx, the 'Hill of Democracy' where a popular assembly was attended by the citizens of Athens who discussed and voted on the laws and affairs of the day. I felt the greatest achievement of Athens was not so much its architecture, philosophy or literature but this example of direct, participatory democracy in action. Unfortunately, it did not last long: Greek democracy was crushed by the Macedonians led by Alexander 'the Great' who then went on to conquer Egypt.

On leaving Greece, my main regret was not having had the time to visit the temple of Poseidon at Sounion where Byron carved his name in the marble in an act of poetic vandalism. It was here that the ancient Greek sailors would offer a last sacrifice to the God of the Sea before leaving the safety of the Saronic Gulf for the perils of the open waters.

We sailed towards the Corinth canal which cuts through the narrow strip of land between the Gulf of Corinth and the Saronic Gulf. Built at the end of the nineteenth century, it meant that ships no longer had to sail around the large south-west peninsula of Greece known as the Pelopponese. We passed through the short canal, cut deeply through solid rock, the next day at noon, and then entered the Ionian Sea and sailed towards the Adriatic port of Bari in Italy.

I caught a train from Bari to Naples where I holed up in a gloomy hotel in the Piazza Garibaldi opposite the railway station. I spent the first night retching my heart up in an airless room – I had caught food poisoning for the second time during my voyage on the luxury Italian cruise ship. Down by the docks, I managed to find a ferry going to Tunis three days later via Trapani in Sicily. I spent the time in between exploring Naples which I found dirty, unfriendly and sweltering. It was the first time I had been back in Europe for six months and it was a disconcerting experience.

To escape the city, I took a train along the Bay of Naples to visit the ruins of Pompeii which had been destroyed in AD 79. I was struck by the continued influence of Egypt passed on by the Greeks into the Roman empire. Several patrician villas had mannered paintings with Egyptian-style buildings and Nilotic scenes of palm trees, hippos and crocodiles. There was also a fine temple dedicated to Isis, first built around the end of the second century BC. Isis had been the patron saint of the sailors of Alexandria while the Greeks and Romans identified her with the goddess of nature.

I went down to the Maritime Station next day, 11 August, to board the MV *Kelibia*, a white ninety-seven-metre, 3,300-ton ferry boat. It was registered in Malta. I spoke to the Polish first officer organizing the loading, and he told me that the officers were Polish and the crew Tunisian. The Italian owner was once again employing cheap labour.

The officer had his work cut out. As far as the eye could see, there were young Tunisian men in expensive new cars – Renaults, Fords, Alfa Romeos – stuffed and piled high with consumer goods. One even had a cooker tied to its bonnet. They were not owned by the men themselves, I learned, but had been paid for by fat cats in Tunis. Like millions of North African guest workers in Europe, they were lost souls; no longer satisfied at home and second-class citizens north of the Mediterranean.

I slept badly that night in a cramped cabin with no porthole next to a noisy concourse and spent the following morning on deck in an armchair in the shade. We arrived at Trapani on the south-west tip of Sicily at one o'clock in the afternoon. Many Italian holidaymakers came on board. We were not allowed to disembark so I had to content myself with a view of a statue of Garibaldi surrounded by palm trees on the waterfront.

A few hours later, I saw Africa again, the brown rocky cliffs of the Cap Bon Peninsula which stretched out into the azure sea. I was on the Barbary Coast, where pirates had long plundered ships travelling from the Western to the Eastern Mediterranean through the narrow strait between Sicily and Tunisia, a reminder of the closeness between Europe and Africa. It was the struggle for control of these trade routes which led to the Punic Wars between the ancient Carthaginians and Romans.

It was a delight to see the happy smiles on the faces of the migrant workers as they leaned over the railings, the sea breeze playing with their curly hair. They stood in shorts, bare foot and bare chested, holding each other's calloused hands or throwing an arm over a friend's shoulder. With the Tunisian crew, it was their ship and they were going home and no one could tell them what to do or think anymore.

We arrived in Tunis at 18.00 hours. It took about an hour to queue up in the main lounge of the ship and get my passport stamped by the immigration officials. The Tunisian authorities let the European visitors jump the queue; it seemed like the returning workers were second-class citizens in their own country.

The ship had docked at La Goulette. On the quayside, I took a taxi and asked the driver to take me to the town centre. This involved travelling along a narrow causeway across Lake Tunis which smelt of rotting salt pans.

'The French built the new city of Tunis on the water,' the driver informed me.

'Are there many French left?'

'After independence, nearly all the French and Italians left when their property was nationalized. Some are still trying to get compensation.'

'How are things these days?'

'We have a high standard of living for a developing country. There's a social security system for the old and sick, and education and health are free. Women have equal rights. But the economy is in trouble and the government's having a lot of trouble with the *intégristes*, the Muslim fundamentalists, right now.'

I asked the driver to drop me at a good hotel in the Avenue Bourguiba, the main street in the centre of town named after the first President of Tunisia after independence. The Hotel El Hana International turned out to be a huge, expensive, four-star hotel, but I had little choice as it was very late.

When I opened the shutters next morning, Tunisia stretched out before me. The main street was lined with solid French buildings with shuttered windows, balconies and wrought-iron railings. This *nouvelle ville* was built on a grid pattern on reclaimed marshes below the old rambling walled Medina which stretched up the hill. Its flat-topped buildings and minarets shone white in the early morning sun.

I went out into Avenue Bourguiba with its central tree-lined walkway. It had been washed down during the night. Newspapers kiosks were beginning to open and flower sellers were laying out their wares. The smell of fresh bread and cakes wafted from the many *pâtisseries*. Opposite, on the terrace of the Café de Paris, the Tunisian middle class – nearly all men – were reading their papers and taking coffee. Violent French films were advertised, such as '*Tous les Coups sont Permis*' (no blows are barred). I could have been on the Left Bank of Paris. There were no beggars or hustlers about; the place had an easy, unhurried pace.

Leafing through my *ABC of Shipping* I discovered that the German company Transeste Lines had a ship sailing from Naples to Felixstowe via Palermo, Algeciras and Oporto. If that failed, I worked out that I could catch a ferry to Marseilles from Tunis and then try to get another boat from there.

I had come to Tunis primarily to visit Carthage. I was particularly interested in exploring the close links in ancient times, many centuries before Vasco da Gama, between Africa and Europe. What had happened in the last five hundred years was only the tip of an iceberg of time.

I wanted to visit Carthage because it was from here in 450 BC that Himilcon went as far north as the British Isles, calling in at Cornwall and probably Wales. Hanno too in the same year undertook a voyage along the West Coast of Africa and reached the Bight of Benin where he had seen Mount Cameroon, the 'Chariot of the Gods'. Even more interesting to me was the voyage undertaken by the Phoenicians employed by the Egyptian king Necos around 500 BC – the first recorded circumnavigation of Africa.

According to Greek historian Herodotus, they had sailed in the opposite direction to me, from the Red Sea down into the southern ocean. Every autumn they put in where they were on the African coast, sowed a patch of ground and waited for next year's harvest. In the third year, they eventually passed through the Pillars of Hercules – the Strait of Gibraltar – and returned to Egypt. The voyage proved 2,000 years before the Portuguese that there was a passage around southern Africa and that the continent was surrounded by water, knowledge lost to Europeans until Vasco da Gama's epic voyage.

Carthage was founded in 814 BC just below Byrsa Hill near modern Tunis, one of several Phoenician colonies along the North African coast which at first remained dependent on Tyre in Phoenicia (Lebanon). By the fourth century BC Carthage had become the greatest power in Africa and the western part of the Mediterranean, controlling the coast all the way to the Atlantic. They also traded indirectly with people in West Africa, leaving goods on the beaches and then retreating to allow the locals to offer gold in exchange. Their attempt to guard the trade routes inevitably led them into conflict first with the Greeks and then with the Romans. The latter culminated in the three Punic Wars, the high point of which was Hannibal's crossing of the Alps in 218 BC with his army and several hundred elephants. In the end, the Romans took Carthage in 146 BC and burnt it to the ground, symbolically seeding its soil with salt to curse it for ever. The world wars of antiquity had ended with their own version of Hiroshima.

The only Phoenician remains were to be found on Byrsa Hill, east of modern Tunis. At the height of Carthage's power, there would have been six-storied houses set alongside wide avenues which went down to the sea, vast defensive ramparts, and stables for 300 elephants and 4,000 horses. All that was left was a few cisterns, broken walls, and pillars which had been used as foundations of Roman Carthage. They were the ruin of ruins, eloquent testimony to the bitter onslaught of the Romans. Not far away, I came across part of an amphitheatre where early Christians martyrs were thrown to wild animals, including St Perpetua.

From the Byrsa hill, I had a wonderful view of the Punic Ports on the shore of the azure Gulf of Tunis. The commercial and military ports had been reduced to two lagoons in one of the most exclusive suburbs of Tunis. I went down to take a closer look. Strolling around Admiral's island of the old military port, I could see the outline of an ancient ship excavated from the earth. Down by the entrance to the sea I sat on the rocks and watched the fishermen leave in the late afternoon in their brightly coloured boats. It was difficult to imagine that their ancestors would have set sail here to try to circumnavigate Africa and to take on the might of the Roman Empire.

The next day I went to the Bardo Museum, a former palace in a suburb of Tunis which housed some of the finest Roman mosaics ever discovered. When the Romans rebuilt Carthage in 44 BC it became a beautiful city, second only to Rome. Its citizens developed North Africa until it provided most of the empire's grain. Roman Carthage not only produced Magon, the father of agronomy, but inspired the first Christian Latin school to appear. It was also the home of the African theologians Tertullian and St Augustine. By the third century AD, Carthage had become so important that the majority of Roman senators were of African origin; indeed, the African colonies provided a line of emperors, notably Septimus Serverus. Carthage then went into a slow decline until it was eventually overthrown by the vandals in the fifth century.

Many mosaics in the Bardo had a maritime theme. There was a second-century portrait of a wild Neptune in a chariot with horses rising out of the water, surrounded by women representing the four seasons. Another depicted Ulysses tied to his ship's mast passing by the sirens. I wondered looking at the mosaic whether when I returned home like Ulysses in the *Odysseus* I too would find trouble in my household and Jenny pursued by suitors in my absence. I lingered in front of another mosaic showing Orpheus charming wild animals with his lute. Not only had the face of Orpheus been erased by anti-pagan Christians, but many of the animals depicted – the lion, leopard, cheetah, bear, baboon, oryx and hartebeest – had long since disappeared in North Africa.

Back at the hotel in bustling Tunis, I found a fax waiting for me from the Hamburg office of the Transeste Shipping Company. It was agreed that I could join the MV *Ulf Ritscher* at Palermo in Sicily, provided that I paid the captain the equivalent of $100 a day on embarkation. The ship would be arriving on 17 August – five days later – and would be calling at Algeciras, Oporto and Felixstowe. Perfect. Then I went back to a travel agency in Avenue Bourguiba and managed to book a passage on the MV *Kelibia* back to Trapani. If all went well, I would now be able to complete my circumnavigation of Africa and return to England by boat.

Before leaving, I contacted Tanya Matthews who lived in Sidi Bou Said, a picturesque Moorish village perched on a cliff guarding the Gulf of Tunis. My Cameroonian friend Jean-Victor Nkolo urged me to meet her: 'Despite her age, certainly well over her mid-seventies, Tanya Matthews should still be strong, brilliant and provocative. She lives in one of the most beautiful houses in Sidi Bou Said, beautiful, and very old. Played golf with Bourguiba. Now plays golf with Ben Ali. Knows every one and every thing, almost.'

She certainly lived in a beautiful place. I took the light railway along the coast, passed the stops for Carthage, and got out in the brilliant sunshine at Sidi Bou Said. I climbed the road to the cobbled village square with its little boutiques and whitewashed terraced cafés, houses with bright blue doors and shutters. The turquoise sea shimmered below; across the gulf, the rocky mountain range of Cap Bon was silhouetted against the azure sky. It was a pure Mediterranean scene.

I knocked on the heavy wooden door of her rambling house, and was admitted by a servant into the inner courtyard which was full of flowering plants. A cooling breeze blew through the coloured windows thrown open to the sea. We sat in the shade of an inner patio under white jasmine flowers which gently snowed on Tanya as we spoke. Swallows were nesting in her house, and flew in and out of the open doors and windows.

Tanya Matthews had had an eventful life which she had described in several books. She had grown up in Russia and during the war fallen in love with Ralph Matthews, a BBC correspondent in Moscow. She eloped with him in 1944, leaving behind her Russian husband and their young daughter. They had come to Tunisia thirty years before. She played golf, as Jean-Victor said, but not with the Presidents of Tunisia. Graham Greene had been a lifelong friend. Her granddaughter Laura, out from London for a holiday, was staying with her at the time of my visit.

It so happened that the day we met was Women's Day in Tunisia, 13 August, and I asked Tanya about their status in the country.

'Legally women have equal rights in Tunisia, but not moral equality. If a woman is seen in a car with a man at night, and she has no marriage papers, she can be arrested. If a man is seen with a neighbour's wife, he too can be arrested. Islam is not very tolerant and Muslims believe that their women should remain at home.'

'Walking around the streets of Tunis, everything seems very quiet.'

'Outwardly Tunisia is an ordered society but it is based on lies. Many Tunisians are friendly only if they think they can get something out of you. The country is a one-party state which allows little freedom of expression. Political life here is run by a Tunisian Mafia.'

Tanya invited me back the next day to have lunch.

I decided in the morning to go for a stroll in the *souks* in the Medina, the old Arab quarter of the city. It had none of the hassle of Marrakesh, nor the vitality of Cairo, with its carefully brushed alleys, polite tradesmen and shops bursting with consumer goods. Following my instincts rather than a map, I eventually came out into a small square opposite the Great Mosque, a large sandstone building dating from the ninth century, with its medieval colleges nearby. I bought a *chechia*, a red felt hat with a black tassle, and some exotic perfumes. I then realized that it was already noon; Sidi Bou Said was at least an hour away and and I would be late for lunch chez Tanya. I started asking shop sellers and passers-by the way back to the *cité nouvelle* but their conflicting directions sent me deeper into the souks until I became completely lost. The maze of alleys grew darker, narrower and more hostile. Hot and flustered, I came to a halt, finally giving up the idea of making it Tanya's. Then I heard a quiet voice say behind me:

'Hello, Peter.'

I spun round to see Laura, Tanya's granddaughter. 'I believe you're invited to lunch. We can give you a lift to Sin Bou Said, if you want. My grandmother likes to be on time. We're running a bit late.'

She said all this as if she quite expected to find me in the souks; I found our encounter was little short of a miracle. I followed my Ariadne, and after many deft turns, she led me out of the labyrinth into the blinding midday sun. I squeezed into a small car with two Italian girls and Laura's Tunisian adopted brother. Three-quarters of an hour later, we were sitting down for lunch by the sea with Tanya, Laura's father who lived in Rome, and two French journalists. When the others had gone to the beach, I asked Tanya when she would be writing her book on modern Tunisia.

'Everybody is asking me about it. I don't think it will ever be written. You know this jasmine – I have an opening. The first line of the next book – which will never be written – is: "It's snowing jasmine on my patio . . ."'

'But you must write the book . . .'

'No. I prefer playing golf to writing books. Nobody reads books any more!'

'But what do you think of Africa?'

'The black Africans I've met struck me as nice, good-natured people. I think the return to good nature is most welcome because we have become selfish. Everybody wants to survive; it's a rat race everywhere. It's a struggle and in this struggle we've lost ourselves. It's not Arab Africa with its conflicts and its Koranic obsessions that can teach the West. I don't think it will ever make a positive contribution. But the Africa of music, of dancing, of relaxation, of good neighbourliness can teach us a great deal . . .'

I left Tanya on her patio, the light playing on her face, jasmine snowing on her hair. If she had her way, she would spend the rest of her days in her white rambling house full of coloured windows, bright blue shutters, tropical plants and singing birds overlooking the turquoise gulf. She wanted to be buried next to her husband in Carthage. As I let myself out, I felt I had met a woman who had grown up in the snow of northern Europe only to realize herself fully on the African shore.

Before returning to Tunis, I went to explore the narrow alleys and steep cobbled streets of Sidi Bou Said. I eventually came to a café perched on a steep cliff and started to film. After about five minutes, three burly men in short-sleeved shirts with walkie-talkies suddenly descended on me and asked me what I thought I was doing.

'*Laisse-moi ton film!*' one of them ordered, using the familiar '*tu*' form. I replied with '*vous*' to maintain my distance.

'There's nothing of interest there, look!' I rewound some of the video tape and showed him the harmless images of the coast.

'*Arrête-toi là*,' he ordered again. '*Efface ce passage!*'

I fiddled about and erased a section of some children in the café. I then asked him what all the fuss was about.

'*Le Palais du Président.* You've been filming the president's palace. It's strictly prohibited.'

It must have one of the tiny villas which I could hardly see stretching out along the coast. In the end, they seemed impressed by my obvious innocence and after making a show of examining my papers and questioning my movements they finally let me go.

I thought it was deeply paranoid of the Tunisian state for secret police to jump on tourists like that, especially as tourism was one of the country's main sources of income. But then I remembered that the Palestine Liberation Front had their headquarters just outside Tunis. It had been badly damaged by an Israeli bombing in 1985. An Israeli hit squad had also tried to assassinate the PLO second-in-command at his home in Sidi Bou Said in retaliation for the Palestinian uprising in the Occupied Territories. Behind the beauty of Sidi Bou Said lurked some unpleasant ghosts.

I left Tunis on 14 August. The MV *Kelibia* gave a blast on its horn, the dockers threw off the thick mooring ropes and we slowly turned towards the Gulf of Tunis, gathering speed as we passed the ruins of Carthage. The last I saw of the African shore was a flock of swallows circling high in the sky over the white, cliff-top villas of Sidi Bou Said.

I wrote in my notebook:

> Go well, Africa.
>
> You have taught me many things
> since we have been together.
> You have taught me that rulers and soldiers
> are the scourge of the earth.
> You have taught me that generosity of spirit
> lies with the poorest of folk.
> You have taught me that the most oppressed people
> can forgive the cruellest of acts.

You have taught me that life is part of death
as the moon is to the night.
You have taught me that all religions are one
and the earth is sacred and whole.
You have taught me that the races of humanity
flow together like the oceans of the sea.
Africa, you have taught me many things
since we have been together.

Go well, until we meet again.

Nkosi Sikelél' iAfrika

Chapter Thirty-Six

Completing *the* Circle

Not long after our departure from Tunis, a small group of Tunisians in the stern of the MV *Kelibia* – named after a coastal town in their country – took out some drums and started playing. To the accompaniment of clapping and singing, a couple of plump women with long black hair began to dance, their hands held in the air, their feet stamping the deck. They were leaving home but determined to keep up their spirits. They were soon joined by a long-haired European with his drum.

It was a glorious day. There was not a cloud in the sky and the lovely breeze made me shiver with delight. I watched some small dark brown birds skimming across the waves, and thought of my seagull in Lisbon who had shown me how to travel independently, without ties, family and friends; how to be centred when all around was uncertain; how to become one with the elements. I mused that in a week I would be forty six, almost half a century. When I now saw children playing, I realized they were in another dimension of life. Most of my life was now behind me and I was ready for the last great voyage ahead.

I spent hours looking at the wake of the ship, the boiling, surging waters which slowly reformed into a smooth expanse towards the horizon. I liked the way a ship moved lightly across the sea and left no trace behind. I also loved the sea for itself, reflecting that in the beginning there was only water. We came from water and one day we might return to water. I sensed the *Chandogya Upanishad* was right when its ancient Hindu author declared: 'It is pure water solidified that is this earth, that is the atmosphere, that is the sky, that is gods and men, beasts and birds, grass and trees, animals together with worms, flies and ants. All these are just water solidified. Reverence water.' It was a view shared by the first Greek philosopher, Thales, and is confirmed by modern science.

I wondered whether my love of water was a result of having grown up by the sea, or of something much deeper, of some dim evolutionary memory of the time when our ancestors crawled out of the sea to live on land. The watercourse way reverberated with profound truth. I had become aware that everything in the universe is in flux and that we cannot put our foot in the same stream twice. And in the long run, the most effective action does not block the flow of energy but yields and adapts like water which wears away the hardest rock.

We arrived in Trapani at 21.00 hours under a full orange moon. After a couple of hours waiting to pass through the immigration officials who came on board, I went ashore and managed to find a room in an old hotel down a dimly lit side street called the Hotel Ruso Moderno. The next day I took a bus across the barren rocky hills of central Sicily to Palermo; I could see why generations had gone abroad to seek their fortune.

I found a small *pensione* near the railway station above a noisy road. In the maze of streets in the old quarter nearby I came across crumbling *palazzi* and closed baroque churches. Palermo had known better days. But the spirit of the people had not been crushed. A demonstration of women in the main square and a spate of posters plastered around the city showed that they were no longer prepared to put up with the grubby *homini d'onore* of the Mafia.

I went down to the docks to look for my ship, but the harbourmaster, the pilots' office and the seaman's mission had no knowledge of it coming. It was Sunday and no one cared. Then I looked out to sea and there sure enough at anchor outside the harbour was a blue ship with a white funnel: the *Ulf Ritscher*.

When I returned to the port the next day, the *Ulf Ritscher* was moored alongside the dock and unloading containers. I went on board and met the Captain Till Hülsbergen in his cabin. He was a handsome man in his forties, with blue eyes and curly brown hair flecked with grey. He had an intense and thoughtful manner. He took his job seriously and wanted everything to be done correctly.

On the bridge, I met the captain's nephew Jonas, a blond, blue-eyed, willowy twelve-year-old. He had come on a round voyage with his uncle during his summer holidays. As we left Palermo, his hand was on the steering lever and he directed the ship as his uncle issued orders from the bridge wing. The domes of the churches and *palazzi* glowed in the late afternoon sun as we left the crescent-shaped harbour and turned west along the rocky coast towards the golden sun. I was homeward bound on my last ship. It should have been a moment of joy but I felt strangely melancholy, uncertain about how I would take up my land-based life again.

There were several other passengers on board the *Ulf Ritscher*, all German. At dinner in the officers' mess, we all sat at a separate table: a middle-aged couple on a honeymoon of sorts, both tall and quiet; a white-haired, pink-faced, plump dentist who owned a factory making braces but whose real passion was making videos; and a large bald man in his eighties, with an anchor tattooed on his forearm. Only the captain and the dentist spoke English well, and my little German was rusty, so we got through the meals mainly by smiles and gestures.

The next day was beautiful – ideal Mediterranean sailing weather – calm seas and blue skies. After a turn around the ship after breakfast, I went to see the captain in his cabin. He was reading a biography of Freud. Unlike most seamen, he was an intellectual. Ater taking his master's certificate, he had left the sea to study social history for eight years at the Free University of Berlin. He had been unable to find a lecturer's job and returned reluctantly to sea, although his wife whom he had met at university continued to do research. They had no children.

'My wife calls herself an anarchist,' he told me, 'but I think anarchists have a problem with organization.'

'Anarchists aren't against organization,' I said, having an interest in the subject. 'They may be against government and the state, but they are confident that people can organize their own affairs.'

'Yes, I know; I've often discussed it with my wife! Have you ever thought that pirates were anarchists; your national hero Francis Drake operated as a law unto himself on the high seas!'

'Is it possible to make life on board more democratic?'

'It's difficult. A sailor is a kind of military man and there's still a strong hierarchy at sea. They work in an authoritarian tradition and are used to being told what to do. It's in the blood of old sailors – a kind of second nature – to see the captain like a god, even though you can become a captain at twenty-eight now.'

'I should imagine all that power must have an effect on you as well.'

'Yes. My wife complains that I am too self-sufficient and not used to co-operation! It's certainly a lonely life being a captain. There's a good description of it in Conrad's *Mirror of the Sea*.'

'But things must have changed since Conrad's time?'

'Even in my own life, things have changed. When I was young the captain had his own space on the starboard side of the bridge; no one would dare go there out of respect. He would come at noon to check the chart and say "very good" and disappear again. He could even disappear for a week in his cabin and no one would say anything. But now the captain has to work as hard as the other officers. On this ship, apart from ultimate responsibility, I have to take a watch, do the work of the radio officer and a lot of paper work. Although much of the navigation is now automated, there's more work to do for fewer officers.'

'What are your main priorities?'

'First, the people on board; second, the ship; third; the owners; fourth, the charterers. In that order.'

Later in the morning, there was a demonstration of fire-fighting equipment with the officers and crew. In the discussion that followed, the captain and the chief engineer openly clashed about their respective responsibilities. In fighting a fire in the engine room, the captain suggested that the chief engineer should be prepared to make his own decisions since he had special knowledge of the situation. The chief engineer, raised in Communist East Germany, refused to accept personal responsibility; he saw himself as a cog in the machine and would make no decision of his own. It was an age-old argument about democracy.

On 19 August at 11.30 hours, we passed the Greenwich Meridian – 0° longitude – off Oran in Algeria. I read in the *Tao te ching* some verses about travelling: 'Be as careful at the end as at the beginning/ And there will be no ruined enterprises'. I thought about it as I paced the decks. I had started the voyage badly, having left my home in disarray and not being mentally prepared. I was determined to be more skilful on my return. It would take some time for all the members of the family to get used to each other after seven months' separation, separation which had changed us all.

On the following day, at 6.30 hours, we passed the Pillars of Hercules and through the Strait of Gibraltar. I saw the lighthouse at Europa Point on the edge of the looming rock of Gibraltar, the most southerly point of the Iberian peninsula. On the other side of the narrow strait, I could make out in the pre-dawn light the dark outlines of the mountains of Africa. As we passed from the Mediterranean Sea to the Atlantic Ocean, it felt noticeably colder, and for the first time since the highlands of East Africa I had to wear a pullover. The rising sun turned the sky purple as we rounded the rock of Gibraltar and entered the Spanish port of Algeciras on the other side of the bay.

At breakfast I asked Herr Kube, the old man with the tattoo, whether he was going ashore. 'Legs *kaput*,' he replied. 'Always the same in port – cars, houses, people!'

We sat next to each other at table and often had coffee in the morning and tea in the afternoon together. I liked being with him although we said very little. He lived in an old people's home in Germany. At eighty-two, he told me, this was his last voyage.

After breakfast we stood looking at a photograph on the wall of the officers' mess of the passenger ship SS *Bremen* being fitted out in the Hamburg docks before the war, the largest of its kind. Herr Kube observed:

'At that time, unemployment, no ships. Then Hitler, work, ships. Ah, but the war . . .'

'But now Germany and Britain are friends,' I said.

'I hope so,' he replied, but he did not sound very sure. He had lived through two world wars and had seen the darkest side of human nature.

Algeciras was very much a frontier town, the gateway to Europe for Africans and to Africa for Europeans. Down by the waterfront, there were many agencies selling tickets on the ferries to Ceuta just over the other side of the strait. Only a few backpackers were around that early in the morning. The faces of the local inhabitants reflected their past Moorish links. Several posters calling for a general strike and '*Por la tierra, el trabajo y la libertad*' (For land, work and freedom) showed that the economic miracle since the fall of Franco had not reached all quarters of Spanish society.

I went to the station hidden behind a hotel and caught a bus to Gibraltar which was about ten miles away on the other side of the bay. The rock dominated life in a wide circle on the mainland, with about 5,000 Spanish workers making the trip daily across the narrow causeway. Although it was one of the last outposts of the British Empire, there were only about 2,000 British people living there, along with about 25,000 Spanish-speaking Gibraltarians descended from Spanish, British, Maltese, Genoese, Portuguese, Jews and Moors.

I had no trouble entering Spain at Algeciras, but the Spanish customs and immigration officials were holding up cars at the Gibraltar frontier, a reminder that the continued British occupation of the rock was opposed by the Spanish government. Although the limestone rock itself was only three miles by half a mile, it had great strategic value at the entrance to the Mediterranean. It also had vast caves and subterranean tunnels which made it a natural fortress.

Once over the frontier, I took a taxi and asked the driver to take me on a tour. I stopped off near the lighthouse at Europa Point which I had seen earlier in the morning from the *Ulf Ritscher*. The wind had picked up a little and there were several ships passing in different directions through the choppy strait. The blue rocky mountains of Africa were now clearly visible. Five million years ago the two mainlands were connected, but a fissure had turned into a gulley and the waters of the Atlantic had gushed into the Mediterranean basin. Here Europe confronted Africa, and Africa, Europe, two continents drifting further apart, despite their common past.

We left Algeciras at 18.00 hours with Jonas at the helm, lying back in the spacious seat, sun glasses on, his feet up on the instrument panel. His uncle double-checked his every move and only gave his young nephew the illusion of being in control of such a vast ship. It was good seeing children and women travelling on cargo ships, although this privilege was only limited to the officer class.

We sailed due west towards the setting sun which cast a purple hue over the choppy sea. When the ancient Greeks and Romans passed through the Pillars of Hercules, they were leaving the the edge of the known world. For me, it was the opposite; I was sailing back into familiar waters. We steamed close to the Spanish coast, port to port with the traffic moving in the opposite direction, and soon passed Tarifa Point where the strong currents of the Mediterranean Sea and the Atlantic Ocean met in a cold and swirling embrace. In the fading light, my last glimpse of Africa was of rugged mountains merging with a dark purple sky and sea. The sun set soon after and a sudden wind chilled my bones; I thought of the cold, wet northern winter ahead.

The next day, 20 August, the sun rose at eight o'clock. I was already up on deck to see its golden rays shine behind the steep cliffs of Cape St Vincent and Sagres about two miles away, the Land's End of Europe. There was a slight swell and only a few clouds in the sky. I had stood on the cliffs of Sagres six and a half months ago. Passing the Cape meant that I had completed my circumnavigation of Africa. I had often wondered, particularly in the early part of the voyage, whether I would ever make it back, but now that I had it came as something of an anti-climax. I had with my own body and mind drawn a circle around Africa, but it still escaped me and I was content that it should be so. No one could confine the energy and variety of that great continent.

After so much time on my own (even with the film crew who had joined me for a total of six weeks I felt on my own) I had developed a degree of self-reliance and self-sufficiency. I had also confronted the prospect of my own death and accepted with a calm mind the fact that it would come sooner or later. I felt not just a member of a family but part of a wider community which embraced the past and the present. Like ripples from a stone dropped in a pool, my community stretched in ever-widening circles from my village, region, country, species, planet, to encompass the entire universe. In occasional moments of heightened awareness, I felt at home in the universe, at the centre and circumference of things.

Later in the morning, I went to see the second officer on watch on the bridge, Ralf Gerdes, a tall fit man in his twenties who would no doubt become one of the new breed of young captains. We got out a chart of Africa and with a pair of compasses and calculator worked out the number of miles I had covered in my circumnavigation. Walking the compasses down from one port of call to another, we came up with the figure of 5,590 nautical miles from Lisbon to Cape Town, excluding the distance by air from Agadir to Las Palmas and including the doubling back from Port Gentil to Douala. From Cape Town to Port Said, we calculated 6,190 nautical miles, including the extra journeys I did from Durban to Maputo and back and from Mombasa to Dar es Salaam.

When all these miles were added to those from Alexandria to Lisbon, we arrived at a total figure of 14,410 nautical miles. Then there was the additional 1,036 nautical miles from Lisbon to Felixstowe to come. In all, I would have travelled by sea in twenty-nine weeks over 15,446 nautical miles, that is to say, 17,7623 statute miles.

We did not call in at Lisbon, where I started my voyage, but at Leixões to the north, the port for Oporto, Portugal's second city. We arrived at 01.00 hours and had to pass through a dock to the container terminal because of the different levels of water. After breakfast, I caught a bus into town. Oporto was a beautiful city which had spread from the banks of the river Douro up the surrounding hills. The main city centre was on the northern bank, with many fine old stone buildings; on the southern side, the port lodges spread along the bank which gave the town its name.

I went in search of the birthplace of Prince Henry the Navigator, in a side street leading down to the old wharfs. Having started from the cliffs of Sagres where Henry spent his last days, it seemed apt at the end of my voyage to visit the place where he began his life.

'Cheers,' I said to myself, raising a fine dry white glass of port, as I sat on the river bank. 'It's taken a long time, but you've made it!'

Perhaps that was my hubris, pride before a fall. The captain had told me that the ship was leaving at five o'clock. On my return from Oporto I asked the bus driver to drop me off at the dock gate, but he hurtled past and would not stop until we had reached a highway two miles away. I could see the *Ulf Rischer* in the distance, still moored, but it was now almost five o'clock.

371

I went as fast as I could, carrying three bottles of port and my bulky camera bag, scrambling down embankments and running across waste plots to reach the entrance of the dock through which I had passed in the morning.

It was closed. In the distance I heard a blast from the ship's horn. I shouted and waved frantically at a policeman on the other side of the fence but he refused to budge, no doubt taking me for a madman or a drunk. The ship was only a few hundred yards away but there was no way I could clamber over the high fence topped with barbed wire. I started to run for the next entrance along the perimeter, about half a mile away. By the time I reached it, my shirt was sticking to me and sweat dripping from my nose. Another blast on the ship's horn. I thought I was done for when suddenly a car skidded to a halt in front of me. The Portuguese driver said:

'Are you Peter Marshall?'

'Yes. Why?'

'I'm the agent. The *Ulf Rischer* is leaving now. Jump in.'

We sped across the dock, narrowly missing the corner of a container and a bollard, and screeched to a halt at the bottom of the gangway. Dockers were already loosening the mooring ropes. I ran up the gangway where several crew members were gathered.

The bosun said smiling: 'We should have left two hours ago. We finished the containers early.'

I went up on to the bridge and the captain declared: 'You've only just made it. We were discussing what to do with your luggage. We're not British Rail you know!'

'But I thought German ships left on time. That's why I'm back at five!'

'Okey do!'

We left at 17.00 hours – sharp.

Chapter Thirty-Seven

Fare Well Africa

D URING the last leg of my voyage on the *Ulf Ritscher* from Portugal to England, I had ample time to try to make sense of my experiences in Africa. Africa was in trouble, there was no doubt about it, but what could be done? What could I do? To begin with, I felt it essential to understand the causes of the mess before considering possible ways out. With this in mind, I wrote down some ideas which had become clearer during my travels.

Africans have a point when they say that the present troubles – political dictatorship, economic decline, civil war and ecological disaster – are largely a result of years of colonialism. The myth of Africa as a savage, dark continent in which life is nasty, brutish and short, was a myth perpetrated by the early colonialists and explorers in order to justify their rule. In fact, pre-colonial societies were for the most part stable, democratic and self-governing, held together by traditions, customs and rituals. The communities were fully sustainable, with violence being contained and conflicts kept to a small scale.

What outsiders considered mumbo jumbo – mere superstition and witchcraft – was usually quite reasonable within the local culture, the result of a long process of trial and error in finding an acceptable balance with nature. Religions provided supernatural sanctions for codes of acceptable behaviour, rewarding those who promoted cohesion in the community and punishing those who upset it. Myths were based on long social experience of a people surviving in their particular environments.

In a world where slender resources had to be shared, it was wrong to take more than a fair share. In the case of wild bees' nests, it was good to find one, better still to find two, but to continue to search and discover three was the work of witchcraft which the powers of good would find a way of punishing. In the same way, justice was not based on revenge – an eye for an eye – but on restoring social harmony. If someone was killed, the main issue was to replace the lost person, not kill the killer.

There were of course many different forms of organization in pre-colonial societies, ranging from anarchies without rulers, to societies with chiefs and kings. But in all communities there was a strong awareness that power corrupts and that rulers by their nature tend to become oppressive. To counter this tendency, different checks and balances were institutionalized and executive power was widely distributed. There was always a high level of popular participation in decision making. Chiefs were accountable and could be removed if they did not meet the needs of their peoples.

It was the slave trade which disrupted these traditions and gave guns and opportunities to chiefs to usurp power for themselves and wage war on their neighbours. The impact of colonialism was even more devastating. In order to govern their subject peoples, colonial governments encouraged the formation of 'tribes' from different ethnic groups in order to 'divide and rule' – a process which culminated in the apartheid system in South Africa. They also adopted a policy of 'indirect rule' by promoting and appointing chiefs who were accountable to them and not to their people.

The colonialists' mission of spreading the three C's – Civilization, Christianity and Commerce – led to the systematic undermining of the inherited values of African societies. Africans were not only dispossessed from their land but alienated from their own history and culture. They were considered, in Kipling's words, to be 'Your new-caught, sullen peoples,/ Half devil and half child'. They were 'lesser breeds' who needed the white man's law. To become civilized was to retreat from the savage forest of their own selves and to take on the language, clothes and mental world of the invader.

When the colonial powers realized after the Second World War that they

374

would be unable to check the growing aspirations for self-determination, they hastily engaged in a rearguard action of 'nation building', hoping to create a centralized and rigid nation-state on their own model out of the disintegrating colony. Who cared that the frontiers of the new states did not reflect natural regions or human cultures but had been shaped by conquest and compromise between the colonial powers? Bound with bands of steel, locked in copper-bottom constitutions, the random slices of scrub, desert and forest covered with a patchwork of tribes would serve.

In the scramble out of Africa, enough 'modernizers' were found to take over the newly created nation states, although there were not enough trained civil servants, engineers, teachers or doctors to go round. That did not matter. In the heady days of independence, the newly enfranchised people, long reduced to silence, subjection and toil, imagined that land, health, education and opportunity would soon be available for all. There were great hopes that one day Africa would be able to catch up with the old colonial powers.

It was not to be. To change the master is not to be free. The new masters took over the state and used it to promote themselves and their own. Although regrettable, it was hardly surprising: colonial government had been by rigid and centralized dictatorship and its bureaucracy hierarchical and authoritarian. The hastily imposed governments were rapidly replaced by military dictatorship or one-party rule. Where multi-parties remained they became riddled with 'tribalism', that is, a system of patronage in which politicians distributed favours to win the support of local leaders of the same ethnic group.

The nation state, the principal means of liberation, has not brought about an open society with equal opportunity in Africa but a closed and crumbling fortress. It does not provide welfare or protection but has become an alien parasite sucking the blood of the people who struggle to survive within its claws. Like a mad elephant crashing through the bush, it sweeps up the available resources, devours foreign aid, destroys its habitat, and finally deposits most of what it consumes in a steaming pile behind it – without leaving any seeds to germinate amongst the destruction. Inherited from the white man, it has become the black man's greatest burden.

I have seen the disastrous results of this process at first hand throughout my voyage. Like toads swallowing jewels, Presidents have blown up into monstrous proportions. Pirates have seized power in the overloaded and leaking ships of state. Bandits called soldiers and police armed with magical AK-47s roam the land, unchecked by law or morality, intoxicated with their instant, new-found power.

The new élites have given priority to the cities where they live while extracting the maximum surplus from the increasingly impoverished countryside. Farmers, alienated from the state, have no wish to produce cash crops when there is nothing to buy with the cash and return to a subsistence economy. Women continue to suffer from a system of discrimination more entrenched than apartheid which condemns them to do the most work and to have the least power. Youth from the countryside flock to the towns where they think the action and jobs are to be found. The 'illegal' or 'parallel' economy has become the only way to survive for the majority of citizens, half of whom are officially unemployed. The gap between rich and poor, town and country, has been steadily growing. In all the major cities of Africa, I have seen oases of private luxury in a desert of poverty, squalor and disease.

With their economies largely geared to producing primary products for their former colonial masters, it comes as no surprise to learn that the attempts of African countries to diversify and industrialize have been largely ineffective. They have been unable to compete with the industrialized nations. Income from their exports of staple commodities have collapsed on world markets. In terms of trade, Africa has remained a net loser; with dwindling production, it has to pay more to Western governments and banks than it receives back in aid and loans. To borrow more would be like a haemophiliac applying leeches to bring about a cure.

But while colonialism has left a devastating legacy in Africa, it is too easy for African rulers to continue to blame the colonialists for all their ills. Most countries in Africa have been independent for over thirty years. Africans themselves have to take responsibility for their own actions. Only if they can draw on their rich and creative past will they be able to shape a better future; only if their imagination is freed from a colonial mentality will the dream of freedom become genuine self-determination.

In the long run, the collapse of the nation state in Africa might well prove a blessing in disguise. The existing imported models – one-party states and multi-party states – have both failed abysmally. Foreign political solutions and values have simply not taken root on the continent. This realization might herald a revival of pre-colonial democratic traditions of popular participation and mutual aid.

The only lasting solution to the present morass in Africa is a radical devolution of power. This can best be achieved through the twin principles of decentralization and federalism. The basic cell of society was and could be again the local neighbourhood or village assembly. They could then federate at the district and regional level in a society organized from the bottom up. Delegates would at all times be accountable and recallable.

All men and women would then be able to participate in the key decisions which affect their lives and shape their own destinies. The arbitrary frontiers left by the colonialists could be redrawn voluntarily on more organic lines, taking into account natural and cultural boundaries.

In this way, tribalism might become a force for good, developing its positive aspects of solidarity, collective responsibility, and self-help. In a few places in Africa, in Eritrea, Uganda, Ghana, Cap Verde Islands – even Nigeria and possibly South Africa – a move towards federalism and decentralization has tentatively begun. If it continues, a map of Africa in the twenty-first century might resemble a tribal map of old, containing hundreds of societies, not just fifty strait-jackets called nation states.

In the meantime, the first priority for Africa is to feed itself, to ensure that food production keeps pace with the growth of the population. The population of Africa stands at some 450 million and has tripled since the last century. Its growth rate at more than three per cent is the highest in the world. At the same time, one in five Africans lives on imported food, and the continent is less able to feed itself than a decade ago.

But the problem is not simply a question of too many people. Africa is still relatively underpopulated compared to other continents. Its regular famines are largely the result of civil wars and man-made ecological disasters. The so-called 'population crisis' is as much a crisis of underproduction and uneven distribution of food as of excessive numbers. Malthus's nightmare of war, famine, disease and vice as the only checks to population growth is not the only scenario. As in the West, if a decent living is assured and survival does not depend on family ties alone, the population of Africa will stabilize as it has done in the past.

Its soils are mostly poor, but Africa could grow enough food for two or three times its present population. There is undoubtedly a problem with the overgrazing of cattle in Central Africa and with the cutting down of tropical forests in West and East Africa for fuel and land, but if farmers can keep off fragile rangeland they should be able to find their own balance. African farmers are no fools and know from their own experience that traditional methods are often more effective than imported wizardry; minimum tillage and intercropping in fragile soils are not backward but ecologically sound.

Africans, not outside experts, know their own countries best. It is Africans who developed the irrigation systems which provided the surplus to build the pyramids, who lived lightly in the deserts of North and South Africa, who merged with the rainforests of Central Africa. They know how to build with local materials, use little energy, and care for the immediate environment. They had been doing it for thousands of years before the colonialists arrived; they can do it again after their departure.

Some commentators have been calling for a 'Marshall Plan' for Africa similar to the one implemented by the United States after the war to kickstart Europe into economic growth. But I offer no plan or blue print of my own. To do so would be to continue the old colonial mentality that implies that the West knows best for the wayward Africans who are so lazy and destructive.

After thinking long and hard about the issue, I believe that Africans should be left to themselves to sort out their own conflicts and problems. If they want to have huge families in Kenya while food production declines, then they must take the consequences of their actions. If warlords want to slaughter each other in Somalia, a country united by language, race and culture, then it is up to their own people to stop them. Why should the United Nations or the United States act as policemen in lands they do not care about or understand, pouring oil on the fires of hatred?

In my view, there are three things, mainly negative, which the outside world can do to help Africa recover from its mess. The first is to cancel all debts – now running in excess of $174 billion. The money loaned lavishly by the World Bank, International Monetary Fund and other Western banks and governments can never be repaid. The payment of the interest alone is in many cases greater than the country's income. Africa is spending more servicing its debt than on its total budget for health and education.

One condition for cancelling the debt should be for governments and rulers to open their books in order to reveal how the funds were used and by whom. But I am realistic enough to realize that this will be opposed as it would show corruption on a grand scale in presidential offices and central banks.

Ideally, the north should be willing to improve the terms of trade with the south. Since independence the industrialized countries have continued the colonial policy of buying raw materials and primary products cheap and selling manufactured and consumer goods dear. The result has been that a third of the world in the north has become richer, while two thirds in the south has become poorer. Since an appeal to good will seems unlikely to reverse this trend, the countries of Africa should form cartels to increase the price of their products. At the same time, they should with other countries on the peripheries of the world market gradually disconnect themselves from the centre in the north and trade between themselves.

The model of development of the industrialized countries – whether capitalist or socialist – is inappropriate in Africa since it assumes expanding markets and resources which no longer exist. There can be no such thing as 'catching up' for Africa, either through the kind of centralized state ownership and command economy tried in Egypt and Algeria, or the *laissez-faire* economies of Kenya and Ivory Coast. Africa cannot expect the high living standards of the north because they are based on the exploitation and impoverishment of the south. Above all, there are simply not enough resources in the world to go around. Africa should therefore aim at self-sufficiency and self-reliance as far as possible, within a context of regional co-operation. This process need not be seen as 'slipping back' but advancing towards a sustainable economy based on local materials, geared to local needs, and embedded in the local environment.

The second thing outsiders can do for Africa is to end all aid. In the past, it has only supported dictatorial governments, entrenched corruption and encouraged uneven development. It feathers the nest of the urban élites and enables politicians to enhance their power and wealth by using aid as a political weapon. Western aid experts develop strategies which assume that wealth trickles down to the poor; in reality, it is invariably sucked up by the rich and powerful. Giving more aid only makes things worse: Tanzania with an official policy of self-reliance has received the highest amount of aid in Africa, and yet has grown relentlessly poorer.

The only exception to the ending of aid for Africa might be the kind of aid provided by voluntary organizations at the village level, but even this continues the myth that the foreign expert knows best. Like all aid, it checks local initiatives and solutions, self-help and self-reliance and encourages a dependent mentality.

The third thing the outside world can do to help Africa is to impose a strict arms embargo. Before the arrival of the slave traders and the colonialists violence in communities was contained. When competing clans or tribes fought each other with bows and arrows only a few died. When they shoot it out with tanks and automatic weapons many more get in the way. When elephants fight, it is the grass that suffers.

Africa is awash with arms and ammunition as a result of the Cold War during which it became a battleground for superpower rivalry. Vast amounts of money were borrowed by dictators to buy their deadly toys and the arms sellers in the West and the East scrambled over each other to oblige. Revolutionary Africa has collapsed into civil wars which are more tribal than anything else. With the social fabric torn apart, the old moralities destroyed, gangs of armed youths answerable to no one but their warlords have been on the rampage in the Congo, Uganda and now in Somalia and Liberia. Having won independence, different factions in Angola and Mozambique continued to destroy each other. Today the greatest scourge of Africa are the rulers and their military forces. No other continent, except perhaps Latin America, has demonstrated so horribly the truths that violence breeds violence and that power corrupts. And in modern Africa power grows invariably out of the barrel of a gun.

Without Western help, you might say, Africa will grind to a halt. The great cities built with Western technology and maintained by foreign experts would collapse. I say, if the people who live in them cannot look after them, why keep them artificially alive to suck the blood of the countryside? Let the rulers pack up their bags and leave and the people return to the quiet and simple life. You say, that would mean returning to a subsistence economy. I say it is better to see the sun set over the savannah than to choke in a traffic jam, to subsist in a village than to die in a gutter.

All this might sound arrogant coming from a European, yet more advice from another would-be expert. But the essence of what I am saying is: 'Hands off Africa. Let Africa sort out its own problems and find its own solutions in its own way'.

I have repeatedly heard the argument during my travels that Africa is not ready for democracy and that Africans only work if they are told to do so. The apparent dislike of work is certainly true when it comes to forced labour and the prospect of endless toil with little reward. Yet businessmen, smugglers, street sellers, farmers and women in Africa have no trouble getting down to work when it is in their interest. It is not work that Africans avoid, but like all other people, meaningless toil.

Another favourite argument, still heard amongst South African whites, is that Africans are not educated enough to be free. But democracy had deep roots in Africa before the arrival of the slavers and colonizers, and Africans have had long experience of organizing themselves in democratic, stable and sustainable societies. Above all, one cannot be educated for freedom; the experience of freedom is an education in itself. People only become responsible for their actions by being free to make mistakes.

After my travels around Africa, I have come to realize that the 'Dark Continent' of the nineteenth-century European explorers and missionaries was only dark because they were blind to the light shining forth from the heart of Africa. The forest is not dark to the pygmies, but a sacred, life-giving presence. The savannah is not a savage wilderness to the pastoralists but their home where they live lightly and their cattle roam amongst the wild animals. Traditionally, Africans believe that the land does not belong to them but that they belong to the land along with others animals and plants. There is no gap between the life of humans and the life of all growing beings; they are all part of nature's bespangled web. And nature itself is a living organism animated by spirit: the earth, the sea, the sky, trees and rocks. They revere it and are thankful for its abundance and fertility. They pray to nature and wish it no harm. They leave the third wild bees' nest alone.

Africa has a great past and enormous potential for the future. Since the arrival of Vasco da Gama, things have not gone well for the continent but the worst is probably over. By its movement of peoples, it has become a melting pot, the meeting place of three continents – Africa, Europe and Asia. It has long experience of tolerating ethnic and cultural differences and being enriched by diversity. Africa can teach us the value of community, community in which the individual is part of wider society and nature itself. It can teach spontaneous generosity, generosity which does not calculate or expect anything in return. It can teach forgiveness, forgiveness of those who have done great wrongs and know no better. Africa, where humanity first emerged, where civilization first developed, where the wilderness last remains, can teach those values which may still save humanity from their headlong rush to global madness and destruction. Light shines from the heart of Africa and can illuminate the darkness of the modern world.

Chapter Thirty-Eight

Rolling Home

AFTER leaving Portugal, we had some rough weather. As we entered the Bay of Biscay the wind increased to a force 7 and the *Ulf Ritscher* began to roll and pitch in the long north-westerly swell.

I went up to the prow of the ship after breakfast and stood for a long time looking at the horizon of the heaving sea, the white caps breaking on the long swell. Although it was rough, the skies were a light blue and it promised to be a warm summer day.

It was 23 August, my forty-sixth birthday. In the mess, the officers came up to me and shook my hand firmly, saying 'Happy Birthday'. They looked at me straight in the eyes; they wanted to make the only Englishman on board feel at home on their German ship.

My best birthday present was sitting after all the others had left with Herr Kube. The anchor tattoo on his forearm had faded in the loose skin but not his appetite. He loved tucking into the fresh rolls, plum jam and piping hot coffee for breakfast. I liked watching him. At eighty-two, his spirit still soared like a seagull.

Before pulling his big frame up the gangways and back to his cabin, Herr Kube said with a chuckle:

'There is a song, Rolling Home!'

Then he added, as if it were an afterthought:

'Happy Birthday, Herr Peter. You are a young man!'

Young? I was forty-six, nearly half a century on the earth. I observed that forty-six was twice twenty-three; add another twenty-three and I would be reaching three score years and ten. I had always considered it lucky to reach this biblical age. If that were to be my allotted time, I still had a third of my life left, twenty-four summers. My voyage had helped me come to terms with the rhythm of life, with ageing, but it had also thrown me more into life, helping me to appreciate the here and now. I did not want to live in the distorting prism of the past or the mirage of a mythical future. Life itself is a voyage, a voyage from nowhere to nowhere, and I had a choice at every moment to be depressed or exhilarated on the way.

I looked forward to becoming an old man, living a simple life with good neighbours and friends in peaceful and creative ways. I had set out on my voyage wanting to return a fitter, wiser and better man. I felt fitter; it was for others to judge whether I was wiser. I would try to be kinder, more forgiving and open. I would remind myself that I belong to the earth, the earth does not belong to me.

I would not try to possess my children. I never wanted to say to them: 'I am a man of experience', or 'I told you so'. They had to learn their own way. If I had accumulated some wisdom over the years, let them help themselves if they wanted to, like water overflowing from a mountain spring. I would not force it on them. I would try to be like a lighthouse, warning of dangerous reefs and rocks of life; it would be up to them what course they chose to steer.

My voyage around Africa had not only involved the discovery of a continent but also had been a voyage of self-discovery. It had undoubtedly been a watershed in my life. I had not realized before how vulnerable I could feel without family, home and country, but on the way I also discovered new reserves of strength. If I had destroyed anything, it was my old restless, egoistic self as I reached out to embrace the larger Self of all beings.

But how long would this new understanding last? I wrote in my notebook on the evening of my forty-sixth birthday.

'Achieve the task but take no merit. Belong to the earth and make no claim. Set free the beings and things called possessions. Seize the day and live in the present. Roll gently home, and dance to the rhythm of the sea. Remember that being at home is to feel at home anywhere in the universe.'

* * *

It took twenty-four hours to cross the Bay of Biscay. It was very rough. During the night all the things on my desk and several drawers crashed to the floor of my cabin. The captain's nephew was very sick and remained in his cabin the next day.

As we entered the English Channel it became noticeably calmer and the rolling decreased. I looked out my porthole to see grey skies, grey sea, grey mist. The clear, bright light of the Mediterranean was far away, but I liked sailing home in the swirling mist: betwixt and between suited my mood.

Off Torbay at 13.00 hours, I rang my mother on the ship's telephone via Peter's Port in Guernsey. She couldn't believe that I was only a few miles away, passing by unseen on the sea. We were both pleased that we had got through the last seven months without too many mishaps and would be seeing each other again soon.

At 22.00 hours we passed Bognor Regis on the Sussex coast where I came into the world and grew up. It was there that I had first developed a love of the sea. But I had joined the Merchant Navy at eighteen to escape the stifling and petty conventions of the town and to go round the world. For most of my life I had despised imperial England and what it stood for: its narrow-minded smugness, its careful accounting, its monarchy and class system, its ruthless military might disguised behind a smoke screen of fair play and decency, its sense of national and racial superiority – all insular, inward-looking, in a word, English. I had never felt English until a man in the Gambia had asked for sixpence and then said 'Fuck off, English!' But I later learned in Wales that not being aware of one's nationality is peculiarly English.

Sailing up the Channel, it felt good to be close to where I had swum as a boy. I was looking forward to seeing the sun rise over England, the England where I felt completely at home, understood all the undertows of meaning and nuances of language. I had been so close to England that I had wanted to get away. I liked living in the mountains of Wales precisely because I was on the edge, half way between heaven and earth, part of society and yet separate from it. I would always be an outsider.

Jonas, the captain's nephew, was at breakfast the next day, feeling much better. At ten o'clock, I heard the BBC home news for the first time: a

Texan financier had been photographed kissing the foot of a topless duchess; a hurricane was heading for Miami; England and Pakistan were having a day match at Old Trafford; the pound had recovered a little after yesterday's fall. I might not have been away! That was depressing. The grey drizzle in the Channel seemed to represent the grey drizzle of the English mind. I was returning to a land not of hope, but of slow decline, unemployment and quiet despair.

As we were sailing passed the white cliffs of Dover, still lost in fog, the captain confessed to me: 'It's a very lonely life at sea. It's become a closed society. Before, the men used to leave the doors of their cabins open after work; now, with TV and videos, the cabin doors are closed and they keep to themselves. A seaman has to be very self-reliant. It okay when you're young, but not when you reach my age.'

'Do you still like the sea?'

'Yes. I don't know why, but it fascinates me. Even on leave, I go down to the sea. It's not just the work, but the sea itself.'

I knew exactly what he meant and my voyage had only increased my fascination. But whenever I tried to grasp the essence of the sea, it slithered away. It can never be encapsulated; it always passes through the net of definition. Perhaps I was fascinated by the sea precisely because it is inconceivable, beyond the grasp of the human mind. Perhaps too because it represents the Other from which we come and to which we may one day return. It is certainly an archetype of wilderness, a place where man is not, a place which escapes his control, quite indifferent to his purposes. And then I thought it to be a symbol of eternity, always changing yet always the same. To dissolve into the sea like a grain of salt is to become absorbed into the whole. Perhaps that was why I had often felt the urge to jump overboard during my voyage and to let go, to breathe in the cool waters and to drift down into the fullness of being.

I knew I would miss the endless horizons, the vast expanses of sky and sea, the sense of air and space, the constant movement, the excitement of danger, the worry of survival, the pleasure of the unexpected. But what would it be like when I returned home? After his travels, Gulliver preferred the company of horses to that of his family; would I spend the rest of the days down on the shore with the seagulls?

At our last meeting for afternoon tea in the empty officers' mess, I asked Herr Kube whether he was returning to his family.

'I am alone. I have no childs. My wife died seven years ago.'

'You must still have some family.'

'I have many nieces and nephews but they live far away and do not visit.'

'At eighty-two, you are still a young man!'

'No, I am an old man. This is my last voyage. I will not go to sea again. Legs *kaput*.'

Herr Kube had brought a dictionary with him. He had pointed out at breakfast the words *Verwöhn dich* on the label of his beloved pot of plum jam. He looked up the words in his little German–English dictionary. Raising his old brown head, he beamed in triumph: '*Verwöhn dich*! Spoil yourself! *Verwöhn dich*! Enjoy yourself!'

The night before we arrived in Felixstowe, I wrote in my notebook:

> In things I know best, I am most content.
>
> My daughter's thumb held in a clenched fist,
> My son's strong left arm,
> Their mother's gentle brown eyes,
> The rain lashing on the window panes,
> Hard-boiled eggs on a Sunday morning,
> Grapefruit on holy days.
>
> Galloping with my daughter
> Across the salt marsh flats,
> Releasing a sheep from the brambles,
> Watching quietly for the kingfisher,
> Sharing sandwiches by a dyke,
> Horses steaming at our side.
>
> Climbing a mountain with my brother
> In scudding clouds and biting wind,
> Wet boots and aching limbs,

Scones and strawberry jam and tea
In a climbers' hotel
By a roaring fire.

Getting up with the sun,
Dew on the grass and bracken,
Sailbag over my shoulder,
Hand in warm hand with my son,
Going for an early morning sail
And a second breakfast.

Lying in my bunk in the Bay of Biscay,
Rolling home on a white-capped sea,
Feeling good about being incomplete,
A book, a poem, a vegetable patch,
A painting, a walk, a friendship,
A person, a life.

In things I know best, I am most content.

The following morning the fog lifted, but it was a cold, windy and wet summer's day. At breakfast, our last together, Herr Kube said:

'You are home. British weather!'

When I got up, he shook my hand firmly. Had it killed other Englishmen as my father's had killed Germans? It would be his last voyage; perhaps it would be mine. His last words were: '*Verwöhn dich!*'

Having packed my bags, I went up to the bridge to see the captain bring the *Ulf Ritscher* through the choppy grey-green waters of the North Sea into Felixstowe, the largest container port in Britain, set in the flat, featureless plains of East Anglia. To save money, his company had asked him to be his own pilot and the authorities of the privately owned port agreed. We went alongside below the giant gantries without a bump.

The agent, a young, cheerful man, came on board immediately and was surprised to find an English passenger the ship. I said goodbye to the captain, the officers, the passengers, and the rest of the crew. Jonas accompanied me down to the bottom of the gangway with my luggage. I had been away for

201 days and he was the only person to see me step on English soil again. He waved goodbye from the top of the gangway, a tiny figure below the great bridge and funnel of the *Ulf Ritscher*.

The agent took me to the immigration office where a girl looked briefly at my passport, leafing through the African visas, and said 'no problem'. How many times had I heard that when it meant the very opposite in recent months! The agent then dropped me off at the local railway station. A poster was advertising a course at a university: 'Come to terms with stress, fatigue, and catastrophic failure'. It could not teach me anything now.

Waiting for the train, I bought some apples, the first English apples of the season. They were delicious – crisp and juicy. I was still swaying from the rough weather in the Bay of Biscay and the Channel and felt distinctly unreal. It was strange to hear everyone speaking English all around me, with such familiar tones and expressions. The sun began to break through the clouds.

The smell of the British Rail train hit me with its acrid familiarity. At Ipswich, it was announced that the London train would be delayed for half an hour: 'British Rail apologize for any inconvenience'. I was in no hurry and had learned how to wait. I was strolling along the platform, enjoying the warm sun, when a member of staff came up and said 'You must not leave your luggage unattended, sir.' There were terrorists around. I had forgotten.

When we moved off I opened the windows and let in the soft and balmy air. I was struck how green everything looked as we trundled passed the hedgerows, fields and copses of East Anglia. It was high summer and some farmers were gathering in hay. There were neat gardens with roses and green runner beans with red flowers. Here there was no drought, no famine, no dictatorship. I had completed my circumnavigation and I was back in England!

Arriving in London was not pleasant, with its noise, grime, and commerce. I caught a cab to the embankment where I got out and walked alongside the grey, oily Thames to Cleopatra's Needle. I had seen Queen Hatshepsut's obelisk in Luxor under the deep blue sky still in perfect condition, the deep hieroglyphs no different from when they had first been carved. Cleopatra's Needle, its sister, was like a rotten tooth, worn away by London fog and acid rain. England had done in a hundred years what Africa had failed to do in five thousand.

I had a very good homecoming in Wales, with a party for all my friends and neighbours. The house was as beautiful as I remembered it, with its back to the mountains, looking out to the sea. The kitchen garden was in good shape and the cherry tree planted in the spring had survived. Some of the governor's beans from South Africa took root.

But once the novelty of being home had worn off, I found it very difficult to settle down to a steady routine: taking my son to school across the fields, writing during the day, cooking an evening meal. I had changed a life of constant movement and adventures for a sedentary and safe existence. For weeks, I dreamt every night that I was back at sea, my bed was a rolling bunk, and I had impossible obstacles to overcome in unknown lands.

My children Emily and Dylan were pleased to have me home. They had grown in confidence and independence. I value greatly their energy, grace and wisdom.

It was more difficult with Jenny. It had been a voyage of self-discovery for her as well. Despite the difficulties at the beginning, she had made the exciting realization that she could cope on her own, doing her work and looking after the children. She had made new friends and developed an independent life without me. Things will never be the same.

I have not lost my love of the sea. I often go down to the shore and watch the gulls soaring in the wild winds. I sail my boat in the Irish Sea and know that over the beckoning horizon its grey waters flow into the deep blue oceans of the world. And down south towards the Equator lies Africa, Africa with golden light streaming from its heart.

*I*ndex